# Linking to the Past
## A Brief Introduction to Archaeology

# Linking to the Past
## A Brief Introduction

# to Archaeology

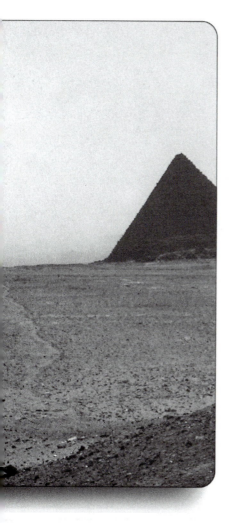

**KENNETH L. FEDER**
Central Connecticut State University

New York     Oxford
OXFORD UNIVERSITY PRESS
2004

*To a house filled with life:*
*Melissa, Josh, Jacob, Randolph, Harpo, Busterella, Groucho, and Aslan*

Oxford University Press

Oxford   New York
Auckland  Bangkok  Buenos Aires  Cape Town  Chennai
Dar es Salaam  Delhi  Hong Kong  Istanbul  Karachi  Kolkata
Kuala Lumpur  Madrid  Melbourne  Mexico City  Mumbai
Nairobi  São Paulo  Shanghai  Taipei  Tokyo  Toronto

Published by Oxford University Press, Inc.
198 Madison Avenue, New York, New York, 10016
http://www.oup.com

Oxford is a registered trademark of Oxford University Press

Library of Congress Cataloging-in-Publication Data

Feder, Kenneth L.
    Linking to the past : a brief introduction to archaeology / Kenneth L. Feder.
        p.  cm.
    Includes bibliographical references (p. ) and index.
    ISBN 0-19-515919-5 (pbk. : alk. paper)
    1. Archaeology.  2. Archaeology—Field work.  I. Title.
CC75.F43  2003
930.1—dc21
                                                                          2003054896


Book design by Cathleen Bennett

Printing number: 9 8 7 6 5 4 3 2 1

Printed in the United States of America
on acid-free paper

# Contents

**PREFACE** • xi

**PROLOGUE:** HOW TO USE *LINKING TO THE PAST* • 1

**INTRODUCTION** • 7

**AN ARCHAEOLOGICAL NARRATIVE:** HOW I SPENT MY SUMMER VACATION • 14

## UNIT 1

What Is Archaeology? • 17

What Do We Mean by the
Term *Culture?* • 20

How Did Archaeology
Get Started in the First
Place? • 24

Is Garbage Really All That
Informative on the Subject
of Human Behavior? • 28

How Do You Get to Be an
Archaeologist? • 29

Who Owns the Past? • 32

What Kinds of People Go
into Archaeology? • 36

## UNIT 2

What Determines What an
Archaeologist Investigates
in the First Place? • 45

What Laws Regulate
Where Archaeologists
Can Dig? • 47

What Is an "Archaeological
Site" and How Do You
Know When You've Found
One? • 50

## UNIT 3

What Kinds of Stuff Do
Archaeologists Find? • 55

How Are Archaeological
Sites Made? • 59

How Can You Find
Archaeological Sites Just
by Walking Around? • 64

How Old Does Something
Have to Be in Order
to Be Considered
"Archaeological"? • 70

Why Do Archaeologists
Need to Dig; Why Are
Most Sites Buried? • 74

How Deep Do You Have to
Dig to Find Archaeological
Material? • 76

# UNIT 4

How Do Archaeologists Know Where to Dig to Find Sites? • 85

What Forms the Basis of an Archaeological "Sampling Strategy"? • 88

How Can Archaeologists Probe the Subsurface without Digging Holes? • 90

What Are the Mechanics of Looking for and Finding Sites? • 93

How Do You Determine the Precise Location of a Site? • 98

What Preliminary Work Goes into an Archaeology Laboratory? • 101

# UNIT 5

What Kinds of Research Goals Do Archaeologists Have? • 108

How Is Archaeological Research Funded, and Why? • 112

What Is It that Archaeologists Want to Find Out? • 115

Is Archaeology Really a Dangerous Pursuit? • 117

# UNIT 6

How Do Archaeologists Know How Old Artifacts and Sites Are? • 124

What Are Relative Dating Techniques? • 125

How Can You Date Sites by Stratigraphic Analysis? • 126

How Can You Determine a Relative Date for a Site by Reference to Artifact Style? • 129

What Are Chronometric or Absolute Dating Methods? • 134

What Are the Most Commonly Used Radiometric Dating Methods Relied on by Archaeologists? • 135

How Does Dendrochronology Work? • 143

How Can You Determine an Absolute Date for a Site by Reference to Style? • 146

# UNIT 7

# UNIT 9

# UNIT 8

How Can the Location
of Archaeological Sites
Be Accurately
Predicted? • 154

How Can Landscape
Characteristics Be
Examined to Help Identify
Places Where Sites Are
Likely to Be Found? • 156

How Are Archaeological
Sites Named? • 159

How Can You Determine
the Size of an Ancient
Habitation? • 160

Who Gets to Dig at an
Archaeological Site? • 162

Why Do Archaeologists
Want to Know about
Ancient Environments and
How Do They Do It? • 167

How Is Archaeological
Research Like Detective
Work? • 172

How Do Archaeologists
Excavate Sites? • 173

How Do Archaeologists
Keep Track of Where Stuff
Is Found at Sites? • 175

What Is an Excavation
Unit and How Is It
Labeled? • 183

Why Do Archaeologists
Save All the Tiny Scraps
of Stone, Bone, and Other
Stuff? • 185

How Can You Identify
Tree Species from Bits
of Burned Wood? • 187

What Tools Do
Archaeologists Use to
Expose and Recover
Artifacts? • 188

# UNIT 10

# UNIT 12

# UNIT 11

What Are the Characteristics That Make a Rock Type Attractive to Tool Makers? • 198

How Can You Determine the Source of a Raw Material Used by Ancient People? • 200

How Do Archaeologists Figure Out How Ancient People Made Their Tools? • 202

How Did Ancient People Make Stone Tools? • 206

Why Are Archaeologists So Painstaking and Slow in Excavation? • 210

How Do Archaeologists Figure Out the Function of an Ancient Tool? • 211

How Do Archaeologists Figure Out the Function of a Site? • 214

Why Is Pottery of Such Great Importance to Archaeologists? • 215

How Do Archaeologists Investigate the Spread of Ideas or Inventions? • 218

How Do Archaeologists Know What Foods Ancient People Ate? • 227

Why Do Archaeologists Want to Know the Animal Species Exploited by Ancient People? • 234

How Can You Tell What Kind of Animal Was Killed or Butchered with an Ancient Stone Tool? • 237

How Can You Tell What Kinds of Plants Were Collected or Processed with an Ancient Stone Tool? • 239

How Can You Determine the Importance of an Animal Species in a People's Diet? • 241

How Does Skeletal Chemistry Help us Reconstruct an Ancient Diet? • 243

How Can the Season of a Village's Occupation Be Determined? • 244

Can Archaeologists Figure Out the Social Relationships of Past People? • 252

Can Archaeologists Figure Out the Roles of Males and Females in Ancient Societies? • 256

How Does an Archaeologist Approach Issues of Economic, Social, and Political Inequality in an Ancient Society? • 261

Can Archaeologists Reconstruct Ancient Religious Practices? • 264

How Can Archaeologists Reveal Ways of Life of People Whose Reality Was So Different from Our Own? • 267

# UNIT 13

Why Are Archaeologists
Interested in Human
Bones and Why Is This a
Contentious Issue? • 273

How Can You Determine
the Sex of a Person from
His or Her Skeleton? • 276

How Can You Determine
the Age of a Person from
His or Her skeleton? • 279

How Can You Determine
the Health of a Person
from His or Her
Skeleton? • 287

How Can You Determine
the Ethnic Identity of a
Person from His or Her
Skeleton? • 292

# UNIT 14

Wood Lily: Portrait of a Life:
Food for Thought • 297

# UNIT 15

Wood Lily: Portrait of a Life:
Tools of the Trade • 304

EPILOGUE: CAN WE RECONSTRUCT THE PAST? • 311

GLOSSARY • 314

REFERENCES • 351

INDEX • 363

# Preface

Considering the abundance of introductory archaeology texts already available, a number of questions likely occur to you about contemplating yet another, beginning with the most obvious: Why bother? What could this author add that might provide a significantly different and attractive option for introducing archaeology?

## The Web Model

I admit it—I love the Internet and am thoroughly addicted to it. Certainly, the Net offers a vast, virtually inclusive information database. I can't remember the last time I searched on the Net for some arcane bit of trivia that I couldn't find. At least as much as I enjoy the universe of data available on-line, I also appreciate the ways in which that information is linked together. Nearly every Web site you visit on a particular topic provides links to other sites that provide complementary information. I have long found it amazing and even exhilarating to go on-line seeking a particular piece of information and, then, by following links to other sites, discovering additional interesting stuff I wasn't even aware of when I began the initial, narrowly focused inquiry. Therein lay my "Eureka" and the beginning of my quest to provide a meaningfully different option for introducing archaeology.

## The Format: Book and CD

By their nature, books tend to convey information in a linear way. Readers move in a more or less straight line from topic to topic and from chapter to chapter. A Web site, however, links together the discussions of connected or related ideas, concepts, and issues and allows individuals to explore a topic along a variety of pathways.

Students are nearly universally Web-literate. Almost all of the students I know spend an enormous amount of time on-line and are very familiar with the nonlinear and flexible style of information gathering that the Internet affords. This book exploits that familiarity and comfort level by using what is essentially a web-based format for introducing archaeology. *Linking to the Past* presents the core content found in an introductory course in archaeology using the format of a web of interconnected concepts, ideas, stories, object lessons, and the like.

Along with a physical book, we provide an electronic version of the text on a CD-ROM where the text can be read within any standard Web browser, and the metaphorical links in the physical book become actual hyperlinks, just like on a Web site. Beyond this, *Linking to the Past* also incorporates the Internet itself, by including links to actual Web pages relating directly to the text. For example, when I discuss the laws that protect archaeological sites, the reader can click on a link in the digital text and be transported directly to a Web page with the text of the cited legislation or regulation.

## Organization: The Archaeological Narrative and Questions

Divided into a series of units, the archaeological narrative describing the discovery, excavation, and analysis of the three-thousand-year-old Wood Lily site in Barkhamsted, Connecticut, represents the core of the book. This discussion provides the framework for explaining how archaeologists do what they do. It is a brief, informal account of the project. However, this book is in no way a case study. The narrative uses my own research project only as a pedagogical device by which the practice of archaeology—survey, excavation, and analysis—can be introduced.

The unique element of the approach consists of a broad series of general questions scattered throughout the narrative relating to the discussion of archaeology at each point in the text. Using the CD, the reader can navigate to the answers to those questions simply by clicking on the question. ("Dig Deeper" labels identify these questions.) In the physical book, the questions and their answers are separated from the narrative as sections marked by a trowel. Icons like the one featured in the margin indicate additional illustrations and text on the enclosed CD that support the in-text discussion.

## How to Use This Book

How might one approach *Linking to the Past*? A typical reading assignment might be: "For next week, read Unit 1 of the archaeological narrative, and visit and read all of the links or questions associated with that unit." (The Table of Contents shows you all the questions associated with each unit.) You'll see that each unit provides a good bit of information that moves from specifics of my excavation to general concepts about archaeology. For example, in Unit 3 when I mention digging test pits as part of our archaeological survey in Peoples State Forest, I pose the question, "How deep do you have to dig to find archaeological material?" When I suggest that the flint from which many of the stone tools were made at the Wood Lily site came from the Hudson Valley of New York State, I link that discussion with the question in Unit 10, "How can you determine the source of a raw material used by ancient peoples?" Although the presentation of information here is nonlinear and readers can follow different pathways, everyone ends up at the same place at the end of a given reading assignment.

Along with providing a novel way of presenting archaeology, this unique format provides an advantage when it comes to studying and testing. The book provides a study guide inherent within its structure. Students preparing for a test need only to go over the questions for the part of the narrative covered in the exam; if they can answer those questions, they are prepared for the test. To provide even more study help, I've added a number of detailed study questions at the end of each unit in the text. (These study questions do not appear on the CD.) Beyond this, assignments can include having students gather additional information about the practice of archaeology from the Web pages linked to the text.

Key terms are highlighted throughout the text. In the book, they are defined in a traditional glossary. On the CD, each glossary term is hot-linked to its definition, which makes checking glossary definitions convenient and is useful in preparing for exams.

Please see the prologue for a detailed description of how to use this book.

## Additional Features and Ancillary Material

In the margins of the text are a number of icons that direct the reader to the included CD. There you will find fifty color images grouped into eight note-books or slide shows. In addition to providing readers with additional visual support for information discussed in the text, these images are freely available for instructors to use and project in class to support their own lectures. Readers may find the Firetown Meadow slide show particularly interesting: it is a visual overview of my 2003 field school and shows students at work on their first excavation.

An Instructors Manual and Test Bank is available on CD for instructors who adopt the text. It includes a list of glossary terms, short essay questions, and multiple choice questions for each unit. In addition, I've provided a kind of "transition guide" that I hope will make it easier to understand how the units in this book correspond to the chapters in other texts.

I had great fun writing and preparing this work. It forced me to consider connections and linkages among the various introductory archaeology topics that I had not previously thought much about. It is my hope that this format causes students to consider these connections and linkages as well. If you have questions or comments, please direct them to me at feder@ccsu.edu.

## Acknowledgments

Writing the acknowledgments for a book can be a daunting task. Invariably, there are more people to thank than the author even realizes, and one always manages to forget to thank individuals whose help materially contributed in ways both small and large. Nevertheless, a number of people fulfill two important criteria: (1) their help was indispensable and (2) I remember their help.

I wish I could tell you that this book was my idea, but actually, it wasn't. Jan Beatty, executive editor at Oxford University Press suggested this book to me in the first place, and I am forever in her debt for that. Thanks, Jan!

I was amazed at the generosity of my colleagues in my search for photographs and figures. Without exception, every email or phone call made, almost always to people who I did not know personally, resulted in my obtaining a photograph, figure, or chart for this book. Many thanks especially to Matthew Barrett, Nick Bellantoni, David Bernstein, Bruce Bradley, Lawrence Conyers, Noel Coonce, Peter Dana, Regina Dardzienski, Gretchen Jones, Harold Juli, Bill Keegan, Keith Kintigh, John Lynch, William McGrew, Cindy McWeeney, Michael Park, Warren Perry, Douglas Scott, John Seidel, Brian Tidey, and Emma Waas.

Deserving my great thanks are those reviewers whose job it was to plow through multiple drafts of the manuscript of this book. Their encouraging criticism made this a pleasant task and, of far greater importance, resulted in a much improved manuscript: Chuck Bollong, University of Arizona; Marcello Canuto, Yale University; Debra Gold, St. Cloud State University; Shannon McPherron, George Washington University; Sarah Neusius, Indiana University of Pennsylvania; Deborah Nichols, Dartmouth University; Cameron Wesson, University of Illinois at Chicago. Many thanks are due as well to the team at GiddyMachine, especially Dave Wolfe and Arne Knudson, who took my simple web format and made it into a thing of beauty for the electronic version of the book.

This is my first book with Oxford, and I couldn't have asked for a better group of folks to work with. Jan Beatty's assistant, Talia Krohn, went above and beyond the call of duty, kept me focused and on track, and was always helpful. Thanks as well to project editor Christine D'Antonio, who held together this very complicated task of book and CD on those few occasions when I thought it couldn't be done. Christine begins a lot of her emails with the phrase, "Just one more thing." Somehow, ten of those go down easier than a single email beginning, "Just ten more things." Thanks also to copyeditor Terri O'Prey, who did a grand job of improving my writing, while allowing it to still be recognizably my writing.

The thanks I convey to my extended family of people and critters is neither perfunctory nor simply obligatory. My wife is a role model for me; her energy and joy are contagious and inspire my work. My two sons, Josh and Jacob, never fail to inspire me with their intellectual curiosity. They'd better never lose that. Kitties, too, those here only in spirit (Harpo and Randolph), and those currently prowling the house (Busterella, Groucho, and Aslan), can inspire my muse as well, though Aslan's tendency to stretch out on the computer keyboard (how comfortable can that be?) can interrupt the writing process or, at least, result in some interesting keystroke combinations. Thanks to you all.

# How to Use *Linking to the Past*

In this book, I am going to tell you a true story. The story is about the discovery and excavation of an archaeological site in north-central Connecticut. Telling that story is not the purpose of this book. This book is intended as a brief, practical guide to the conduct of archaeological research in general. It is not a "case study" in archaeology. It is not a detailed accounting of one archaeological research project that is intended as a model for how archaeologists conduct their research. The entire book will not focus on this one project; this piece of research will be the central character only in the narrative of the chapter following the introduction. What I am going to tell in the narrative is just a story, an interesting one, I hope, about finding, excavating, and analyzing a rather ordinary, ancient village site. It's the kind of a story you might read in a magazine or newspaper, with just enough detail to give you a sense of the process and the results of the project. There aren't even any obviously sensational finds to distract you from the focus of the story, which is the process by which archaeological research is conducted. No great king's burial was found, no hoard of gold coins, no evidence of a lost civilization; just the remnants of a small village of Native Americans who lived in southern New England about three thousand years ago. In a sense, the story is primarily a pedagogical device, a teaching tool that I am using to get you interested in archaeology and to introduce the practice of that science.

In telling the story, I can't help but use terms and concepts that reside at the core of what archaeology is all about. You don't need a detailed explanation of these, at least not initially, to enjoy, appreciate, or understand the essence of the story. In fact, an immediate, in-depth discussion of every one of these details of method and theory would distract you from the narrative. It's like reading a popular magazine article on some topic in science; you recognize that there's lots of deep context for what you're reading about, but you can still appreciate what's going on and can investigate particular details of the story later.

Although the book is structured somewhat like a magazine article, of course, it isn't one. Most of you will likely be reading the hypertext version of this work on your computers, but either by book or CD you are reading it, not necessarily because you have some deep and abiding interest in my work in particular, or even in archaeological methodology in general. Most likely, you are reading this because a professor has assigned it in a course you are taking. In other words, you're reading it because you are required to do so to get a good grade in the course. Fair enough. I am going to assume, however (I hope not too naively), that you are taking the archaeology course in which this book is required because, among those courses in a list that you had to select from to fulfill a general education requirement for your undergraduate degree, the topic of archaeology sounded interesting. So, as long as you have to read this book to pass the course, you might as well gain an appreciation for archaeological methodology and achieve an understanding of the interesting field on which the text focuses. You will continue that process by reading the story in the next chapter.

The bad news is that, by itself, reading a breezy account of an archaeological research project won't be nearly enough to inform you of the necessary intricacies of how archaeologists go about their task of illuminating the story of the human past. Let's continue the analogy of an article in a popular publication. Whenever you read a newspaper or magazine article about some scientific undertaking, whether it is in physics, biology, astronomy, or archaeology, much of the background work—the methodological and intellectual "heavy lifting"—is left out of the telling. Essentially, these stories focus on the conclusions, the fascinating results of the research, and not so much on the often laborious process by which those conclusions and results were reached. Did you ever find yourself asking, when reading one of these intentionally superficial treatments of some complex scientific topic, assorted versions of the question, "That's cool, but how do they know that?" For example, a popular article about comets might mention that astronomers believe that these remarkable objects consist primarily of ice. "Dirty snowballs," you may have seen them called. Well, that's certainly interesting, but how did they figure that one out? When is the last time one of those scientists actually visited a comet and checked? Or how about this: a television documentary about brown bears might state that males travel around in a territory that is as much as 500 square miles in area. Okay, while not exactly riveting stuff, it is sort of neat, but how did they measure that? Or you might read in a Sunday supplement piece on forestry that the oldest tree in the world is exactly 4,844 years old (as of February 2003, anyway). That's breathtaking, in fact, mind-boggling, but how did they determine that? You shouldn't take such pronouncements as absolute truth, simply because you read them in an article or heard them announced on the television news, and especially not because you saw them on a Web site—the Internet is great, but there is an enormous amount of misinformation on the Web.

This bit of skeptical advice applies equally to this book. In the course of my story, I am going to include a lot of information about an archaeological project that I directed. I want you to enjoy the story and the last thing in the world I want to do is interrupt the telling every other line to explain exactly how I know what I just told you or to clarify some detail of the process by which our archaeological work unfolded. The dilemma, of course, is that you do need to know and understand these details to become educated about archaeology. You are not just a casual reader of a human interest story in a newspaper. You are a student in a class, probing in far greater depth the process of the science of the human past and you should be asking how I know or figured out what I am telling you. Does that put too much pressure on you? You just want to find out what happened so you can answer questions on the test? Okay, I'm going to make it easy on you. Instead of your having to ask the questions, I will. No extra charge. That's correct; throughout this book, following along with the narrative of the story, I have posed the very questions that you, as an intelligent, probing, curious, inquiring, and critical thinker should ask, not necessarily because you are a skeptic—though that alone is a very good reason to ask such questions, whether you are reading a college textbook or the *National Enquirer*. No, these are questions that should be asked and answered in order to fully appreciate and truly understand my story of archaeological research in the first place.

Of course, it is not enough for me simply to provide the questions that you should be asking. The questions are only the first part of the puzzle. Rather obviously, I need to provide the answers to each of these fundamental questions related to the practice of archaeology. I have done so in a traditional format in the hard copy of this book. Reading along in the print version of the narrative discussing the discovery, excavation, and analysis of an archaeological site, you will come to boldfaced questions marked by trowels. Each of these questions relates specifically to the discussion in the narrative. Beneath these headings, phrased as questions and set in a font different from the narrative, are the answers that represent a discussion of general archaeological practice, method, and theory. Further, these answer sections often are layered with additional queries focused on the particulars of the primary question. The questions follow a logical progression with increasingly detailed and specific information and ultimately lead you back to the descriptive narrative.

There is, however, another way of reading this text—on your computer. An electronic version of this book is provided on the enclosed CD-ROM. You will find on this e-version of the work that each of the posed questions is itself an active link, just like a hyperlink you can find on a Web site, which, when engaged by the click of a mouse, transports you to the section of the work that presents a detailed answer to the question. When you have finished reading the answer, you can easily return to the narrative exactly where you left off. There is no need to thumb through pages or stick adhesive flags on sections so you can find them again. Everything is immediately available and findable with the click of a mouse. Because this book is intended to introduce you to the field of archaeology, not just my particular site, I won't answer each question narrowly, describing only how I answered it in my research. Instead, I will discuss the many and diverse ways in which archaeologists answer each of these questions. At the end of each answer to a primary link, there is another link titled "Return to . . . ," which, when clicked, returns you to precisely where you left off in the narrative. At the end of secondary links there is a link that returns you to where you left off in the primary link answer. The Table of Contents on the CD version provides a map depicting the pathways linking each of the sections. In some of the answers, there are secondary question/links that provide more detailed and specific information about the general topic addressed in the primary link.

Knowledge is not necessarily linear, with each piece of information having a readily definable spot on a single pathway leading from ignorance to enlightenment. Knowledge is interconnected and I have attempted to organize the electronic version of this book in recognition of that. In other words, rather than organized in a strictly linear fashion, it is arranged as a web of information. The web format emphasizes connections between the various aspects of the science of archaeology. The format is intended to enable you to move around within the information—and always to be able to get back to where you started. Certainly, everyone ends up reading the same things and the format of the narrative chapter forces everyone to be on the same page, both literally and figuratively. But you are not confined to that format. For example, you will notice that scattered throughout are boxes that enable you to **JUMP AHEAD** to links that contain discussions that, though they fit later in my telling of the process of archaeological methodology, might be interesting for you to look at before that. Use a JUMP AHEAD and, after reading it, click the return link on the bottom and you will be transported back to where you just came from. You will also see **BOUNCE BACK** links, where you can readily return to a discussion you have already read simply to remind yourself of the material presented previously, to reinforce your understanding of the topic, and because it is relevant to a discussion later on in the narrative. Read a BOUNCE BACK and, at the bottom, click the return and you will be transported to the place you were before you "bounced back." Within some of the answer sections are links to actual Web sites where more detailed information related to each particular answer is available. To engage these links, rather obviously, you need to be online. All of the internal book links are useable whether you are online or not; they merely provide a convenient and efficient way to navigate through the information on the CD.

Here is an example of how it all works. I begin the narrative chapter simply mentioning the fact that I am an archaeologist. You might not care that much about how I got to be an archaeologist, but this statement might—maybe even should—inspire you to ask something like: "This guy's an archaeologist; I wonder how you get to be an archaeologist anyway?" But you don't have to intuit the right question here because I have already placed it there in the narrative for you: "How do you get to be an archaeologist?" And sure enough, if you move your pointer over to the question and give your pointing device (mouse, trackball, touchpad) a single click, you are transported to a section titled "How do you get to be an archaeologist?" The answer is not going to focus on my career path—how boring would that be?—but it will be a general discussion of the training necessary to become a professional archaeologist. Within the answer to this primary question ("How do you get to be an archaeologist?") is a secondary question and associated secondary link: "What kinds of people go into archaeology?" with some statistics about, obviously enough, the kinds of people (their sex and ethnicity) who become archaeologists. There's even a link within the primary question ("How do you get to be an archaeologist?") to a professional organization (the Register of Professional Archaeologists) where a set of ethical standards are presented to which archaeologists should adhere. None of the organizations who produced and maintain these linked Web sites have anything to do with this book—they don't recommend or sanction my work. These sites are merely valuable for furthering your investigation of the science of the human past.

Some of the primary and secondary questions are rather obvious and probably would have come to you anyway. When I told you earlier in this discussion that the site that is the focus of the narrative core of the book is three thousand years old, you might have wondered: "Three thousand years old? How do archaeologists know how old a site is? What's that based on?" If you didn't wonder about that, you should have, out of simple interest, intellectual curiosity, or even just plain irascible skepticism. Even if it didn't occur to you to ask this question, it's okay; I ask it and provide a detailed answer to the many ways in which archaeologists assess the age of archaeological materials.

I have to admit that, in order to maintain the scheme of the book, I also will be posing questions that perhaps would not obviously come to mind. That's okay. Obvious or not, the questions are relevant and they will move you toward a better understanding of archaeology. And that is the point of the book.

If you choose to read along with the electronic version of this text, you have a number of choices on how to proceed. You can read the narrative straight through, initially ignoring the questions entirely. Later, you can read each answer section in sequence, where the details of archaeological research are presented as answers to the posed questions in a linear fashion, presented much the same as the printed version. The advantage of this approach is that it makes the narrative flow more readily. The disadvantage is clear as well; you may encounter topics or concepts in the narrative that intrigue you, but that you will gloss over initially because the details of methodology are not provided. Later, when you read the answers to the questions posed in the narrative margins, you might not recall the context of the question in the story and you may have to skim back to the narrative to find that context. This strategy, rather obviously, does not take advantage of the web format of the book.

Another approach involves reading the narrative, stopping at each question, clicking it, reading its linked answer, and then returning to the story. This will achieve essentially the same effect as reading the print version of the text, in which each question is posed, then answered, right in the narrative. The advantage of this approach is that you will be able immediately to collect details of the concept or technique when it appears in the progression of the narrative. The disadvantage of the approach is that it interrupts the flow of the story; the overall experience might seem a bit choppy and by the time you finish reading one of the more detailed answers, you might have forgotten the context of the question in the narrative. You could, of course, use a combination of these two strategies, saving for later the detailed answers and clarifications for those issues that don't perplex you and immediately exploring the details only for those questions that seem most meaningful or engaging. Yet another approach is to read the entire narrative through first, glancing at the questions but trudging along without reading each answer. When you are finished with the narrative, go back to the beginning of the story and read it again—it's not all that long. This time, stop at each question and navigate to its answer further along in the book. This last approach would be my personal preference, but ultimately it's up to you and your professor; he or she might have another strategy that conforms better to class lectures, scheduling, or the individual approach to teaching the material.

However you elect to read this book, I hope you enjoy it and come away from your reading with a deeper appreciation for the study of the human past.

# Introduction

Our first house was built in 1924. It was a sweet little place, with clapboard siding, black wooden storm shutters, and, our favorite feature, a time-worn tin roof. That roof provided a charmingly rustic, antique look to the house. I tried to remember that during heavy downpours when rain falling against that roof produced a noise not unlike that of a machine gun going off directly above our heads. It was during one of those intense storms with associated high winds that one of the oak trees adjacent to the house photosynthesized its last and fell over. The fallen oak was one of several similar trees left standing when the house was built and which, though having seen better days, were still alive when my wife and I bought the place in 1985.

In the thirteen or so years we lived there we became depressingly familiar with an affliction common to old oaks in the northeast: those industrious and aptly named "carpenter" ants who carve out extensive galleries for their nests in the trunks and limbs of these trees. The large oak near the driveway simply could not withstand the complex network of tunnels the ants had excavated through its massive trunk over the years, succumbing to the combined effects of wind, gravity, and the relentless ant species *Camponotus pennsylvanicus*.

Luckily, no one was injured—other than the tree—and after the town-contracted tree service cleared the road all that was left behind, along with enough wood to fuel our woodstove for the following heating season, was a large stump adjacent to the end of our driveway. The top of the stump was vaguely circular and about 3.5 feet in diameter. Across its surface marched the familiar parade of annual growth rings. We counted more than one hundred in all, some thick, some thin, each one demarcating a year in the life of an old tree with which we had shared our half-acre lot for more than a dozen years (Figure I.1).

Our oak had left behind a record of its life in the form of annual growth rings, loops of new wood added by trees each year they are alive. The tree had lived through more than one hundred snowy New England winters and an equal number of long, humid summers. More than one hundred times, its leaves had turned brown, withered, and fallen to Earth and an equal number of times buds had formed on the tree's branches and leaves had unfolded to capture the warming solar energy of spring with which the tree maintained its life. The rings on the stump were each like the pages of a book, telling in their own alien language the story of the tree's life: the droughts, insect infestations, lightning strikes, and the industrious ants it had encountered and ultimately surrendered to.

**FIGURE I.1** A cross-section of a downed tree, showing annual growth rings. (*Kenneth L. Feder*)

## Archaeology: The Study of the Human Past

This book is not about oak trees. It is a brief guide to the practice of **archaeology,** the science that studies the human past. By looking at the rings on the stump of our old oak, however, we were conducting a sort of archaeology of the life of that tree—studying the past by examining the remains left behind by a once living thing. There is even a method of analysis used in archaeology called **dendrochronology** that does precisely this, reconstructing ancient environments by examining tree rings. We'll look at how this form of analysis works later in the book.

Though they don't leave a year-by-year record of their passing, animals, like trees, also leave a trail of their existence, as bones within ordered layers of rock and soil. Their biographies are written on those bones, just as surely as our oak tree's biography was written in its rings, in a code that scientists attempt to translate.

Human beings are animals and, like other such organisms, we also leave behind our bones, which can, under the right conditions, preserve for long stretches of time to be examined by scientists in future generations. Like other animal bones, ours record our histories, telling stories of disease, nutrition, labor, trauma, and even family ties. Part of the job of the archaeologist is to study those bones for the stories they can tell of the times and lives that make up the human past. We'll discuss how scientists interpret human remains later in this book.

Like other life forms, we humans possess inborn, biological **adaptations** to our environments. These adaptations are physical characteristics we are born with that allow us to live. In this sense, we are no different from polar bears, butterflies, or, for that matter, oak trees, who, like all animal and plant species, possess physical adaptations, inborn strategies for survival. Some of these adaptations—for example, the way we walk on two feet and the ways in which we can hold and manipulate objects with our hands—are reflected by the form of our bones. Those who study the human past examine how our ancestors lived, in part, by the analysis of their skeletons.

Unlike animals or oak trees, we human beings leave behind something more than just the remnants of our physical selves because the human adaptation is not only inborn, it is also invented, reinvented, and learned in each generation. It can be argued, in fact, that our primary adaptation is not strictly biological but cultural. We do not adjust to our environment only through the slow-acting biological process Charles Darwin labeled "natural selection," by which individual members of a species who happen to possess advantageous characteristics are more likely to survive life's struggle and pass those characteristics down to subsequent generations. We humans also can actively and nearly instantly adjust to our physical environment by using our great intelligence to figure out how to make the most out of what nature has to offer. We invent and make tools that enable us to better extract resources from our surroundings, not in generations removed but right here and right now. We construct homes from wood, stone, and earth that buffer us against the cold of winter and the heat of summer. We make and wear clothing and footwear from animal hides and plant fibers. We manufacture vessels of clay in which we cook our food, and containers of bark, wood, and fiber to store our valuables. We differentiate, distinguish, and identify ourselves with items of adornment made of every imaginable raw material—bone, antler, ivory, metal, stone, wood—that communicate to others our marital status, social standing, religion, and group membership. The raw materials from which we build these structures and manufacture these objects often are more durable than the raw materials from which nature has constructed our bodies. The houses that enclose us, the tools we hold in our hands, the pots in which we cook our food, the rings we wear on our fingers, and the symbols we suspend from chains around our necks often outlast us and may serve, like the tree rings of our old oak, to convey in their own language the story of who we are and who we were. The science that attempts to read this language of objects—those things that make up our **material culture**—is archaeology, and we will spend much of the remainder of this book discussing the methods archaeologists use to find, recover, and study the material culture that was left behind by past people and that has fortuitously preserved.

## The Context of Antiquity

Though old in comparison to a human lifespan, our fallen oak was not a particularly ancient tree. Living examples of the justifiably famous giant sequoias (*Sequioadendron giganteum*) of the American west that reach dizzyingly into the sky can be more than three thousand years old. Dendrochronologists can extract thin slices across the radius of a tree's trunk, allowing for a ring count without causing harm. Using this method, the oldest living giant sequoia has been calculated to be 3,266 years old. That's enormously old, but even that pales in comparison to the true longevity champions among trees, the bristlecone pines (*Pinus longaeva*), also in the American west (Figure I.2). One of the oldest living bristlecones has been named "Methuselah" for the biblical patriarch who is supposed to have lived for 969 years. In fact, he would have been a real youngster compared to the tree named for him; Methuselah the bristlecone pine is a stupendous 4,789 years old (see the Web site http://www.rmtrr.org/oldlist.htm for a listing of the oldest known trees for a number of species).

It is remarkable to consider that those of us alive today share the planet with living organisms so breathtakingly ancient. The old grove bristlecone pines, Methuselah among them, were alive in 1901, at the turn of the twentieth

**FIGURE I.2** The oldest living trees on our planet are bristlecone pines, some of which are nearly five thousand years old. The growth rings on a bristlecone pine and on other trees as well present a version of their life histories. (*Kenneth L. Feder*)

century. Remarkably, these very same trees were alive during the American War of Independence in 1776. It is amazing to consider that living trees you can see today were happily photosynthesizing when Columbus's ships plied the waters of the Atlantic in 1492. William the Conqueror invaded England in 1066. Blissfully unaware of this crucial historical event memorized by high school history students everywhere, bristlecones alive today collected solar energy with their needles and drew up moisture through their roots in that same year. The birth of the Muslim prophet Muhammad (A.D. 570) and the birth of the Christian savior Jesus Christ (most likely 4 B.C.) occurred during the lifetimes of bristlecone pines that continue to live in the twenty-first century. The Bible story recounted in the Old Testament of the Hebrew prophet Moses leading his people out of bondage in Egypt relates to historical events that likely occurred in the thirteenth century B.C.—sometime soon after 3300 years ago. Living bristlecone pines that you can walk by today and smell the fragrance of their needles were already more than a thousand years old when Moses implored the Pharaoh to let his people go. The Egyptian pharaoh Khufu ascended to the throne in 2589 B.C. soon thereafter initiating construction of the Great Pyramid, truly one of the wonders of the ancient world and emblematic of human antiquity (Figure I.3). Today you can hike the trail to the old grove bristlecone pines in Inyo National Forest in central California and stand in the shadows of living trees that had already been casting shadows for nearly two hundred years when Khufu built his pyramid.

The Bible characterizes a reasonable human lifespan as "three-score and ten" or seventy years, not quite 1.5% of the longevity of an ancient bristlecone pine tree, and therein lies an interesting insight. Like all living things—like our

**FIGURE I.3** Bristlecone pine trees still alive in California were already thriving when these icons of the ancient world were constructed by the ancient Egyptians on the Giza plateau overlooking the Nile. (*Kenneth L. Feder*)

oak tree—we humans are temporary residents of this planet, and not particu-larly long-lived ones at that. Unlike all other living things, however, we are conscious of our transience. Among all Earth's creatures, we likely are the only ones who are aware that there is more to time than our own "now." All human beings know that we have a future where we will succeed or fail in what we attempt—and probably do a little of both. If we're lucky we will live a happy and successful life, be surrounded by good friends, and live to a ripe old age. But, lucky or not, successful or not, long-lived or not, we all eventually die.

Along with a future, each one of us also is aware that we have a past, a period of personal development during which we are born and slowly mature. Beyond this, we know that we have more than an immediate, personal past; we have a family history as well. Certainly you recognize—though it may be chal-lenging to imagine—that there was a time, not so very long ago, when your parents were your age, a time when they experienced some of the same pres-sures, confusions, frustrations, and yes, some of the same joys that you do now. Of course, your parents had parents too. Your grandparents were young in a time even more different and distant from yours. Consider, when you look at the fading, seemingly ancient photographs of your grandparents taken when they were young that the seemingly enormous amount of time since your grandparents were your age is only the tiniest of fractions of the time that the human lineage has walked this planet. The human family has substantial time depth and our lives today represent only the current page of an ongoing and ancient story.

## Shadow of the Past

Every generation of human beings asserts sovereignty over its time on life's stage. But the members of each generation pass, succumbing to the inexorable unwinding of time. It may be a burden to know our fate, but it also provides our species with an opportunity—and a rationale—to know even more. Although the only time we can live in is now, the past casts its shadow into the present. We can contemplate and even explore the time before our own because, in a sense, there is an element of immortality to everything that rises up for its brief stint on the center stage of existence.

Simply put, the past does not simply disappear, receding into an invisible horizon and preserved only in mind and memory. In fact, life leaves behind physical traces of its passing. *Linking to the Past* is about the science that in-vestigates these traces of the human past. It is a short book. It is not encyclope-dic or all inclusive. It cannot, in its relatively few pages, tell you everything there is to know about archaeology. Reading this book will not make you an archaeologist. Not even close. Its entire purpose simply is to get you to think about how we study human history in its broadest sense, beginning long before our ancestors developed the capacity to actually write down that history. The subject matter of archaeology comprises a story that we cannot read directly. We can recover that history only from the "library" of objects people left be-hind. That library of objects is the archaeological record and how we study that record is the focus of this book.

## Study Questions

1. What was the point of the story of the old oak tree that crashed down on my property?

2. How can the old, dead oak tell the story of its life?

3. Trees and animals (including human animals) leave behind physical remains in the form of wood and bones that can be studied long after they are dead. What else do human beings leave behind?

4. I assert that "the past casts its shadow into the present" allowing those of us residing in that present to study the past. How does the human past cast its shadow into the present?

# An Archaeological Narrative
## How I Spent My

# Summer Vacation

June 1986 marked a starting point for two long-term undertakings with which I was intimately associated. The first of these—and the more relevant to this discussion—was a research project involving **archaeological fieldwork** in Peoples State Forest, located in the town of Barkhamsted, in north-central Connecticut (Figure 1.1).

The second project of June 1986, the birth of my son Josh, initiated my wife and me into the world of parenting. The only significant and relevant connection between Josh's birth and the subject at hand has to do with timing. As the result of astonishingly bad planning, our first child was due

**FIGURE 1.1** Overview of the Farmington River; the major watercourse in Barkhamsted, Connecticut. (*Kenneth L. Feder*)

to arrive exactly as I was to begin work as the **principal investigator** of an archaeological **survey** project. Beginning on June 1, my wife's due date, I was supposed to be deep in the woods of north-central Connecticut, directing a team of archaeological field-workers, digging **test pits** throughout 4,000 acres of state forest land.

## What Is Archaeology?

A few years ago I received a phone call from a reporter who some months previously had spent a few hours with my students and me at a five-thousand-year-old archaeological site in the town of Avon, Connecticut. In preparing an article about the work I was doing in the Farmington River valley, the reporter had asked lots of questions about what I do and I had done my best—or so I thought—to convey what it is that archaeologists hope to accomplish by spending their summers digging in the dirt.

We talked a lot about what archaeology is and what it isn't. "The dry, textbook definition," I told him, "usually presents archaeology as the study of the material remains of human behavior. People live and work at a place, using things that they have made. These things end up in the ground as people lose them, throw them away, or even put them away for safekeeping and archaeologists attempt to figure out the nature of their lives by recovering and analyzing what remains of these things."

I tried to elaborate on this—let's face it—pretty boring description of the discipline to which I have devoted my life. "It's really all about passion," I told the reporter, "a passion for knowing about the past times and past lives of the human family." Where'd we come from and when? How have people survived for thousands, hundreds of thousands, and, if you include our most ancient ancestors, even millions of years? How did we, as a species, develop ways of life, a breathtaking variety of different **cultures?**

How did we, as a species, go from making tools that were little more than busted up rocks to creating things like Stonehenge and the pyramids? "Archaeology," I told the reporter, "focuses on the vast history of humanity and it just so happens that we go about this by finding and analyzing some really cool stuff." The recognition that there was anything left from which to recover the ancient human story is, in itself, relatively recent and archaeology, therefore, is really a rather young discipline, just a bit more than a century old.

As a result of this "immaturity," we don't have the answers to all of the questions we might pose about the human past and new and exciting discoveries are constantly being made. Archaeologists are always rewriting the past. That's part of what makes the discipline so exhilarating. I thought I did a good job of conveying my genuine excitement about the study of the human past and the resulting article prepared by the reporter was well done. So, needless to say, I was more than a little perplexed when, just a few months later, this same reporter called me, hoping to get a quote or two from me, as the resident expert on all things old and crumbly, for an article he was doing on a fascinating

**FIGURE 1.2** Dinosaur footprints, indeed, are "really neat," but my succinct characterization to the newspaper reporter belied my general ignorance. I am, after all, an archaeologist and not a paleontologist. (*Kenneth L. Feder*)

discovery that had just been made in Connecticut; dinosaur footprints behind the new mall being built just down the road from my university.

Dinosaur footprints. I don't know anything about dinosaur footprints (Figure 1.2). Dinosaurs became extinct some 65 million years ago. The earliest fossil forms of human ancestors have been dated to a little more than 4 million years old. I reminded the reporter of our lengthy discussion of just a few months before about what it is that I do, about how archaeology focuses on the *human* past. There had been nothing in our previous conversation that even hinted at a connection between archaeology and dinosaurs.

"You may find it surprising to learn," I good-naturedly chided the reporter, "that *The Flintstones* is not based on a true story. Brontosauruses have never been used by people as excavating equipment at rock quarries and nobody ever kept a dinosaur as a pet. There's a more than 60-million-year gap between the dinosaurs and what I study. It sounds like a fascinating discovery but I really can't help you on your article about the footprints."

The poor reporter was crushed. He genuinely thought that, as an archaeologist, of course I would know all about dinosaur footprints and could provide him with an informative and juicy sound bite for the next day's paper. I tried to help out and gave him the name and number of a geologist who would be a far more appropriate source of information about dinosaurs and their footprints, but the reporter was not entirely satisfied. He was on a tight deadline to get the article into the next day's paper. He promised that he would try to contact the geologist but asked me for any insights that I could give him about dinosaurs. Feeling somewhat responsible for not making it clearer the last time we spoke that archaeologists are not **paleontologists** and we don't study dinosaurs, I told the reporter, "Look. Dinosaur footprints are really neat. You can learn a lot about dinosaur behavior by looking at the prints. Now go and call a real expert and you'll get something a lot more intelligent than that." You probably can guess the punch line for this story. The reporter was unable to contact the geologist and, rather predictably, there I was in the paper the next day, the "expert" quoted—painfully accurately I might add—as characterizing dinosaur footprints as "really neat." I have yet to live that one down among my colleagues in geology and paleontology.

Okay, so archaeology is not paleontology. It's not geology either. Though archaeologists need to know a fair amount about the various earth sciences, we are not necessarily expert in any of them. People bring me rocks on a regular basis, expecting me to be able to expound on their age and origin. In one case, a gentleman tracked me down because he needed an archaeologist to confirm his identification of a rock he had found as being a part of a meteorite. What possible connection this guy had made between the science that studies the human past and rocks of extraterrestrial origin that have fallen to Earth, I have no idea. I professed ignorance of meteors and sent the fellow to the meteorology professor on campus. Meteorology is, of course, the study of weather and has nothing to do with meteors, but at least meteorology has the word "meteor" in it.

A more common misconception about archaeology involves a narrowing of the geographic and temporal focus of the field. People are regularly surprised when they learn that I dig in Connecticut and not Egypt or Greece. My dentist confessed that he assumed that the archaeological research he knew I was conducting in Connecticut represented little more than practice, a sort of rehearsal for the really important work I might someday do in Egypt. Certainly there are archaeologists who excavate sites in Egypt and Greece, not to mention Rome and Israel. But there also are vibrant, active archaeology programs in India and China, England, Zimbabwe, Australia, Peru, Mexico, and all places in between and, oh yeah, Connecticut, New Jersey, Arizona, Alaska, and the rest. Anywhere people lived in the past, archaeology can help us discover the nature of their lives (Figure 1.3).

Further, contrary to most people's assumption, archaeology is not restricted to any particular period of time in the past. Archaeology is not the study of people before the birth of Christ or before the Bible or before agriculture or before the development of urban life or necessarily before anything. Archaeology cannot even be defined as the study of the past before writing. The first written records of king lists, palace inventories, genealogies, tax roles, calendars, and so on do not replace the archaeological record of these ancient societies, they complement and supplement it, adding to the database of our study of the human past.

I often have a difficult time convincing people that I am not looking for jewels or treasures that will one day make me fabulously wealthy. Many people assume a stereotype of archaeology based on what they may have heard about King Tut's fabulous tomb or people who call themselves "archaeologists" and plunder old ships for profit, looking for gold coins, precious stones, and other valuable cargo. The truth is that the vast majority of what I have dug up in the more than nearly three decades I have been involved in archaeological fieldwork has been not treasure but trash, stuff people thought so little of, they disposed of it in a garbage pit, tossed it on the disposal pile, or simply left it where it dropped. But in that trash archaeologists find a narrative, written in the language of **material culture,** a text that tells the story of ancient lives and past cultures.

Finally, I suppose I will never quite understand what inspired a property owner in a nearby town to leave a frantic message on the department voicemail, expressing the immediate need for an archaeologist because giant bees were burrowing a hole in her backyard. Archaeology is not about dinosaurs (or their footprints), rocks, meteors, or giant burrowing bees. It is about the study of the material record left behind by past people in an attempt to shine a light on the human experience, a story whose origins stretch back across the millennia.

**FIGURE 1.3** Assortment of archaeological sites: Pueblo Bonito (New Mexico, top); Wood Lily (Connecticut, bottom left); SkaraBrae (Scotland, bottom right). (*Kenneth L. Feder*)

## What Do We Mean by the Term *Culture?*

*Mesa Verde*

Archaeologists use the word "**culture**" a lot. It comes with the territory; we are, after all, **anthropologists** and culture is a concept central to that field. We anthropologists argue a lot and you probably would have a hard time getting any group of us to come up with a universally accepted or approved definition of culture, but many would agree at least in principle with the following: culture is the extra-somatic means of adaptation. The prefix "extra" means "beyond" and the word "somatic" means "the body." A "means of adaptation" is just another way of saying "a strategy for survival." Translating our original definition then,

**FIGURE 1.4** Wild chimps using stone hammers and stone anvils in Liberia, West Africa, to crack open nutritious nuts, the shells of which litter the ground. Chimps use tools, refine them, and teach their offspring how to use them, and chimps living in different territories have even developed their own different styles of tools. (*Courtesy of William C. McGrew; Alison Hannah, photographer*)

our characterization of the word "culture" becomes "the beyond-the-body strategy for survival," in yet other words, those elements of human existence beyond what our body offers that enable us to live. Culture, therefore, represents the totality of those things we are able to produce with our minds, through the application of our intellect: the things we invent, develop, refine, solve, produce, teach, and pass down to subsequent generations.

Human beings are not the only organisms that have culture. A good argument can be made that chimpanzees rely to some extent on their invention of tools (which they have been seen to refine, improve, and elaborate), whose manufacture adults explicitly assist their young to master, and the styles of which vary from group to group (Mercader, Panger, and Boesch 2002; Figure 1.4).

We humans, however, are the only species for whom culture is the primary means by which it adapts to its surroundings. Human beings can live anywhere on the face of the planet and, for that matter, underwater and even in outer space, not because we have developed physical or somatic adjustments to life in these places, but because we have *invented* ways to survive. Consider the following comparison of two species of mammals that inhabit the Arctic: polar bears (*Ursus maritimus*) and people (*Homo sapiens*). Polar bears thrive in the extreme conditions that characterize the Arctic because they are supremely well adapted to life there; that is, they are somatically tailored to life under the Arctic's frigid conditions (Figure 1.5).

**FIGURE 1.5** Polar bears are supremely well adapted to life in the harsh conditions of the Arctic. Their adaptation is biological; nature has provided them with the physical characteristics necessary for their survival. (© *John Conrad/CORBIS*)

Perhaps most obviously, polar bears are supremely well adapted hunters as a result of their great size, enormous strength, sharp claws, and powerful jaws. Beyond this, polar bears have a thick coat of fur and each hair is actually hollow. The air trapped inside provides an additional boost in the fur's insulative properties. Polar bears also have a thick layer of fat as much as 11.5 centimeters (4.5 inches) thick beneath their protective fur. Between the fur and the blubber, polar bears suffer virtually no heat loss; apparently the bears can scarcely be picked by infrared tracking devices because they experience so little heat loss from their bodies. Polar bears may look white, but their fur is actually free of pigment; each strand is transparent. The hollow shaft of each strand of fur scatters visible sunlight, producing the appearance of whiteness much in the way that snow looks white even though it is just a form of frozen water without any color. The white appearance of a polar bear is highly advantageous for a predator who needs to be able to sneak up on its prey in an environment with lots of snow-covered, white backgrounds.

Further, polar bear skin exudes a thick, waterproofing oil that serves as a protective barrier against moisture. I recently spent a cold and rainy day at a zoo where one of the resident polar bears was leisurely and quite comfortably swimming in the frigid waters of its artificial pond. When the bear came out of the water, a quick shake almost instantly removed nearly all of the water from its fur.

Polar bears also have roughly circular, enormously broad feet, up to 30.5 centimeters (12 inches) in diameter. This feature allows polar bears, which can weigh nearly 700 kilograms (1,500 pounds) in the case of large adult males, to walk efficiently on top of a relatively thin skim of ice overlying a powdery snow base. Other animals—caribou, for example—will quickly exhaust their

**FIGURE 1.6** The Inuit people have adapted to life in the arctic, not by any particular physical adaptation, but by their intelligence and ingenuity. Their strategy for survival has resulted from their ability to respond intellectually to the challenges of life in their environment. (© *Galen Rowell/CORBIS*)

energy cracking through the ice while attempting to escape from a hungry polar bear. Further, polar bear toes are webbed, making them handy and efficient paddles when the polar bear goes for a swim, which is often, seals being a favorite food.

The natives of the American Arctic, the Inuit people (more commonly called Eskimos) have none of the polar bear's somatic adaptations to life in the Arctic: no dense layer of blubber underlying their skin, no thick coat of insulative fur, no large webbed feet, and so on. However, the Inuit have something the polar bears don't: a human brain that affords them the ability to respond to the challenges of the Arctic intellectually, to invent a culture that is brilliantly well adapted to life under the same conditions in which polar bears live (Figure 1.6).

Inuit people may not have a thick layer of fur, but they know who does and they know how to get it from them (polar bears, among other animals), by techniques of hunting, butchering, hide preparation, and the production of clothing. Similarly, unlike the polar bear, Inuit feet aren't particularly well adapted to walking on snow, but the Inuit figured out the practical physics behind the advantages of a broad distribution of body weight for walking on top of snow and ice and applied this knowledge in their invention of snowshoes. The parka, a knee- or thigh-length outer garment that includes a fur-lined hood, is another invention of the Inuit. The igloo (an Inuit word), which is an efficiently designed little domed domicile that retains heat and is manufactured from the most abundant raw material available in the Arctic—ice; the kayak (another Inuit word), a boat used in their tradition of hunting marine mammals;

harpoons; waterproof clothing; and even eye protection against the bright Arctic sun (not quite sunglasses, but a wrap-around piece of bone or ivory with a thin slit that lets in just enough light to see but not enough to produce snow-blindness) all are elements of Inuit inventiveness and resourcefulness. These objects and the behaviors that led to their invention, elaboration, refinement, and application are part of Inuit culture, indeed, their "extra-somatic means of adaptation."

So, when archaeologists dig up stuff, the items we painstakingly recover, return to the lab, and intensively analyze represent the material remains of a people's culture, the physical remnants of their extra-somatic means of adaptation. By studying these objects, in other words, archaeologists reveal the nature of past people's strategy for survival.

## Read More

To learn more about how anthropologists think about culture—and to see how the study of chimpanzee tool-making traditions are causing us to reassess how we define what makes us uniquely human—any of the following resources offer a good start:

Haviland, W. 2001. *Cultural Anthropology.* Wadsworth, Belmont, California.

Kottak, C. 2004. *Anthropology: The Exploration of Human Diversity.* McGraw-Hill, New York.

Mercader, J., M. Panger, and C. Boesch. 2002. Excavation of a chimpanzee stone tool site in the African rainforest. *Science* 296:1452–55.

Park, M. A. 2003. *Introducing Anthropology: An Integrated Approach.* McGraw-Hill, New York.

Schultz, E. A., and R. H. Lavenda. 2000. *Anthropology: A Perspective on the Human Condition.* McGraw-Hill, New York.

## How Did Archaeology Get Started in the First Place?

The presumption that is at the core of archaeology—that there is a past that is not written down or spoken, but that we can nevertheless learn about, a past that can teach us things about ourselves and our species—is not exactly self-evident. After all, the present is fleeting and it isn't all that obvious that much remains materially of the present once it becomes a part of the past. The science of archaeology, however, (as well as the focus of this book), is all about retrieving and studying those material remains of the past that endure. If we hope to answer the question posed by the title of this section, we need to learn when people first recognized the fundamental fact of a materially enduring past upon which all archaeology ultimately is based.

It is probably fair to say that the origins of archaeology, long before it earned that name, can be traced to the recognition that some elements of the past—abandoned structures, things people lost or discarded, items left behind and simply not reclaimed—continue to survive in the present and can be recovered and studied for the insights they may provide about the lives lived before our own. Of course, it is impossible to determine exactly when this recognition was made, when a human being, perhaps walking along the eroding edge of a stream channel, first picked up a broken piece of pottery whose style and form were unrecognizable. The discoverer may have wondered about the person who made it, and in so doing presaged the work of archaeology. We cannot know when someone burying the remains of a comrade first encountered the bones of an unknown individual, coincidentally interred at that same spot at some time in the past, and then wondered who this past person was and when they lived. Events like these must have occurred on countless occasions in the past but they have left little evidence for us in the present. It is clear—at least in terms of the development of the historical sciences in Western societies—that an explicit recognition of a material manifestation of the past surviving into the present, enabling "modern" people to study the past directly, became obvious and important at least as far back as the Renaissance.

The Renaissance of the 1300s though 1500s involved an explicit attempt on the part of Europeans to recapture the knowledge of the ancients, specifically the Greeks, Romans, and, before them, the Egyptians, knowledge that was supposed to have been lost and forgotten after the fall of Rome in the fifth century A.D. Though travel was difficult, with parts of the land afflicted by difficult and unstable political conditions, a small handful of Europeans were able to travel to Egypt before the end of the eighteenth century. These visitors returned with stories of the remnants of a spectacular antique civilization, whose obvious great age and level of architectural achievement seemed to provide evidence for the notion of a past "golden age" whose study might allow for the recapture of lost knowledge and wisdom (Fagan 1994; Stiebing 1993). The trickle of European visitors to Egypt became a torrent after Napoleon Bonaparte led a military campaign there in 1798. In his ultimately failed attempt at conquest, Napoleon brought along a contingent of scholars as well as soldiers who spent their time measuring, mapping, drawing, and studying the monuments of ancient Egypt (Figure 1.7).

Closer to home, Greek temples and Roman ruins abounded, and not just in Greece and Rome. The Romans, especially, had a far-flung empire and the aboveground ruins of Roman roads, baths, and walls are found in much of Europe. It certainly made sense for Europeans during the Renaissance to study these material remnants of the past if they wished to recover and rejuvenate the art, architecture, and science of the perceived golden age of classical civilization (Figure 1.8).

An awareness of a surviving material manifestation of the past, a sort of ancient history written in crumbling walls and ruined Roman temples, alerted scholars of the time to the existence of a much broader and far more ancient language of human antiquity written not in crumbling roads and deteriorating temples but in bronze daggers, shards of pottery, and stone spearheads and axes, all things that substantially predated classical civilization.

The stone tools found in deep deposits especially perplexed and fascinated European scholars. The Old and New Testaments of the Bible represent not just blueprints for how people should live their lives, but also a chronology for the history of the world beginning with its creation by God. That chronology had no opening for a period of time in human history in which tools were made

**FIGURE 1.7** Engraving depicting the great emperor of France, Napoleon, contemplating the sculpted visage of one of the great pharaohs of ancient Egypt as presented in the Great Sphinx. Napoleon's attempt at conquest in Egypt was a military and political failure, but it played an important role in encouraging the study by Europeans of that nation's ancient history. (© *Bettmann/CORBIS*)

primarily of stone; in fact, according to Genesis, brass metallurgy was used at least as far back as Noah's time. In 1650, James Ussher, Archbishop of Ireland, had managed to cram the entire history of the world as represented in the Old and New Testaments of the Bible into a little more than 5,600 years. Ussher had determined that God began the creation week in 4004 B.C. In Ussher's calculation, the entire universe that modern scientists believe to be something like 15 billion years old was actually only about 0.00004% of that age.

So, with no existing concept of a "stone age" and an incredibly compressed time scale to work with, it was not apparent to many European thinkers who examined the often quite artfully rendered stone axes found in deep deposits that these objects were the product of human craft from some ancient age. Some actually believed that the stones had resulted from the recent activities of gnomes and elves, going so far as to call the finely crafted stone axes "fairy stones." Others took a more "scientific" approach, ascribing them to natural causes, especially lightning strikes, calling the symmetrical stone axes "thunderstones." Of course, a few discoverers who found these objects in the soil and then analyzed them realized that no natural process could

**FIGURE 1.8** Ancient features of the historical landscape, like this well-preserved segment of a wall built by the Romans under their emperor Hadrian (A.D. 122–126) in England, provide physical evidence of ancient societies. (*Courtesy of Michael A. Park*)

have crafted them and, barring a belief in fairies, the objects had to be the work of human artisans.

A young Englishman, John Frere, found some of these objects at the bottom of a deep shaft in a quarry in the English village of Hoxne in 1797 (Figure 1.9). The tools were located at a depth of at least 12 feet and beneath three distinct layers of soil. Furthermore, the soil layer directly overlying the stone tools contained marine shells and the bones of extinct animals (Stiebing 1993). Frere reported on the appearance and context of the stone tools he had excavated to the London Society of Antiquaries, deducing that their context led to the inevitable conclusion that they dated to "a very remote period indeed; even beyond that of the present world," and clearly indicated the existence of an ancient race of human beings who, again as Frere phrased it, "had not the use of metals" (Frere 1800:204).

Frere's report and the work of others who discovered and reported on stone tools and weapons in contexts that implied great antiquity played a significant role in opening and broadening the vista of the past. Most significantly, in the context of the discussion here, whatever debates ensued about the specific meaning of the stone tools, they clearly showed that items made in what turned out to be an ancient period had survived into the present. The discovery at Hoxne and those that followed showed absolutely that ancient objects could be found in the soil where they had been left by their makers in a remote period, and could be studied, analyzed, and argued about; in other words, these objects could make a contribution to our understanding of the past and this forms the basis for the science of archaeology.

**FIGURE 1.9** One of the finely crafted stone tools recovered and analyzed by John Frere deep in a clay pit in the English village of Hoxne in 1797. Objects like these caused a stir because the possibility that there had been a time in history when stone tools dominated human material culture seemed not to fit the accepted biblical chronology of the world.

## Read More

The following sources (including John Frere's own discussion of his discoveries and a compendium of first-hand accounts of many of the most significant archaeological discoveries in Fagan 1996) provide a wealth of information about the roots and history of archaeology:

Fagan, B. M., ed. 1996. *Eyewitness to Discovery: First-Person Accounts of More than Fifty of the World's Greatest Archaeological Discoveries.* Oxford University Press, Oxford.

Frere, J. 1800. Account of flint weapons discovered in Hoxne in Suffolk. *Archaeologia* 13:204–5.

Stiebing Jr., W. H. 1993. *Uncovering the Past: A History of Archaeology.* Oxford University Press, New York.

Van Riper, A. B. 1993. *Men among the Mammoths: Victorian Science and the Discovery of Human Prehistory.* University of Chicago Press, Chicago.

Willey, G. R., and J. A. Sabloff. 1993. *A History of American Archaeology.* W. H. Freeman and Company, New York.

## Is Garbage Really All That Informative on the Subject of Human Behavior?

Calling A. J. Weberman a fan of songwriter, singer, poet, philosopher, and folk-rock icon Bob Dylan is not nearly an accurate enough representation of Weberman's obsession with the music and life of the composer of so many anthems of the 1960s and 1970s (http://www.rollingstone.com/news/newsarticle.asp?nid=13566). At some point in the 1960s, after careful and relentless—and, it has been suggested, chemically enhanced—listening to the then collected works of the master songwriter, Weberman decided that he—and maybe he alone—had cracked the cleverly obscure "code" that he—and, again, maybe he alone—believed lay at the heart of the often startlingly layered lyrics of Bob Dylan's compositions. During this period, Weberman came to the realization that it should be his role in life to disseminate the true meaning behind Dylan's songs. As part of that task, he established in his Greenwich Village, New York, apartment what amounted to a Bob Dylan "database" that incorporated a colossal amount of Dylan-related material, including tapes of unreleased recordings, newspaper and magazine articles, and, as it turns out, stuff he swiped from Bob Dylan's trash cans.

Apparently, while passing by Dylan's Greenwich Village apartment one day in late 1970, Weberman experienced an epiphany, a sudden and intuitive flash. Oh sure, Dylan had granted his share of interviews and had revealed aspects of his life to the press. But who could trust the veracity or utility of a secretive Bob Dylan providing obscure answers to the insipid and self-serving questions of reporters who didn't truly understand the meaning of Dylan's work? Dylan could control an interview, answering only those questions that he wished to and in ways that revealed little about his true self. However, in front of the apartment house were Dylan's garbage cans, containers of items of great power and value, housing items that had actually been used by Bob Dylan, material reflections of the true life lived inside the walls of his apartment. Dylan could lie and obfuscate when confronted with questions about his life and work, but garbage cannot lie, it cannot mislead. Garbage is pure data, revealing truths about the people who used the items before discarding them.

Weberman walked over to the trash cans that day in 1970, opened the lids, and stole (if that is the correct word for taking material out of the trash) some of Dylan's material culture. Weberman brought the stuff home and analyzed it the way an Egyptologist might pore over a hieroglyphic text. Thus initiated a new front in the struggle to both understand and reveal the essence of Bob Dylan. Weberman made numerous subsequent field trips to "excavate" artifacts that had passed through Dylan's hands and house to the miniature and temporary archaeological "sites" of the great songwriter's trash cans. Weberman even offered classes in Dylan "garbology" and conducted expeditions to Dylan's house to train students in his brand of fieldwork. He published articles in a number of underground—and not so underground—1970s publications wherein he presented his fantastic interpretations of the meaning of what Bob Dylan had thrown away in the trash.

Weberman's seemingly single-minded obsession with Bob Dylan expanded to include other celebrities whose garbage he collected, analyzed, and reported on. The trash of former vice presidents (Spiro Agnew, who had re-signed in disgrace under President Nixon), the garbage of the wives of former presidents (Jackie Kennedy), and the refuse of writers (Norman Mailer) and actors (Dustin Hoffman) all became part of Weberman's garbology archive.

Weberman certainly was and, as nearly as I can tell, continues to be, one strange dude. Until recently, he produced a Web site discussing his lifework in garbology; unfortunately, the URL has gone dead, apparently after Weberman was arrested for drug possession. I will leave it to you to assess the irony here: the evidence used to convict Weberman was obtained by federal agents when they trawled through, of course, his trash.

I will not pass judgment on any of his seemingly bizarre interpretations of Bob Dylan's lyrics, nor do I have much to say about the legality of mining living people's trash to obtain insights into their lives. I will say, however, that Weberman discovered, albeit in an odd and interesting way, an axiom at the core of archaeology: there is a comprehensible relationship between human behavior and the objects they made, used, and discarded. Weberman did not have access—at least not much—to Bob Dylan himself because Dylan elected not to talk to him after their one conversation, which ended rather disastrously. So Weberman collected Dylan's trash and allowed the discarded materials to "talk" to him instead. Archaeologists, similarly, do not often have access to people who lived in the past for the rather obvious reason that most of them are long dead. We have little choice but to fall back on the material remains of their behavior, much of it their garbage, to talk to us in the present about lives lived long ago. Weberman's term garbology, after all, is not all that inaccurate in describing what it is that archaeologists do.

## Read More

To see just how insights about a culture—including our own—can be derived from the study of garbage, read the article that started it all or get the terrific book co-authored by Mr. Garbologist, William Rathje:

Harrison, G. G., W. L. Rathje, and W. W. Hughes. 1975. Food waste behavior in an urban population. *Journal of Nutrition Education* 7(1):13–16.
Rathje, W., and C. Murphy. 1992. *Rubbish: The Archaeology of Garbage.* HarperCollins, New York.
Sullivan, R. 1998. *The Meadowlands.* Scribner's, New York.

##  How Do You Get to Be an Archaeologist?

I call myself an archaeologist and have undergraduate and graduate training in archaeology, along with more than twenty years' experience conducting archaeological research. That makes me an archaeologist. But, the fact of the matter is, there is no universally accepted, legal definition of the term "archaeologist," no formal or binding prerequisites for calling yourself an archaeologist. In truth, anyone can have a set of business cards and some stationary printed saying that they are an archaeologist and they can excavate sites on private property as long as they have obtained permission from the landowner (see *What Laws*

*Regulate Where Archaeologists Can Dig?* in Unit 2). And, in fact, while you rarely will find neurosurgery hobbyists or avocational nuclear physicists, there likely are more amateur archaeologists than there are trained professionals.

On the other hand, the federal and most state governments, in a sense, do legally define "who is an archaeologist" through a set of regulations and guidelines determining who can conduct archaeological research, at least on federal or state property. Most governmental agencies also have policies concerning who can participate in archaeological projects mandated by those agencies to conform to federal, state, or local laws protecting archaeological or historical sites. You may call yourself an "archaeologist" but if you don't fulfill the requirements for training and experience established by the federal or local state government, you cannot practice archaeology on public lands, although, under most circumstances, these restrictions do not apply on private property. For example, in the group of federal regulations labeled 43 CFR 7, Section 7.8a, a less than catchy title, I will admit (http://www.cr.nps.gov/lawlinks.htm), the federal government lists the training and experiential requirements for an applicant who proposes to excavate an archaeological site on federal property. These include, among a number of guidelines: a graduate degree in anthropology, archaeology, or equivalent training and experience; at least 16 months' experience or training in archaeological fieldwork, laboratory work, or library work; and a demonstrated ability to conduct research to its timely completion. These regulations are in place to insure that any individual applying for a permit to dig on public lands, or any person submitting an archaeological proposal in response to a call for bids for legally required research has adequate training and enough experience to properly conduct the work.

These governmental policies concerning the qualifications of an archaeologist who wants to dig on federal land or participate in a federally funded archaeological project make a lot of sense. Archaeological sites on federal land are perceived to belong to us all, in essence, held in trust by the government for the communal good, resources from which all American citizens can learn and be inspired. The government takes its responsibility seriously and a fundamental goal of policies and regulations concerning who can excavate archaeological sites on federal property is that of protection, insuring that if sites are excavated, they are done so proficiently and the information they contain is shared with the public who, after all, "own" the sites and pay, through taxes, for their study.

The cardinal rule for physicians in their Hippocratic Oath applies equally well to archaeologists: "First, do no harm." Archaeological evidence is rare, precious, and of enormous scientific value. Without careful data recovery, objects can be damaged or destroyed and their **contexts** and **spatial associations** may be lost. Archaeological data can be likened to a nonrenewable, endangered resource; in fact, archaeological materials are often called **cultural resources.** No one is making any more two-thousand-year-old pottery or ten-thousand-year-old stone tools. It would be a terrible irony if, in the attempt to recover these kinds of objects, they are destroyed by someone ignorant of the best ways of preserving the information they can provide.

To maintain the integrity of the information provided by the archaeological record, it certainly is best for an archaeologist to have appropriate training and experience. In the United States, a trained archaeologist ordinarily will have obtained an undergraduate degree, most often in the discipline of **anthropology,** the general study of humanity, although there are archaeologists with undergraduate degrees in history, geography, geology, art history, classical studies, or even archaeology itself. A few universities in the United States offer a separate degree in archaeology, but most archaeology programs continue to be subsumed under anthropology departments. Undergraduate training ordinarily will include an extensive and diverse program of coursework in the study of **culture, prehistory,** history, **material culture,** geology, **osteology,** ecology, statistical analysis, and archaeological theory and method. Virtually all archaeology programs require laboratory and field experience before conferral of a degree. Many universities offer field schools in archaeology—intensive projects, ordinarily offered in the summer, where students are trained in the basic skills of archaeological **site survey, excavation,** mapping, lab work, and analysis. It is learning by doing and it is the only way to train in archaeological fieldwork. Field school training is not a one-way street, and students make a valuable contribution to the research. My own field research has been made possible by the labor of countless students who were being trained in archaeological field methods.

Individuals with an undergraduate degree in anthropology or a related field and training in fieldwork or lab work as a part of that degree program can gain employment in archaeology or work as a volunteer in a project, usually as a digger on a field crew or as a lab assistant cleaning and cataloging artifacts and preparing samples for more detailed analysis. An individual with a great deal of field experience might serve as a field crew chief, directing those digging **test pits** or in **excavation units.**

Ordinarily, to progress in archaeology and to go on to conduct one's own research, eventually to be the **principal investigator** of a project or to teach at a university, a graduate degree is essential. Like all sciences, archaeology has a vast and growing database and in general one needs an intensive exposure to what is already known about the human past and its study before one can direct a complex field project. Though some archaeologists conclude their academic training at the master's degree level, completion of a doctoral dissertation is sometimes perceived as a necessary indicator that an individual is capable of designing a research project, conducting research, and conveying the results of the work. A Ph.D. is often a requirement for employment as a professor at a university.

Finally, there is a private and voluntary listing of qualified archaeologists called the Register of Professional Archaeologists (RPA). This listing compiles the names of archaeologists who have applied to and been accepted for inclusion on the basis of their academic training in archaeology, their experience, and their conformance to basic ethical standards of archaeological research and reporting. Membership in the RPA requires a commitment to a set of rules of ethical behavior toward the archaeological record and toward the descendants of the people who left that record behind (http://www.rpanet.org).

I invited a number of my colleagues to share the story of the pathway they took into the field of archaeology and published their short essays titled, "Who Is an Archaeologist?" as segments of my book *Lessons from the Past*

(Feder 1999b). All of us share one guiding perspective: an overriding passion for the past and its study.

## Who Owns the Past?

In the provocative title of one of her courses, University of Wisconsin–Milwaukee anthropology professor Bettina Arnold poses the question: "Who Owns the Past?" A PBS documentary and accompanying Web site ask the same question regarding the archaeological record (http://www.pbs.org/wotp/). The question of who owns the past can be narrowly interpreted, focusing on ownership of the actual objects recovered by archaeologists. Phyllis Messenger (1993) calls these objects "cultural property" in the title of her book: *The Ethics of Collecting Cultural Property: Whose Culture, Whose Property?*

And, indeed, it can be a vexing legal, not to mention, moral question: to whom do the objects that archaeologists recover belong legally? To whom should they belong morally? Should the rule of the playground, "finders, keepers," apply and, therefore, should "cultural property," wherever it is found, always become the property of the archaeologist or arrowhead collector who found it? Should artifacts belong to the owner of the land on which the materials were found, though they were left there long before the current owner took title to the property? Should, instead, archaeological material belong to the state or nation in which the land is located? Should archaeological artifacts accrue to the person, organization, governmental agency, or museum that funded the project? Or, how about this: should objects found by archaeologists or artifact collectors revert to the descendants of the people who left the materials in the ground in the first place?

In the United States, archaeological material found on federal land (for example, national parks, forests, or on military bases) belongs to all American citizens communally, not to any one of us individually. Most archaeological material found on private property, no matter how scientifically or monetarily valuable, belongs to the owner of the property on which the material was found. Legally, the property owner can keep archaeological material found on his or her land, display it, sell it, give it away, or even destroy it.

Human remains, however, are not considered property—at least they are no longer so treated—and human skeletal remains don't belong to a landowner simply because they are located on his or her land. Certainly this makes sense. After all, how would you feel if it were your great-grandfather whose remains were being used as a conversation piece on someone's fireplace mantle, displayed to tourists at a roadside museum, or used as a Halloween decoration, all with the justification that they were found on private property and, therefore, belonged to the property owner for use as he or she saw fit?

Most people agree that human remains should not be considered property or mere specimens, but things can get pretty dicey when we move beyond human bones and consider objects that may be deemed sacred by the descendants of the people who left them behind. Instead of your great-grandfather's bones, the found objects could be the crucifix he wore around his neck when he was buried or the wedding ring he wore for more than fifty years in life and which he intended and expected to continue to circle his finger in death, expressing for eternity his bond with your great-grandmother. Would you view these things as artifacts, mere specimens for people to collect, however noble their intention?

This is not an easy issue. Fortunately, the overwhelming majority of the materials archaeologists find were disposed of as trash by ancient people and almost certainly were not considered sacred or meaningful by the folks who tossed them in the garbage pit or compost heap. Nevertheless, I was once told by a Native American that everything archaeologists dig up is sacred and was intended by his ancestors to remain in the ground forever (Feder 1999a). A corollary to the question "Who owns the past?" raised by this individual might then be "Who owns the right to decide what is sacred among the things found by archaeologists?" And, if everything left in the ground by ancient people is sacred, there can be no archaeology. It is a quandary, indeed, and there are no easy answers, and, perhaps, not even difficult answers.

The mistrust many Native Americans feel and express about the motives behind archaeological research is understandable. The U.S. government, for example, has much to atone for in terms of its treatment of the skeletal remains of Native Americans. Curiosity about racial differences—and an indifference to the lives and belief systems of the indigenous people of the New World—led to a skeleton collecting frenzy on the part of U.S. government agencies in the nineteenth century. Fresh graves were robbed and ancient graves despoiled, all in an attempt to produce a huge database of "scientific materials" that also happened to be the remains of human beings (Thomas 2001). Many of these complete and partial skeletons (in some cases only the skulls were kept) ended up at the Smithsonian Institution; others were housed at various museums and university laboratories throughout the United States. Certainly, these bones were of value for the scientific information they provided. Equally certainly, these bones were the remains of people whose loved ones were and are understandably aggrieved that they are lying in drawers in museums and laboratories.

Largely as a result of the efforts of Native Americans and sympathetic nonnative people, the **National Museum of the American Indian Act** of 1989 (http://www.nmnh.si.edu/anthro/repatriation/nmaiact.htm) and the **Native American Graves Protection and Repatriation Act (NAGPRA)** of 1990 (http://www.cr.nps.gov/nagpra/MANDATES/25USC3001etseq.htm) were passed by the U.S. Congress to redress the nineteenth-century grave-robbing policies of the federal government. As a result of NAGPRA, the National Museum of Natural History at the Smithsonian Institution established a repatriation office in 1991, whose function continues to be the careful inventory of human remains and sacred funerary objects curated by the museum, and the return of these remains and artifacts to the tribes from which they originated (http://www.nmnh.si.edu/anthro/repatriation/). Many Native American tribes have availed themselves of the opportunity to bring their ancestors and sacred objects home for reconsecration and, sometimes, reburial (Figure 1.10). A state-by-state and regional listing of the enormous numbers of individuals (to date, the bones of more than eighteen thousand people) whose remains have been returned to their tribal groups for reconsecration can be found at http://www.nmnh.si.edu/anthro/repatriation/.

**FIGURE 1.10** Human bones may be viewed as valuable scientific specimens and stored in universities, museums, and laboratories, but they also may be the revered remains of living people's ancestors. The solemn ceremonies shown here depict the reconsecration and reburial of human remains excavated by archaeologists and returned to the descendants of the people represented by the bones: Eyak Indians (Cordova, Alaska, top; CORBIS/Natalie Forbes) and Euroamericans (the Walton Family Cemetery, Griswold, Connecticut; courtesy, Nick Bellantoni).

Beyond the issue of who owns the actual skeletons and artifacts, the question of "Who owns the past?" as Bettina Arnold poses it has far broader implications. It's not just ancient things, but the interpretation of those ancient things that also is at issue. Who owns the right to "parse" the past, to provide the definitive description and explanation for what happened in antiquity? Who has the right to be the "official" authority about a group's past and who is the rightful mediator between the archaeological record and an interested citizenry? Is it tribal elders? Professional archaeologists? Textbook authors?

Consider a complete stranger, someone who doesn't know the language of your ancestors, has little if any shared cultural experiences with your family, and is ignorant and even dismissive of the stories told within your family of its own history. Would you be totally (or even a little) comfortable with such a person being the official chronicler and interpreter of your story, the source everyone relies on for information about your family's history? Probably not, and many Native Americans feel exactly this way about the stories white archaeologists tell of their native history (Biolsi and Zimmerman 1997). Then again, should those outside of your family, who are interested in its history, accept without reservation the family's own version with its likely closeting of episodes and individuals whom the family is uncomfortable with, and without sufficient objective or empirical evidence to support the family's version? Again, probably not.

Once, the oral histories and traditions of descendant groups were ignored by many archaeologists. This made no sense. The oral, traditional history of a group of people should not be dismissed and certainly can contain important and accurate information of value to archaeologists and historians. On the other hand, it also makes no sense to accept uncritically all oral traditions about the past as fact, simply because the people telling the stories are the biological and cultural descendants of those who produced the archaeological sites being studied.

Roger Echo-Hawk, an archaeologist and a Native American, coordinates repatriation for the Denver Art Museum and the Colorado Historical Society. He has used tribal oral histories extensively in the process of connecting recovered skeletal remains with descendant tribal groups. Echo-Hawk (1997) clearly recognizes the great historical value of these oral histories but he does not accept them unconditionally or uncritically, explicitly maintaining that the truth can be reached only by the combined use of oral history and archaeology. In fact, he labels the perspective that "Indian" knowledge based on oral history is superior to "white knowledge" based on archaeology, a "racialist paradigm" (Echo-Hawk 1997:101).

For example, despite seemingly overwhelming archaeological evidence, some Native Americans reject the notion that their ancestors arrived in the New World from Asia sometime before fifteen thousand years ago, in part because their oral histories record no such migration (Deloria 1995). Merely because it is their history does not make them right in their interpretation, however, any more so than would be the assertion that Egyptians did not build the pyramids more than 4,000 years ago because the modern residents of Egypt have no collective memory preserved in their oral traditions of having done so.

Oral traditions are great sources of hypotheses, possible explanations for elements of a people's past. Archaeology provides the physical evidence by which the historical veracity of such hypotheses can be tested.

If you are looking here for an authoritative, definitive answer to the questions "Who owns the past?" and "Who should own the past?" I am afraid that you are going to be disappointed. As the title of yet another book on this issue phrases it, Indians and archaeologists are still in the process of attempting to find "common ground" on the issue of who owns the past (Swindler et al. 1997). Perhaps it will be through recognizing a multiplicity of ownerships of the past and a diversity of interpretations by descendants, historians, and archaeologists that we may be able to more fully and objectively assess and understand the stories that the archaeological record can tell us.

## Read More

To learn about the broad diversity of views on the issue of who "owns" the past—some written by archaeologists, some written by Native Americans, and some written by archaeologists who are Native Americans—check out any and all of the following sources:

Biolsi, T., and L. Zimmerman, eds. 1997. *Indians and Anthropologists: Vine Deloria, Jr., and the Critique of Anthropology.* University of Tucson Press, Tucson.

Deloria Jr., V. 1995. *Red Earth, White Lies: Native Americans and the Myth of Scientific Fact.* Scribner's, New York.

Echo-Hawk, R. 1997. Forging a new ancient history for Native America. In *Native Americans and Archaeologists: Stepping Stones to Common Ground,* edited by N. Swindler, K. E. Dongoske, R. Anyon, and A. S. Downer, 88–102. AltaMira Press, Walnut Creek, California.

Feder, K. L. 1999a. Indians and archaeologists: Conflicting views of myth and science. *Skeptic* 5(3):74–80.

Jemison, G. P. 1997. Who owns the past? In *Native Americans and Archaeologists: Stepping Stones to Common Ground,* edited by N. Swindler, K. E. Dongoske, R. Anyon, and A. S. Downer, 57–63. AltaMira Press, Walnut Creek, California.

Messenger, P. M., ed. 1993. *The Ethics of Collecting Cultural Property: Whose Culture? Whose Property?* University of New Mexico Press, Albuquerque.

Swindler, N., K. E. Dongoske, R. Anyon, and A. S. Downer, eds. 1997. *Native Americans and Archaeologists: Stepping Stones to Common Ground.* AltaMira Press, Walnut Creek, California.

Thomas, D. H. 2000. *Skull Wars: Kennewick Man, Archaeology, and the Battle for Native American Identity.* Basic Books, New York.

Watkins, J. 2000. *Indigenous Archaeology.* AltaMira Press, Walnut Creek, California.

## What Kinds of People Go into Archaeology?

Almost every generation comes up with a popular—and thoroughly misguided—impression of who archaeologists are and what they should look like. In American movies made in the 1930s and 1940s, for example, archaeologists were almost universally Egyptologists. Quite eccentric, these white-haired, bearded gentlemen ordinarily had beautiful daughters who, of course,

**FIGURE 1.11** Though it seems to happen all the time to archaeologists in Hollywood epics like the 1932 black-and-white classic, *The Mummy*, personally, I have been an archaeologist for more than twenty-five years and I have yet to awaken a mummy in suspended animation. (© *Bettmann/CORBIS*)

accompanied their fathers on expeditions to godforsaken parts of the world, searching for secret or mystical knowledge possessed by ancient people. In revealing this occult information through their research, these archaeologists unleashed terrible calamities upon an unsuspecting world (Figure 1.11).

In another caricature, as most clearly exemplified in the *Indiana Jones* movies and, more recently, in *The Mummy* and *The Mummy Returns*, archaeologists are dashing, rather romantic, madcap adventurers, swashbuckling a swath across the Middle East or Egypt, finding glorious treasure, and fighting Nazis while continuing their tendency to inadvertently unleash the demons of some ancient hell. Oh, and in this version of the caricature, the archaeologist always "gets the girl."

It should go without saying that Hollywood's primary goals rest in selling tickets and popcorn, not in verisimilitude. To begin with, archaeologists are not necessarily, or even most often, men. Though in the past often counseled against going into archaeology (Claassen 1994), women, in fact, have long made a significant contribution to the discipline, more than enough, in fact, to base a book on their achievements and exploits in revealing the secrets of the ancient past (Williams 1981). In 1997, the Society for American Archaeology (SAA; http://www.saa.org) published a statistical analysis of its more than five thousand members and about a thousand nonmember archaeologists written by Melinda Zeder (1997), herself a highly regarded archaeologist at the Smithsonian Institution and a member of the SAA. This census of American archaeologists was rather striking in showing that, while among older archaeologists—and, therefore,

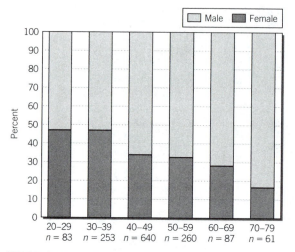

**FIGURE 1.12** Graph showing the percentages of male and female archaeologists (vertical axis) within each age group by decade (horizontal axis). Note the steady increase as you move to the left along the graph in the percentages of female archaeologists in each age group until we find that, among archaeologists in their twenties, nearly half are women. (*Melinda Zeder and AltaMira Press*)

people who became archaeologists fifty, sixty, or even seventy years ago—the majority, indeed, were men, among successively younger generations of archaeologists, women represented an increasing fraction of the field (Figure 1.12). In the youngest cohort among those sampled, people in their twenties and likely still in graduate school when the survey was taken, women represented almost exactly half of the field (Zeder 1997:11). Although Lara Croft is, by the labeling of her originators, a "tomb raider" and not an archaeologist, I suppose one could argue that her rise to prominence among video game and movie action heroes who get involved with antiquities parallels the rise of female archaeologists in the late twentieth and early twenty-first centuries. I do not know of any archaeologists, however, who view Lara Croft as a role model for young women interested in pursuing a career in archaeology.

Most stereotypes also represent archaeologists as white Europeans or Americans, studiously yet romantically revealing the ancient past, most often of non-European peoples. In a sense, unfortunately, this caricature resonates with not just a little truth. European and American archaeologists have long traveled to Egypt as well as Africa south of the Sahara, Mexico and Peru, Cambodia and India/Pakistan, and, like an invading colonial army, appropriated the prehistories and ancient histories of the native peoples, removing the artifacts recovered for display in European museums, and monopolizing all conversation about their antiquity. In America, archaeology has long tended to be a rather exclusive club with, once again, "foreigners" (that is, white folks of European descent) dominating the research and discussion of the ancient history of a native people, in this case American Indians. In Zeder's (1997:13) analysis of SAA members, as of 1997, people of white, European ancestry accounted for about 98% of the group. Members of the SAA who characterized their ethnicity as African American, Asian, or Native American could be counted on the fingers, if not of one hand, then of three: there were only two African Americans, four Asians, and ten Native Americans out of the 1,700 or so surveys returned for analysis. There were only fifteen Hispanics in the group, and five of them were from Latin American countries, conducting archaeology in their own nations.

Archaeology has much work to do in this regard, but the field is transforming in many ways. Today, though much of the paleoanthropology of Africa conducted in search of our earliest human ancestors continues to be carried out by European and American scholars (or African scholars of European

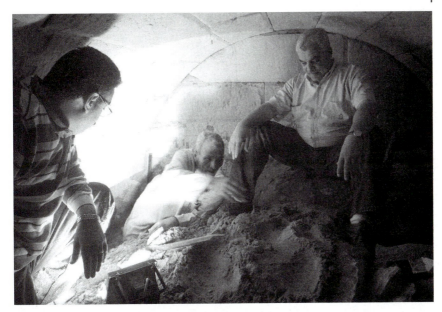

**FIGURE 1.13** Undersecretary of the State for the Giza Monuments, archaeologist Zahi Hawass (right) is seen here supervising the excavation of a 2,500-year-old tomb found in 2001 during construction in a Cairo neighborhood. (*Reuters NewMedia Inc./CORBIS*)

descent), they now work in collaboration with native African archaeologists and paleontologists. It is almost impossible to see a television documentary about the latest discoveries regarding ancient Egypt that does not include the substantial participation of native Egyptian archaeologists led by the guiding hand of researcher Zahi Hawass (Figure 1.13), whose official Egyptian government title is Undersecretary of the State for the Giza Monuments (these are the three large pyramid complexes—including the sphinx—located along the Nile at Giza, http://www.guardians.net/hawass/).

In essence, throughout the world, people are reclaiming the archaeological study of their ancestors and archaeologists come in all ethnicities and nationalities. In the United States, where archaeologists of European descent continue to statistically dominate the archaeological investigation of the Native American past, a small, dedicated, and growing cadre of Indian archaeologists are telling the story of their own ancient ancestors. (For example, see the book *Indigenous Archaeology* by Joe Watkins 2000, an archaeologist who works for the federal government; he is a Choctaw Indian.) The Navajo Nation in Arizona even has its own archaeology department (http://www.nau.edu/nnad) that conducts archaeology and trains Navajo and other native archaeology students in the study of their own past.

In a similar vein, the historical context of the "peculiar institution" of slavery has become grist for the mill of historical archaeology (Ferguson 1992; McKee 1995). Because slaves were compelled in many states to remain illiterate as a matter of law, they could not tell their own story through the written word. In fact, generally, it was those who *owned* slaves and not those who *were* slaves who wrote about slavery in the American North and South. Certainly, the objectivity of these historical descriptions of the institution of slavery by slave owners cannot necessarily be trusted.

As a result, some archaeologists have focused their attentions on the institution of slavery. The archaeological record of plantations, including the remains of slave quarters, is in this sense a far more democratic and objective source of data than the written record, especially concerning such physical qualities of slave life as diet, housing, and material culture. Also, items of material culture that were intentionally hidden from slave masters by African captives, especially items related to the practice of forbidden non-Christian, native African religious behaviors, provide a unique perspective on the nature of the intellectual resistance to captivity practiced by captives in a way the written record cannot.

Although the majority of archaeologists conducting this work have been of European descent simply because the vast majority of archaeologists in the United States are of European descent, this too is changing. A colleague and friend, Warren Perry (Central Connecticut State University), is one of a growing group of African American archaeologists. Perry has conducted research in Africa and the United States and is the director of the archaeological component of the African Burial Ground project, in which the graves of more than four hundred African captives buried in the southern end of Manhattan Island in New York are being examined (Perry and Blakey 1997). In a sense, in this project, it is the children of slaves, not the children of slave masters, who are revealing the nature of captivity as reflected in the archaeological record.

The point is, neither of the sexes and no particular ethnic group has a monopoly on a passion for the past. A fascination for antiquity knows no gender, cultural, or political boundaries. As in all other fields of human intellectual endeavor, archaeology can only benefit from the multiplicity of perspectives that results, at least in part, from the diversity of the life histories of its practitioners (Feder 1999b).

## Read More

For a hint at the diversity that characterizes the community of archaeologists, any of the following sources would be a good place to start:

Claasen, C. P., ed. 1994. *Women in Archaeology.* University of Pennsylvania Press, Philadelphia.

Feder, K. L., ed. 1999b. *Lessons from the Past.* Mayfield Publishing, Mountain View, California.

Ferguson, L. 1992. *Uncommon Ground: Archaeology and Early African America, 1650–1800.* Smithsonian Institution Press, Washington, D.C.

McKee, L. 1995. The earth is their witness. *The Sciences* 35(2):36–41.

Perry, W., and M. Blakey. 1997. Archaeology as community service: The African Burial Ground Project in New York City. *North American Dialogue* 2(1):1–5.

Watkins, J. 2000. *Indigenous Archaeology.* AltaMira Press, Walnut Creek, California.

Williams, B., ed. 1981. *Breakthrough: Women in Archaeology.* Walker and Company, New York.

Zeder, M. A. 1997. *The American Archaeologist: A Profile.* AltaMira Press, Walnut Creek, California.

# Study Questions

1. What is archaeology? Define the term in a single sentence. And not a run-on sentence!

2. What kinds of data are the focus of archaeological analysis?

3. Do archaeologists study dinosaurs? (Here's a hint: No.) Why not?

4. Are archaeologists also geologists?

5. On what world areas do archaeologists focus their energies? Which areas are they not interested in studying?

6. On what time period(s) do archaeologists focus their energies? Which time periods are they not interested in studying?

7. How do anthropologists define culture?

8. What is adaptation? How do human beings adapt?

9. Is culture uniquely human? Do any other species exhibit behaviors that we can call cultural?

10. Contrast the adaptation of any wild animal species with which you are familiar and human beings who live in the same region as that species.

11. How did the Renaissance contribute to the development of the science of archaeology?

12. How did people in Europe in the eighteenth and nineteenth centuries explain symmetrically shaped pieces of chipped stone (today called hand axes) found deep in the soil, often associated with the bones of extinct animals?

13. What was important about John Frere's discovery at Hoxne in the late eighteenth century?

14. The author Donald K. Grayson (1983) titled his book, *The Establishment of Antiquity*. How did thinkers in the eighteenth- and nineteenth-century establish the great antiquity of the Earth, life, and of the human presence on Earth?

15. Who is A. J. Weberman? What does Weberman's interesting methodology for studying the life of Bob Dylan have to do with archaeology?

16. What is garbology?

17. What are the legal requirements for becoming an archaeologist?

18. What training and experience are required by the federal government for anyone applying to excavate an archaeological site on federal land?

19. Explain the concept of "cultural resources." How does this concept relate to archaeological site preservation?

20. By what rationale is archaeology course work and research, at least in the United States, included in university anthropology programs?

21. In what fields are professional archaeologists ordinarily trained?

22. How does an archaeologist become a member of the Register of Professional Archaeologists?

23. What is meant by the question: "Who owns the past?"

24. By law, who owns archaeological material found on private property? By law, who owns archaeological material found on public property?

25. Describe the demographic profile of archaeologists today. How has that demographic profile changed over the past several decades?

We were searching for remnants of previous human settlement and activity in the wooded upland that became a Connecticut state forest in the early decades of the twentieth century.

Luckily, I had a terrific crew of fieldworkers, a great **crew chief,** and an amazing **field director.** Although it was difficult to hand over a project I had designed and shepherded through an agonizing funding and planning process, at least I knew that I was leaving the day-to-day work to an exceptionally competent crew of archaeologists. Also luckily—not for my wife, but for me—Josh was born about two weeks late. My wife was comfortable with me going out into the field with the crew a

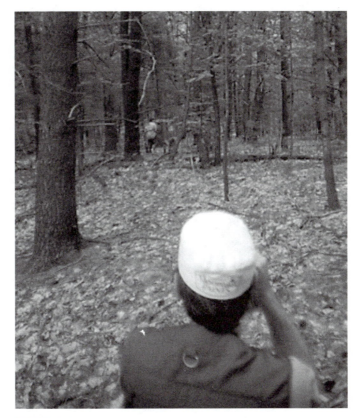

**FIGURE 2.1** Setting up a test pit transect. Using a sighting compass, the crew chief (in the foreground) is shooting in a line for the crew (in the background). Test pits were excavated every 10 meters along this line. (*Kenneth L. Feder*)

**FIGURE 2.2** Topographic map of Peoples State Forest, Barkhamsted, Connecticut.

few times during the twelve-day period between the beginning of our re-search on the first of June and Josh's delayed arrival on the twelfth, so, though admittedly more than just a little bit distracted—okay, I was a wreck—I wasn't entirely isolated from the initial fieldwork.

Though I couldn't spend as much time in the field as I might have wished that summer, I nevertheless continued to play an active role in the project from my home. Often, the entire crew would stop off at my house on their way out into the field in the morning (expecting doughnuts!) and we would go over the particular plan for the day, discussing the established survey lines or **transects** along which they would search for **sites** during the next eight hours or so (Figure 2.1).

Though we had a fairly detailed plan outlining our strategy in the search for sites, as in any scientific project, we needed to be flexible and our plans regularly changed as a result of inclement weather or impossible field conditions that were not initially recognized on our **topographic maps** (Figure 2.2).

Beyond this, on a good day, the discovery of some interesting "stuff" that required additional work and time in an area might also cause us to alter our strategy. So, though we had a good general plan and rough schedule, that plan and schedule needed to be reassessed each day and changed accordingly.

## What Determines What an Archaeologist Investigates in the First Place?

There are many different reasons why an archaeologist may choose to conduct research at a given place. We chose to examine the land within the boundaries of Peoples State Forest for several reasons. We had a research goal in mind; we wanted to study the ways in which the ancient inhabitants of southern New England used upland tracts of land and Peoples State Forest was well suited to our purpose. The land contained within Peoples represents a noncoastal, primarily nonriverine, inland and upland locale, which, when we started the project in 1986, was not the kind of habitat that had been extensively investigated by archaeologists in southern New England. It also is relatively undisturbed habitat and presented us with an opportunity to investigate a large chunk of real estate that had not been completely made over into roads, shopping plazas, and general suburban sprawl. Essentially, we elected to dig in Peoples State Forest because we believed that we could learn new things about the pattern of land use by the aboriginal people of Connecticut. This is an important point to make. Archaeologists don't just go out and dig because we enjoy fieldwork or even just because we need to train students. We conduct research to answer specific questions and to test hypotheses about the lives of ancient people.

Because ours was a university project, supported by our institution and funded largely through the tuition paid by students obtaining six college credits and archaeological training through our program, we had the luxury of pursuing our interest in the settlement patterns of the aboriginal inhabitants of southern New England for no other reason than the fact that we were intensely interested in that issue. Many university-based archaeological research projects have a similar advantage: the educational institution recognizes the significance of such projects and supports its archaeological faculty in the pursuit of their research interests everywhere in the world.

Other archaeological research universes may be chosen for far more practical reasons. Much of the archaeology conducted in the United States today may be characterized as **compliance archaeology.** The federal government of the United States has, since at least 1906 (http://www.cr.nps.gov/local-law/anti1906.htm) enacted extensive legislation protecting archaeological sites on public lands and, especially since the early 1960s, laws requiring the determination of possible impacts on archaeological "resources" that might result from federally funded, mandated, or permitted (in the sense that formal permits are required from the federal government before a project may commence) projects. (Look at Thomas King's 1998 book, *Cultural Resource Laws and Practice* for an insightful discussion of historic preservation legislation, and visit http://www.cr.nps.gov/linklaws.htm for links to the actual text of the most important federal laws protecting archaeological sites.) This legislation acts to protect archaeological sites that may be affected by government activity by contracting with archaeologists to look for and conduct at least a preliminary examination of sites in a project area. Here, the research universe is determined not simply on the basis of an archaeologist's curiosity or desire to cover a particular area. Instead, it is defined by the practical concerns involved in answering a very specific question: Are there any sites in the specific area to be affected by activity carried out by or enabled by (through funding or permitting) the federal government?

For example, when the federal government, in its application of the Clean Water Act, requires a local municipality to respond to a pollution problem through the construction of a sewage treatment system, the government legally requires an assessment called an **Environmental Impact Statement** that provides a detailed analysis of the possible negative impacts of a project on historical resources within or adjacent to the project area. In this example, the government may sponsor an archaeological investigation restricted to the area to be directly affected by the construction of a water treatment facility and the placement of sewer pipes. Simply put, many archaeologists do not independently decide where they will dig on the basis of their own research interests or analytical goals; they are contracted to look in particular places because any sites that might be in those places are threatened by a construction project—an interstate highway, an airport, a sewer system—funded, mandated, or permitted by the U.S. government.

Local governments, including states, counties, and even towns, may have their own diverse regulations requiring an assessment of the potential for damage or destruction of archaeological sites in an area where construction is planned. It is becoming increasingly common for town governments to include consideration of archaeological sites in the impact assessments required by conservation commissions or other town boards that must approve construction projects before they can proceed. Here, too, archaeologists may be hired to make such assessments and the areas they are contracted to study are determined by the geographical scope of the construction project. The point here is that, although you might think that most or even all archaeological work is inspired by the particular geographical interests of archaeologists, this is not the case. A fair portion of the archaeology conducted in the United States is located according to the agendas of those who are paying the bills for the archaeological work, and those agendas are often dictated by laws that have been passed to protect archaeological sites endangered by federally or state mandated projects.

 ## What Laws Regulate Where Archaeologists Can Dig?

I think many archaeologists would like to be awarded special badges upon conferral of our Ph.D.s that bestowed on us the unfettered right to conduct fieldwork wherever our research interest directed us. Instead, unfortunately (or maybe fortunately), archaeologists are like everybody else and must obey local property laws. In the United States, the rights of private property owners are highly regarded, legally protected, and supercede our research interests and intellectual curiosity. Any archaeologist who ventures onto private land to conduct research without getting the permission of the property owner is guilty of trespassing and subject to the penalties for the commission of that crime as meted out by the municipality in which the trespassing took place.

It should be pointed out that in the United States, and in contrast to the laws of many other countries, holders of real estate own not just the surface of the land, but virtually everything buried on their property, including oil, minerals, and archaeological material. The only exception to this relates to human burials that might turn up on private land. Most states have laws that protect human remains and a landowner usually does not have the right to disturb or remove burials on his or her property without going through a legally mandated process. For example, when graves are located on private land in Connecticut, a formal process is initiated. The police and state medical examiner must be notified; they will determine if the remains are associated with a crime or those of a missing person (Figure 2.3).

If the bones are not those of a murder victim or an accidental death, the state archaeologist is called in to help determine the affiliation of the deceased. If the remains are those of a Native American, a formal council made up of representatives from a number of tribes is convened to decide the disposition of the bones. If the bones are not Native American, the law requires that the descendants of the deceased, if they can be found, must be contacted. The landowner ordinarily cannot simply move human remains to a more convenient location to allow for development without first obtaining permission from the descendants of the deceased. Also, there is a federal law—the **Native American Graves Protection and Repatriation Act**—that specifically protects the physical remains of American Indians and Native Hawaiians.

The bottom line here is straightforward: an owner of a piece of property has the right to allow or deny access to his or her property to anyone (at least anyone without a warrant), including an archaeologist who might want to dig

**FIGURE 2.3** The first skeleton at what turned out to be the lost Walton family cemetery was found by a couple of kids riding their bikes down the embankment of a gravel quarry. Once the state medical examiner determined that the remains were not those of a missing person, a crew from the Office of the State Archaeologist commenced excavation and preservation of the more than two dozen graves shown in this map. After descendants were found and notified, the remains were studied and then reburied in a church graveyard nearby. (*Courtesy of Nick Bellantoni*)

there and, except for human remains, anything found on private property is considered to belong to the property owner. An archaeologist must obtain permission to conduct research on private property, always aware of the fact that any archaeological materials found on private land remain the property of the landowner, unless some other legally binding arrangement has been made.

The rules concerning archaeological work on public lands are far different. The federal government owns a tremendous amount of property, especially in the form of national parks, forests, monuments, and military bases. Archaeological sites on federal lands are considered to be part of our national heritage and the property of all U.S. citizens as a group. The government, through the Department of Agriculture, the Defense Department, and especially the National Park Service (an agency of the Department of the Interior), protects sites on the land it administers and closely regulates archaeological access to these lands through the **Archaeological Resources Protection Act of 1979** (http://www2.cr.nps.gov/laws/archprotect.htm). A regulation of that act, 43 CFR 7, titled The Protection of Archaeological Resources (http://www.cr.nps.gov/local-law/43cfr7.htm), provides a detailed set of rules (Section 7.8a) about who can conduct archaeological research and how they need to go about justifying such research on federally administered land.

These regulations stipulate that an archaeologist must obtain formal permission to conduct archaeological research on public lands. Federal agencies charged with the duty of protecting sites have strict rules concerning to whom they will grant archaeological permits. Along with possessing the level of training and experience required by 43 CFR 7, he or she must submit a proposal for research on public land, which is evaluated by archaeologists who serve on the staff of the government agency in charge of the land in question. Perhaps of greatest importance, the regulation makes it clear that archaeological research on federally administered lands will be permitted only when that research has the potential to contribute to our understanding of the human past and only if the researcher agrees to share the results of the research with the true owners of the property, the citizens of the United States. As the regulation indicates:

> The proposed work is to be undertaken for the purpose of furthering archaeological knowledge in the public interest, which may include but need not be limited to, scientific or scholarly research, and preservation of archaeological data.

The **American Antiquities Act of 1906** (http://www.cr.nps.gov/local-law/anti1906.htm) initially established a fine of no more than $500 and a maximum of ninety days in jail for anyone convicted of excavating without official permission and thereby injuring or destroying an archaeological site on federal property. More recently, the penalties have become far more severe: anyone found in violation of the **Archaeological Resources Protection Act of 1979** is subject to an initial fine of up to $10,000 and one year in jail. If the monetary value of the artifacts taken from federal lands exceeds $500, the penalty may double. Penalties dramatically increase with any subsequent violations and convictions. Obviously, the federal government takes very seriously its responsibility to protect archaeological resources on lands it administers.

There are many different rules that regulate archaeological access to lands owned by states or local municipalities. Almost always, formal permission must be obtained from those municipalities for archaeological investigation. To obtain permission to conduct our archaeological research in Peoples State Forest in 1986, we submitted a formal request to the Department of Environmental Protection (DEP) of the State of Connecticut, the agency that administers state forest land. Today, such a proposal would need to be assessed by both the DEP and the Office of the Connecticut State Archaeologist.

## Read More

Because laws are in a constant state of flux, the best place to read about the current state of historic preservation legislation is on the homepage of the National Park Service, in particular, their list of historic preservation laws (http://www.cr.nps.gov/linklaws.htm). The following books provide good historical context for these laws:

King, T. F. 1998. *Cultural Resource Laws and Practice: An Introductory Guide.* Altamira Press, Walnut Creek, California.

King, T. F., P. P. Hickman, and G. Berg. 1977. *Anthropology in Historic Preservation: Caring for Culture's Clutter.* Academic Press, New York.

McGimsey III, C. R. 1972. *Public Archaeology.* Seminar Press, New York.

## What Is an "Archaeological Site" and How Do You Know When You've Found One?

*Carnac*

An archaeological **site** is a place where people once lived or worked or where they carried out specific tasks like hunting animals; collecting edible nuts; collecting fish; quarrying for metals, minerals, or clay; fighting a battle with their enemies; worshipping their gods; grinding meal; milling lumber; and burying their dead. Crucially, a site is a place where the material remnants of these activities and behaviors can be found. "Villages," "quarries," "cemeteries," "hunting camps," "mill towns," "sacred locations," "battlefields," and the like are the places where people carried out their tasks and where the events of their lives took place (Figure 2.4).

**FIGURE 2.4** Archaeological sites—like the burial mound (top), the ruins of a barn with a stone silo on a nineteenth-century Connecticut estate (bottom left), and the Giza plateau in Egypt where resides the Great Sphinx—are places where people once lived, worked, or carried out a task, and where physical evidence of those activities can be found, recovered, and analyzed (bottom right). (*Photos by M. H. Feder*).

These terms—cemeteries, hunting camps, battlefields, and so on—represent human **behavioral contexts,** reflecting how ancient people perceived and utilized these places. The site, the thing archaeologists look for and investigate, represents what's left behind by people as a result of their having buried their dead, collected resources, planted crops, hunted game animals, disposed of their trash, and so on. The site, in other words, represents the physical remnants of these human activities, the spoor or trail of a community of people living their lives at a particular place and time. If the village, camp, or quarry represents the behavioral context of a group of people, the site reflects the **archaeological context** of these same folks.

These material manifestations of behavior occur accidentally: people do not set out to produce archaeological sites. People do not ordinarily leave things behind with the deliberate purpose of giving future archaeologists something to find and analyze. Today we may set aside time capsules with a selection of items that exemplify our time and place for future people who might be interested in what life was like "way back when." Change is so rapid these days, our cultural attention span is so short, and we seem so anxious to connect to the past that time capsules tend to be opened just a few decades after they were sealed up. The inhabitants of the dim mists of the 1990s seem quaint and foreign with their CRT computer monitors and Pokémon. Archaeological sites do not reflect the self-conscious attempt by past people to communicate through material objects the essence of their time on life's stage to an unimaginable future generation of scientists. Sites come into existence through largely unintentional cultural processes.

There are no archaeological "road signs" alerting the inquiring archaeologist to the presence of a site. Archaeologists know they are at a site when, in the course of survey, they encounter physical evidence in the form of **site constituents** (**artifacts, ecofacts,** and/or **features**). *Site constituents* is just a fancy way of describing the things and facilities that people made and used and then lost, discarded, or simply left behind and that have preserved into the present (McManamon 1984). When an archaeologist finds flint flakes or pottery shards while screening the dirt from a test excavation, he or she knows that the location is an archaeological site. In the subsequent **excavation,** the archaeologist hopes to determine the cultural meaning of the site, its function and significance to the people who left behind the material remains that today represent the archaeological record of their lives.

# Read More

Although "archaeological site" might seem like a difficult concept to define, you certainly would know when you encountered one. Archaeologists have attempted to explain the "site" in formal ways. I have always employed an article by Frank McManamon who, in his capacity as the director of the federal archaeology program of the National Park Service, ought to know:

McManamon, F. P. 1984. Discovering sites unseen. In *Advances in Archaeological Method and Theory,* edited by M. B. Schiffer, vol. 7, 223–92. Academic Press, New York.

## Study Questions

1. Why was my crew of archaeologists digging test pits in Peoples State Forest in Connecticut?

2. What are the most common reasons for conducting an archaeological survey in a given region?

3. What is "compliance archaeology"? With what are archaeologists complying?

4. What is an Environmental Impact Statement?

5. What special rights do archaeologists have to gain access to private property to look for sites?

6. How does the law relate to the archaeological excavation of human remains?

7. What is the Native American Graves and Repatriation Act?

8. What does the Archaeological Resources Protection Act of 1979 require of archaeological work proposed on federal land?

9. What was the purpose of the American Antiquities Act of 1906?

10. In what ways did the Archaeological Resources Protection Act of 1979 expand upon or toughen the American Antiquities Act of 1906?

11. Define the term "archaeological site."

12. Provide a list of ten different entities for which the term "archaeological site" would be appropriate.

13. What is "behavioral context"? What is "archaeological context"?

14. Name the "constituents" of archaeological sites.

15. The site concept represents the archaeological context of what?

At the end of each day, my field director would stop by my house, dropping off paperwork consisting of maps, **test pit forms,** and paper bags containing any archaeological material recovered during the field day—mostly **artifacts** that, through any one of a number of **site formation processes,** had been transformed from their original functions as tools and objects people used in everyday life in the distant and not-so-distant past to their present incarnation as elements of the archaeological record.

Part of our **research strategy** that summer involved a walkover of the entire forest surface, looking for above-ground evidence of historical use of the area. In our walkover, called a **pedestrian survey,** of Peoples, we found house foundations, the remains of old mill buildings and their associated facilities, animal pens, stone walls, historical trash dumps, and even an old burial ground (Figure 3.1). These were visible on the surface because they were large, built-up features composed of durable material, and because they weren't particularly ancient, dating to only the last few hundred years. Not nearly enough time had passed to cover these sites in their particular settings and they were visible to anyone who took the time to walk around off trail deep in the woods.

Though archaeologists can in some instances find sites, including quite ancient sites, through above-ground, visual inspection (in southern New England where our survey took place and elsewhere) a series of entirely natural processes serves to cover material that rests on the ground for very long.

Thus, except for relatively recent materials, the archaeological remains that we sought had been buried and the only way we could find them was

**FIGURE 3.1** This small cemetery, with graves indicated by simple fieldstones, is located in our pedestrian survey in Peoples State Forest. (*Kenneth L. Feder*)

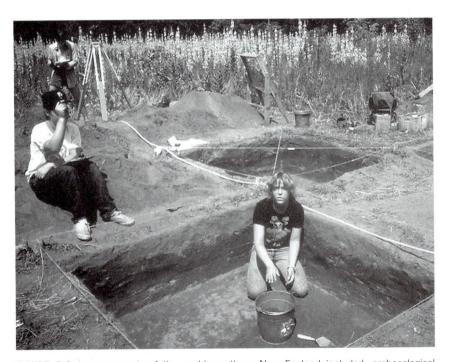

**FIGURE 3.2** In many parts of the world, southern New England included, archaeological material is buried by a broad array of natural processes. In order to find and recover this evidence of past life, archaeologists need to dig using a series of careful and controlled procedures. (*Kenneth L. Feder*)

to peer beneath the surface. Even now, with various high-tech devices at our disposal for mapping and analysis, in most places the best way to do that—meaning the way in which most sites in an area can be found and described—is simply to dig (Figure 3.2).

Of course, we couldn't excavate an entire 4,000-acre forest in our search for archaeological sites. We didn't have the time, the personnel, or the money—and we certainly wouldn't want to destroy 4,000 acres of forestland merely to satisfy our archaeological curiosity. Much of the time my crew members spent in the field they investigated only a **representative sample** of the subsurface soil in the forest.

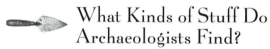

# What Kinds of Stuff Do Archaeologists Find?

Archaeologists usually divide the materials we find into the following (or similar) categories: **artifacts, ecofacts,** and **features.** Archaeologist Frank McManamon (1984) has labeled these items the "constituents" of archaeological sites. During the survey phase of an archaeological project, where we are examining an area for the possible presence of **sites,** these constituents are essentially what we are looking for most directly, the first clues of a past human presence. The site represents the big picture. Artifacts, ecofacts, and features are the pieces of the puzzle, the bits we find and put together to reveal the big picture.

Artifacts are defined simply as the things people made and used and that have by various processes become part of the archaeological record. Artifacts usually are further distinguished by the fact that they are portable; people could pick them up and carry them from place to place. Before these objects actually became "artifacts," they were, among other things, hardware, tools, weapons, items of personal adornment (like jewelry or religious symbols), storage containers, cooking apparatus, fasteners, as well as broken bits and pieces of all of these items, and any of the waste fragments produced in their manufacture. Archaeologist Michael Schiffer (1972, 1976) refers to the actual function of items in a society—what they were used for and what they meant to the people who made and used them—in essence, what they might have called these things—as their cultural or **behavioral contexts.** People make and use hardware, tools, weapons, and so on; they don't set out to produce artifacts, anymore than you would consider the pen in your pocket, the watch on your wrist, the clothes you are wearing, or the computer on which you may be reading this book an artifact. Those things, in fact, are not artifacts—at least, not yet. In fact, all of your tools, utensils, jewelry, keepsakes, toys, treasures, knickknacks, gear, junk—all of your possessions, all of your stuff—are "artifacts in waiting." *Artifact* is the general term archaeologists apply to these things once they have entered into the archaeological record (Figure 3.3). The term *artifact* reflects what Schiffer labels the **archaeological context** of these items in the present.

**FIGURE 3.3** Each of the sculptures in this spectacular clutch of jade figurines of the Olmec culture of Mesoamerica is an archaeological artifact, like a potsherd, a spear point, or a stone flake. (© *Gianni Dagli Orti/CORBIS*)

Ecofacts include any environmental elements that become part of the archaeological record as a result of human activity, generally reflecting their use without substantial or goal-oriented modification. It can sometimes be a subtle distinction, but it is an important one to recognize. Ecofacts are not, in the strict sense of the term, artifacts because they were not so modified by people that we would consider them to have been manufactured. These items weren't, in the strict sense of these words, tools or weapons or treasures made by people to serve a particular purpose. Instead, they were used and deposited by people in the conduct of their activities without being *made* into anything. A good example of an ecofact is a piece of wood burned in a hearth fire. Certainly, its presence in the hearth and its burning are the result of human activity—a person collected the wood and put it in a fireplace, using it as fuel—but one wouldn't call the burned wood a tool per se, as you would had the piece of wood instead been shaped and used as a spear. Ecofacts include unmodified (in the sense of not intentionally made into something) wood, nutshells and nutmeat fragments, seeds, pollen, and animal bones if their presence at a site is the result of human activity (Figure 3.4). If an unmodified animal bone is found in the trash heap at an archaeological site, perhaps exhibiting cut marks where a stone tool was used to remove meat, the bone

**FIGURE 3.4** Part of an extensive bed of ancient bison bones found at the Certain Site in Oklahoma is shown here as it is being excavated by archaeologists. This level of bone concentration resulted from a mass killing of these large animals at this spot. (*Courtesy of Kent Buehler*)

itself is an ecofact. It is an element of the environment—part of an animal—whose presence and appearance are the result of human activity (in this case, hunting and butchering).

On the other hand, an animal bone found at a site and bearing engravings of lunar phases, perhaps used as a calendar, clearly is an artifact, an item modified by people to serve a particular purpose. So, the left foreleg of a deer killed, butchered, cooked, and eaten by a group of people, and then disposed of in the kitchen trash is an ecofact; the right foreleg of the same animal if, for example, it was modified for use as a tent stake and then tossed in the trash after it cracked, is an artifact.

A feature is an accumulation of material at a particular place and, therefore, represents a different level of analysis than an artifact or ecofact. Features often are concentration of artifacts and/or ecofacts as well as structural remains (Figure 3.5). Features are nonportable and spatially bounded, often resulting from an activity or set of activities in which items used together or disposed of together were deposited. For example, the ground where a stone tool maker removed sharp flakes from a stone **core** by **percussion flaking** with a stone hammer and then shaped and sharpened some of those flakes into particular tool types will become littered with **debitage** (waste flakes of stone too small to be of use), battered chunks of **hammerstone,** nearly complete tools broken

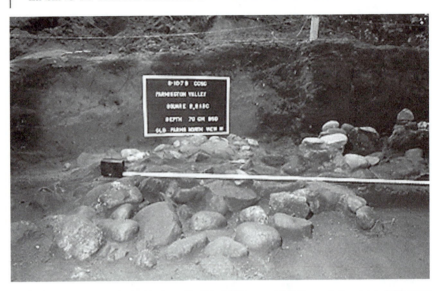

**FIGURE 3.5** An archaeological feature, like this 4,250-year-old platform of stones on which meat was roasted, represents a combination of artifacts and/or ecofacts (in this case, the stones themselves, charcoal, bone fragments, and a spear point) demarcating a place where people once carried out an activity. (*Kenneth L. Feder*)

in the final stages of manufacture and then abandoned, and pieces of antler ground off in **pressure flaking.** Each of these items individually—waste flakes, snapped tools, hammerstone chunks, ground antler fragments—are artifacts. Together, they demarcate space that we might call an **activity area**—that is, its behavioral context, a place where people conducted an activity—whose archaeological manifestation is a **feature.** Hearths, burials, workshops, and house remains are all archaeological features.

Taken together, the presence of artifacts, ecofacts, and features define an archaeological site, which was, in life, a place where people may have lived, worked, or carried out a particular task, and even where they died and were buried—and in some instances where they did all of these things.

## Read More

For more details on how archaeologists formally label the categories of material that constitute the archaeological record, the following sources are most helpful:

McManamon, F. P. 1984. Discovering sites unseen. In *Advances in Archaeological Method and Theory,* edited by M. B. Schiffer, vol. 7, 223–92. Academic Press, New York.

Schiffer, M. B. 1972. Archaeological context and systemic context. *American Antiquity* 37:156–65.

———. 1976. *Behavioral Archaeology.* Academic Press, New York.

# How Are Archaeological Sites Made?

In his book *Behavioral Archaeology* (1976), his book *Formation Processes of the Archaeological Record* (1987), and in a number of articles he authored in the 1970s and 1980s (Schiffer 1972, 1975, 1983), archaeologist Michael Schiffer formally laid out the processes by which archaeological sites come into existence. In the overwhelming majority of cases, these processes of **archaeological site formation** operate entirely unintentionally. People do not ordinarily set out to create archaeological sites; they do not consciously or intentionally contribute to the archaeological record, hoping that sometime in the future someone will excavate and analyze their leavings. An exception to this general rule in the modern era would be time capsules. For the most part, however, stuff ends up "archaeological" by accident, through a number of often rather obvious, commonsense processes. Schiffer enumerated these **site formation processes** as (1) loss, (2) discard, (3) caching, and (4) abandonment.

Obviously enough, people lose stuff and, if no one picks up these lost items, another set of processes works its magic and ensconces them in the archaeological record. Loss is a process by which even today's modern material culture is being transmitted into the archaeological record. Walk across your campus, for example, especially on dirt paths, keeping your gaze on the ground. See how many pens, pencils, and coins you can find, lost by your cohorts. Much of this stuff is dirty, broken from people stepping on it, and generally ignored. Over time, the items may be covered by loose soil or mud after a rain and become part of the archaeological record of your campus. Consider also those folks who trawl popular beaches with metal detectors, looking for lost money, keys, class rings, and other jewelry that became covered in sand almost instantly upon being dropped. People have always dropped and lost things, a simple process that has long contributed to the archaeological record.

Here's an example. A few years ago a local landowner called me. The previous year, the gentleman decided to re-sod his lawn and thought it would be a good idea to first remove the stones and pebbles from the soil. To accomplish this, he constructed a screen, coincidentally similar to the kind of device archaeologists use to aid in the recovery of artifacts during test pitting and excavation. Apparently, early in the process the landowner found the tip of a chipped stone spear point. Naturally, he was fascinated by the discovery and hoped to find more evidence of ancient artifacts in his soil. He continued screening the soil for the better part of a year—not as an archaeological enterprise, but as preparation for new sod. He never found anything else. Nothing. He wondered how a single, broken object could end up in a large expanse of land (Figure 3.6).

Had the man's property been the location of an ancient village inhabited for a long period of time by a sizeable population of people, we would expect there to be plenty of physical evidence of that occupation: all of the stuff the inhabitants lost, discarded, secreted away, or simply abandoned. It was pretty clear that, though the man was not an archaeologist and might have missed some of the subtler clues of ancient activity, after screening all of the soil on his property over the course of a year, he would have found a lot more than a single

FIGURE 3.6 This broken spear point was an isolated find; no other archaeological artifacts were found in spatial association with it. (*Courtesy of Marc Banks*)

broken spear point if he was in the middle of an ancient village site. It seems to be an inviolable rule of human behavior: wherever people live or work, they make and leave a mess behind. Archaeologists are grateful for that tendency, because such a "mess" of artifacts, ecofacts, and features together constitutes the archaeological record.

Though we cannot say for certain how the broken spear point ended up in soil that many years later became part of this man's suburban house lot, loss is a reasonable possibility. Maybe at some time in the past, at that spot, a hunter threw a spear at an animal and missed. The spear struck the ground, perhaps hitting a rock, and the stone point snapped in two. The spear shaft was easy to find, with the base of the stone point still attached, and the hunter likely recovered it. But the tip, broken off and lost in the leaves or pine needles, wasn't worth searching for and might not have been worth the effort even if it could have been found. It likely was left where it fell, to be incorporated into the soil and to be found by sheer accident and coincidence many years later by someone curious enough about its meaning to contact the closest archaeologist: me.

Perhaps the most significant site formation process that contributes to the creation of archaeological sites is discard. For example, in the course of making stone tools, a certain amount of wastage called **debitage** is produced. These stone waste chips, perhaps too small to be of any use or too awkwardly shaped to be salvaged by the tool maker, are simply left where they fall in the process of removing stone flakes from a core. Trash left like this, where it initially falls to earth, is called **primary refuse** (Figure 3.7).

Once made and part of a **tool kit,** tools may simply wear out or break. A dull stone edge can be resharpened for a while, but eventually can become useless and the tool will be discarded. Some stone tools may break in such a way as to make their reworking or mending impossible or more time consuming than simply starting from scratch and making a new one.

**Ceramic** fragments are often found in prodigious numbers at archaeological sites. At a recent excavation of a tiny site covering only about 50 square meters (a little more than 500 square feet, the area of a good-sized living room) in the Farmington River Archaeological project, we found only a handful of stone tools but more than two hundred broken pieces of pottery, likely all from one or two smashed pots. Pottery, though extremely useful as waterproof vessels, fireproof cooking containers, and generally durable serving dishes, is breakable and will shatter into sometimes hundreds of pieces when dropped on a hard enough surface.

**FIGURE 3.7** Lithic scatter. Note the scatter of pieces of chipped stone, particularly in the upper-right corner of this photograph. These bits of stone—the largest of which is no more than 5 centimeters (about 2 inches) across—represent primary refuse, waste flakes left just where they fell to the ground during the process of stone tool production at, in this case, a nearly five-thousand-year-old site. (*Kenneth L. Feder*)

I occasionally make pottery. It's a lot of work and there are many steps in the production of even a simple utilitarian piece. I am certain, however, that throwing and trimming a new pot, bisque firing, glazing, and then glaze firing it are much easier and more sensible then trying to mend and make useful again an old pot that has smashed into a hundred small fragments. What happens when a pot breaks? The broken fragments or **sherds** may be left where they fall or, more often, swept up and placed in a trash pit or pile. Left where they fell, the potsherds would be primary refuse as we just defined. Discarded material that is gathered and deposited in a special trash pit or pile is said to be **secondary refuse.**

Some activities produce garbage as a matter of course, when people extract the useful part of a resource from the useless. People may find walnuts, chestnuts, or hickory nuts tasty, but the shells that enclose the nutmeats are not digestible and may simply be thrown away. Corn kernels are nutritious, but the cobs on which they grow are not edible and may be viewed as nothing more than rubbish. Deer meat may be packed with protein; the antlers may be useful as pressure flaking tools for sharpening the edges of stone knives, scrapers, or arrow points; and some of the bones contain large amounts of nutritious marrow, but many of the bones, especially the smaller ones, may be of little utility to people. Much of this stuff—nutshells, seed hulls, bone fragments, shells, and so on—though useful in certain technologies, may also be perceived by people

**FIGURE 3.8** Looking down into an excavated trash pit found at a more than three-thousand-year-old site in Ohio. Here, the pit matrix—the trash that was thrown into the pit by the inhabitants of the site—is in the process of being recovered and returned to the lab for analysis. Broken stones, white flecks of bone, and black fragments of burned wood can still be seen at the bottom and along the walls of the pit. (*Kenneth L. Feder*)

as useless trash and may end up in a **kitchen midden** or dump. As soon as these materials end up in the pile, pit, dump, or midden, they enter into the archaeological site formation stream and, if not dragged away by an animal or recovered and recycled for use by someone else centuries or millennia later, they may, as archaeological objects, contribute to our knowledge of the diet, technology, or other practices of a group of people (Figure 3.8).

Another behavior of human beings that can contribute to the formation of archaeological sites is the practice of stashing away stuff intended for later use. The French verb "to hide" is *cacher,* and in English the word "cache" is used both as a verb (meaning "to hide away for safekeeping") and as a noun (for the actual place—a "cache"—where something is hidden away). When we find a pit with a stash of projectile points or crystals or some other material at an archaeological site, we often interpret it as just such a **cache,** a feature that reflects an accumulation of stuff that was put away or stored. In the case of a true cache, we often assume that the person who stored the material had every intention of returning to retrieve it when needed, but for one reason or another—and lucky for the archaeologist—they never did, and neither did anyone else. When we find a discrete accumulation of artifacts, not broken bits that obviously made their way into the ground as refuse but material that the maker likely intended to retrieve, we call it a cache. This behavior is yet another process by which objects move from the realm of a living culture to the world of the archaeological record.

A cache may also represent a desire to remove objects or remains from the above-ground secular world in which we all live to a sacred realm sometimes

**FIGURE 3.9** Seven stone blades of the total of thirty that were found in the Glazier Blade Cache located in the town of Granby, Connecticut. These blades were neatly stacked in a shallow pit approximately sixteen hundred years ago. (*Figure by Kenneth L. Feder*)

represented by the Earth itself. In a sense, an intentional human or animal burial is an example of such a cache: the placement of the remains of a loved one in a way that serves a practical sanitary purpose by disposing of a corpse and that also produces a memorial to the deceased, consecrating and, perhaps, marking the place where their mortal remains are housed.

Even objects alone, without human remains, may be buried for ceremonial purposes, essentially put into the Earth as offerings to gods or spirits. It seems the only explaination for the Glazier Blade Cache (Figure 3.9), a neatly arranged, tight cluster of thirty large stone blades that we excavated in Granby, Connecticut, in 1993 (http://archnet.asu.edu/archnet/uconn_extras/lithic/blades/glazier.html). At a mean length of more than 13.5 centimeters (5.3 inches), with the largest measuring more than 18 centimeters (7 inches), it seems unlikely that these objects were ever intended for use, and, indeed, there is no evidence along their edges that they ever had been used. The Glazier blades were placed into an isolated pit in the ground about sixteen hundred years ago. The pit itself was not part of a site; no additional archaeological material was found anywhere nearby. It is at least plausible that these blades were placed into the ground as an offering, the details of which we will never know.

Finally, people sometimes abandon material for reasons we may never fully understand. Tools, food, and personal possessions may be left where they were being used or stored when people abandoned a place as the result of a catastrophe. A house may catch fire and many of the items stored there may be abandoned, burned, and become part of the archaeological record. A natural cataclysm (for example, a volcanic eruption) may inspire the inhabitants of a community to flee, leaving their possessions behind to be covered by ash or lava. An aggressive enemy might descend upon an unsuspecting village whose inhabitants abandon their homes and most of their possessions. The attackers may cart away many of the valuables and ignore everyday items, which then become part of the archaeological record through abandonment.

The site formation processes described contribute to the production of the archaeological record. It would seem that without tragedy, destruction, forgetfulness, carelessness, sloppiness, and catastrophe the archaeological record wouldn't amount to much.

## Read More

To find out more about how archaeologists explain the ways in which human behavior becomes transformed into an archaeological record of that behavior, the following books and articles—most, but not all by archaeologist Michael Schiffer—are an enormous help:

Dunnell, R. C. 1992. The notion site. In *Space, Time, and Archaeological Landscapes*, edited by J. Rossignol and L. Wandsnider, 21–41. Plenum Press, New York.

Ebert, J. I. 1992. *Distributional Archaeology.* University of New Mexico Press, Albuquerque.

Schiffer, M. B. 1972. Archaeological context and systemic context. *American Antiquity* 37:156–65.

———. 1975. Archaeology as a behavioral science. *American Anthropologist* 77:836–48.

———. 1976. *Behavioral Archaeology.* Academic Press, New York.

———. 1983. Toward the identification of site formation processes. *American Antiquity* 48:673–706.

———. 1987. *Formation Processes of the Archaeological Record.* University of New Mexico Press, Albuquerque.

## How Can You Find Archaeological Sites Just by Walking Around?

The common conception of an archaeologist is that of a scientist dusted in dirt, searching for specimens at the bottom of a perilously deep pit, oblivious to the imminent and obvious danger posed by the tons of loose soil precariously mounded up all around. In fact, although archaeological material may be found deeply buried in the soil, it is also quite common to find sometimes even extraordinarily ancient material right under our noses, resting on the exposed, modern surface.

This variation in the depth at which archaeological materials are discovered exists for two very different reasons. On the one hand, human beings, especially when they work together in large, organized groups, can dramatically and drastically alter the face of the earth. They can produce features that are, using the term of Schiffer et al. (1978), archaeologically **obtrusive.** Whether through carving out deep gouges of the earth's surface to make canals; altering the flow of a stream to divert its water to power a mill wheel; building up and shaping the soil to produce huge, three dimensional images of animals to worship the gods; or constructing monuments, temples, pyramids, or houses people leave behind sometimes massive, durable traces of their labors, too deep, too tall, or too extensive to be covered by natural processes of soil accumulation on any kind of a human time scale. The Great Pyramid of the pharaoh Khufu, for example, consists of more than 2.5 million stone blocks stacked to a height of nearly 150 meters (500 feet; Figure 3.10; Lehner 1997).

*Stonehenge*

**FIGURE 3.10** The cliff dwelling, Square Tower House, at Mesa Verde, Colorado (top), and the Pyramid of the Magician at the ancient Maya site of Uxmal in the Yucatan Peninsula, Mexico (bottom), are quintessentially "obtrusive" archaeological remains. They are large, above-ground structures made of durable material. Even centuries after their construction, use, and abandonment, they are clearly recognizable. Although archaeology has long been conducted in their proximity, no digging was necessary to find them. (*Kenneth L. Feder*)

The huge adobe structure called Pueblo Bonito at Chaco Canyon in New Mexico was three stories tall, made of regularly sized, durable brick, and comprised more than eight hundred rooms (Cordell 1994; Sebastian 1992). Though it is only an urban legend that the Great Wall of China is visible to the naked eye from the moon (or something like that), the structure really does epitomize the term "stupendous": it is about 7,000 kilometers (4,500 miles) long, ranges from 4.5 to 9 meters (15 to 30 feet) high, and is as much as 7.5 meters (25 feet) wide. It simply doesn't take much digging—in truth, it doesn't take any digging—to find features like these. Walking around with open eyes is all that is required.

Such archaeological remains can be found simply by walking around with your eyes open for another reason: the environments in which they were found are of high archaeological **visibility.** In some regions, processes that serve to cover things left on the surface very quickly remove archaeological remains from the visible landscape, enfolding them in leaf litter, pine needles, sand, silt, and rock. Clearly in those places, if a sufficiently long time has passed to cover items, archaeologists must dig to find that stuff and a pedestrian survey may not readily pinpoint the location of archaeological material (Chartkoff 1978; Chartkoff and Chartkoff 1980; McManamon 1984).

On the other hand, there are regions in which these natural processes that cover material on the surface act very slowly or not at all. Items left on the surface for hundreds or thousands of years—in some instances even longer— may continue to reside in full view, exposed at the spot where human beings left them.

At the same time, even in regions where material left on the surface is fairly quickly buried, there may be broad areas with high archaeological visibility as a result of erosion and other geological processes. For example, where a river erodes its bank, even deeply buried archaeological material may be exposed, rendering previously hidden items highly visible. Ancient episodes of land movement due to tectonic activity like earthquakes can also contribute to archaeological visibility, tearing apart a section of the earth's surface and exposing ancient layers of soil. Many of the most ancient hominid sites at Olduvai Gorge in Tanzania, Africa, were found through pedestrian survey (M. Leakey 1971; M. Leakey and A. Walker 1997; R. Leakey and R. Lewin 1992). The deeply buried remains of ancient skeletons and stone tools, enclosed in ancient strata hundreds of thousands and even millions of years old, have been exposed at the surface when the land was ripped apart by earthquake activity. Where the ancient layers were torn open, their edges are exposed to the surface and paleoanthropologists scan them for signs of ancient human ancestors (Figure 3.11).

We can see another example of the usefulness of a surface inspection for archaeological remains on the largest of the Orkney Islands of Scotland (Ritchie 1995). Local residents of the island in the mid-nineteenth century were familiar with what they presumed to be a natural feature of the landscape, a mound of earth they called Skerrabra located on the shore of a protected bay on the island's west coast. An enormous northern Atlantic storm pounded the Orkneys in the winter of 1850 and the combined effect of an especially high tide and the fierce winds that accompanied the storm managed to peel the turf from the top of the mound. When residents left the safety of their homes to

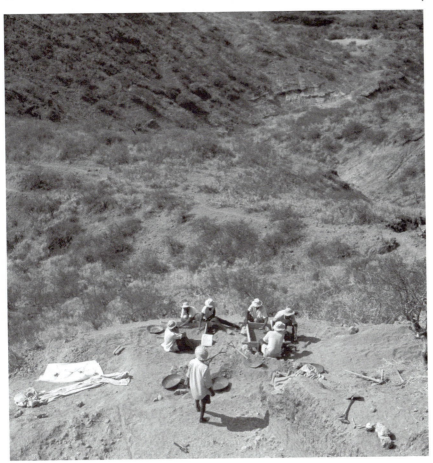

**FIGURE 3.11** Olduvai Gorge in east Africa is a geological gash across the earth, exposing ancient strata and their contents. Paleoanthopologists have found ancient sites containing the skeletal remains and tools of ancient human ancestors without digging deeply, but by perusing the ancient soil layers exposed in the gorge. (© *Ric Ergenbright/CORBIS*)

assess the damage after the storm, they found exposed in the truncated mound a maze of stone walls demarcating the remnants of a warren of eight interconnected rooms (Figure 3.12; Clarke and Maguire 1995).

Since then, the ancient village so revealed has attracted the interest of archaeologists. Now called Skara Brae, the site has been excavated, revealing a village that was first occupied more than five thousand years ago and that had been enclosed in a protective blanket of sand for about four thousand years (http://www.orkneyjar.com/history/skarabrae/).

Vegetation growth can render the archaeological visibility of even large-scale, obtrusive remains quite low. For example, the Maya of Mesoamerica (Coe 1993; Schele and Freidel 1990; Schele and Mathews 1998) and the Khmer civilization of Southeast Asia (Higham 2001) both developed in tropical regions where vegetation grows quickly—and thickly. In both of these cultures, people carved communities out of the thick, humid forest, clearing trees for cities,

**FIGURE 3.12** The walls of the five-thousand-year-old village of Skara Brae lay buried beneath the beach sand near a bay on the main Orkney Island, Scotland, until the gales of a powerful north Atlantic storm revealed them in 1850. (*Kenneth L. Feder*)

temples, pyramids, and tombs. These remains are obviously highly obtrusive, built on a monumental scale (Figure 3.13). The Maya city of Tikal is estimated to have had a population of fifty thousand in A.D. 650 and is marked by beautiful and massive pyramids and temples of stone (Sabloff 1989).

Built in the twelfth century A.D., the Khmer temple of Angkor Wat has been called the largest religious structure ever built, covering several acres and characterized by five massive towers more than 60 meters (200 feet) tall (Mannikka 1996; Figure 3.14). Obtrusive, indeed, but when in the ebb and flow of great civilizations these sites were abandoned, the tireless and relentless jungle claimed both the Khmer and the Maya, cloaking their massive statues and edifices in vines, roots, and lush greenery. Their archaeological obtrusiveness was trumped by the low visibility of their respective regions and both civilizations were forgotten and unknown, at least to the world beyond their own borders, until the forest was entered by explorers and scientists with machetes and the forest was once again forced back to reveal hidden archaeological treasures.

The utility of a pedestrian survey, therefore, is a complex product of the interplay of the obtrusiveness of the archaeological remains to be found and the archaeological visibility presented by the local environment. Where obtrusiveness and archaeological visibility both are high, a pedestrian survey can be an effective strategy in the search for archaeological remains (Feder 1997b). Where both obtrusiveness and visibility are low, rather obviously a pedestrian survey may be of little utility. The usefulness of a pedestrian survey must be

**FIGURE 3.13** The Maya site of Chichen Itza is an example of an obtrusive archaeological remain located in a tropical rainforest where vegetation grows so quickly and densely that, given sufficient time, it can overwhelm even a large pyramid, an expansive temple, or an entire city. (*Kenneth L. Feder*)

**FIGURE 3.14** Long since cleared of the enfolding tropical forest, the monumentally scaled temples of the ancient Cambodian civilization of Angkor Wat are examples of obtrusive archaeological remains. (© *Kevin R. Morris/CORBIS*)

assessed on a case-by-case basis when obtrusiveness is high but visibility is low, or when visibility is high and obtrusiveness is low.

## Read More

To find out more about pedestrian survey and how it can contribute to the discovery of obtrusive and/or highly visible archaeological remains, check out any of the following books and articles:

Chartkoff, J. L. 1978. Transect sampling in forests. *American Antiquity* 43:46–52.

Chartkoff, J. L., and K. K. Chartkoff. 1980. *The Discovery of Archaeological Sites: A Review of Methods and Techniques.* U.S. Forest Service.

Clarke, D., and P. Maguire. 1995. *Skara Brae: Northern Europe's Best Preserved Prehistoric Village.* Historic Scotland, Edinburgh, Scotland.

Coe, M. D. 1993. *The Maya.* Thames and Hudson, New York.

Cordell, L. 1994. Ancient Pueblo peoples. In *Exploring the Ancient World.* Smithsonian Books, Washington, D.C.

Feder, K. L. 1997b. Site survey. In *Field Methods in Archaeology,* edited by T. R. Hester, H. J. Shafer, and K. L. Feder, 41–68. Mayfield Publishing, Mountain View, California.

Higham, C. 2001. *The Civilization of Angkor.* University of California Press, Berkeley.

Leakey, M. 1971. *Olduvai Gorge 3.* Cambridge University Press, Cambridge, Massachusetts.

Leakey, M., and A. Walker. 1997. Early hominid fossils from Africa. *Scientific American* 276(6):74–79.

Leakey, R., and R. Lewin. 1992. *Origins Reconsidered: In Search of What Makes Us Human.* Doubleday, New York.

Lehner, M. 1997. *The Complete Pyramids.* Thames and Hudson, New York.

Mannikka, E. 1996. *Angkor Wat: Time, Space, and Kingship.* University of Hawaii Press, Honolulu.

McManamon, F. P. 1984. Discovering sites unseen. In *Advances in Archaeological Method and Theory,* edited by M. B. Schiffer, vol. 7, 223–92. Academic Press, New York.

Ritchie, A. 1995. *Prehistoric Orkney.* B. T. Batsford, London.

Sabloff, J. A. 1989. *The Cities of Ancient Mexico: Reconstructing a Lost World.* Thames and Hudson, New York.

Schele, L., and D. Freidel. 1990. *A Forest of Kings.* Quill William Morrow, New York.

Schele, L., and P. Mathews. 1998. *The Code of Kings: The Language of Seven Sacred Maya Temples and Tombs.* Scribner's, New York.

Sebastian, L. 1992. *The Chaco Anasazi: Sociopolitical Evolution in the Prehistoric Southwest.* Cambridge University Press, Cambridge, New York.

# How Old Does Something Have to Be in Order to Be Considered "Archaeological"?

A local business in central Connecticut is hoping to demolish an office building constructed not quite fifty years ago and designed by a well-known and respected architect. Many local residents and aficionados of architecture have objected, asserting that the building is historically significant, having won a prestigious architectural award upon its completion and been the focus of much discussion—and emulation—soon after construction. Debate about this issue even reached the state capital, where one skeptical, sixty-something state legislator has said that for anything to be historically significant it must be older than him. Perhaps he has a valid point, perhaps not, but it is an interesting general question: how old does something have to be in order to be archaeological or historical?

I should remind you that archaeology does not just focus on ancient sites or sites of a particular time period or degree of antiquity. Prehistoric archaeology is only one of the subfields of the discipline. Historical archaeology, where researchers excavate relatively recent sites (some that may be less than a century old and that have voluminous associated written documents), is a vibrant and growing part of the field. This subfield includes the archaeological investigation of presidents' homes (McKee 1995), African American cemeteries (Perry and Blakey 1997), battlefields (Scott et al. 1989), and locations of historical tragedies (Hardesty 1997), the analysis of legends (Feder 1994), solving mysteries (King et al. 2001), and chronicling the history of a great modern metropolis (Cantwell and Wall 2001).

At least in a theoretical sense, therefore, there is no age restriction for archaeological material. Anything can be considered part of the archaeological record, from 2.5-million-year-old stone chopping tools to literally yesterday's trash. In fact, an entire subfield within archaeology focuses on modern garbage. For more than twenty-seven years, archaeologist William Rathje and his students have been examining the rubbish folks throw out in their trash cans as part of the Garbage Project (Harrison, Rathje, and Hughes 1975; http://bara.arizona.edu/gs.htm). These archaeologists of modern rubbish have been showing up at peoples' curbs and doorsteps before the regular trash pickup in a number of cities, taking the material collected to the archaeology lab for a detailed analysis.

More recently, Rathje has been conducting actual archaeological excavations at modern landfills and trash dumps (Figure 3.15; Rathje and Murphy 1992). Though it doesn't match most common expectations

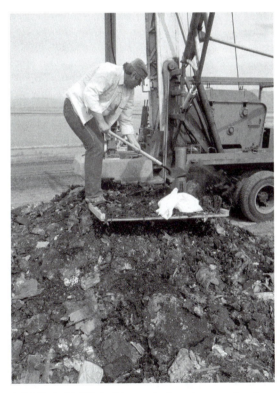

**FIGURE 3.15** Bill Rathje conducting dump archaeology. (© *James A. Sugar/CORBIS*)

about the romance of archaeology, the archaeology of modern society has made significant contributions to our understanding of the kinds of information that might be coded into garbage, regardless of its age, and has revealed important and practical insights about our own culture's trash, waste, and recycling habits.

Of course, while theoretically there is no required degree of antiquity for something to be considered archaeological, in practice we do apply some commonsense standards, though these generally are not absolute. Recall the Archaeological Resources Protection Act of 1979, the purpose of which is to protect archaeological material on federal property. If that law did not specify how old something had to be in order to qualify as archaeological then—because essentially all material culture is potentially of archaeological importance—you would be in violation of the act if, for example, you picked up a dollar bill you saw lying on the ground in a national park. For that matter, even picking up trash that a thoughtless hiker left along a trail might be seen as a violation of the Archaeological Resources Protection Act; after all, today's litter is tomorrow's archaeological treasure! Avoiding any such problems, the act specifies that to qualify as archaeological, by statute, items must be a minimum of one hundred years old. Anything younger than that, at least according to the regulations is, in fact, just trash.

The federal government, even within its own regulations, is not consistent regarding the necessary age of archaeological or historical significance. Another federal regulation stipulates that for a historical site to be technically eligible for inclusion on a national honor role called the **National Register of Historic Places** (http://www.cr.nps.gov/places.htm), established by the federal **National Historic Preservation Act of 1966** (http://www2.cr.nps.gov/laws/NHPA1966.htm), it must be a minimum of fifty years old, half the age of that required in the Archaeological Resources Protection Act. Even here there is some wiggle room and the regulations allow that a site may be eligible for the register even if it is less than fifty years old if it can be established that it is of "exceptional significance" (Figure 3.16).

In fact, the structure I discussed at the start of this section—the Wilde Building on the campus of the CIGNA corporation in Bloomfield, Connecticut—is being considered for inclusion on the National Register, even though it was built in 1957 (and, therefore, is a few years shy of the fifty-year rule).

Please note that whatever fixed stipulation related to age is made concerning the archaeological status of an artifact or location, time moves ahead as does the status. A forty-nine-year-old building that doesn't technically qualify for the National Register today becomes eligible in one year. A ninety-nine-and-a-half-year-old artifact that you can legally pick up in a National Park becomes a protected object in a few months. If this book is successful and is used for several years as a required textbook in university archaeology courses, I will have to alter the discussion of the Wilde building; any technical argument about its eligibility for the National Register becomes moot in 2007 when it turns fifty. The bottom line is that any determination of a minimum age for something to be considered archaeological is going to be arbitrary and rather subjective, and we need to apply a bit of common sense.

**FIGURE 3.16** The oldest continuously operated McDonald's with the original double-arch design turned fifty in 2003. Considering the impact McDonald's has had on American eating habits specifically, and on culture, in general, it should come as no surprise that this outlet, located in Downey, California, is eligible for inclusion on the National Register of Historic Places. (© *Reuters NewMedia Inc./CORBIS*)

## Read More

Any of the following sources are good examples of the study of sites that don't match the stereotype of archaeology's focus only on sites that are enormously old:

Cantwell, A.-M., and D. d. Wall. 2001. *Unearthing Gotham.* Yale University Press, New Haven, Connecticut.

Feder, K. L. 1994. *A Village of Outcasts: Historical Archaeology and Documentary Research at the Lighthouse Site.* Mayfield Publishing, Mountain View, California.

Hardesty, D. L. 1997. *The Archaeology of the Donner Party.* University of Nevada Press, Reno.

Harrison, G. G., W. L. Rathje, and W. W. Hughes. 1975. Food waste behavior in an urban population. *Journal of Nutrition Education* 7(1).

King, T. F., R. S. Jacobson, K. R. Burns, and K. Spading. 2001. *Amelia Earhart's Shoes: Is the Mystery Solved?* Altamira Press, Walnut Creek, California.

McKee, L. 1995. The earth is their witness. *The Sciences* 35(2):36–41.

Perry, W., and M. Blakey. 1997. Archaeology as community service: The African Burial Ground project in New York City. *North American Dialogue* 2(1):1–5.

Rathje, W., and C. Murphy. 1992. *Rubbish: The Archaeology of Garbage.* HarperCollins, New York.

Scott, D., R. A. Fox Jr., M. Conner, and J. Harmon. 1989. *Archaeological Perspectives on the Battle of the Little Big Horn.* University of Oklahoma Press, Norman.

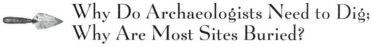

# Why Do Archaeologists Need to Dig; Why Are Most Sites Buried?

As we have already discussed, sites come into existence through a number of processes that lead to the deposition on the surface of the stuff that people made and used. And, as discussed in the section on pedestrian survey, in some regions there may be no active natural process by which these materials become covered. In most places, however, a diverse array of natural processes conceal cultural material left on the ground by burying it.

For example, rivers and streams regularly burst over their banks and deposit a layer of silt that covers everything over which the water flows. A single flood episode may leave only a fraction of a centimeter deposit that may, in turn, blow away once it becomes dry, but large-scale floods have been known to deposit more than a meter of silt. Multiple floods over many years can build up thick deposits over archaeological material, producing a chronological sequence in the soil with a series of archaeological layers representing different episodes of occupation of a particular place separated by deposits laid down during flooding.

Outside the limits of a river or stream's **floodplain,** other natural processes can cover archaeological material. Leaves and pine needles build up on the surface of a forest floor and decay, ensconcing the stuff that people lost or discarded in a blanket of humus. Humus eventually becomes the soil in which archaeologists probe for those objects left behind by past peoples. Generally, this all happens rather slowly so in most places recent and built-up features are often still visible on the surface, but ancient material dropped or deposited by people many hundreds or thousands of years ago becomes covered up. Those materials that preserve while covered up make up the subsurface archaeological record.

Other processes of waterborne deposition occur along the shores of lakes as well as in coastal regions. Like rivers, lakes are affected by fluctuations in precipitation and may expand and contract as a result. Sites that are located close to a lake shore may end up being inundated during periods of high water level and may be covered entirely by the sand, gravel, and silt carried by the expanding lake waters. These are called **lacustrine** deposits.

Just as lake levels may fluctuate, resulting in the inundation of sites, the world's ocean levels change, in some cases quite dramatically. When sea level rises (as it has been doing for the last twelve thousand years or so), sites located along coasts may become covered not only by rising water but by marine deposits of sand, gravel, silt, and rock moved around by tide and wave action. For example, we know that about fourteen thousand years ago, worldwide sea level was at least 100 meters (nearly 330 feet) lower than it is today because a much larger proportion of the world's ocean waters was locked up in the ice sheets that covered much of northern North America and the higher elevations of South America, Europe, and Asia. As a result, continental coasts were located much farther out, in places that are miles out to sea today. Archaeological sites actually have been found by probing those areas now underwater, but that in antiquity were coastal regions. Using submersible vehicles, researchers Daryl W. Fedje and Heiner Josenhans (2000), for example, have explored a section of ancient coast off Alaska and recovered a ten-thousand-year-old spear point at a site that today is 53 meters (about 175 feet) below the ocean's surface, but that was, rather obviously, dry and very hospitable land in the distant past.

Nearly everything eventually goes downhill, certainly literally (and some might argue figuratively as well). Gravity acts to move soil, gravel, and even rock downslope and this material can blanket archaeological material, in some cases protecting the stuff left behind at abandoned habitations. A village located at the base of a hill or foot of a mountain may be slowly (and sometimes not so slowly) covered with soil and rock eroding off the high ground. Even very large rocks can move downhill as a result of gravity, covering archaeological materials at the base of the hill. These covering deposits pulled downslope by gravity are called **colluvium.**

Though wind cannot ordinarily move heavy rocks or boulders, it can push around enormous quantities of **unconsolidated** (loose) **material,** for example, sand, which can cover and protect archaeological sites. These **aeolian** deposits play a major role in covering sites, especially in such dry parts of the world as areas of the Middle East, where there is a shortage of plant life holding the soil in place. Windblown sand can accumulate and cover over an abandoned village, producing a natural time capsule of a community.

Catastrophic processes may act to cover archaeological material. An erupting volcano may eject tons of ash, which can cover a village almost instantaneously, killing thousands and creating and covering an archaeological site in the process. The eruption of Mt. Vesuvius in 79 B.C. obliterated the Roman city of Pompeii in a virtual heartbeat, destroying and forever freezing the moment of destruction of an ancient metropolis (Figure 3.17; Guzzo, D'Ambrosio, and Foglia 2000).

**FIGURE 3.17** In the case of Pompeii, an entire city was destroyed in a virtual instant as the volcanic mountain Vesuvius erupted in 79 B.C. It is amazing to consider the fact that, in this photograph, you are looking down the street of a city whose preservation for archaeological analysis was made possible by the agency of its death. (*Courtesy of M. H. Feder*)

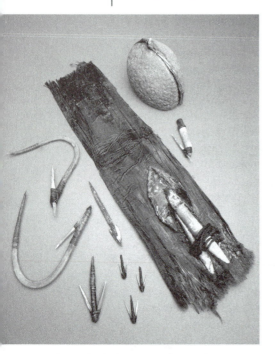

**FIGURE 3.18** The remarkable preservation of materials encapsulated in a catastrophic mudslide five hundred years ago can be seen even in the organic materials used by the Ozette villagers to make their fishing equipment. (© *Richard A. Cooke/CORBIS*)

Sometime near A.D. 1491, a Native American village in what is today the state of Washington was blanketed by a landslide (Pascua 1991). Like a coating of slip smeared onto a pot, a slush of waterlogged earth rushed down the hillside above the village, plowing down everything above ground and enfolding everything on the surface in a thick slurry of mud. The village was destroyed by the mudslide, but the archaeological manifestation of that village produced by the catastrophe (now called the Ozette site) was remarkably well preserved by being packed in mud until its rediscovery five hundred years later in A.D. 1991. Ozette, like Pompeii, represents a moment frozen in time, a village of people destroyed and an archaeological site created in the same instant (Figure 3.18).

Whichever natural process is at work blanketing the surface at a given place, archaeological material gets covered up and archaeologists must adopt the motto of the utility provider in New York City, Consolidated Edison, which is forever apologizing for disrupting the flow of traffic in the city by fixing underground utilities: "Dig We Must." And dig we do, as well.

## Read More

To learn more about the processes that serve to bury archaeological sites, read virtually any geology textbook. For more information on the specific examples mentioned in this section, check out the following resources:

Fedje, D. W., and H. Josenhans. 2000. Drowned forests and archaeology on the continental shelf of British Columbia, Canada. *Geology* 28:99–102.
Guzzo, P. G., A. D'Ambrosio, and A. Foglia. 2000. *Pompeii.* Getty Trust Publication, Los Angeles.
Pascua, M. P. 1991. A Makah village in 1491: Ozette. *National Geographic* 180(4):38–53.

 ## How Deep Do You Have to Dig to Find Archaeological Material?

I can remember one field season scraping back the soil at the bottom of an excavation unit that was just a little more than 75 centimeters (almost 2.5 feet) deep. An elderly man with a small dog walked by, peered down at me, and asked what

I was doing. I told him that we were conducting an archaeological excavation and showed him some of the artifacts that had been left in place in the soil for mapping at the bottom of the excavation unit. The old man shook his head and said to me, "You know; I never would have thought the Indians would have buried their stuff so deep." Right.

Of course, ancient people did bury trash as well as the bodies of their deceased compatriots, but most of the archaeological material we find becomes buried by natural processes. This raises the question of how deeply archaeological material is buried and, in turn, how deeply we need to dig to find it.

There really is no one single answer to this question primarily because each of the various processes proceeds at a different rate and even the same processes proceed at different rates depending on the particular set of circumstances that apply in each instance. In southern New England, for example, for two sites of equal age, one located within the **floodplain** of a large river like the Connecticut ordinarily will be buried far more deeply than one situated in the uplands. Especially before the institution of flood control procedures by local municipalities and, especially, by the Army Corps of Engineers (a federal agency), rivers left behind substantial flood deposits called **alluvium,** consisting of very fine-grained soil called **silt,** on a yearly basis. Alluvium can build up in a hurry and sites along rivers can be buried fairly quickly and fairly deeply. The formation of a layer of soil outside of the floodplain of a river usually occurs far more slowly because the processes that bury material on the surface proceed much more slowly.

Human activity, too, creates layers of soil. Especially when people live in large numbers in settled communities and where they construct durable buildings, material tends to pile up. When these communities are abandoned and where, for example, wind-blown sand covers the ruins, a later group may settle on the top, not necessarily aware that the remnants of a previous village lie under their new settlement. Over many years, a series of communities may be established at the same location, one superimposed on top of the other as people elect to build their communities on the artificially created high ground. They may choose to settle the high ground because it is drier than the surrounding area and because it provides a better outlook for the presence of attacking enemies. Called **tells** in the Middle East, there can be more than a dozen villages so positioned on these high mounds (Figure 3.19). Obviously, archaeologists may have to dig very deeply before they encounter the archaeological remains of the earlier settlements.

Make no mistake; none of these processes of soil formation or deposition are entirely consistent or regular. None of them functions like a clock. You cannot simply measure the depth of an **occupation layer** at a site and plug the result into a universally applicable formula to come up with an age (Figure 3.20). Along a floodplain, for example, a series of years with minimal winter snowfall and dry springs will result in small floods or none at all in individual years and, as a consequence, there will be very little, if any, deposition of silt. You can have a situation in which, over the course of decades, only a fraction of a centimeter is deposited. On the other hand, though rare, a single, enormous rainstorm resulting, for instance, from a hurricane, may cause a devastating flood that may deposit several feet of alluvium all at once.

**FIGURE 3.19** The hill in the foreground of this photo of Tel Hazor, Israel, on top of which ruins can be seen, is not natural, but is the result of the accumulation of living debris from a sequence of occupations—twenty-one, to be precise—one on top of the other. (© *Richard T. Nowitz/CORBIS*)

Along with processes of deposition, there are processes that work to strip away soil and slice through soil layers. Rivers and streams cut into their banks, heavy rains can wash away soil, a storm surge can tear up a shoreline and expose a buried site, and, especially where there are no trees or heavily rooted vegetation, the wind can remove enormous quantities of soil. Deeply buried, sometimes quite ancient sites can be exposed on the surface by these processes. As mentioned previously, in 1850 an enormous storm surge that struck the Orkney Islands (just north of the north-Scottish coast) exposed remains of a previously completely unknown five-thousand-year-old archaeological village site, a place called Skara Brae. Sites where the remains of human ancestral forms, dating back not thousands but millions of years have been found not by digging deeply—at least not initially—but by walking over the surface in areas where ancient deposits one million, two million, and even more years old, were exposed by slow processes of erosion.

There is no hard and fast rule concerning how deep an archaeological site may be buried and, therefore, how deeply we need to dig in order to find it except for this: an archaeologist needs to be knowledgeable about the stratigraphy of an area being surveyed or excavated in order to insure that he or she is digging deeply enough. Knowing the soil layers in which other sites in a region have been found and being familiar with the geological or **stratigraphic** sequence in an area is crucial. Archaeologists need to excavate to a depth sufficient to insure that nothing archaeological would be found any deeper. Even adhering to this rule, it must be admitted that most of us have experienced that twinge when, about to fill in a test pit or excavation unit we wonder: "What if I dug down just another centimeter?" (Archaeologists obsess in metric, of course.)

Test pits may be excavated until a recognizable glacial deposit is encountered in regions where human occupation post-dated the last period of glaciation. In some places, the deepest testings of a region's stratigraphic sequence may reach bedrock. And in other places, test pits may be excavated to a depth that reaches the water table.

Ultimately, we do have to draw the line somewhere and our approach should be realistic. If, based on the solid evidence of a substantial amount of previous work in an area, we are pretty sure no humans lived there before a certain point in the geological history of a region, then when we excavate down to those geological deposits we need dig no more deeply.

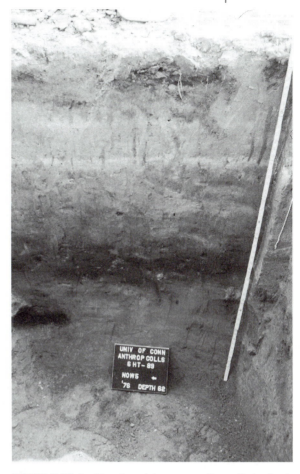

**FIGURE 3.20** Looking down into an excavation unit at a floodplain site, one can readily see the occupation layer marked by stones and dark soil in a discernible layer among other layers free of stones. The layer shown here is approximately 3,200 years old. The soil above it has accumulated over the course of that 3,200-year period, the result of yearly flooding and alluvium deposition by a nearby river. (*Kenneth L. Feder*)

## Study Questions

1. What is an artifact?
2. What is an ecofact?
3. What is a feature?
4. What is the fundamental difference between an artifact and an ecofact?

5. Provide a general list of possible archaeological features.

6. How does an area where an activity was carried out (stone tool making) become transformed into the archaeological context of a feature?

7. The terms *artifact, ecofact,* and *feature* denote the archaeological contexts of things unearthed by archaeologists. Name some possible behavioral contexts of artifacts, ecofacts, and features.

8. What is a site formation process? What does it do?

9. What are the primary archaeological site formation processes enumerated by archaeologist Michael Schiffer?

10. After carefully screening all of his topsoil to allow for a better lawn, a local landowner finds a single, isolated stone spear point. What are some possible ways in which that spear point became part of the archaeological record? What site formation processes may have been at work?

11. What is the difference between primary and secondary refuse? From the perspective of an archaeologist excavating a site, what are the advantages and disadvantages of these different elements of the archaeological record?

12. What is a cache? In what way is a cache a unique kind of archaeological feature?

13. Discuss the concept of archaeological visibility. What world areas provide a high level of archaeological visibility? What world areas provide a low level of such visibility?

14. What does the term *obtrusive* mean in its archaeological use? What kinds of archaeological sites are obtrusive? What kinds of sites are not obtrusive?

15. Provide a listing of cultures that have produced an obtrusive archaeological record. Provide a listing of cultures that have produced nonobtrusive material.

16. What is "pedestrian" archaeology? What kinds of sites can be found in pedestrian archaeology? In what kinds of environments can pedestrian archaeology be found?

17. What natural processes might act to reveal archaeological remains even in environments that are otherwise characterized by low archaeological visibility?

18. The discovery of the village site of Skara Brae is an instance in which a natural phenomenon revealed an archaeological site in an environment otherwise characterized by low archaeological visibility. Explain what that means and what happened in this case.

19. What is the minimum age a site or artifact must be, from a theoretical perspective, for it technically to be "archaeological"?

20. What is the minimum age a site or artifact must be, for it to be archaeological according to the Archaeological Resources Protection Act of 1979?

21. What is the minimum age a site must be in order to qualify for the National Register of Historic Places? Are there exceptions? If so, under what circumstances are they granted?

22. By what *general* natural processes are archaeological materials covered over?

23. How was the village of Pompeii transformed into an archaeological site? How was the village of Ozette transformed into an archaeological site?

24. As a general rule, how deep do archaeologists need to dig to find all of the materials at an archaeological site?

25. What is the "occupation layer" of a site?

# UNIT 4

$W$e defined the representative sample in the early planning stages of the project by subdividing the forest lands into a number of zones based on the characteristics each possessed that might have been of importance for human use. Applying our modern perceptions to land patterns, we divided Peoples into the following categories: major river floodplain, small streams and their associated terraces, uplands, and bedrock exposures (Figure 4.1, left). Next, we established a series of transects through each of these zones, lines along which we planned to excavate regularly spaced **test pits.** In establishing the transects along which we planned to test the subsurface, we made sure that we covered each of these subdivisions of forest land (Figure 4.1, right). Furthermore, we sampled the forest in a manner that insured that each of the defined zones was investigated at a level of intensity that reflected its spatial proportion in the forest.

After my son's rather eventful entry into the world on June 12—everything turned out just great in the end—we maintained our established pattern in the survey project. I continued staying home most days for my son's first few weeks of life, having a great time getting to know the new member of our family. On most mornings—we weren't getting any sleep then anyway—the crew would drop by the house to go over the planned work for the day and to make funny faces at the baby. In the evenings—we weren't getting any sleep then either—the crew would drop by the house and I went over the field forms and did a preliminary examination of whatever had been recovered in the test pits on that day, before the material was transported to the archaeology laboratory at my university.

On one otherwise uneventful day, my field crew chief stopped by in the morning, with map in hand, to discuss the fieldwork planned for that

**Peoples State Forest**
SAMPLING ZONES

Farmington River

1 kilometer

N

**Peoples State Forest**
Testpit Transects

Farmington River

Transects

1 kilometer

N

☐ Farmington River     ▨ Streams and terraces
   floodplain and terraces

▨ General uplands       ▨ Bedrock exposures

**FIGURE 4.1** Divisions of Peoples State Forest. (*Kenneth L. Feder*)

day in a part of the forest we had not previously entered. The section in question was just to the east of a paved, public road that crosscut state forest land. Eastward, the land was quite flat, the exception rather than the rule in north-central and northwest Connecticut, and then after about 100 meters dropped off rather abruptly to another flat terrace of land, far narrower than the first. Another quick drop to the east brought the crew down to a small, unnamed but permanent stream (Figure 4.2) flowing south into a larger watercourse (Beaver Brook) which, true to its name, was impounded by a textbook-perfect little beaver dam (Figure 4.3).

Beaver Brook, in turn, flowed into the Farmington River, the major watercourse in north-central Connecticut (Figure 4.4) and the environmental feature that bounded and gave a name to our Farmington River Archaeological Project (FRAP). (When we started this project, we had considered naming ourselves the Farmington Archaeological Research Team, but we suspected that the acronym wouldn't work all that well on our project T-shirts).

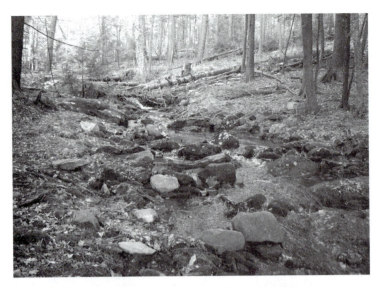

**FIGURE 4.2** The unnamed brook that flows into Beaver Brook, the major drainage stream in Peoples State Forest. (*Kenneth L. Feder*)

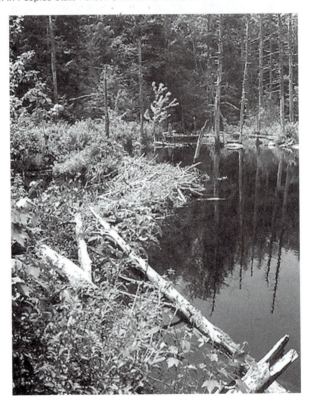

**FIGURE 4.3** Beaver Brook is impounded by a textbook-perfect Beaver Dam, part of which can be seen in the left-center of this photograph. The beaver pond can be seen on the right. This area has long been beaver habitat and is indicated as "Beaver Meadow" on maps going back to the mid-1800s. (*Kenneth L. Feder*)

**FIGURE 4.4** The Farmington River, the major watercourse that flows through north-central Connecticut and that has served as a focus for my archaeological research. (*Kenneth L. Feder*)

The positioning of our planned transect that day in early July was determined by a combination of our **research strategy** and the practical concerns of the Connecticut Historical Commission, the agency that was funding our project with monies provided by the United States Department of the Interior.

 ## How Do Archaeologists Know Where to Dig to Find Sites?

In a regional archaeological survey like the one we were conducting in Peoples State Forest, we were not simply looking for sites, we were attempting to understand an ancient pattern of land use. This pattern of land use or **settlement pattern** of ancient people leaves behind what archaeologists William Marquardt and Carol Crumley have called a **landscape signature** (1987:7). That landscape signature will consist of the geographical locations of cities, towns, villages and camps, quarries, mills and factories, sacred places, shrines, burial grounds, battlefields, and so on. These entities were established by past people in various places for different reasons. Cities may have developed where transportation and trade would have been easiest; quarries were placed—obviously enough—where the resources being quarried were located; sacred places may have been located

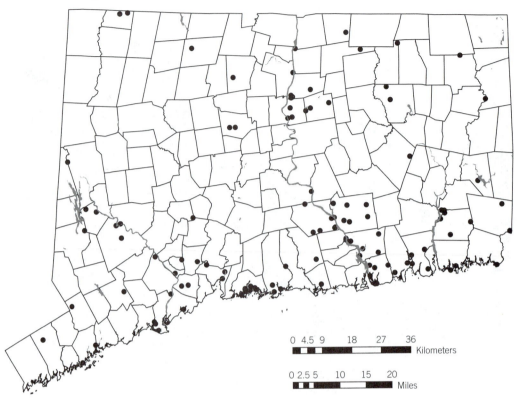

**FIGURE 4.5** Distribution of Native American sites in Connecticut that date to the early period of contact with European settlers of the state. Some of these sites are located along the coast, some are inland along major rivers, and some are situated in what were the forested uplands of seventeenth- and eighteenth-century Connecticut. (*Courtesy of William Keegan, Keegan Associates*)

far from a population center, near an awe-inspiring view or impressive rock formation that was imbued with sacred meaning by the ancient people; a fishing camp may have been positioned near a fall line along a stream where anadromous fish would be easy to collect during their spawning runs. People use the landscape in ways that are both sensible and predictable, at least from their own perspective. No one type of landscape will have monopolized the attention of past people and, therefore, no one type of landform will have a monopoly of sites (Figure 4.5).

Looking for sites in the kinds of places where we have always found sites while conducting previous research—for example, in the land adjacent to a major river—will insure that we find sites in only those kinds of places. Our prophecy of finding sites in particular spots will be self-fulfilling, but our picture of a past people's land use will be incomplete. Even though we may be fairly certain where, for example, village sites with their rich artifact assemblages might be discovered because of a distinct pattern in the location of villages already found, we cannot restrict our search only to those kinds of areas. We need to investigate a broad diversity of landscapes in our hope to illuminate the concomitant diverse nature of an ancient human land use pattern.

Because the places where people lived, worked, worshipped, extracted resources, fought battles, and buried their dead were selected for consistent, comprehensible—and often sensible—reasons, when we can figure out these reasons we can predict the location of as yet unknown archaeological sites reflecting these same activities. People are attracted, in part, to settle or use particular places as the result of a constellation of environmental variables that we can identify in the present. The significance of each of these variables will differ in the calculations ancient people made about the placement of their settlements, location of resource extraction facilities; hunting stands; fishing camps; seed, root, nut, or fruit gathering stations; farmsteads; industrial zones; and so on, depending on their particular circumstances—whether they were foragers or farmers, made ceramics or metal tools and thus required proximity to a source of clay or ore, were nomadic or sedentary, needed to harness the energy of running water to provide power for their industries. Generally, the following environmental variables are considered when assessing the likelihood of the presence of a site at a particular place: access to fresh water; richness of available food sources, including wild plant and animal resources; presence of raw materials like stone, clay, or metal; proximity to transportation routes like large navigable rivers; fertile soil; gentle relief with flat areas suitable for the location of a village; and defensibility of a place (Dincauze 1978; Feder 1997b; Schiffer, Sullivan, and Klinger 1978).

As we will soon see, I accurately predicted the location of the Wood Lily site in Peoples State Forest because three significant features of the surrounding landscape were readily apparent on the topographic map we were using in the field: (1) proximity to a fresh water stream; (2) the presence, within an area of rather rough and uneven topography, of a flat surface sufficiently large to allow for a number of structures; and (3) a terrace immediately to the west of the location high enough to provide a windbreak, adding an element of protection from the weather for anyone living east of the ridge. In other words, Wood Lily would have been a clever place to live and one can almost always rely on the cleverness of ancient people whose lives depended on choosing wisely the locations of their villages, encampments, and locations for resource extraction. Once we recognize the elements of an area that were attractive to people of a given culture in a particular period of time, we can both explain the locations of the archaeological sites that we have found and accurately predict the most reasonable locations to look for sites that we have yet to find.

# Read More

To delve more deeply into the ways in which features of the environment signal the likely existence of archaeological sites, and how these environmental signals help us craft site surveys, read any of the following sources:

Dincauze, D. F. 1978. Surveying for cultural resources: Don't rush out with a shovel. In *Conservation Archaeology in the Northeast: Toward a Research Orientation*, edited by A. Speiss, vol. 3, 51–59. Peabody Museum of Archaeology and Ethnology, Cambridge, Massachusetts.

Feder, K. L. 1997b. Site survey. In *Field Methods in Archaeology,* edited by T. R. Hester, H. J. Shafer, and K. L. Feder, 41–68. Mayfield Publishing, Mountain View, California.
Schiffer, M. B., A. P. Sullivan, and T. C. Klinger. 1978. The design of archaeological surveys. *World Archaeology* 10:1–28.

# What Forms the Basis of an Archaeological "Sampling Strategy"?

Consider the 4,000 acres of Peoples State Forest. That is a large tract of land, densely covered with trees and with irregular and rough topography—by the standards of southern New England, anyway. The archaeological record representing past human use of the forest is, for the most part, obscured, having long ago been covered by soil. In order to reveal that record, we needed to peer under the leaf and needle litter, beneath the humus, and within the rich, rocky, and rooty soil.

Of course, we would have been very happy to have a high-tech method for imaging the subsurface of all of those 4,000 acres without excavating, but, sadly, we have no such ability, at least not one that is effective and efficient in the literal neck of the woods where I do most of my fieldwork. To be sure, there are a number of procedures that collectively fall in the category **remote sensing** where, without digging, the subsurface is probed for the presence of artifacts and, more usually, buried features, but we do not yet have the ability to accurately and thoroughly image the soil beneath our feet.

Even if we could produce what amounted to an x-ray, CT scan, or MRI of the subsurface of our entire 4,000-acre study area down to bedrock, we would still be unable, in all likelihood, to distinguish cultural materials like artifacts and ecofacts from the natural background noise of roots and rocks that populate the soil in incalculable numbers. Though I someday may be—and hope to be—proven wrong on this, the bottom line is that the time-consuming, backbreaking approach of **test pitting** is and will likely remain the most effective method for finding buried sites in rocky soil. **Shovel test pits** (sometimes just called **STPs**) represent an incredibly laborious but successful strategy for peeking below the surface in our search for archaeological material. There are really no other alternatives that work as well.

In small projects and especially when an entire parcel of land is to be developed and all archaeological sites located there will likely be destroyed, we may excavate test pits across the entire area, distributing pits in a dense grid pattern. In many other situations, we simply cannot test at this level of intensity. Certainly, we could not excavate all 4,000 acres of Peoples State Forest and, equally certainly, archaeologists looking for sites almost everywhere else similarly cannot strip away all of the soil down to bedrock, extracting a 100% sample of the subsurface in a project area to look for sites. This means that in our search for buried archaeological material we almost always can examine only a small fraction or "sample" of that subsurface. Because of the constraints of time, money, and a desire to cause as little ecological disruption to a place as possible, we usually rely on test pits dispersed across the expanse of a research area. The question then becomes: Where do we place those pits that we dig in the search for sites and how densely do we distribute them? The answers to these questions are resolved by developing a **sampling strategy.**

Sampling strategies may differ depending on the research goals of the archaeologist (Orton 2000; Shafer 1997b; Whalen 1990). Sometimes, the concentration may be on only a particular kind of landform in a region, or sites from only a single time period may be the focus. Usually, however, whether we are talking about the search for buried archaeological sites or the attempt to figure out who is ahead on election night, the goal of sampling is to produce a **sample** that is both **random** and **representative.**

Let's consider the example of sampling a small fraction of the electorate in order to get a statistical sense of how the entire **population** of voters is going to cast their ballots. Here, researchers design a sampling strategy that produces a sample that, though it represents only a small fraction of the population, in a statistical sense "looks like" the population in miniature. Everyone has an equal chance of being included in the sample because individuals are chosen randomly. Further, it doesn't discriminate against any categories of people because it is representative. For example, if 50% of the entire electorate is female, then 50% of the sample should be too. If 1% of the electorate is made up of millionaires, the sample should have about that same percentage of wealthy people. Men and women have been known to vote differently and rich and poor people may vote differently as well. If you include proportionally more men or women, or more poor people or millionaires in the sample than there are in the entire population, your poll may not reflect accurately how the electorate as a whole will vote on election night. The sample will be skewed—it won't look like the population— and the results may be far different from those of the population.

We face a similar challenge in archaeological testing. When surveying a region, we hope to find a representative sample of the population of archaeological sites—a sample in which the relative proportions of sites of differing cultures, functions, and ages are very similar to those proportions in the entire population of all of the sites in the region being investigated. Of course, we don't really know what the population of sites in a region looks like—we're conducting our archaeological research to figure this out. We can, however, increase the probability of obtaining a representative sample of sites by designing a strategy that tests different kinds of landforms and habitats in a region at the same level of intensity and by making sure that coverage is proportional to the percentage of land in a project area represented by each kind of land form and habitat. In other words, we randomly choose those specific areas within our sampling universe of property where test pits are excavated and proportions of the different kinds of land tested are represented in the sample in the same proportions in which they are found in the entire research area. For example, if only about 20% of a region can be characterized as floodplain and 50% is upland, then about those same proportions of test excavations should be located in the floodplain and the uplands (20% and 50%, respectively). If we skew our sample and excavate mainly on the floodplain (because its easier to access, the soil passes through the screening much more readily, and floodplain sites produce rich artifact assemblages) we may find great sites and lots of them, but our overall sample of sites will not be representative and our general impression of the pattern of ancient land use may be grossly distorted. You don't find sites where you don't look and a host of special activity sites used by folks whose floodplain villages we do find, as well as the settlements of societies whose land use pattern was focused away from the floodplain, may remain unknown to us. So the key factor in assuring a useful and informative sample of the population of archaeological sites in a research area is to employ a strategy that produces an array of sites that are representative of the population as a whole. We do this by sampling land types in the research area that are measurably representative of the landforms in the area.

## Read More

Sampling is a vast subject; most of the important works on sampling are not written by archaeologists but by statisticians. For sources directly related to how archaeologists deal with the fundamental problem that we can't dig up the entire world, but only bits and pieces of it, consult any of the following resources on sampling strategies in archaeology:

Mueller, J. 1975. *Sampling in Archaeology*. University of Arizona Press, Phoenix.

Orton, C. 2000. *Sampling in Archaeology*. Cambridge University Press, Cambridge, England.

Shafer, H. J. 1997b. Research design and sampling techniques. In *Field Methods in Archaeology*, edited by T. R. Hester, H. Shafer, and K. L. Feder, 21–40. Mayfield, Mountain View, California.

Whalen, M. E. 1990. Sampling versus full-coverage survey: An example from western Texas. In *The Archaeology of Regions: A Case for Full-Coverage Survey*, edited by S. Fish and S. Kowalewski, 219–36. Smithsonian Institution Press, Washington, D.C.

## How Can Archaeologists Probe the Subsurface without Digging Holes?

The stereotype of the archaeologist, pick-ax in hand, smashing through the door of a tomb, has long since been abandoned and replaced by the equally stereotypical image of a digger at the bottom of an enormous shaft, slowly and carefully brushing away soil with a whisk broom, painstakingly removing thin slices of earth with a razor-sharp mason's trowel, and exposing the tiniest of clues about antiquity with a dental pick. There is more than just a little reality to this more recent stereotype, but these simple, time-worn methods for conducting archaeological excavation can be supplemented with several more technologically advanced procedures.

As complex as an excavation may be, all excavations are essentially about removing the soil from over and around the stuff left behind in the past for discovery in the present, analyzing the spatial organization of the items, and re-covering the ancient material for detailed study back in the laboratory. Moving soil carefully is made possible by the application of fairly low-tech procedures and pretty primitive tools like shovels, brushes, and trowels. On the other hand, there are a number of ways in which we can reveal artifacts, ecofacts, and features from a distance (even though we do not actually move the soil or pro-duce images of what the subsurface looks like) by discovering anomalies in the physical structure and/or chemical makeup of the soil that may have resulted from past human activity in an area (Weymouth 1986).

For example, in **electrical resistivity survey,** an electrical current is passed through the soil between two probes. The conductivity of the soil between the probes (the ability of the soil to sustain an electrical current passing through it) and its related resistance to that current (its inherent opposition to the passing of an electrical current that is then translated into heat or some other form of energy) is controlled by a host of variables, water content being key.

Even long after someone in the past dug a pit or a trench and then filled it in, the soil in the pit can display a different degree of compaction than the surrounding soil. In fact, an experienced field archaeologist is often able to feel that difference when excavating even a very ancient pit; a trowel scraped across undisturbed soil simply feels different than when scraped across soil that was dug up to create a pit that was then filled back in. The difference in compaction causes a difference in water content, which, in turn, alters the conductivity of the soil in the filled pit or trench. Similarly, the conductivity of, for example, a buried stone wall and the resistance it presents to an electrical current passing through it will also be quite different from the conductivity of the soil in which the wall is buried, as will be its resistance to an electrical current.

In an electrical resistivity survey, we put probes in the ground and pass a current between them, move them regularly, and repeatedly pass an electrical current for each positioning of the probes, producing a detailed map of the conductivity of the subsurface soil. Based on deviations in soil conductivity, areas of soil disturbance or the presence of a large buried structure may be recognized, all without digging any test pits but instead by sticking metal probes into the ground and passing an electrical current between them. Where electrical resistivity surveying measures the soil's ability to conduct an electrical current, in **ground penetrating radar,** the soil's response to an electromagnetic pulse is analyzed. In above-ground applications of radar such a pulse is directed out into the air where it encounters objects that are dense enough to bounce the pulse back to where a receiver can measure it to determine the distance and shape of whatever object the pulse bounced off of. In ground penetrating radar, the electromagnetic pulse is directed into the ground and, at least in theory, a receiver measures the depth and size of whatever the pulse encountered that was dense enough to reflect it back to a receiver (Figure 4.6; Conyers 1995; Conyers and Goodman 1997). If the object or objects encountered by the electromagnetic pulse possess a shape that appears to be artificial (that is, not a product of nature), the archaeologist may elect to dig at its location to determine whether it is, in fact, the result

**FIGURE 4.6** Remote sensing capabilities are rapidly growing in archaeology. Here, researchers using ground penetrating radar look for eighteenth-century graves among the replica buildings at Fort Vancouver, Washington. (*Courtesy of Larry B. Conyers*)

**FIGURE 4.7** Map produced using ground penetrating radar, revealing the presence of an architectural feature at the site of Petra, Jordan. The buried walls, not discernible on the surface, are clearly visible in this image. It's not magic, but it comes pretty close. (*Courtesy of Lawrence Conyers*)

of human activity (Figure 4.7). Ground penetrating radar has been used successfully to locate and identify buried walls, foundations, and the compacted floors of houses (Weymouth 1986).

Instead of actively inserting energy into the ground in the form of an electrical current or an electromagnetic pulse, in **proton magnetometry** the Earth's own magnetic field is used in the search for buried archaeological material. In theory, when the magnetic field measuring device called a magnetometer is pulled along over a homogeneous soil body, the Earth's magnetic field is the same on the path along which the magnetometer is pulled. If, however, the soil is not homogeneous (for example, if there are burials, subterranean passageways, infilled canals, and so on) the Earth's magnetic field may deviate slightly and this deviation turns up as an anomaly when the field is measured and mapped.

Although these approaches have had great successes, in many parts of the world the subsurface is quite complex, is not naturally homogeneous, and is loaded with rocks. Even without the presence of alterations wrought by past people, soil resistivity may vary greatly in different parts of a research area, radar may show the presence of dense buried objects, and magnetometers may reveal anomalies in the Earth's magnetic field. Unfortunately, many of these results cannot be distinguished from cultural materials, limiting, at least for the present, the applicability and utility of these remote sensing technologies in the search for buried archaeological sites.

## Read More

For more information about remote sensing in archaeology, any of the following works would be a good place to start (especially Conyers and Goodman):

Conyers, L. B. 1995. The use of ground penetrating radar to map the buried structures and landscape of the Ceren Site, El Salvador. *Geoarchaeology* 10:275–99.

Conyers, L. B., and D. Goodman. 1997. *Ground-Penetrating Radar: An Introduction for Archaeologists*. Altamira Press, Walnut Creek, California.

Johnston, R. B. 1964. *Proton Magnetometry and Its Application to Archaeology: An Evaluation at Angel Site*. Research Series. Indiana Historical Society, Indianapolis.

Shapiro, G., and J. M. Williams. 1982. *A Search for the Eighteenth Century Village at Michilimackinac: A Soil Resistivity Survey*. Mackinac State Parks, Mackinaw City, Michigan.

# What Are the Mechanics of Looking for and Finding Sites?

The search for archaeological sites in any survey ordinarily progresses through a number of steps (Feder 1997b). Archaeologists often begin, perhaps rather obviously, with a **literature search.** Have other researchers—professional archaeologists or hobbyists—encountered archaeological material in an area and then published or in other ways shared the details of their discovery? Professional archaeologists often publish the results of their research in journals geared to other professional archaeologists. Some of these journals concentrate on broad issues in archaeology, but others are focused more narrowly on regional prehistory and are a great source for site-specific information. Many local archaeological societies that have among their members both professional and avocational archaeologists publish newsletters or bulletins and articles concerning the research conducted by members. Research reports unpublished in traditional outlets may be available in local libraries, museums, State Historic Preservation Offices, state archaeologists' offices, or may be viewable online (for example, there is a wealth of such material housed at the ArchNet Web site: http://archnet.asu.edu/archnet).

Where material concerning the location of sites has not been published or even recorded, artifact collectors may be approached directly for any information they are willing to supply. Many hobbyists do not actually dig to find sites but take advantage of already disturbed soil layers. Probably most commonly, many collectors walk farmers' fields soon after plowing, looking for artifacts that had been buried but are now exposed in the furrows, brought up to the surface by the plow blade (Figure 4.8). Newspaper articles about ongoing research may encourage local collectors to identify themselves and share their knowledge about the location of sites.

**FIGURE 4.8** A sharp eye, a tight focus, and a strong back are valuable assets for an archaeologist walking a recently plowed field, looking for archaeological evidence of a previous occupation of the area. (*Kenneth L. Feder*)

Sometimes the discovery of important archaeological sites relies on serendipity. The Glazier Blade cache site mentioned previously is a textbook example: the site itself was located by sheer luck and only a string of coincidences led to my involvement. By chance, the small, ancient pit in which the stone blades had been so carefully stacked by the ancient inhabitants of the Farmington River valley was located at the base of a slope, just below where a storm pipe exited the soil, directing storm runoff from the street down to the wetland behind the houses in a quiet neighborhood. A few years ago a torrential downpour had pushed quite a bit of water through that drain and the swiftly flowing water washed away the soil that rested, coincidentally, on top of the pit where the blades had been cached. Had the drainpipe poked out of the slope a few inches farther north or south, the water would not have eroded and exposed the top of the pit, and the artifacts, in all probability, would not have been discovered.

Mr. Ron Glazier, the property owner, takes great pride in his landscaping and was concerned about property damage from the storm. He examined his yard after the downpour and found that the water that had funneled through the storm drainpipe, indeed, had caused erosion on the slope behind his house. By another stroke of luck, Glazier had grown up in Ohio farm country and as a boy had collected arrowheads in agricultural fields. As a result of those experiences, and unlike most people, Glazier was primed for distinguishing artifacts from naturally broken rock. You would be amazed at how often I have been called on by local people who are sincerely convinced that they have discovered wonderful ancient artifacts that turn out to be nothing more than plain old rocks. The fact that a stone "fits nicely in the hand" seems to be the primary distinguishing characteristic for many would-be artifact discoverers. I have seen quite a few rocks that have, indeed, fit rather nicely in my hand, but they have been nothing more than that: rocks that were picked up by collectors precisely because they fit in the hand or were fortuitously shaped. Glazier, however, clearly recognized that the large, symmetrical slice of stone exposed by the drainage pipe water was no ordinary rock but actually the finely flaked tip of a huge spear point. Glazier immediately cleared away the surrounding soil and exposed an enormous, **bifacially** flaked stone blade, which he then pulled from the ground.

In another useful coincidence, Glazier had recently purchased an automobile from a local dealer, Dick Wagner, who happens to have a great interest in archaeology. Aware of this interest, Glazier excitedly contacted Wagner about the stone blade and brought it to the dealership. Wagner is more specifically interested in Mesoamerican prehistory and, though he ooed and aahed about the size of the stone blade, he couldn't tell Glazier much about the artifact: he didn't know what the raw material was, couldn't guess its age, and wasn't sure about its cultural affiliation. And now another lucky happenstance: because of his general interest in archaeology and history, Wagner is a member of the local historical society which, on occasion, has invited me to give slide lectures on local archaeology. Wagner and I had spoken on a number of occasions about archaeology and he advised Glazier to contact me as a local "expert."

While all this was going on, a few more storms struck the area, a few more deluges passed through the storm pipe, and, as luck would have it, a few more blades were exposed and recovered by Glazier. On Wagner's recommendation, Glazier called me and described his discovery; by then he had pulled no fewer than sixteen gargantuan stone blades from the base of the slope and he invited me to come and take a look. It all sounded far too good to be true. Based on Glazier's information, the artifacts were larger by far than anything we had found in the Farmington Valley and I visited his home to examine what I fully expected to be a handful of large, naturally fractured rocks that

GBC-001 '93 N.COONCE          GBC-006 '94 N.COONCE

**FIGURE 4.9** Examples of two of the thirty Glazier Blades, extraordinarily large, flaked stone tools recovered from a cache discovered in Granby, Connecticut. (*Courtesy of Noel Coonce-Ewing*)

just happened to "fit nicely in the hand." Much to my surprise, when I met with Glazier, he brought me into his living room and showed me sixteen of the largest spear points I had ever seen. They were all neatly symmetrical, finely flaked, and huge, indeed more than four times the length of the spear points we had been finding in the Farmington Valley. Needless to say, I was floored by the size of the artifacts, by the expertise reflected by the work of the toolmaker or toolmakers, and by the concentration of the spear points in one spot. Glazier invited us to conduct a formal excavation in the area where he found the artifacts and, by the time we were done, there were thirty blades in all (Figure 4.9). And it all happened due to a series of lucky breaks.

Certainly, as exciting as the Glazier Blades experience was, archaeologists cannot simply linger hopefully by the phone waiting for archaeological lightning to strike. We need to be proactive and seek out the knowledge of other people. Questionnaires mailed to landowners in an area may generate valuable information about the discovery of artifacts by amateurs actively looking for artifacts or accidental discoveries by people digging into the soil for entirely mundane reasons like putting in a swimming pool or planting a vegetable garden.

Of course, one needs to word the questionnaires carefully. A local farmer, the owner of a substantial tract of agricultural land in an area where others had found sites, did not initially return a survey I sent. When I ran into him later in the field season, I introduced myself and inquired about the survey, concerned that he may not have received it. He informed me that he had, but didn't think it would help for him to return it because he had certainly never found any artifacts on his property. I expressed my surprise, explaining that a number of his neighbors had, indeed, found interesting artifacts on their land. The farmer was shocked, expressing his extreme skepticism about any such discoveries. "Well, I certainly haven't found any artifacts," he assured me. "Lots of arrowheads," he went on, "but never any artifacts." Whoops. I picked my jaw up from the floor and explained that the question about "artifacts" also included arrowheads (and pottery, stone drills, bone awls, soapstone bowls, and the like). The farmer rather reasonably chided me: "Well, why didn't you say so?" Of course he was right and I had been foolish to use a term not necessarily familiar to all people. It should go without saying that all subsequent versions of my questionnaire ask people about their discovery of arrowheads (and pottery, stone drills, and so on), and not artifacts.

Despite the poor wording of my initial questionnaire, I have experienced an extraordinary amount of interest and cooperation from local landowners. It has often been the case that local people have found interesting artifacts (there's that word again) while plowing, planting, digging footings for an outbuilding, and so on, and have stored them in old cigar boxes or coffee cans, always intending to ask someone about the relics but not knowing where to begin. Many of these people are more than happy to allow us to look at the material and some even end up donating it to our university for research or teaching purposes. More than once, these "accidental archaeologists" have been able to identify the precise location where the archaeological remains in their possession were found and further excavation by us has led to astonishing discoveries.

Historical records may also be useful in the search for sites. Property and tax records stored in county or town offices may pinpoint the locations of old houses, factories, mills, and cemeteries that have long ago been abandoned, fallen into disrepair, burned to the ground, or become overgrown and largely forgotten. Treaties may indicate the location of the villages of Native Americans that today, on the surface, appear to be little more than cornfields, woodlots, or suburban developments (Figure 4.10; Feder 1983). Historical documents may direct us to locations where our hidden history can be revealed by archaeological excavation.

We employed all of these information sources in our survey of Peoples State Forest but, as in all archaeological surveys, we needed to go out into the field. In the analysis of aerial photographs, researchers talk about "ground

**FIGURE 4.10** Part of a 1673 treaty citing a tract of land, "ye Indian Neck which ye Indians stand possessed of." Indian Neck was located, and a pedestrian survey confirmed the presence of a seventeenth-century Indian village.

truth," establishing the veracity and significance of features seen in aerial photographs by actually putting people down in those spots and seeing what they look like on the ground. In the field, an archaeological survey crew similarly attempts to assess the ground truth of the collected anecdotal, historical, and documentary evidence concerning the location of archaeological sites in a project area by putting people on the ground. Surface walkovers in areas suggested by background research can reveal the locations of foundations, old mill dams or raceways (the engineered, often stone-lined channels directing water to the mill wheel), overgrown and abandoned cemeteries, trash dumps, middens, and so on.

In most places, any sites except for the most recent are buried by a series of natural processes and we need to dig to find them. Archaeology in the twenty-first century may be a high-tech enterprise, with computers, laser transits, and GPS devices, but even so, the most common tool used in the search for buried sites is still the shovel. There is no universally applicable, efficient, or accurate way to see beneath the surface of the earth in the search for the constituents of archaeological sites—we need to dig to find buried sites. **Shovel test pits** (sometimes simply referred to as **STPs**) are the decidedly low-tech method most archaeologists use to find buried archaeological remains (Krakker, Shott, and Welch 1983; Lightfoot 1986; Lovis 1986; Nance and Ball 1986).

There is no universal standard for the size and placement of shovel test pits, or for how the soil brought up in these pits is examined for the presence of artifacts or ecofacts. In the Farmington River Archaeological Project (FRAP), our test pits are 50-centimeter square holes. Some researchers dig larger test pits, some dig smaller ones; it often depends on the size of sites in a region and how intensively an area is to be sampled. In FRAP, all soil in a test pit is passed through one-eighth-inch mesh hardware cloth that has been attached to a small wooden frame. Many archaeologists use screening with quarter-inch mesh. To cover a broad area, test pits are often placed along a straight line or **transect.** Individual transects may be located entirely within subsections of a research area defined on the basis of similar characteristics (river floodplain, lakeside habitat, upland with steep slope, wetlands) or they may intentionally cut across several habitats. The goal is to extract a representative sample of sites to enable us to produce an accurate picture of whether and to what extent people in different time periods utilized these different environmental zones. Once a site is found, its precise location is measured and recorded.

Because we are testing only a fraction of the subsurface in a project area, we would like to find all of the sites located within each of the transects along which we dig test pits. Certainly, if our test pits are extremely close together, we can find every site a transect actually intersects (Nance and Ball 1986). Such an intensive strategy, however, would represent what amounts to digging, not a sampling of holes in the ground, but instead a continuous trench, sometimes across miles of territory. We can't really accomplish this in most circumstances, so we end up having to place test pits some distance apart and there almost always are compromises to make between the desire to find all sites located along a transect and the need to accomplish a survey project before we reach retirement age and, ultimately, become archaeological specimens ourselves. There is no perfect, universally applicable figure for test pit interval that solves this dilemma. In an interesting mathematical simulation, archaeologist Ken Kintigh (1988) showed

**FIGURE 4.11** The graphic results of a simulation showing that the percentage of existing archaeological sites actually discovered or "intersected" by a test pit in a test pit transect increases as the distance between the test pits approaches the diameter of the sites. (*Courtesy Ken Kintigh*)

that as the distance between test pits approaches the actual linear extent of a site (the distance across which artifacts or ecofacts are found), site discovery approaches 100% (Figure 4.11). In other words, if the smallest sites in a region have archaeological material spread out across a length of about 20 meters, then you will find nearly all of the sites a test pit transect cuts across if the distance between test pits is about 20 meters. We made every effort to adhere to that strategy in our survey of Peoples State Forest.

## Read More

There is a vast archaeological literature concerned with site survey and the various methods archaeologists employ in the systematic search for sites. Read any and all of the following resources for a brief perspective on how archaeologists look for—and discover—archaeological sites:

Feder, K. L. 1983. "The avaricious humour of designing Englishmen": The ethnohistory of land transactions in the Farmington Valley. *Bulletin of the Archaeological Society of Connecticut* 45:29–40.

Feder, K. L. 1997b. Site survey. In *Field Methods in Archaeology*, edited by T. R. Hester, H. J. Shafer, and K. L. Feder, 41–68. Mayfield Publishing, Mountain View, California.

Krakker, J. J., M. J. Shott, and P. D. Welch. 1983. Design and evaluation of shovel-test sampling in regional archaeology. *Journal of Field Archaeology* 10:469–80.

Lightfoot, K. G. 1986. Regional surveys in the Eastern United States: The strengths and weaknesses of implementing subsurface testing programs. *American Antiquity* 51:484–504.

Lovis, W. A. 1976. Quarter sections and forests: An example of probability sampling in the Northeastern woodlands. *American Antiquity* 41:364–71.

Nance, J. D., and B. F. Ball. 1986. No surprises? The reliability and validity of test pit sampling. *American Antiquity* 51:457–83.

Shott, M. J. 1989. Shovel test sampling in archaeological survey: Comments on Nance and Ball and Lightfoot. *American Antiquity* 54:396–404.

## How Do You Determine the Precise Location of a Site?

I suppose it is rather ironic that, as an archaeologist who spends quite a bit of time directing fieldwork deep in the forests of southern New England, I am pretty much hopeless when it comes to finding my way in the woods. With the proper equipment, even just a simple compass, I'm fine, but I have zero innate sense of direction. This became embarrassingly apparent a couple of years ago when I led a troop of dedicated archaeology students to begin work at a site located deep in the McLean Game Refuge in Granby, Connecticut. After walking for twenty minutes in what I thought was the direction of the site, I led the crew to the top of a rise where I expected to find our datum stake demarcating the zero point of the site from which all other measurements were taken. Instead, we looked back down on our truck: I had managed to make a complete circle through the woods back to where we had started. I felt like a homing pigeon.

Of course, the ability to precisely determine a site's location is important if you hope to find it again (duh!). Equally important is the task of being able to record the precise location of a site on a map on which important environmental variables (slope, distance to fresh water, soil type, bedrock characteristics, and so on) have already been identified. By pinpointing the location of a place used by past peoples, we can accurately convey the positioning of a site in an environmental context, and that context includes the most likely factors on which a people in the past based their land use decisions.

Typically, archaeologists bring actual paper copies of United States Geological Survey (USGS) topographic quadrangle maps into the field or they carry digital versions on laptop computers. In fact however, these quite useful maps are of a scale that does not really allow for sufficient precision when attempting to pinpoint the location of an archaeological site, especially a small one. The quad sheets are produced from aerial photographs and the scale is 1:24,000. Though quite good for conveying significant topographic and hydraulic features—these maps show all major elevation changes as well as rivers, streams, brooks, lakes, ponds, and wetlands—the scale at which they are drawn is a bit large for accurately and precisely mapping the location of small archaeological sites. At their scale, 1 inch on the map is about 2,000 feet on the ground (1 centimeter on the map translates into 240 meters). Put another way, a straight line on the map about 2.625 inches in length represents a mile on the ground (1 centimeter on the map is the equivalent of about .24 kilometers on the ground). At this scale, a site relatively large by New England standards, for example, one about 50 meters (164 feet) across would be proportionally only about 2 millimeters (about 0.08 of an inch) across on the map. The point of all this annoying math is simple: it is extremely difficult to eyeball the exact location of a site on a USGS topographic map, especially when the site itself may be no more than a few tens of feet across. At this scale, many archaeological sites are barely pinpoints; when we mark a site's location with a pencil, in some cases the mark itself is bigger than the site (Feder 2001).

Fortunately, we no longer need to "guesstimate" the location of a site. Our ability today to far more accurately place a site on a broader landscape is made possible through the **Global Positioning System (GPS).** Initiated in 1973, the GPS currently consists of a web of at least twenty-four satellites orbiting Earth at an altitude of about 12,600 miles (20,000 kilometers; Figure 4.12). At any given time and from any location on the planet, the signals of between five and eight (and sometimes even more) of the satellites can be received. These satellites emit radio signals that can be processed by GPS receivers here on Earth and from those

**FIGURE 4.12** Schematic diagram showing satellite positioning in the Global Positioning System. A very accurate measurement of your location (and the location of an archaeological site you are standing on top of) can be determined by using a hand-held GPS device when it can "see" five or more of the satellites. (*Courtesy of Peter H. Dana, The Geographer's Craft Project, Department of Geography, The University of Colorado at Boulder*)

**FIGURE 4.13** Photo of the screen of my eTrex GPS handheld device, showing the location and elevation of the Wood Lily archaeological site in the UTM system. (*Kenneth L. Feder*)

readings GPS receivers can provide precise and accurate information concerning location in three dimensions (latitude, longitude, and elevation).

Generally, with handheld receivers, locations can be measured accurately to within a range about 20 meters. Additionally, the Federal Aviation Authority is developing the **Wide Area Augmentation System,** which uses ground stations in conjunction with the satellites to improve accuracy to within between 7 and even 2 meters. With corrections available from known, fixed locations, even greater accuracy can be achieved and locations pinpointed to within a remarkable 1 meter on our planet's 510,000,000,000,000 square meters!

One can readily see how useful the ability to pinpoint to within just a few meters the location of friendly and hostile troops would be in a battlefield situation. It should come as no surprise, therefore, that the GPS is funded, maintained, and controlled by the U.S. Department of Defense. Its original and still primary purpose is one of military support, and GPS signals originally were encrypted so that only the U.S. military and our allies could access the signals. Recognizing the great potential of the GPS system for civilian use, the signals were made available to everyone in the mid-1980s, but for a time only the U.S. military and our allies could access the *pure* signal from the satellites. Called "selective availability," the Department of Defense degraded the signal available to everyone else (remember, "everyone else" included Iraqi troops in the 1991 Persian Gulf War engaged in combat against American soldiers), allowing for less accuracy. Under selective availability, nonmilitary measurements were accurate only to within about 100 meters, still not bad on a rather large planet, but of limited use to archaeologists who needed to locate their sites much more precisely.

As a result of newly developed abilities to block the signals to an enemy during combat, degrading signal accuracy became unnecessary and the selective availability program was ended in May 2000. Since that time, pure satellite signals have been accessible to anyone with a GPS receiver. An experiment was conducted at a fixed point at a known location just before and immediately after selective availability was suspended. With the degraded signal, 95% of the measurements taken over a twenty-four-hour period at a known location fell within a circle whose radius was measured at 45 meters. After selective availability was turned off, measurements taken over the next twenty-four hours fell within a circle whose radius was only 6.3 meters around the actual location (http://www.colorado.edu/geography/gcraft/notes/gps/gps_f.html).

Handheld GPS receivers are widely available, sell for as little as $200, and are about the size and weight of a cell phone (Figure 4.13). Most of these truly remarkable and useful devices can be connected to a computer and the locational information collected and stored in the handheld receiver can be uploaded and automatically indicated on digital maps that can be purchased in various software packages. These maps are at a far smaller scale than that provided by USGS topographical maps. Along with the ability to accurately position the archaeological sites my group has surveyed, for me there is an added bonus to using a GPS handheld device: I no longer walk in circles attempting to find sites in the woods.

## Read More

With a handheld GPS device and any of these comprehensive guides to GPS systems and approaches you'll nearly always be able to locate an archaeological site with enormous precision—and you will hardly ever get lost in the woods:

El-Rabbany, A. 2002. *Introduction to GPS: The Global Positioning System.* Artech House, Boston.
Hotchkiss, N. J. 1999. *A Comprehensive Guide to Land Navigation with GPS.* Alexis Publishing, Leesburg, Virginia.
Letham, L. 2001. *GPS Made Easy.* Mountaineers Books, Seattle.

## What Preliminary Work Goes into an Archaeology Laboratory?

Finding "stuff" (archaeological artifacts, ecofacts, and features) at places where people once lived, worked, or extracted resources (sites) represents the data collection phase of archaeological analysis; a fun phase, to be sure, but only one step in the process. Much of the work of extracting information from the raw data of archaeological site components—and enabling us to say something interesting and perhaps even important about the lives of a past people—occurs not in the field but in the laboratory (Sutton and Arkush 2002).

A commonly used metaphor in archaeological research maintains that, with careful enough analysis, the artifacts and other materials we study can "speak" to us and tell us about the lives of the people who made, used, and left these things behind. It is important to realize, though, as the title of a popular archaeology book suggests (*Making Silent Stones Speak,* Schick and Toth 1993) the materials we recover at archaeological sites sometimes jealously guard their secrets. These objects are not always forthcoming; we have to "make them speak," and they speak not in any human tongue but in the alien language

**FIGURE 4.14** Field crew members in the lab, inventorying artifacts that have been brought in from the field. (*Kenneth L. Feder*)

of material culture. Before we can translate that language and interrogate the archaeological materials we have recovered, we need to spend a bit of time doing some essential housekeeping. Traditionally, artifacts were cleaned as a first step upon arrival in the archaeology lab. Chipping patterns on a stone tool or finely etched designs on a potsherd may be obscured by dirt adhering to their surfaces. Rather obviously, this dirt needs to be removed to facilitate analysis of the objects. However, archaeologists have increasingly recognized that microscopic residues of plant material (for example, pollen and, especially, **phytoliths**) and even of animal remains (especially blood) may lie hidden in the pits and crevices of an artifact's surface. At least a sample of objects may remain uncleaned in order to extract possible residues for analysis.

Once artifacts and ecofacts arrive at the archaeology lab, the materials recovered at a site need to be logged in and inventoried (Figure 4.14; Feder 1997a). Every object may receive its own, unique **accession** or inventory designation. That unique identifier may be written directly on the object itself.

The next time you visit a museum with archaeological specimens, look carefully at each of the displayed objects and you most likely will see a number, often written in India ink. On a broken pot that has been reassembled, you may even be able to find separate numbers on each of the pieces. Some coding systems employ a system of colored dots, and more recently some have employed machine readable barcodes. Whatever technique is used, the purpose is the same; to assign every object with a unique identifier that itself may be written in a readable code that conveys important information about the artifact, for example, the site, excavation unit, and stratigraphic unit in which it was found. For instance, a numerical prefix in an inventory number may identify the site from which an artifact was recovered, the next column may represent the excavation unit, the next the stratigraphic unit or level, and the next set of numbers may simply be a running tally of artifacts recovered in a given unit.

Beyond this basic "geographic" information about an object, a tremendous amount of information can be recorded for even quite small archaeological specimens, far more than can be coded into an accession or inventory number (for example, the precisely measured location of its discovery, the exact depth at which it was recovered, the appearance of the soil in which it was found, other objects located nearby, its raw material, the name of the excavator, the date of its discovery, and so on). This information certainly cannot fit on the object itself, even in a coded form, but it can be recorded in a paper or digital inventory. A unique identifier, along with supplying basic information about the location where an object was recovered, also allows the archaeologist to permanently conjoin each object with the information recorded about that object in the inventory.

As we analyze, compare, synthesize, and place in context the material recovered from a site, which may include thousands of individual specimens with many attributes measured or recorded for each, the database of even a small site quickly attains great size and complexity. A site inventory allows us to manage that complexity and creates a format in which patterns and correlations among artifacts and their locations can be recognized (Figure 4.15).

The actual inventory for a site may take the form of a standard computer software spreadsheet (Microsoft Excel may be the most common commercial program) or database management software (for example, File Maker Pro) (McPherron and Dibble 2002). The first column in a spreadsheet may be reserved for the inventory number of each specimen, the unique designator for each object that has been written or printed on the object itself or on the bag, envelope, canister, box, or other container in which it is stored. The next column may represent the raw material of the object (stone, ceramic, wood), the next a descriptor (spear point, potsherd, burned wood), the next its weight, then a precise horizontal location or provenience, then its stratigraphic level, and so on. The resulting simple database allows us to perform statistical analyses on the raw data encoded in the materials recovered at the site. Use of a computer spreadsheet or database allows us, for example, to determine quite easily the percentages of different lithic raw materials used by the site's inhabitants to make spear points, or to separate for analysis materials found in different stratigraphic layers. The preliminary work in the lab allows us to keep track of the materials we have laboriously recovered in the field and begins the process of extracting the information about an ancient lifeway encoded in those materials.

# Read More

Some people find lab work to be the most fascinating part of archaeological research. Others find it tiresome and tedious. Everyone recognizes, however, that data collection in the field is only one part of the process by which we illuminate the past. For a far more detailed discussion of what goes on in the archaeology laboratory, check out any of the following resources (other than the Schick and Toth reference, which is an interesting read, but not about archaeological laboratory methods):

Dillon, B. D. 1993. *Practical Archaeology: Field and Laboratory Techniques and Archaeological Logistics.* Institute of Archaeology, Los Angeles, California.

Feder, K. L. 1997a. Data preservation: Recording and collecting. In *Field Methods in Archaeology,* edited by T. R. Hester, H. J. Shafer, and K. L. Feder. Mayfield Publishing, Mountain View, California.

McPherron, S. P., and H. L. Dibble. 2002. *Using Computers in Archaeology.* McGraw-Hill, New York.

Rice, P. C. 1998. *Doing Archaeology: A Hands-On Laboratory Manual.* Mayfield Publishing, Mountain View, California.

Schick, K. D., and N. Toth. 1993. *Making Silent Stones Speak: Human Evolution and the Dawn of Technology.* Simon and Schuster, New York.

Sutton, M. Q., and B. S. Arkush. 2002. *Archaeological Laboratory Methods: An Introduction.* Kendall/Hunt Publishing, Dubuque, Iowa.

| Inventory # | Artifact type | Excavation unit | Depth below datum | Structure |
|---|---|---|---|---|
| 1001 | CERAMICS | 1 | 23 | 1 |
| 1002 | CERAMICS | 1 | 28 | 1 |
| 1003 | CERAMICS | 1 | 28 | 1 |
| 1004 | CERAMICS | 1 | 28 | 1 |
| 1005 | CERAMICS | 1 | 28 | 1 |
| 1006 | CERAMICS | 1 | 28 | 1 |
| 1007 | W.GLASS | 1 | 28 | 1 |
| 1008 | W.GLASS | 1 | 28 | 1 |
| 1009 | NAIL | 1 | 28 | 1 |
| 1010 | CERAMICS | 1 | 33 | 1 |
| 1011 | CERAMICS | 1 | 33 | 1 |
| 1012 | W.GLASS | 1 | 33 | 1 |
| 1013 | CERAMICS | 1 | 38 | 1 |
| 1014 | CERAMICS | 1 | 38 | 1 |
| 1015 | CERAMICS | 1 | 38 | 1 |
| 1016 | CERAMICS | 1 | 38 | 1 |
| 1017 | CERAMICS | 1 | 38 | 1 |
| 1018 | CERAMICS | 1 | 38 | 1 |
| 1019 | CERAMICS | 1 | 38 | 1 |
| 1020 | CERAMICS | 1 | 38 | 1 |
| 1021 | CERAMICS | 1 | 38 | 1 |
| 1022 | CERAMICS | 1 | 38 | 1 |
| 1023 | CERAMICS | 1 | 38 | 1 |
| 1024 | CERAMICS | 1 | 38 | 1 |
| 1025 | CERAMICS | 1 | 38 | 1 |
| 1026 | W.GLASS | 1 | 38 | 1 |
| 1027 | METAL | 1 | 38 | 1 |
| 1028 | METAL | 1 | 38 | 1 |
| 1029 | METAL | 1 | 38 | 1 |
| 1030 | METAL | 1 | 38 | 1 |
| 1031 | METAL | 1 | 38 | 1 |
| 1032 | METAL | 1 | 38 | 1 |
| 1033 | METAL | 1 | 38 | 1 |
| 1034 | METAL | 1 | 38 | 1 |
| 1035 | METAL | 1 | 38 | 1 |
| 1036 | PIPE | 1 | 43 | 1 |
| 1037 | PIPE | 1 | 43 | 1 |
| 1038 | CERAMICS | 1 | 43 | 1 |
| 1039 | CERAMICS | 1 | 43 | 1 |
| 1040 | CERAMICS | 1 | 43 | 1 |
| 1041 | CERAMICS | 1 | 43 | 1 |
| 1042 | CERAMICS | 1 | 43 | 1 |
| 1043 | CERAMICS | 1 | 43 | 1 |
| 1044 | CERAMICS | 1 | 43 | 1 |
| 1045 | CERAMICS | 1 | 43 | 1 |
| 1046 | CERAMICS | 1 | 43 | 1 |
| 1047 | CERAMICS | 1 | 43 | 1 |
| 1048 | W.GLASS | 1 | 43 | 1 |
| 1049 | W.GLASS | 1 | 43 | 1 |
| 1050 | W.GLASS | 1 | 43 | 1 |
| 1051 | W.GLASS | 1 | 43 | 1 |
| 1052 | NAIL | 1 | 43 | 1 |
| 1053 | BUTTON | 1 | 43 | 1 |
| 1054 | CERAMICS | 1 | 43 | 1 |
| 1055 | CERAMICS | 1 | 43 | 1 |

**FIGURE 4.15** Example of a simple artifact inventory.

# Study Questions

1. Because the areas we search for sites often are vast, ordinarily we can only actually dig test excavations in a limited sample of those areas. How do we ensure that the results of our sample (in terms of site locations and types) are an accurate reflection of the reality of an entire region?

2. What are shovel test pits (STPs, or just test pits)?

3. In a test pit survey, how does an archaeologist make sure that the sample of the land tested is representative of the region as a whole?

4. You have 4,000 acres of a state forest to survey for archaeological sites and you have money enough for only one thousand test pits. How do you distribute the pits in the forest?

5. What are the advantages of locating test pits at a random sample of points? What are the disadvantages?

6. Define "representative sample" in terms of an archaeological survey.

7. Why do archaeologists hope to obtain a random and representative sample of sites in a regional survey?

8. What is "remote sensing" as applied to archaeology?

9. List and describe some remote sensing procedures used in archaeology.

10. Why hasn't remote sensing replaced soil removal (in test pits and in excavation units) in archaeology?

11. Using the example of the Glazier Blade Cache, what role is played by serendipity or luck in site discovery?

12. How do archaeologists obtain the knowledge of local people concerning the location of archaeological sites in a region?

13. How far apart should test pits be in a test pit transect? What does archaeologist Ken Kintigh's mathematical simulation tell us about optimum test pit interval?

14. What are the key characteristics and features of United States Geological Survey quadrangle maps?

15. Of what use are GPS handheld devices in archaeological surveys? How accurate are current devices in mapping locations on the surface of the Earth?

16. Describe the function of a site inventory. What are accession numbers?

O ur funding required us to test state forest lands broadly. Although the particular plot through which the day's transect cut across might otherwise have been overlooked (it was a rather narrow appendix of property surrounded to the north and the south by private holdings that abutted the public lands), it was a section we had promised to investigate in our grant proposal.

During the first two weeks of fieldwork, my crew had not found any substantial archaeological evidence of occupation of the forest. That's not terribly surprising. In some regions, sites are few and far between and difficult to find. Surprising or not, after a little more than two weeks digging test pits, the crew was getting a bit crabby over the lack of any exciting discoveries.

I certainly could empathize, but it is important to understand that archaeology is not a scavenger hunt and that "finding stuff" is not the goal. Our purpose, instead, is to "find out stuff," which may be an entirely different thing. There is a rule in archaeology that all field crews understand, at least on an intellectual level, that states that not finding any archaeological evidence in a given spot is every bit as important as finding spectacular archaeological remains. "Negative information is just as important as positive information," is a virtual mantra for field archaeologists, intoned, albeit, with a bit of a wink and a sigh.

Certainly, in large measure the rule is true. Knowing that human groups did not inhabit a given region or microenvironment—and trying to understand why they didn't—is an important part of archaeological analysis. Emotionally, however, it must be admitted, this can be a little difficult to accept at times. Negative information may be important, but not many of us are so intellectually disciplined that we leave the field, after a long day digging dry test pits, enthusiastic about the contribution we have made to our understanding of the ancient past—by not finding anything. Even the most serious-minded archaeologist has to admit, finding stuff is a hell of a lot more fun than not finding stuff. This doesn't make archaeology a treasure hunt. Really. It's just that in the humid, buggy, muddy, sweaty, exhausting reality of archaeological fieldwork with mosquitoes, ticks, broken bones, poisonous snakes, poison ivy, poison sumac, food poisoning, and so on, it just feels so much better if instead of negative information at the end of the day you have something tangible (ancient stone tools, potsherds, butchered animal bones, anything) to show for your literal blood, sweat, and tears.

When Marina Mozzi, the chief of my increasingly whiny crew, and I looked over the **United States Geological Survey (USGS)** topographic map of the area the crew was scheduled to test that morning, I noted the location of the east-west transect line we had drawn on the map previously, starting at the paved road, cutting across the flat, briefly ending at the steep slope, continuing again across the lower flat, and terminating at the stream. I took my pencil and marked an "X" on the lower terrace, just west of the stream (Figure 5.1), telling Marina not to despair, but that, at long last, the field crew would be finding a **prehistoric** site exactly where I had marked the map. Marina smiled and nodded, saying that she was going to hold me to that "promise."

It was all done in a joking manner, of course, but I was, at least in part, quite serious. Certainly, I had no way of knowing whether an ancient site really was located where I predicted, and the location of the "X" I had scrawled on the map that morning was not all that exact anyway, but I believed that there was a fair probability of my crew's finding evidence of past human habitation of the forest somewhere on the lower terrace adjacent to the stream.

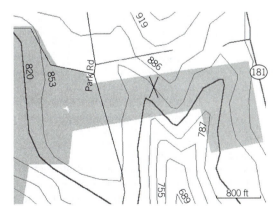

**FIGURE 5.1** The section we were about to survey was located in this narrow swath of land in Peoples State Forest.

My stock as a "psychic archaeologist" rose considerably several hours later. The entire crew made it a point to stop by my house at the end of their workday to lay themselves prostrate at the feet of their great guru archaeologist. Well, nobody actually did that, but they were appropriately impressed by my apparent clairvoyance. A few skeptics even accused me of having advance knowledge of the site and sending them to it boost morale. But, in truth, I had no foreknowledge of the site and merely used standard archaeological reasoning to hypothesize where a site would be located. "X," indeed, did "mark the spot," and the crew encountered a number of three-thousand-year-old artifacts almost exactly where I had marked the map that morning.

## What Kinds of Research Goals Do Archaeologists Have?

As mentioned in earlier sections, archaeology is not a treasure hunt. Our purpose is not just to look for interesting or impressively ancient things and our goal is not simply to fill displays with moldy objects that museumgoers will find captivating. As scientists, archaeologists seek to answer questions about the lives lived by past peoples, and we propose and then attempt to test hypotheses explaining those lives. In the broadest sense, our ultimate research goal is knowledge and we endeavor to attain that knowledge as all scientists do, first by observing (in our case by observing the world of the human past by finding and analyzing the material remains left behind by human beings), then by proposing explanations for what those remains signify (these are our hypotheses, explanations we propose for why people lived as they did in the past), and finally by testing the validity of those proposed explanations with additional evidence (Shafer 1997).

Though not our only concern, archaeologists in one way or another have always had as a research goal constructing, modifying, and fine-tuning the **culture history** of the regions in which they work; the story of what happened and when. In other words, archaeologists attempt to write a "history" for a region, often where no written history, in the usual sense of that word, exists because the people left no written record behind. One of the classic works of archaeology, written by one of the icons of the profession, V. Gordon Childe (1942), said it as forcefully and as simply as possible; the book in question was titled and was about *What Happened in History*.

In some parts of the world the study of prehistory has a lengthy history, and a local chronological sequence of what happened when is fairly well established. Revision is always possible, of course, and every archaeological project in an area can contribute to the goal of constructing culture history, sometimes by clarifying or refining an existing well-documented sequence and sometimes by overturning a chronology that had been accepted previously.

It is sometimes the case that chronological issues that one might have thought—or at least hoped—would already have been resolved continue to vex researchers and continue to be in need of basic research and data collection. For example, much to the chagrin of American archaeologists at least, the question of when human beings first entered into the New World remains unanswered, at least in any kind of a definitive way. For a long time, many archaeologists, though by no means all, believed the question had finally been laid to rest: the data seemed to indicate an initial migration sometime around twelve thousand years ago from Asia across a land bridge in an area called **Beringia** (sometimes called the **Bering Land Bridge**) connecting northeast Asia (Siberia) and northwest North America (Alaska) that was exposed during the end of the Pleistocene or Ice Age. However, a number of sites that may be far older than twelve thousand years have been located, and in some cases intensively excavated, in the New World. Some of these sites are thousands of kilometers distant from the area of Beringia, indicating that even older sites necessarily remain to be found in that region, if, in fact, that was the point of entry for ancient people into the New World. The chronology and nature of human movement into the Americas is a fundamental research question that remains unresolved. Not just a little research time and money continues to be invested in attempting to settle this fundamental issue of the culture history of the New World (Dillehay 2000; Dixon 1999; Meltzer 1993, 1997).

Culture history, however, is not the only research issue that intrigues archaeology and not the only concern that guides our work. Many modern anthropologists view culture as a means of adaptation, a complex series of strategies that enable the survival of the people who practice the culture. Where most other animal species rely almost entirely on their physical characteristics for survival, human beings also have as a strategy the ability to invent, develop, and refine behaviors that enable their continued existence. Making tools, building houses, controlling fire, trading for valuable raw materials with our neighbors, and making alliances are all behaviors that are made possible by our vast intelligence. These behaviors differ from group to group, are all elements of culture, and both directly and indirectly enable our survival. Humans think these things up and teach them to their children, who continue to develop and refine the ways of carrying them out. These behaviors leave material manifestations in the form of artifacts, ecofacts, and features: past people made spear points that were useful in hunting the animals on which they subsisted; they constructed domiciles that enabled them to withstand the long cold winters or blazing summers of their home territories; they built hearths to warm their houses and cook their food; they traded with neighbors to obtain valuable raw materials for making the tools they needed to hunt, build houses, or start fires. Understanding the nature of the cultural adaptation—being able to describe an ancient way of life of a particular group of people at a particular place at a particular period of time—and being able to explain why they lived as they did is another of the goals of archaeological research.

Understanding the great diversity of the human adaptation is an important goal of anthropology in general and of the anthropological archaeologist in particular. Cultural anthropologists conduct **ethnographic research** among living

**FIGURE 5.2** Ethnographer in the field. Anthropologist Margaret Mead is shown here with a Manus mother and child in 1953 during a visit to the Admiralty Islands. (© *Bettmann/CORBIS*)

people, observe and describe a lifeway, and then attempt to explain the nature of the adaptation of the people they study (Figure 5.2).

In the case of ethnographic research, however, the amount of time various human groups have been studied is only a tiny proportion of the time these groups have been around. The earliest ethnographers began living with cultures different from their own just a bit more than a hundred years ago, so, at best, ethnographic data has a time depth of only about that long. In contrast, the archaeological record of individual groups of people reflects a far greater amount of time. By excavating a series of sites from different time periods, archaeologists can follow the evolution of a group of people for hundreds or even thousands of years. Over such a long period of time, a group likely encountered great changes in their natural environment, their technology may have undergone enormous change, and they may have come into direct contact with a diverse array of other human groups. Only the archaeological record possesses a breadth of time sufficient to reveal how people adjust to changes in their natural and cultural environments over not just decades or centuries but millennia. Only the archaeological record provides the researcher with the totality of a people's chronology, a sufficiently large chunk of their story to assess the evolution of their technology over not just one or two generations but across their entire history. And only the archaeological record presents a thick enough slice of time to expose the lengthy story of the impacts of the movement of ideas across cultural boundaries. Studying an ancient people across a lengthy expanse of time can illuminate how they responded to great change and may even provide insights for facing such change in the present (Binford 1962, 1968).

Consider one of the most important issues facing the modern world: climate change. Whether or not human beings are the root cause of what appears to be planetary warming—especially since the inception of the industrial revolution—is vigorously debated, but there seems to be little controversy among climatologists on the existence of global warming. What will be the long-term consequences of this warming? What economic dislocations will result over, not just years or even decades, but centuries during which time the map of agricultural lands constantly changes and the soil in regions that once earned the deserved characterization "bread basket" dries up and blows away? It is important to know that periods of vast, planetwide climate change have challenged human beings in the ancient past. It is at least potentially important to understand how our ancestors responded to such changes in the past to provide insights into how we might respond—and how we might plan to respond—in the future (Butzer 1982).

Understanding the nature of human behavioral change, and stability, over long periods of time, during which the rules of the game may be altered dramatically, is a significant goal of archaeological research. Like most archaeological projects, our research goals in Peoples State Forest included culture history, culture description, and the nature of change over a lengthy period of time.

# Read More

Archaeologists, perhaps none more then Lewis R. Binford, have thought long and hard about how the study of the ancient past can contribute to our understanding of humanity. Binford's seminal articles, first published in the 1960s, resonate in the discipline more than thirty years later and are more than worth a read. I have also included a few citations of popular publications focusing on one of the cultural historical goals of those interested in New World archaeology: figuring out when, how, and from where people first entered into the Americas.

Binford, L. 1962. Archaeology as anthropology. *American Antiquity* 28:217–25.

Binford, L. R. 1968. Archaeological perspectives. In *New Perspectives in Archaeology*, edited by S. R. Binford and L. R. Binford, 5–32. Aldine Publishing, Chicago.

Butzer, K. W. 1982. *Archaeology as Human Ecology*. Cambridge University Press, Cambridge, England.

Childe, V. G. 1942. *What Happened in History*. Pelican Books, Baltimore.

Dillehay, T. D. 2000. *The Settlement of the Americas: A New Prehistory*. Basic Books, New York.

Dixon, E. J. 1999. *Bones, Boats, and Bison: Archaeology and the First Colonization of Western North America*. University of New Mexico Press, Albuquerque.

Meltzer, D. J. 1993. Search for the First Americans. In *Smithsonian: Exploring the Ancient World*. Smithsonian Books, Washington, D.C.

———. 1997. Monte Verde and the Plesitocene peopling of America. *Science* 276:754–55.

Shafer, H. 1997a. Goals of archaeological investigation. In *Field Methods in Archaeology*, edited by T. R. Hester, H. J. Shafer, and K. L. Feder, 5–20. Mayfield Publishing, Mountain View, California.

# How Is Archaeological Research Funded, and Why?

What is arguably the most famous archaeological discovery of the twentieth century almost didn't happen because the money supporting the project was about to run out. Archaeologist Howard Carter's excavations in Egypt in the second two decades of the twentieth century were funded, as were many archaeological projects during this period, by a wealthy benefactor, in this case the Earl of Carnarvon, a member of the British nobility (Buckley 1976; Fagan 1994; Hoving 1978).

After fifteen years of providing the financial backing for Carter's expeditions in an unsuccessful search for the unplundered tomb of a pharaoh, Carnarvon was running out of patience and the will to keep funding the project. In fact, it was with Carnarvon's displeasure and increasing impatience in mind that Carter left Egypt and returned to England in the summer of 1922 to implore the Earl to continue providing financial support for his work.

Carnarvon would hear none of it. The Earl told Carter that, barring any major discoveries, this would be the final season of excavation that he would fund. But Carter's luck changed dramatically in November of that same year when one of his workers discovered the entryway to the spectacular and justifiably famous burial chamber of the Egyptian pharaoh Tutankhamen; at last, he and Carnarvon had their unspoiled tomb (Figure 5.3).

Wealthy individuals like Carnarvon funded archaeology for many and varied personal reasons. Though not trained in archaeology, and often not willing to endure the rigors of full-time fieldwork, many benefactors simply were

**FIGURE 5.3** Archaeologists removing artifacts from the unspoiled tomb of the Egyptian pharaoh Tutankhamen. (© *Underwood & Underwood/CORBIS*)

fascinated by antiquity and wished to contribute in the best way they could, by paying for archaeological research. Certainly, many benefactors hoped to achieve notoriety and not just a little personal aggrandizement by providing such financial backing. Furthermore, wealthy patrons commonly signed contracts with their archaeologists, allowing the benefactors to personally donate recovered materials to museums (where their names would adorn the displays) and even to keep whatever they wished for their personal collections. In fact, Carnarvon had such a contract with Carter.

This pattern of funding necessarily colored archaeological research for a long time. Wealthy patrons funded projects that they found interesting. Commonly, and not coincidentally, these were projects that illuminated the lives of wealthy people in antiquity. After all, the archaeological remains of the homes and burial chambers of the rich and famous of the ancient world were where the most spectacular artifacts could be found. Gold and lapis lazuli death masks, alabaster vases, and ebony chairs inlaid with ivory (all objects found in Tut's tomb and the kinds of things desperately sought after by museums) simply are not found in the houses or graves of common people, workers, and slaves.

As a result, the houses and graves of common people, workers, and slaves—in fact, the majority of the population in ancient societies—were not the focus of most such archaeological work. Few wealthy patrons wanted to subsidize research that would illuminate the lives of the poor and downtrodden of antiquity, if only because the material culture of the lower classes was plain, simple, and not nearly as impressive as that of the nobility. Wealthy patrons were happy to see their names associated with museum displays of spectacular gold, silver, and alabaster objects found in a pharaoh's tomb. Few such patrons hoped to see their names associated with a similar display of plain pottery or wooden tools found in the house of a worker or farmer.

An additional consequence of this pattern of funding is that archaeological objects often were taken from their place of origin and deposited in museums located in the countries of the benefactor. Many archaeological **assemblages** (for example, the objects that together made up the grave furniture and goods of a pharaoh's burial chamber) became dispersed, scattered to various locations, removed from their association with all of the other objects with which they were found, torn from their contexts. Many important artifacts, housed in private collections, were not available for study or even public viewing and became isolated *objets d'art* (art objects), rather than scientific components of a unified package reflecting a particular set of behaviors at a single place and time. It was, in fact, concern that the Tutankhamen funerary assemblage would meet a similar fate that inspired the Egyptian government to require that it remain in Egypt, the property of the Egyptian people. The stipulations of the contract Carnarvon had signed with Carter were not carried out when the Egyptian government insisted that the objects found in Tut's tomb remain together in Egypt, rather than be removed piecemeal to various museums in European capitals and the personal collections of the wealthy.

Although wealthy benefactors continue to subsidize archaeological research, the major financial support today is from universities, museums, private institutes and societies, as well as governments. Because their motives for supporting archaeology differ significantly from those of most of the wealthy patrons of the eighteenth, nineteenth, and early twentieth centuries, the kinds of archaeological investigations possible have changed and expanded. Private organizations like the National Geographic Society (see http://www.nationalgeographic.com/ for the NGS homepage, and see http://www.nationalgeographic.com/research/grant/rg1.html for detailed information about the Society's funding of research) and federal funding agencies like the National Science Foundation (http://www.nsf.gov/) have as their fundamental goal the expanding of our scientific understanding of the world, including our understanding of the ancient world, and they fund projects accordingly.

As mentioned previously, universities also fund archaeology directly and indirectly as they would research conducted by any of their faculty, indirectly by supplying laboratory space, equipment, and supplies, as well as directly through money for salaries, graduate students, and support services. Again, much of the archaeology conducted in the United States today is categorized as "compliance archaeology," which is required of governmental agencies, states, local municipalities, and even private developers in order to comply with a broad array of historic preservation legislation on the federal, state, county, and town levels. Perhaps most significant of these laws is the **National Environmental Protection Act** (http://ceq.eh.doe.gov/nepa/regs/nepa/nepaeqia.htm). This law requires that when the federal government is funding a project (for example, a highway, a flood control project, or a community septic system), the potential impact on archaeological resources must be assessed, much in the way the act requires the assessment of a project's impact on natural resources like air, water, vegetation, and animal life. Archaeologists are hired to examine particular tracts of land that will be affected by these projects to pinpoint sites that might be adversely impacted, to assess the severity of impact, to weigh that against the significance of the site, and to help mitigate any such impacts.

In the United States, a growing number of Native American groups are supporting the archaeological investigation of their own histories. For example, the Navajo Nation, whose reservation is in Arizona and New Mexico, has its own archaeology department (http://www.nau.edu/nnad/) with a self-proclaimed goal to preserve and protect the cultural heritage of the Navajo people. The Mashantucket Pequot tribe of southeastern Connecticut has used some of the proceeds of its enormously successful gaming operation to build a state-of-the-art cultural heritage center whose focus is, in part, on the archaeological heritage of the tribe (http://www.pequotmuseum.org/). There is an archaeology research facility at the museum and tribal archaeologists conduct research both on the current reservation and on land that once was part of the Mashantucket homeland. The Mashantuckets, like many Native American tribes in the east, came close to extinction and they view archaeology of their homeland as one way in which they can recapture a part of their ancient history that might otherwise have been lost.

The funding of archaeological projects becomes far more democratic when, rather than being obliged to fulfill the personal goals or motivations of an individual patron, the kind of work attempted is determined: (1) by an anthropologically or historically trained archaeologist who is approaching particular research questions; (2) when private funding agencies simply wish to support the accumulation of knowledge about the past; (3) when government agencies fund research as part of a general policy of preservation, study, and dissemination of information about the past to an interested citizenry; or (4) when people hope to recapture their own lost history.

Our research in Peoples State Forest was supported by a combination of university and federal resources. Some summers, my university paid my salary as I taught the archaeology field school and students paid tuition for taking the course. My university also provided laboratory space, equipment, and supplies, as well as a vehicle for transporting students. In addition, the project was supported by money supplied by the National Park Service (http://www.nps.gov/) in the form of a preservation and planning grant wherein money was provided for archaeological research, in a sense before the fact, to determine the archaeological sensitivity of an area before any sites were threatened by development. There were no Tut tombs to be found in Peoples State Forest, and it is enormously unlikely that a wealthy patron of archaeology at the turn of the twenty-first century would have been enamored of the bits and pieces of stone tools and ceramic vessels we found in our research. Our work was made possible by the way such research is funded today, where the potential scientific contribution of a project—not the promise of finding pretty things—is the most significant variable in determining funding.

## Read More

The search for and excavation of Egyptian pharaoh Tutankhamen is emblematic of how major archaeological expeditions were funded in the early years of the discipline. The following sources, along with conveying the excitement of discovery, reflect the fact that archaeology was conducted in the first place because wealthy benefactors supported the work.

Buckley, T. 1976. The discovery of Tutankhamun's tomb. In *The Treasures of Tutankhamun*, edited by K. S. Gilbert, J. K. Holt, and S. Hudson, 9–18. The Metropolitan Museum of Art, New York.

Fagan, B. 1994. *Quest for the Past: Great Discoveries in Archaeology.* Waveland Press, Prospect Heights, Illinois.

Hoving, T. 1978. *Tutankhamun, the Untold Story.* Simon and Schuster, New York.

 ## What Is It that Archaeologists Want to Find Out?

In a sense, archaeologists serve in the manner of journalists reporting on the lives of past peoples. In the cliché, journalists need to ask and answer the following questions when reporting a story: where? when? what? who? how? and why? In fact, at least a couple of archaeology textbooks have organized their discussion of the purposes of archaeology around these (or similar) journalistic questions (Feder and Park 2001; Renfrew and Bahn 2000). Archaeologists attempt to find out the answers to these same questions about people in the past. Where did past people live? (Where can we find the locations of their former villages, burial grounds, hunting camps, farmsteads, quarries, mills, battlefields, and sacred places?) When did a people live at a particular place? (When did they arrive? When did they adopt new behaviors? When did they leave?) Who were the people who lived at the sites we excavate? (Who were their ancestors? Who are their descendants?) What remains did they leave behind of their tools, weapons, jewelry, clothing, structures, icons, and even of their own bodies? (What can we find of these things to use as evidence of their ways of life?) How did they live their lives? (How did they survive? How did they feed their children? How did they get along with their neighbors? How did they govern themselves? How did they obtain the raw materials needed to make their tools, construct and heat their houses, cook their food, and store their valuables? In essence, how did they respond to the challenges of their world?) Finally, why did they live as they did? (Why did they come to this spot? Why did they change or why did they remain the same? Why did they leave and not return, or why did they die off?)

Every human society represents what amounts to an experiment in survival. By asking and attempting to answer the previous questions, archaeologists hope to illuminate and comprehend those experiments in survival. All groups of people develop their own strategies for dealing with the challenges that life presents. Finding sufficient clean water to drink and food to eat, collecting enough wood to provide fuel for fires or raw materials for homes, collecting the stone or metal to make the tools necessary to hunt or to prepare the soil for planting, extracting clay from the earth to make pots in which to store or cook food, harnessing the energy of a stream to power a sawmill or gristmill, organizing families and coordinating the labor of a group of people, governing themselves, raising children to become competent adults, responding to life's tragedies, and producing a safe, protective, and secure cultural environment into which people can be born and can develop as individuals—these are all things that culture must enable and each culture finds its own way of accomplishing these tasks.

Archaeologists hope to illuminate the cultures of past people, to puzzle out their many and varied strategies for survival. It is probably naive to believe that from the lifeways of past people archaeology will reveal great insights about the human condition that will enable our own survival. I find it unlikely that our survival into the future will be facilitated in some way by the work of archaeologists. Nevertheless, humanity is characterized by its ability and, perhaps, need, to reflect upon itself. The goal of understanding the lengthy and fascinating pathway we all have taken to reach our current state is an honorable one. There is great value in exposing the enormous diversity of the human approach to survival and in illuminating the story of how groups of people across the vast stretches of time represented by the archaeological record developed ways of life that enabled their survival. Essentially, then, archaeologists hope to find out how human groups developed ways of life by finding and analyzing the material objects that were a part of that strategy for survival.

## Read More

To see how various archaeologists perceive the fundamental questions we can pose about past cultures, take a look at any of these textbooks:

Ashmore, W., and R. J. Sharer. 1999. *Discovering Our Past: A Brief Introduction to Archaeology.* Mayfield Publishing, Mountain View, California.

Fagan, B. M. 2000. *In the Beginning: An Introduction to Archaeology.* 7th ed. Prentice Hall, Upper Saddle River, New Jersey.

———. 2002. *Archaeology: A Brief Introduction.* 4th ed. Prentice Hall, Upper Saddle River, New Jersey.

Feder, K. L., and M. A. Park. 2001. *Human Antiquity: An Introduction to Physical Anthropology and Archaeology.* Mayfield Publishing, Mountain View, California.

Renfrew, C., and P. Bahn. 2000. *Archaeology: Theories, Method, and Practice.* Thames and Hudson, New York.

Sharer, R. J., and W. Ashmore. 2003. *Archaeology: Discovering Our Past.* 2d ed. McGraw-Hill, New York.

Staeck, J. 2002. *Back to the Earth: An Introduction to Archaeology.* McGraw-Hill, New York.

Thomas, D. H. 1998a. *Archaeology.* 3d ed. Wadsworth, Belmont, California.

———. 1998b. *Archaeology: Down to Earth.* Wadsworth, Belmont, California.

 ## Is Archaeology Really a Dangerous Pursuit?

During the course of an archaeological field season, hundreds upon hundreds of field schools, museum and university research projects, as well as government mandated archaeological surveys are conducted across the face of the globe. Thousands upon thousands of experienced, professional archaeology field-workers, serious archaeology students, and casual, one-shot volunteers participate in field projects and are paid or trained or simply have a wonderful life experience. For the vast majority of these people, the worst that happens is a bad sunburn, some annoying insect bites, tired muscles, and the occasional sprained ankle. It is important to note, however, there are serious dangers, both natural and artificial, facing anyone who spends a substantial amount of time outdoors, and archaeology field-workers need to be aware of issues that pose a serious danger to their health and the health of the people they teach or employ (Poirier and Feder 2001).

For example, insect bites are almost an inevitable consequence of being outside in the spring, summer, or fall. The various benefits and drawbacks of bug spray with DEET (the official cologne/perfume of my field crew), vitamin B supplements, and products like Skin-So-Soft are the subject of vigorous debates among field crews. Obviously, bee stings are dangerous for those who are severely allergic, but for most people, stings and bites are little more than an irritation.

In some areas and in some years, however, encounters with local insects can have far more serious consequences. The field season that has just passed (as I write this segment of the book in October 2002) appears to have been the year of the West Nile virus. Unknown in the Western Hemisphere before 1999, the virus is spread by mosquitoes, who can infect birds, horses, some other mammals, and human beings, some of whom get sick with flu-like symptoms and a few of whom even die as a result. West Nile is so recent a danger that when a colleague and I edited a book on health and safety in archaeology (*Dangerous Places: Health, Safety, and Archaeology*, Poirier and Feder 2001), we didn't cover it at all as a threat to the health of archaeological fieldworkers. A year later, at least where I sit in New England, mosquitoes carrying West Nile have pushed aside ticks carrying Lyme disease as the major topic of conversation regarding insect-borne disease. With the exception of Arizona, Nevada, Utah, Oregon, and Idaho, all of the other contiguous United States have reported cases of West Nile in mosquitoes, birds, or people. By October 2002, there were more than 2,700 human cases and 146 deaths attributed to West Nile (http://www.cdc.gov/ncidod/dvbid/westnile/index.htm). It is a serious public health issue and one that is of particular concern to archaeologists who, by the nature of their field of study, must spend lots of time outside where the risk of mosquito bites is high.

An entire chapter of the book I co-edited was devoted to the debilitating bacterial disease *Borrelia burgdorferi*, which is carried by deer ticks (*Ixodes scapularis*, Bellatonni 2001). The bacteria that cause the disease enter your body while the tick is attached, collecting your blood. The disease can begin as a rash, develop into flu-like symptoms and, if untreated with a vigorous course of antibiotics, can lead to arthritis-like symptoms, nerve damage, and worse. Lyme disease, named for the Connecticut town where it was first diagnosed, is primarily seen in the northeast, mid-Atlantic, and north-central states of the United States; according to the Centers for Disease Control, of the more than 16,000 cases reported in 1999, more than 90% were from the states of Connecticut, Rhode Island, New York, Pennsylvania, Delaware, New Jersey, Maryland, Massachusetts, and Wisconsin (http://www.cdc.gov/ncidod/dvbid/lyme/, Figure 5.4).

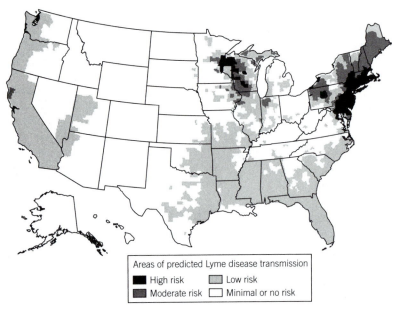

**FIGURE 5.4** Distribution of human cases of Lyme disease in 1999 as reported by the federal agency the Centers for Disease Control.

I find it somewhat amusing, in an admittedly dark sense, when the local health officials recommend to people that for protection against Lyme disease and West Nile virus, it is best to stay out of the woods. We can't get very much archaeology done anywhere else, so complete avoidance simply isn't an option for archaeologists—we stoically perceive these dangers as occupational hazards. We slather ourselves in spray—whose side effects I choose not to think about— and do regular tick checks. We are careful, not panicked about the dangers presented by insect-borne diseases.

Rabies is a disease that justifiably terrifies people: it is virtually 100% fatal if not treated (Morganti and Tartt 2001). According to the Centers for Disease Control, dogs are the primary carriers worldwide, responsible for about 90% of the human infections each year. Due to a vigorous program of vaccinating our canine and feline pets against rabies, dogs are not the primary carriers in the United States. Here the primary rabies vectors are raccoons (37.7%), skunks (30.1%), bats (16.8%), and foxes (6.1%) (statistics for the year 2000 are available at http://www.cdc.gov/ncidod/dvrd/rabies/Epidemiology/Epidemiology.htm), though the significance of each of these species varies regionally (Figure 5.5).

Other animal-borne viruses also pose a hazard to archaeologists in the field. Carried by mice and deposited in their feces, for example, the hantavirus can lead to serious consequences when it is inhaled, leading to pulmonary distress and even death when not treated immediately.

Obviously, even healthy wild animals can present a danger to archaeologists. Terry del Bene, a good friend and esteemed colleague, tells of conducting

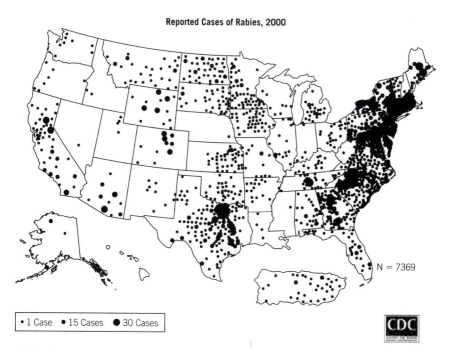

**FIGURE 5.5** Distribution of cases in the United States of rabies in animals for the year 2000 as reported by the United States Centers for Disease Control.

archaeological survey work in Alaska and being given, as a part of his archaeological tool kit, a hand gun. He was told to keep the pistol loaded when in the
field and when encountering an angry grizzly bear to always remember that
only the first five bullets in the barrel were meant for the bear. Apparently, if
those first five shots merely annoyed the rampaging beast, the final bullet was
intended as the escape of last resort for the unlucky archaeologist. I assume
they were pulling Terry's leg—or perhaps he was pulling mine. Poisonous
snakes are another source of potential danger. There are four species of poisonous snakes in North America: rattlesnake, cottonmouth, copperhead, and coral
snake. Numerous subspecies, like the western rattler, can kill even a healthy
adult not treated with the antivenom. Other snakes don't pack enough punch to
kill an adult, but can make you feel pretty awful. In more than twenty-five
years of archaeological fieldwork experience in New England, I have never
encountered a venomous snake, at least not while actually in the field. I
recently ran into a meter-long copperhead while weed-whacking in the front of
my house, but never in the field.

Dangerous viral and bacterial infections and diseases can be carried by
molds, spores, and fungi. Valley fever, for example is a condition caused by
inhaling the spores of a soil-dwelling fungus, *Coccidioides immitis*. Coccidioides has been reported primarily in the American southwest (Fink and
Komatsu 2001). For most, the resulting disease consists of little more than what
passes for a bout with the flu. However, in some instances chronic disability can
result and, though rare, even death. Histoplasmosis is another airborne fungal
disease present in the soil, resulting, rather unpleasantly, from the accumulated
excrement of bats and birds. It can result in the usual flu-like symptoms but in
rare instances it spreads beyond the lungs and may require hospitalization.

Historical archaeologists, in particular those who work in the abandoned
mines, factories, workshops, and even cemeteries of societies that used potent,
poisonous chemicals in their industrial processes, may be exposed to levels of
contaminants far beyond what we would allow under modern regimes of work-
place protection regulations. For example, embalmers historically used arsenic
to preserve the remains of the deceased, and this poisonous chemical can lie
hidden in the cemetery soils archaeologists encounter (Konefes and McGee
2001). Lead used in paint manufacturing (Saunders and Chandler 2001) as well
as mercury and lead used in ore processing (Reno, Bloyd, and Hardesty 2001)
all pose dangers to those who disturb the soils in which these toxic elements
repose. Archaeologist Michael Roberts (2001:160–64) has compiled an extensive list of chemicals that were used in various industries in Boston (including
shipping, woodworking, metal, paint, leather, rubber, felt, textiles, printing, and
plastics manufacturing, not to mention the chemical industry itself) long before there were regulations concerning their disposal. After perusing the list, it
should come as no surprise that archaeologists in urban areas increasingly are
trained in handling hazardous wastes and conduct archaeology in HAZMAT
(hazardous materials) suits.

Battlefield historians and archaeologists need to be concerned about
safety as well. Unexploded ordinance labeled UXO (in other words, bullets

and bombs that were fired but that did not detonate) often lie buried at battlefields. Enormously unpredictable, scraping with a trowel or striking with a shovel may be all that is needed to detonate them. As archaeologists Dana Linck and Joe W. Vann III (2001:169) put it, archaeologists of historical battlefields who do not contact experts in unexploded munitions to clear an area before they excavate "dig fast," and "die young." No archaeologist in the twenty-first century wants to be remembered by a footnote in history texts as the final casualty of the Civil War, so great care is advised for battlefield archaeologists.

Finally, it is not just elements of the natural environment or hazardous wastes left behind by past peoples that pose danger to archaeologists. Archaeological field methods themselves may also endanger the lives of members of a field crew. Construction crews must obey OSHA (Occupational Safety and Health Administration) regulations concerning the digging of deep pits in which people will work. The danger of wall collapse is always present and virtually every year workers are seriously injured and even killed when laboring at the bottom of an excavation—for a house foundation, a mine or quarry, or underground tunnel—when the walls collapse on top of them. Archaeologists may not usually dig as deeply or extensively as miners, quarry operators, or house builders, but our pits are sometimes more than deep enough to pose a danger to those who work within them if they are not carefully monitored and their walls adequately supported.

The point of this discussion is merely this: archaeological fieldwork presents dangers to the health and safety of people working in the field. Awareness of these dangers and a proactive approach should minimize the danger and insure that the field is as safe a place as it is interesting.

# Read More

If you would like to become scared out of your wits about the prospect of actually participating in archaeological fieldwork, read any of the following. The point is not to scare anybody away from archaeology, but to alert archaeologists to the potential and too-often ignored but very real dangers in the field:

Bellantoni, N. F. 2001. Ticked off: Lyme disease and archaeologists. In *Dangerous Places: Health, Safety, and Archaeology*, edited by D. Poirier and K. L. Feder, 3–10. Bergin and Garvey, Westport, Connecticut.

Fink, T. M., and K. K. Komatsu. 2001. The fungus among us: *Coccidioidomycosis* ("Valley Fever"). In *Dangerous Places: Health, Safety, and Archaeology*, edited by D. Poirier and K. L. Feder, 21–30. Bergin and Garvey, Westport, Connecticut.

Konefes, J. L., and M. K. McGee. 2001. Old cemeteries, arsenic, and health safety. In *Dangerous Places: Health, Safety, and Archaeology*, edited by D. Poirier and K. L. Feder, 79–106. Bergin and Garvey, Westport, Connecticut.

Linck, D., and J. W. Vann III. 2001. Dig fast, die young: Unexploded ordnance and archaeology. In *Dangerous Places: Health, Safety, and Archaeology*, edited by D. Poirier and K. L. Feder, 169–88. Bergin and Garvey, Westport, Connecticut.

Morganti, T., and N. Tartt. 2001. Rabies: A short discourse. In *Dangerous Places: Health, Safety, and Archaeology,* edited by D. Poirier and K. L. Feder, 11–20. Bergin and Garvey, Westport, Connecticut.

Poirier, D., and K. L. Feder. 2001. *Dangerous Places: Health, Safety, and Archaeology.* Bergin and Garvey, Westport, Connecticut.

Reno, R. L., S. R. Boyd, and D. L. Hardesty. 2001. Chemical soup: Archaeological hazards at western ore-processing sites. In *Dangerous Places: Health, Safety, and Archaeology,* edited by D. Poirier and K. L. Feder, 205–20. Bergin and Garvey, Westport, Connecticut.

Roberts, M. 2001. Beneath city streets: Brief observations on the urban landscape. In *Dangerous Places: Health, Safety, and Archaeology,* edited by D. Poirier and K. L. Feder, 157–68. Bergin and Garvey, Westport, Connecticut.

Saunders, C., and S. R. Chandler. 2001. Get the lead out. In *Dangerous Places: Health, Safety, and Archaeology,* edited by D. Poirier and K. L. Feder, 189–204. Bergin and Garvey, Westport, Connecticut.

# Study Questions

1. How did I, with remarkable precision, predict the location of the Wood Lily site? Am I psychic, or what?

2. What were the environmental characteristics of the area in which Wood Lily was found that made predicting its location, if not a slam dunk, a pretty good bet?

3. What are the research goals of archaeology? What do archaeologists hope to learn about the human past through the study of the material remains of human behavior?

4. What is "culture history"? Why does that continue to be at least one of the goals of many archaeological research projects?

5. Describe how archaeological research contributes to our knowledge of the diversity of human cultural adaptations.

6. How does archaeology contribute to our understanding of culture in ways that the ethnography of living groups of people cannot?

7. List some challenges facing people in the modern world. How might archaeology uniquely contribute to our examination of these problems?

8. I suppose some archaeologists get filthy rich by having wildly successful books published, but how do the others fund their research?

9. Use the project that discovered the tomb of Egyptian pharaoh Tutankhamen as an example of how archaeological projects were supported in the past. What problems accompanied such funding?

10. What are the major funding sources for archaeological research today?

**11.** What is the rationale of the federal government of the United States for funding archaeological projects?

**12.** List the one-word questions that journalists ostensibly ask and hope to answer when writing a news story. Phrase those questions in terms of the archaeological record, viewing the archaeologist as the journalist of humanity's past times.

**13.** What are the most common—and rather mundane—health issues faced by field archaeologists?

**14.** Discuss the serious bacterial and chemical dangers faced by field scientists, especially those who dig up dirt.

**15.** What are the particular concerns of archaeologists who work in historical sites where the effluvia of past industries and manufacturing processes yet reside in the soil they excavate?

**16.** Researchers Dana Linck and J. W. Vann write, "dig fast, die young"? What's that about?

To be honest, while being spot-on in locating the Peoples State Forest site (the result of luck as well as a bit of archaeological pre-science), accurately predicting the location of archaeological remains is something archaeologists do on a regular basis. There is nothing super-natural or extrasensory about it; a commonsense understanding of the **settlement patterns** of an ancient group of people is all one needs to per-form this apparent act of magic.

## How Do Archaeologists Know How Old Artifacts and Sites Are?

People are fascinated by antiquity; the older the better for most. It should come as no surprise, therefore, that one of the first questions I hear people ask when they show me an artifact that they have found or when I talk about a specimen discovered in my fieldwork is: "How old is it?" And, indeed, that question is one of the first that comes to the mind of the professional archaeologist as well when confronted with a newly discovered site or specimen.

Would that it were the case that, like our modern coins, ancient people stamped the year of manufacture on all of their objects. Archaeological dating would be quite simple, indeed, if all one needed to do upon recovery of a spear point or potsherd was to apply a little spit to the surface or wipe with a damp cloth to reveal an object's date, though we probably would be quite skeptical of the authenticity of an object that bore a date like 2000 B.C.

Artifacts are generally not conveniently dated, so we need to assess age in other ways. For example, archaeologists have long employed procedures of artifact sequencing in their preliminary attempts to date sites. These sequenc-ing procedures, called **relative dating,** whereby artifacts or sites are placed in chronological order or sequence without specific age assignment, often con-tinue to be the first step in attempting to date archaeological material.

An arrangement of artifacts or sites into a chronological sequence is use-ful, but of course we hope to do more than simply put things in order; we also would like to be able to assign accurate and precise dates to the materials we recover. In fact, we archaeologists also have techniques at our disposal that enable the assignment of an actual year or range of years to an artifact or site. **Chronometric** or **absolute dating** methods have inspired a revolution in archaeological analysis, enabling our discussion of the prehistoric past to parallel the analysis by historians of the more recent past.

If you hope to figure out "what happened, when?" as one of your research goals, you need to be able to solve for the "when" variable. Relative methods are a start, providing the archaeologist with an order to "what happened." Absolute methods take us a significant step beyond this, allowing us to position the events of antiquity onto a continuous and objective calendar.

## Read More

For broad-based discussions of dating methods in archaeology, these books are good place to start:

Fleming, S. J. 1977. *Dating in Archaeology: A Guide to Scientific Techniques*. Palgrave Macmillan, New York.
Michels, J. W. 1973. *Dating Methods in Archaeology*. Seminar Press, New York.
Taylor, R. E., and M. J. Aitken, eds. 1997. *Chronometric Dating in Archaeology*. Plenum Publishing, New York.

## What Are Relative Dating Techniques?

For much of the long history of archaeology, determining the age of a site or artifact was extremely difficult and ordinarily a rather imprecise, indirect, and even subjective enterprise. Unless the site was from a culture and time period characterized by writing and a calendar, sites were often dated by reference to their geological context: how deeply the site materials were buried and in what stratigraphic layer they were found.

In other instances, sites were arranged in chronological order based on the invalid assumption of an inevitable increase in sophistication of technology through time. For example, the painted cave sites of Europe, with their fabulous tableaux of ancient animal life, were long sequenced on the basis of an assumed pattern of increasing artistic sophistication; more primitive art renderings were assumed to be older than those that modern viewers perceived to be more artistically advanced. The caves bearing this artwork were arranged in a hypothetical chronological order on this basis.

You can imagine how inaccurate this turned out to be. Consider the subjective nature of the notion "level of artistic sophistication." Also consider the evolution of Western art over the last few centuries. Imagine attempting to place art since the Renaissance in a chronological sequence solely on the basis of personal perception of the degree of "sophistication" or complexity or technological skill reflected in the art. It is unlikely that we would get the chronological order right. It is likely, in fact, that we would often get it precisely backwards. In all probability, for example, we would place the simple geometric forms of an artist like Paul Klee of the late nineteenth and early twentieth centuries sequentially before the exquisite realism of Michelangelo, who actually painted four hundred years before Klee was even born. As it turns out, in fact, some of the oldest ancient cave art discovered in Europe appears to be among the most technically and artistically sophisticated in terms of the realism of the depictions of Ice Age animals. Specifically, the stunningly splendid paintings of animals found in Chauvet Cave in France date to 32,000 years ago and are among the most sophisticated of the images found in the caves, far more realistic and beautifully rendered than most of the cave paintings that date to more recent times (Chauvet, Deschamps, and Hillaire 1996).

The moral is that you simply cannot safely arrange sites or artifacts in chronological sequence based solely on a presumed pattern of an increase in sophistication through time. You will derive incorrect chronologies as often as not. That doesn't mean that patterns of stylistic change cannot be used to help us figure out chronological patterns. In fact, there seem to be common blueprints for how styles replace one another, which we can use in developing at least relative chronological sequences. These blueprints are based, not on any assumption of the inevitable evolution of greater technical or artistic abilities or expertise, but on more general patterns of change through time. Again, the result is a relative sequence of sites without any firmly associated calendar or year dates, providing us with a temporal framework for a region or ancient culture.

## How Can You Date Sites by Stratigraphic Analysis?

Attempting to put archaeological materials in a chronological sequence has long been a goal of archaeological research. As long ago as 1799, British surveyor William Smith recognized that the rock and soil beneath our feet come in distinct layers and that these layers, laid down in sequence, were not just local phenomena but could be traced for miles (Grayson 1983). These layers, called **strata** (each one called a **stratum**), can be mapped and studied across an extensive region. Individual layers are distinguishable on the basis of color, texture (rocky, gravelly, sandy, silty, clayey), and chemical makeup. The sequential arrangement of strata is called their **stratigraphy.** Though no year date can be determined directly, where archaeological materials are found within distinct layers in a stratigraphic sequence, their age can be determined relative to other materials found in lower (older) layers, higher (younger) layers, or to objects found in the same layer (Harris 1979; Harris 1993; Harris, Brown, and Brown 1997).

Archaeologists still use the basic principles of stratigraphic sequencing that William Smith discovered more than two hundred years ago. Essentially, when excavating a site, archaeologists are extremely careful about maintaining the stratigraphic integrity of all materials found, keeping track of the precise level from which each artifact and ecofact is recovered. If you have seen photographs of archaeological excavations or video documentaries about archaeological research, you may have wondered why the walls of excavation units are usually precisely vertical and why, in large excavation units there may even be quadrilateral blocks of soil left unexcavated. Those excavators' obsession with flat, straight, cleanly scraped unit walls and intact soil blocks represent an attempt to maintain precise and accurate stratigraphic controls, intact soil layers that can serve as reference points of overall site stratigraphy.

When stratigraphic sequences are more or less intact and undisturbed, it should be fairly obvious that archaeological materials can be placed in a relative chronological sequence on the basis of their position in layers superimposed one on top of another. If, for example, the same location was occupied on several occasions, the chronological order of those occupations can be determined by the stratigraphic position of the archaeological material left behind in each occupation.

Remember, as we dig down, archaeologists reveal the stratigraphic sequence in reverse order, encountering the most recent levels first, and successively older layers as we dig more deeply. Take, for example, a chronological sequence of human activity revealed in the soil layers of a small test excavation adjacent to the Farmington River in the town of Avon, Connecticut. The first artifact encountered in the test excavation (and, therefore, the most recent of the items we recovered) was very close to the surface, situated within the root mat of the vegetation growing there. This first artifact was a broken yellow plastic toy motorcycle, likely lost by a kid playing near the Farmington River. Okay, so it wasn't a particularly ancient artifact, or one that might inspire someone to pursue a career in archaeology. The excavator, an archaeology student, was actually surprised that I instructed him to treat the object the way we would any archaeological specimen, measuring its precise depth and location, placing it in a small artifact bag, and carefully labeling the bag with site and excavation unit information.

If my student was amused by this first artifact encountered in the stratigraphic sequence revealed in our excavation, he was embarrassed by the next find, nestled in a distinct soil layer underling the root mat. In that somewhat older layer my student uncovered the fragmentary but unmistakable remains of an empty condom wrapper. Try as I might to convince the student that this was, in fact, an archaeological artifact—after all, archaeology is defined as the study of the material remains of human behavior and the wrapper was, most certainly, a material remain of human behavior—I'm not sure he ever actually accepted my argument. He had no choice, however, and went about the process of measuring the location of the discovery and gingerly placing the condom wrapper into a specimen bag for return to the lab.

Beneath the layer of soil in which the wrapper was found, a cluster of more obviously artifactual material was recovered in the excavation. My digger found fragments of white-glazed ceramics, some window glass, and rusty, square-cut nails. Though not the kinds of material that generate National Geographic television documentaries, at least this was clearly old stuff and its location in a soil level below the condom wrapper (which was, in turn, below the toy motorcycle) showed very nicely the sequence of activities that had transpired at this spot along the Farmington River.

Beneath the layer in which the crockery, glass, and nails were found we encountered a number of layers, distinguishable by slight differences in soil color and texture in which no artifacts were encountered. Then, in our progression down through additional layers, back through time, yet another stratum was found bearing evidence of a past human presence. In this lower layer, we found fragments of thick-walled pottery, this time without glaze, along with stone chips and a triangular object of chipped stone that looked like it had been used as the tip of an arrow, the business end of a hunting weapon (Figure 6.1).

**FIGURE 6.1** Stratigraphic profile of a test pit located along the Farmington River in the town of Avon, Connecticut. Note that there is evidence of four temporally distinct episodes of activity at this spot.

Clearly, in this example we could enumerate four temporally distinct episodes of human activity at the place where we were digging. Moving forward through time, from the oldest stratum to the most recently deposited, it appeared that a person or persons dropped or intentionally left behind part of a hunting weapon and some pottery. Sometime later—we cannot tell how much later, we only know it happened later because we found the evidence in a soil layer that was superimposed on a number of other layers laid down in sequence—a person or persons bearing a different material culture that included glazed pottery, glass, and metal disposed of or dropped some of their stuff. Sometime after this, again we cannot be certain how long after, another activity took place (this one involving a condom, and I will leave it to your imagination to speculate exactly what happened). Finally, again at a later time, a child lost, left behind for safekeeping, hid, or simply threw away an object made of yellow plastic, a toy motorcycle reflecting the diagnostic material culture of yet another society.

To be sure, we might have looked for a date or company stamp on the toy and this might have enabled a determination of an actual date for the toy. The same might be true for the condom wrapper. The glazed ceramics bore a particular design and there could have been a maker's mark, which would have allowed for a year date for its manufacture. The arrowhead was of a particular shape and design whose age could be identified by comparison to other, similar looking artifacts. This tale shows how, based on the relative position of objects recovered in soil layers, a chronological sequence of events or occupations can be determined.

You may have noticed that in this discussion of stratigraphy I have labored mightily to avoid saying that, essentially, the deeper something is found, the older it is. Though this often is the case, it sometimes is not because of natural and cultural phenomena that disturb stratigraphic sequences. For example, ancient people can—and did—dig deep holes that cut through older deposits, and their artifacts may end up in the bottom of those pits at a substantially greater depth than older artifacts whose layer was inadvertently and unknowingly cut through by the more recent hole diggers.

Animals can also add to the confusion—and, I guess, the fun. I can remember excavating a beer bottle at the same measured depth as the artifacts from a site dated to just shy of two thousand years old. Though it might be fun to report the archaeological discovery of beer bottling and drinking during the ancient Woodland period of southern New England, alas there was a more mundane explanation. The beer bottle actually dated to a far more modern period and ended up at the same depth as the ancient artifacts because it was located at the bottom of a filled-in woodchuck burrow. I also cannot report that this provides new insights into the behavior of social drinking among woodchucks. More likely, the bottle fell or was dropped into the burrow by a human beer drinker. The burrow was later filled in with silt by river flooding.

Instead of saying that the deeper an object is found, the older it is, the **law of superposition** in stratigraphic analysis maintains that the relative position of an archaeological object in a sequence of layers determines its age (the same, younger, or older) relative to other objects found in the stratigraphic sequence. Objects are as old as the layers that were the living surface when they were deposited and that is not always necessarily the layer in which they ended up.

## Read More

You can find the particulars of stratigraphy, including the history of the concept as well as the methods by which it is exposed, analyzed, and interpreted, on the pages of the following sample of publications:

Adams, R. E. W. and Fred Valdez Jr. 1997. Stratigraphy. In *Field Methods in Archaeology*, ed. T. R. Hester, H. J. Shafer, and R. L. Feder, pp. 235–52. Mayfield Publishing, Mountain View, California.
Grayson, D. K. 1983. *The Establishment of Human Antiquity*. Academic Press, New York.
Harris, E. C. 1979. The laws of archaeological stratigraphy. *World Archaeology* 11:111–17.
———. 1997. *Principles of Archaeological Stratigraphy*. Academic Press, New York.
Harris, E. C., G. J. Brown, and M. R. Brown III, eds. 1993. *Practices of Archaeological Stratigraphy*. Academic Press, New York.

## How Can You Determine a Relative Date for a Site by Reference to Artifact Style?

One relative method of dating relies on technological or stylistic change through time, but avoids the overly simplistic assumption that objects that look more sophisticated or advanced to us are necessarily younger than objects that appear to reflect a perceived simpler technology or artistic ability. Rather than assuming a particular direction of change, the relative dating technique called **seriation** relies instead on a common statistical pattern of technological or stylistic change.

In many cases, when a new way of accomplishing a task is introduced into a culture, whether through invention or by adopting it from another group, it starts off small, with most folks skeptical and resistant to the new idea. Few people even attempt the innovative approach, whether it involves designs on gravestones, methods of illuminating buildings, making spear points, or burying the

**Beverage Can Evolution**

Flat-top can          Pop-top can          Push-in can

Can opener          Disposable pull tab

**FIGURE 6.2** Twelve-ounce beverage cans, seen from the top. From left to right, a can that needs a can opener to get to its contents, a pull-tab can, and the current push tab.

dead. However, if the new way of making tools, decorating pots, producing food, storing seeds, or designing gravestones is objectively recognized to be more efficient than the old method, or if the new style is subjectively perceived to be more attractive by the ancient people, the initial resistance is overcome, its degree of penetration in the community increases, and people may begin to abandon the old practice and embrace the new. Eventually, this new and revolutionary technology or style becomes widely accepted, reaches a peak in popularity, and attains the level of common practice; almost everybody does it that way and it has become the norm. In the nearly inevitable process of change, however, an even newer way of achieving the same result may be introduced. This new practice again starts out small, is met with skepticism and resistance, and few people try it. If the new approach is recognized to be more efficient than the old, it begins to increase in use and replaces the old way, and the cycle continues.

Consider our own history, for example, the ways in which we store and sell carbonated beverages (Figure 6.2). In the 1950s, soda and beer could be purchased in cylindrical, 12-ounce cans that could be opened only with a separate tool, a can opener that punched a triangular hole in the top of the can (actually, two holes were punched, the second of which facilitated the pouring of the beverage through the first). Though the can was a convenient, lightweight, and durable container (it didn't break like a glass bottle does when dropped), needing a separate tool to open it was a drawback. Though I was just a kid in the 1950s, I can remember too many picnics and beach outings where the desperation was palpable upon the realization that our powerful summer thirst could not be slaked because we had forgotten the opener (called the "church key" for rather obvious reasons).

To address the inconvenience of a container that needed a separate tool to open it, in the early 1960s, a new can type was introduced for which no discrete opening tool was needed. The top of the new cans contained an oddly curving outline incised into the metal. The incised shape was riveted at one end to a metal ring, which—when it worked properly—could be bent up from the can top. When the metal ring was pulled up and away from the can, the "pop top" ripped cleanly away from the can along the incised outline and, voilà, the can was now open and ready to be poured. Well, in theory. Too often, when bent back and up to enable gripping, the ring simply broke off, making entry into the can problematic at best. The new can design did make can opening easier though and, over a period of just a few years, the technology was tweaked and opening the can became a bit easier and more reliable. The old opener-dependent can design disappeared, having been replaced by the new type.

The new design, though an advance over the old, was far from perfect and created a new, initially unforeseen problem. Though the can could be opened easily, without the need for a separate tool, the design created a separate piece of metal that needed to be discarded: the so-called pop-top. Unfortunately, the metal pop-tops became ubiquitous pieces of litter, a significant new tributary to the waste stream of the 1960s, scattered across the beautiful beaches and parks where people brought their carbonated beverages. Of course, the ecologists among the soda and beer drinkers came up with a solution to the pop-top dilemma: instead of littering the pop-tops on the ground, they merely dropped the pop-top back into the can immediately after opening and then proceeded to drink from the can. I have no data to back up my assertion that trips to emergency rooms for stomach x-rays took a sharp upturn after the inception of this practice, but I imagine that, especially among heavy beer drinkers, this could have become a significant public health issue if drinkers found it difficult to remember when they found no loose pop-top jingling in the can of beer they had just drained whether they had thrown it away or swallowed it.

Perhaps in response to the problems created by tens of millions of sharp pieces of metal created by the pop-top can, in the early 1970s canning companies came up with yet another can design, a version of the one we are all familiar with today. Instead of a can that opened by removing a piece of the top, the new design caused part of a roughly circular section of the top to push down and in, remaining attached to the top of the can while opening a hole large enough to pour or drink from directly. This design was produced initially in small numbers and, as the technology was perfected and people got used to the new cans, it replaced the pop-top design, which over a period of just a few years disappeared almost entirely.

How does any of this apply in the practice of archaeological dating? The pattern of introduction of a new design (first the pop-top can and then the push-in can), its initially small penetration in the marketplace, and its slow acceptance, growth, and eventual complete replacement of the old way is a pattern seen almost universally in stylistic change through time. The pattern exhibited in the changes in soda and beer cans is a model and even an archetype for changes in ancient artifact styles and technologies, and that pattern reflects not just change, but change through time (Figure 6.3).

Suppose you have a number of sites, each of which dates to a different, narrow slice of time in the history of a culture. Each site represents a point along a temporal continuum of technological and stylistic change, during which different ways of accomplishing the same task may overlap. At each site,

| | Flat-top can | Pull-tab can | Push-tab can |
|---|---|---|---|
| 1995 | | | ▭ |
| 1985 | | ▯ | ▭ |
| 1977 | | ▭ | ▯ |
| 1973 | ▏ | ▭ | ▏ |
| 1968 | ▭ | ▭ | |
| 1963 | ▭ | ▯ | |
| 1955 | ▭ | | |
| 1945 | ▭ | | |
| 1935 | ▭ | | ▭ = 20% |

Data from http://bcca.com/bccacans.html and T. V. Carley, personal communication

**FIGURE 6.3** A seriation graph showing the slow replacement, in temporal sequence, of the initially ubiquitous opener-requiring can with the disposable pull-tab can, and then the inevitable replacement of that container type with the currently used push tab. (*Kenneth L. Feder*)

differing percentages of folks achieve the same results (how they open beverage cans, paint images on cave walls, manufacture spear points, decorate pottery, or mark their graves) in a number of different ways that, at different times, are "old fashioned," "modern," or "cutting edge." If you measure at each site the popularity of the various overlapping ways of achieving the same result (for example, the percentage of artifacts showing cans that need can openers, the percentage of disposable pop-top cans, and the percentage of push-in cans at each site, with each site representing a slice of time), you can consistently arrange the sites in order based on the pattern of new ideas starting small, growing in acceptance, reaching a peak, and then declining as they are replaced by a newer way. You can visualize this with a standard **seriation graph,** where the prevalence of each style or technological method is represented in a column of the graph. Horizontal bars whose lengths are proportional to the percentages of each method (how many cans at a particular site are opened with a tool, how many are pop-tops, and how many are push-in) within each narrow band of time are drawn in each column.

Consider the seriation graph representing the style of carving on gravestones (these are artifacts) found in graveyards (these are sites) dating from the early 1600s through the early 1900s throughout New England (Dethlefsen and Deetz 1966). In this case, of course, we have actual dates on the gravestones, but suppose we didn't. We could still arrange the individual gravestones into a sensible chronological order because the percentages represented by the lengths of the bars on the graphs for each style (skulls, cherubs, and urn-and-willow designs) change in a patterned way, reflecting a steady increase or decrease across time (Figure 6.4).

*Gravestones*

Examine the graph shown in Figure 6.4. There is really only one way to arrange the order of the bars to produce a pattern of steady increase and decrease (and the reverse is equally plausible). The death's heads show up first and are at a peak in their popularity when the cherub design is introduced. Slowly but surely, having an angelic face carved on the top of a tombstone increased in popularity, at the expense of the death's head design. Over several decades, an increasing segment of the graveyard population have a cherub carved on the top of their markers and a decreasing segment have a death's head. By the

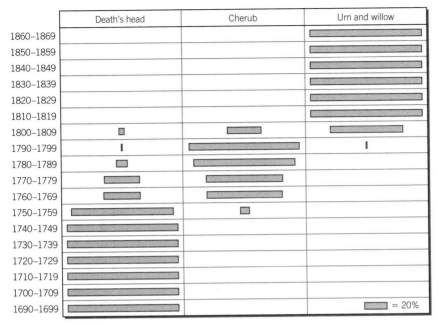

| | Death's head | Cherub | Urn and willow |
|---|---|---|---|
| 1860–1869 | | | ▭ |
| 1850–1859 | | | ▭ |
| 1840–1849 | | | ▭ |
| 1830–1839 | | | ▭ |
| 1820–1829 | | | ▭ |
| 1810–1819 | | | ▭ |
| 1800–1809 | ▪ | ▭ | ▭ |
| 1790–1799 | ∣ | ▭ | ∣ |
| 1780–1789 | ▪ | ▭ | |
| 1770–1779 | ▭ | ▭ | |
| 1760–1769 | ▭ | ▭ | |
| 1750–1759 | ▭ | ▪ | |
| 1740–1749 | ▭ | | |
| 1730–1739 | ▭ | | |
| 1720–1729 | ▭ | | |
| 1710–1719 | ▭ | | |
| 1700–1709 | ▭ | | |
| 1690–1699 | ▭ | | ▭ = 20% |

**FIGURE 6.4** Seriation graph of a sample of seventeenth-, eighteenth-, and nineteenth-century New England gravestones. Just as surely as the beverage can evolved in terms of the technology of its opening, the designs carved onto gravestones also evolved, with themes being replaced to fit the fashion of their time. (*Kenneth L. Feder*)

end of the 1700s the death's head designs are no longer being made and nearly everybody is having a cherub carved on their gravestone. Just as surely as the cherub replaced the death's head, a new pattern takes hold at the end of the 1700s and beginning of the 1800s. Instead of a skeletal or angelic face, people began placing a willow tree on their gravestones, usually depicted bending over what looks like an urn. This urn-and-willow design takes hold and increases in popularity over the decades, eclipsing the cherub design and, ultimately, replacing it altogether. This design can be found on stones that mark the graves of people who died into the second decade of the twentieth century (Figure 6.5).

Following this common pattern, with a few sites representing slices of time and where a style or technology changed through time, the sites themselves can be placed in a chronological sequence based on the patterned change in the percentages of the styles through time.

**FIGURE 6.5** The urn-and-willow design was used by people to adorn the tombstones of their loved ones well into the twentieth century. The date on this stone reads 1915. (*Kenneth L. Feder*)

## Read More

You can find a nicely detailed discussion of seriation in the textbook by O'Brien and Lyman. The gravestone article is a fascinating example of the application of seriation.

Dethlefsen, E., and J. Deetz. 1966. Death's heads, cherubs, and willow trees: Experimental archaeology in colonial cemeteries. *American Antiquity* 31:502–10.
O'Brien, M. J., and R. L. Lyman. 1999. *Seriation, Stratigraphy, and Index Fossils: The Backbone of Archaeological Dating.* Kluwer Academic Publishers, New York.

## What Are Chronometric or Absolute Dating Methods?

**Absolute dating** methods are those procedures that provide an actual age in years for an archaeological artifact, ecofact, or site. Labeling a date as "absolute" does not imply that it is precise (it can be a broad range of years) or even that it is necessarily accurate. To avoid confusion on this point, some archaeologists prefer the less ambiguous term **chronometric dating** (literally, the "measurement of time") for dating methods that provide a year or range of years.

I sit in front of my computer and write this, on October 11, in the year A.D. 2002, an accurate and precise date. I was born fifty years ago, another accurate and precise date. I received a Ph.D. in anthropology in 1982 (accurate and fairly precise). I'm not exactly certain when my ancestors migrated to the United States from Europe, but I know it was more than one hundred years ago (accurate, but not so precise). The first people to enter the New World arrived sometime between twelve thousand and thirty thousand years ago (I think that's accurate but it isn't very precise). Our human ancestors began making stone tools sometime between 2.4 and 2.5 million years ago (probably accurate, but certainly not precise). The human (**hominid**) evolutionary line diverged from the line that led to the modern apes (**pongids**) sometime between 5 and 7 million years ago (probably accurate but not at all precise). All of the dates just listed, from the actual calendar date when I wrote these words to the broad, 2-million-year range for the split between the hominids and the pongids, are absolute or chronometric because we can apply numbers, even an imprecisely broad range of numbers, to the events, artifacts, ecofacts, or sites.

Within absolute methods of dating, there is an entire category called **radiometric.** These methods are based on natural processes of radioactive decay and rely on the fact that the decay itself (as well as the resulting impacts of the decay on archaeological specimens) occurs at measurable, constant rates. The constant rate of radioactive decay as well as the rates at which the changes caused by the decay accumulate can be viewed as natural clocks (or at least natural calendars) that we can use to date archaeological specimens.

Another absolute, and by far the most accurate and precise dating method, is not radiometric but can be labeled a biological technique based on a highly regular, measurable, and dependable natural calendar built into trees. Called **dendrochronology,** this method relies on the addition of a distinct growth ring for each year of a tree's life. Our discussion of ancient trees in Chapter 1 and my reference to the precise ages of some of the oldest trees in North America were based on data produced through dendrochronology.

Additionally, we can determine an absolute date for an artifact with which we cannot directly associate a radiometric or dendrochronological date when the object reflects a style with a narrowly constrained period of popularity that has been so dated: in other words, when artifacts of a given, easily recognized style have been recovered at lots of archaeological sites where they have been dated to the same period of time. For example, by the application of radiocarbon dating, when you are confronted with an artifact with precisely the same form or style it is a good bet that it dates to the same period.

Individual artifacts, ecofacts, or features at a site can be dated using whatever techniques apply in particular circumstances, depending on the time period of the object being dated, the materials actually recovered and datable, and the budgetary constraints of a given project. That's an important point. Even the best-funded excavation can derive dates for only a very small fraction of the material actually recovered at a site. Based on careful stratigraphic analysis, however, we may be confident that the dates we obtain directly on a few objects (all, for example, recovered from a single stratigraphic level) can be associated with and applied to all of the other objects recovered from the same stratum. Though we may state that a site is a particular age, we don't really date the site directly, only individual objects recovered at the site. When an archaeologist states, for example, that a site is one thousand years old, that means that a small sample of individual artifacts or ecofacts have been absolutely dated and the full extent of the occupation (all of the other artifacts and ecofacts) occurred in a narrowly constrained stratigraphic level. Those few directly derived dates are then associated with everything else and are used to measure the date of the occupation of the site.

## Read More

For broad-based discussions of dating methods in archaeology, these books are good places to start:

Fleming, S. J. 1977. *Dating in Archaeology: A Guide to Scientific Techniques.* Palgrave Macmillan, New York.

Michels, J. W. 1973. *Dating Methods in Archaeology.* Seminar Press, New York.

Taylor, R. E., and M. J. Aitken, eds. 1997. *Chronometric Dating in Archaeology.* Plenum Publishing, New York.

## *What Are the Most Commonly Used Radiometric Dating Methods Relied on by Archaeologists?*

More than likely, you have heard of **carbon dating** (or **radiocarbon dating** or **C-14 dating**), which is probably the most widely used absolute dating method and certainly is the most commonly applied radiometric procedure in archaeology (http://www.c14dating.com). Radiometric dating techniques rely on the fixed rate of decay of an unstable (**radioactive**) variety (**isotope**) of an element into a stable variety of that same element or another element altogether. That fixed rate of decay, expressed as a **half-life** (the time it takes for half of the unstable portion of an element to change into a stable substance), provides a natural clock by which we can measure the age of some categories of artifacts and ecofacts (Bowman 1990; Libby 1952; Taylor 1987).

For example, carbon is an abundant element in the atmosphere (in the form of carbon dioxide or $CO_2$). Along with oxygen, nitrogen, and phosphorus, carbon is one of the so-called building blocks of life and is found in all living things. As you probably remember from high school biology, plants respire; in a manner of speaking, they breathe. When we breathe, our lungs extract oxygen from the air, supply it to our blood, and our bodies ultimately combine that oxygen with carbon, which we exhale as carbon dioxide. In photosynthesis, plants do the reverse, taking in carbon dioxide from the air, breaking the chemical bonds between the carbon and the two oxygen atoms in $CO_2$ and, together with water, producing carbohydrates which become stems, bark, fruits, seeds, roots, branches, and so on. Having extracted the carbon in $CO_2$ through photosynthesis, plants exhale the oxygen as a waste product.

Carbon comes in a few varieties or isotopes. The most common isotope is C-12, the stable form of the element, with an atomic nucleus consisting of six positively charged particles called protons and six neutral particles called neutrons. Carbon also comes in unstable or radioactive varieties, including the isotopes C-13 and C-14. C-12, C-13, and C-14 have six protons in their nuclei. That number is what makes them carbon; if their number of protons was different, they would be an entirely different element (for example, boron if they had five protons, nitrogen if they had seven, or oxygen if they had eight). What differentiates the nuclei of these different isotopes of carbon is their number of neutrons. The math here is easy: C-12 has six neutrons (6 protons + 6 neutrons = 12, C-12's atomic weight), C-13 has six protons and seven neutrons (6 protons + 7 neutrons = 13), and C-14 has six protons and eight neutrons (6 protons + 8 neutrons = its atomic weight of 14). (See Figure 6.6.)

Almost all of the carbon on our planet is the stable variety, C-12, with an equal number of protons and neutrons in its nucleus. There is, however, some

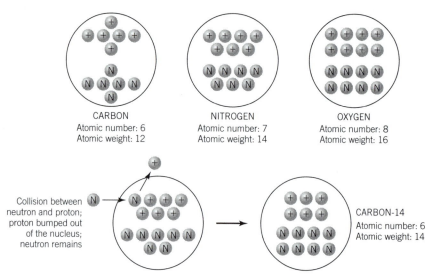

FIGURE 6.6 Schematic drawing of the atomic nuclei of a carbon, nitrogen, and oxygen atom, showing the number of protons in the nucleus of each of these elements, as well as the number of neutrons in their most common, stable isotopes. Not actual size.

C-14 produced in the air when atoms of the element nitrogen (making up about 78% of the atmosphere) collide with swiftly moving free neutrons that stream out of the sun, a result of the nuclear reactions by which the sun radiates energy. Nitrogen has seven protons in its nucleus and its most common isotope has seven neutrons, for an atomic weight of 14. Some of the collisions between solar neutrons and atmospheric nitrogen result in the neutron's crashing into and displacing a proton in the nucleus of a nitrogen atom. The struck proton streams out of the nucleus and the invading neutron stays put. (Think of the solar neutron as a cue ball imparting all of its forward momentum to the nine ball, a proton in the nitrogen nucleus; the nine ball zips off into the corner pocket and the cue ball stays put at the point of impact.) Nitrogen atoms that have this happen to them cease being nitrogen. Their nuclei no longer consist of seven protons and seven neutrons because they have lost a proton and gained a neutron in the collision. Their nuclei now have six protons (the original seven minus that one that got bumped out) and eight neutrons (the original seven plus the one that crashed into the nucleus and stayed put), making them carbon (six protons), not the common variety with six neutrons, but a variety with eight. In the designation "C-12," the twelve represents the isotope's atomic mass (6 protons + 6 neutrons). The atomic mass of the transmuted nitrogen is fourteen (6 protons + 8 neutrons), making it C-14.

Chemically, C-14 is virtually identical to C-12. It combines with oxygen to form carbon dioxide, just like C-12. The isotope C-14 carbon dioxide is just like C-12 carbon dioxide and is used much the same as C-12 by plants in photosynthesis. When ingested in the form of seeds, roots, berries, fruits, nuts, and so on, C-14 carbon is digested and then used in the bodies of animals, just like C-12, to make bone, blood, muscle, nerves, and skin. All living things consist in part of the carbon atoms they obtained by respiring (if they are plants) or by eating plants or other animals (if they are animals), and all living things have the same ratio of C-12 to C-14, which, in turn, is in the same proportion in the atmosphere (for those dying to know, only about $1.3 \times 10^{-10}$ percent of all of the carbon on Earth is of the C-14 variety, and that same proportion is found in the atmosphere, in plants, in animals, and in you).

This percentage remains the same as long as an organism lives and continues to respire (if it's a plant) or eat (if it's an animal). But C-14 is unstable and, therefore, radioactive, decaying back to nitrogen over time. In fact, the decay rate has been carefully measured for C-14. It takes about 5,730 years for half of any quantity of C-14 to decay back into nitrogen. In another 5,730 years, half of what was left after the first 5,730 years then decays to nitrogen. Half of that decays after another half-life, and so on.

When an organism is no longer respiring or eating, it can no longer replace the C-14 that is decaying to nitrogen while it is alive. As a result, we have what amounts to a natural hourglass. We know the rate at which the sand pours out of the top (the decay rate measured as a half-life), we can figure out how much sand (C-14) must have been in the hour glass in the first place, we can measure how much of the sand on top (C-14) has poured (decayed) into the bottom (turned to nitrogen), and from that come up with a pretty accurate estimate for how long it has been since the hourglass was turned over (the length of time since the plant or animal that produced the sample being dated died and, therefore, stopped ingesting "fresh" carbon). For example, the mass of a fragment of burned wood recovered from an archaeological site can be precisely measured and from this we can determine how much C-14 would be in the sample if it were part of a living plant today. We then can measure how much of the C-14 yet remains in the archaeological sample and, based on the known rate of decay, we can figure out about how long ago the wood was cut off of a living tree or how long ago the tree it was part of died and, therefore, about how long ago a human being used the wood to make a fire. When you ask "how old is that archaeological site" and I say, "Oh, three thousand years," my succinct answer is really shorthand for "The wood that we found in the fireplace comes from a branch of a tree whose C-14 content indicates that it was no longer taking in fresh C-14 (the branch was cut off or fell from the tree or the entire tree was cut down) about three thousand years ago and, therefore, we think that this is about the time a human being gathered that wood and made a fire to cook some food, so the site is about that old."

Radiocarbon dating requires a sophisticated laboratory setup and labs charge for the procedure: the going rate for a standard date is about $250. You can learn more about the details of sample sizes, preparation, and specific procedures on the Web site of Beta Analytic Corporation, the world's most active C-14 lab, processing more than twelve thousand samples each year (http://www.radiocarbon.com).

Based on what you know, you should have figured out that radiocarbon dating works on things that once were alive or part of living things (wood, bone, leather, hair, seeds, nuts, fruits, skin, antler, horn, teeth). Its range of temporal applicability also is limited. Very recent items have not experienced enough C-14 decay to accurately determine their age. At the other end of the continuum, after too many half-lives, virtually no C-14 is left to measure and the age cannot be determined accurately. In practice, specimens younger than a few hundred years or older than about forty thousand years (about seven half-lives) fall outside of the range of radiocarbon dating.

Radiocarbon dates require a little interpretation before they can be converted to true calendar dates. It turns out that the proportion of C-14 to C-12 in the atmosphere varies through time. As a result, specimens that date to periods when the C-14 proportion in the atmosphere, and, therefore, in everything that was alive during that period, was higher than it is today, will produce carbon dates that are too young. Conversely, specimens that were alive during periods when the C-14 proportion was lower will appear to be older than they actually are.

A fix for this, at least for the last eleven thousand years or so, has been calculated using tree rings (Bowman 1990). Individual tree rings, whose precise year age can be determined based on a master sequence, have been radiocarbon dated. For a large number of individual tree rings for which we can determine a precise age in years, dendrochronologists have also determined age by radiocarbon dating. Once a tree ring has been laid down, no new carbon is incorporated into it. This means that C-14 dates for interior rings—the earlier rings in a tree's life—will be older than those derived for exterior rings. This is most recognizable in very old trees and adds another possible error factor to radiocarbon dating, the so-called "old wood" effect. For example, if a person cut down a two-hundred-year-old tree for firewood a thousand years ago and used the interior segment of the trunk, the radiocarbon date will likely read twelve hundred years of age, dating to when the portion of the tree used in the fire grew, not when the tree was cut down. This is why archaeologists prefer using short-lived parts of plants in radiocarbon dating (for example, seeds or nuts), rather than trunks of old trees.

In any event, because individual tree rings stop taking in new carbon after the year in which they are laid down, dendrochronologists working with those who perform radiocarbon dates can produce two dates for a large number of tree rings: one based on dendrochronology (these are absolutely precise and accurate dates so they serve as the control or independent variable) and one based on radiocarbon dating of those same rings for which they can determine tree-ring dates (the carbon dates are the dependent variable). A graph can be drawn depicting the relationship between the tree-ring true calendar dates and the C-14 dates for those same rings (Figure 6.7). The resulting graph, called a **calibration curve,** shows the degree of correspondence between tree-ring and C-14 dates across a long stretch of time. This allows us to apply a correction factor to the C-14 dates (http://www.cio.phys.rug.nl/HTML-docs/Verslag/97/ CD-01.htm). As can be seen in Figure 6.7, from recent times until about twenty-five-hundred years ago, C-14 dates are a pretty good match for tree-ring calendar dates. Beyond that, it is apparent that C-14 dates undershoot the actual age of items by an increasing amount, up to several hundred years. Along with providing the results of a C-14 analysis, radiocarbon labs also provide the corrected dates based on the tree-ring calibration curve.

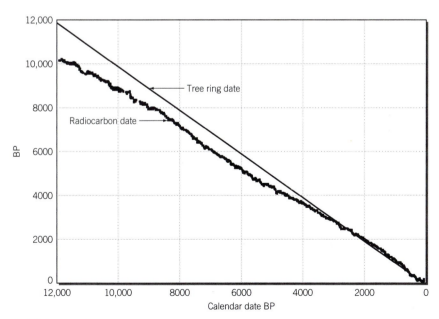

**FIGURE 6.7** Calibration curve worked out for radiocarbon dates for the past 12,000 years based on dendrochronology. (*University of Groningen, Center for Isotope Research*)

Less precise radiocarbon calibrations have been worked out for the period before eleven thousand years ago. For example, carbon dates have been calculated for organic remains extracted from **varves,** sediments laid down annually along lake and ocean shorelines. Varves can be counted back through time in a manner analogous to tree rings. Each varve represents one year so its actual year date can be precisely determined by counting back to it from the varve deposited in the current year.

One of the most important of these varve sequences stretching from eleven thousand to about forty-five thousand years ago has been worked out at Lake Suigetsu in Japan (Kitagawa and van der Plicht 1998). Each of more than 250 carbon dates was compared to the calendar years determined for each of the varves from which the carbon dated material was recovered. A calibration curve based on varves was then produced in the same way the one derived from tree rings is; the varve date is the independent variable and the carbon date is the dependent variable in the equation. The Lake Suigetsu calibration shows that from eleven thousand years ago to about forty-five thousand years ago, C-14 dates are consistently too young when compared to the very accurate varve dates, on the order of a few thousand years with the difference increasing for older dates (Kitagawa and van der Plicht 1998).

Calibration has also been extended beyond eleven thousand years ago by comparing C-14 dates and those determined through an extremely precise and accurate dating procedure based on the radioactive decay of uranium to thorium. Specifically, a sequence of layers sliced from an ancient stalagmite from the Bahamas has been dated by uranium-thorium and radiocarbon dating (Beck et al. 2001). Though stalagmites are cave formations and not organic, the process of their formation results in the inclusion of atmospheric carbon dioxide. The amount of C-14 in the layers of the formation (stalagmites grow by accretion from bottom to top) can be measured and the layer dated (because of radioactive decay, lower slices taken from older layers of the stalagmite have successively less radiocarbon). Following the general pattern revealed in the Lake Suigetsu results, older radiocarbon dates consistently and increasingly undershoot the actual calendar date and need to be adjusted upward. For example, a radiocarbon age of thirty-one thousand years may actually represent a calendar year of closer to thirty-eight thousand years ago (Bard 2001). The Lake Suigetsu results and those derived from analysis of the Bahamian stalagmite, however, differ in how much they indicate that radiocarbon dates underestimate age in the period before about twenty-five thousand years ago (the stalagmite analysis suggests a larger error factor). I am hopeful that these differences will be worked out as additional varve and uranium sequences are determined.

Other radiometric methods are used by archaeologists to determine the age of a site. For example, **potassium/argon (K/Ar)** dating is based on the known rate of decay of an unstable isotope of the element potassium into the gas argon (Deino, Renne, and Swisher 1998). Potassium is an abundant element in the Earth's crust and can be found in **igneous** rock. When lava comes out of a volcano, any argon that had previously accumulated in the rock is released into the atmosphere, essentially setting the natural clock in the lava to time zero. When the lava solidifies, argon begins accumulating as the unstable potassium atoms decay, getting trapped in the now-solid rock. The age of the rock itself can be determined by measuring the amount of argon that has built up and calculating the length of time it would have taken for that amount to accumulate based on the half-life of radioactive potassium, which has been measured at 1.25 billion years.

A chunk of volcanic rock like basalt or rhyolite, or even an entire lava flow, can be dated in this way, but the K/Ar method ordinarily doesn't date an archaeological site, at least not directly. We might be able to age the rock itself from which a human crafted a tool, but that doesn't really date the artifact. Think about it: I can collect a sample of basalt today from the mountain that brackets the eastern margin of the Farmington River valley in central Connecticut. The eruption that resulted in the lava flow that produced our local basalt occurred about 200 million years ago and K/Ar produces dates of about that age for the Talcott Mountain basalt. Suppose I were to make a spear point out of a chunk of that basalt today. Then suppose I sent off the point to a lab that conducted K/Ar dating. The spear point sample would produce an age of about 200 million years, but that certainly isn't how old the tool itself is; I just made it!

So K/Ar dating is not usually used to date an artifact, but it can be applied to rock in an intact level. Here's where our understanding of stratigraphy comes in handy. When archaeological materials are found in a stratigraphic layer above one lava flow and below another, we can bracket the age of the site by reference to K/Ar dates derived for both of the layers (Figure 6.8). If, for

**FIGURE 6.8** Combining stratigraphic analysis with potassium/argon dating has enabled scientists to bracket the ages of ancient hominid skeletons and artifacts. In this hypothetical example, the remains of a human ancestor have been found in a layer overlying a lava flow dated through potassium/argon to 2.15 million years ago and underlying a subsequent flow dating to 1.65 million years. The hominid remains must date, therefore, to some time between 1.65 and 2.15 million years ago.

example, the volcanic deposit that underlies the site dates to 2.15 million years ago, and if the overlying layer dates to 1.65 million years ago, we know that the archaeological site dates to sometime between those two dates.

In one spectacular instance, the K/Ar method actually dated a site directly. At the site of Laetoli, in Tanzania, Africa, a series of human-like footprints were found in a hardened deposit of volcanic ash (Leakey and Hay 1979). Two, and possibly three, individuals had walked across a newly laid bed of ash in the distant past. The ash hardened to the consistency of concrete after a gentle rain and later was covered by additional deposits. When the footprint trail was discovered and excavated by paleoanthropologists Mary Leakey and Tim White, samples of the hardened ash were dated using the K/Ar method. The result: the ash was deposited 3.5 million years ago. The footprints are virtually indistinguishable from those made by modern human beings, showing that, though their brains were the size of chimpanzees', even at this early date our human ancestors walked much in the manner of modern people.

As a result of the extremely long half-life of radioactive potassium, this technique has no effective upper limit; nothing on Earth is too old for the procedure. On the other hand, however, anything younger than a hundred thousand years or thereabouts is too young for the technique to produce accurate results; not enough of the radioactive potassium has decayed to argon.

Carbon and potassium/argon dating techniques are based on measurement of the decreasing amount of an unstable isotope remaining in a substance (C-14) or in the increasing amount of what the unstable isotope decays to (K/AR). Another set of dating procedures relies instead on the measurement of the regularly occurring changes or damage that results during the process of radioactive decay. **Electron spin resonance (ESR),** for example, calculates the accumulation of electrons (the negative particles that make up an atom) that become trapped at higher than normal or "ground state" energy levels in crystalline material (including fossilized bones or teeth) as a result of radioactivity in the surrounding environment (Grün 1993). Based on measurements of the background radiation in the area immediately surrounding the artifact or ecofact, the rate at which the electron trapping occurs can be calculated. From that, the age of the material can be determined: we know the rate at which the trapping occurs and how much has occurred, thus enabling a calculation of age.

**Thermoluminescence (TL)** and **optically stimulated luminescence (OSL)** also are radiation damage dating techniques. Here, the background radiation in the soil surrounding, for example, a buried ceramic or stone object produces energy that becomes stored in the atomic structure of the object. When the archaeological object is recovered, the energy that has accumulated as a result of the background radiation can be released, through the application of heat (thermoluminescence) or laser light (optically stimulated luminescence), and then measured. As was the case for ESR, knowing the rate of energy accumulation in an archaeological object once it ended up in the soil, and then knowing how much energy has actually accumulated, allows for a calculation of how long the object has been accumulating the energy; in other words, how old it is (for details about the procedures from a laboratory that conducts TL analysis, see http://www.users.globalnet.co.uk/~qtls).

# Read More

There is an enormous number of publications on the general topic of radiometric dating methods in archaeology, with each technique generating its own literature. A very brief sample follows:

Bard, E. 2001. Extending the calibrated radiocarbon record. *Science* 292:2443–44.

Beck, J. W., D. A. Richards, R. Lawrence, B. W. Silverman, P. L. Smart, D. J. Donahue, S. Hererra-Osterheld, G. S. Burr, L. Calsoyas, A. J. Timothy, and D. Biddulph. 2001. Extremely large variations of atmospheric 14C concentration during the last glacial period. *Science* 292:2453–58.

Bowman, S. 1990. *Radiocarbon Dating*. University of California Press, Berkeley.

Dalrymple, G. B., and M. A. Lanphere. 1969. *Potassium-Argon Dating*. W. H. Freeman, San Francisco.

Deino, A., P. R. Renne, and C. C. Swisher III. 1998. 40Ar/39Ar dating in paleoanthropology and archaeology. *Evolutionary Anthropology* 6(2):63–75.

Grün, R. 1993. Electron spin resonance dating in paleoanthropology. *Evolutionary Anthropology* 2(5):172–81.

Kitagawa, H., and J. van der Plicht. 1998. Atmospheric radiocarbon calibration to 45,000 BP: Late glacial fluctuations and cosmogenic istope production. *Science* 279: 1187–90.

Leakey, M. D., and R. L. Hay. 1979. Pliocene footprints in the Laetolil Beds at Laetoli, northern Tanzania. *Nature* 278:317–23.

Libby, W. F. 1952. *Radiocarbon Dating*. Chicago University Press, Chicago.

Stuiver, M. and J. van der Plicht. 1998. Intcal 98: Calibration issue. *Radiocarbon* 40(3).

Taylor, R. E. 1987. *Radiocarbon Dating: An Archaeological Perspective*. Academic Press, London.

## How Does Dendrochronology Work?

In Unit 1, I used the study of an old tree through the examination of its annual growth rings as a metaphor for the study of past peoples by the examination of the material culture they left behind. As mentioned in that chapter, the actual study of tree rings to determine the nature of past climates and as a dating method is called **dendrochronology.**

Although it might be obvious that the age of a living or newly felled tree can be determined simply by counting its rings, it is not so obvious how a tree-ring count can help date an ancient archaeological site, especially one that dates to long before any living tree. The key to accomplishing this rests in the creation of a regional **master sequence** of tree rings (Baillie 1990; Schweingruber 1988).

The width of individual tree rings in a region tends to vary on a yearly basis as a result of variation in climatic variables crucial to tree growth. In some areas, the amount of precipitation in the spring is the most important determinant of tree-ring width in any year. In other areas, spring temperature is the determining factor. For example, in a year of substantial spring rainfall, most of the trees in the **four-corners** region of the American Southwest (a wide area around the intersection of Arizona, New Mexico, Utah, and Colorado) add a proportionally wide ring. When the spring rains are sparse, most of those same trees will add a proportionally thinner ring. When timbers that include a portion or even all of the diameter of the tree trunks from which they were cut were incorporated into ancient structures, and where those timbers have preserved, archaeologists can extract cross-sections, showing a sequence of the tree rings produced during part or even all of the tree's lifetime. Looking across a section of tree rings, you can see the ebb and flow of rain across the years.

Good enough, but that still doesn't explain the use of dendrochronology as a dating method. Luckily for archaeologists who rely on dendrochronology, there is no repeating pattern of rainfall variation and, therefore, no chronological sequence of ring width sizes that repeat across time. In other words, any sufficiently long period of years has a unique sequence of rainfall amounts that is never repeated. As a result, any sufficiently long sequence of tree-ring widths also is unique and never repeated. That unique sequence is what makes dendrochronology a viable and highly accurate dating method. It all begins with a living or newly felled tree where the tree-ring sequence can be anchored in time; the most recent tree ring represents the current year (Figure 6.9).

Suppose a tree is one hundred years old. We can cross-section the tree, revealing a sequence of thin, intermediate, and thick rings. Our next task is to look at the tree rings of a number of dead trees. With a little bit of luck, we can find a tree with a pattern of tree-ring widths toward the end of its life that matches the sequence of ring widths of the early years of the old living tree. Because we know that the matching part of the sequence of varying widths is unique in time and has never been repeated, we can safely conclude that the two trees were contemporaries for the period of time their rings show the same varied sequence of thin and thick rings. That knowledge enables us to tie in the dead tree with the sequence that we have already anchored in time. So, for example, if the last ten rings of the dead tree show the same sequence of ring widths as the first ten rings of the live, one-hundred-year-old tree, we can

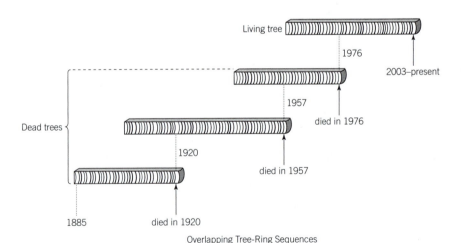

**FIGURE 6.9** Tree-ring sequence of four trees. The top sequence is that of a living tree; its most recent ring, on the far right, represents the current year. The other trees overlap successively with one another, allowing us the ability to place them all in a continuous, master sequence of time.

determine when the dead tree died or was cut down. The final ring of the dead tree corresponds to the tenth ring of the live one. The live tree is one hundred years old, this year is 2005, so its first ring grew in 1905. The dead tree's final ring corresponds to the tenth ring of the live tree; the tenth ring of the live tree corresponds to 1915; the dead tree's last ring grew in 1915. If that dead tree ended up as a log found in a structure (for example, the remains of a log cabin), we have a precise, absolute date for when the tree was cut down and, by inference, a date for when the cabin was built. At least we know it was built sometime after the tree was cut down and we can gauge precisely when that occurred.

The same process of finding successively older trees whose ring sequences overlap at least a part of those exhibited by trees already incorporated into the regional sequence is applied to produce a master sequence. Though overlapping the tree-ring sequences of hundreds of trees, both living and dead, is a painstaking process, master sequences for tree-ring widths have been developed for various parts of the world.

Consider, for example, a relatively short tree-ring master sequence developed in Massachusetts (Steinitz 2002). Using a stand of living old-growth red oaks identified on Mt. Wachusett as recently as 1997, a slightly more than three-hundred-year master sequence was produced, dating back to A.D. 1672. This master chronology of tree-ring thickness in red oaks has enabled the precise and accurate dating of the felling of red oak trees from which timbers were milled and then used in house construction in Massachusetts beginning in the late seventeenth century. Red oak timbers in a series of historic structures were cored and the resulting sequences of tree-ring thicknesses compared to the thickness sequence presented in the master chronology. In this way, for example, important historic structures like the Saugus Iron Works house (A.D. 1683) and the Capen House (A.D. 1681 and 1682) had their ages as indicated in the documentary record confirmed and complemented.

Master sequences arching back to far earlier periods are available in a number of parts of the world. The Laboratory of Tree Ring Research (LTRR) at the University of Arizona is one of the best-known dendrochronology labs in the world and has worked out much of the master sequence for the American Southwest (http://www.ltrr.arizona.edu/). The master sequence derived by LTRR from bristlecone pines in the American west goes back thirty times further than the Massachusetts chronology to more than nine thousand years ago. Sheffield University in Great Britain has produced a master sequence for England that spans the last seven thousand years (http://www.shef.ac.uk/uni/academic/A-C/ap/dendro/dendinfo.html). The master sequence derived from pine trees in Germany now extends to more than ten thousand years ago and, when linked to the oak series, allows for a sequence of tree rings that can be used to calibrate radiocarbon dates back to more than 11,800 years ago (Kromer and Spurk 1998).

In each application of dendrochronology, when a section of a timber is found in an archaeological or historical context (for example, in a hearth or in a standing structure) the sequence of tree-ring widths is compared to that presented by the geographically closest master sequence. Where the width sequence in the archaeological specimen matches a section of the master sequence, the years of that tree's life can be firmly placed in time. Its final year, represented by the last ring it grew, obviously is the first year the tree could have been incorporated into an archaeological structure or facility. Barring any great delay between the year of the tree's death and the year it was used by a past people, we can confidently assign a date to a site based on the year the tree died.

## Read More

To learn more about dendrochronology, check out any of these sources:

Baillie, M. G. L. 1990. *Tree Ring Dating and Archaeology.* University of Chicago Press, Chicago.
Kromer, B., and M. Spurk. 1998. Revision and tentative extension of the tree-ring based 14C calibration, 9,200–11,855 cal BP. *Radiocarbon* 40(3):1117–26.
Schweingruber, F. H. 1988. *Tree Rings: Basics and Applications of Dendrochronology.* D. Reidel Publishing, Boston.
Steinitz, M. 2002. Tree-ring dates offer insight on Massachusetts buildings. In *Preservation Advocate*, pp. 1, 6–7, 10.

## How Can You Determine an Absolute Date for a Site by Reference to Style?

The ways in which people decorate their pots, make their spears, build their houses, bury their dead, prepare their food, and so on, change over time. Sometimes these changes represent genuine progress in the complexity or efficiency of a technology. Some changes reflect little more than the vicissitudes of fashion. Whatever the case, when we are familiar with a culture and aware of when these changes in style or ways of doing things took place, we can date objects or even entire sites on the basis of these styles.

For example, I am certain that your university keeps copies of their catalogues of years past. Suppose the year has been ripped from the cover of a couple of the catalogues so there is no written indication of the catalogue's year date. Now suppose I describe the covers of a couple of the catalogues to you. One has a photograph on the cover of two students, one male and one female. The male has a short haircut with a big wave in the front, sticking up and obviously kept in place with some sort of gel. He is wearing a sweater with the university's initials sewn onto the pocket, white pants with a thin belt, and penny loafers on his feet. The female has her hair in a ponytail, is wearing a skirt appliquéd with the image of a poodle, and on her feet wears two-tone, so-called saddle shoes. You will immediately know that the catalogue dates to the 1950s, not because you lived through that period, but because you are familiar with

**FIGURE 6.10** We can apply the same analysis to video game systems. As technology has improved, one of the biggest names in video gaming, Nintendo, has released increasingly sophisticated hand-held systems. Depicted here in the order of their release are: (A) Gameboy, (B) Gameboy pocket, (C) Gameboy Color, (D) Gameboy Advance, and (E) Gameboy Advances SP.

the styles of the period from photographs of your parents, or endless, merciless high school productions of the musical *Grease*.

Suppose, I next describe a copy of your university's annual catalogue with a photograph, again, of two students, and again a male and female. Now the male has wild, scraggly hair hanging down his back, a beard, tie-dyed t-shirt, ripped jeans with an American flag sewn on the knee, and, well, there is no need to describe his shoes because he isn't wearing any. Except for the beard, the female looks just like the male. Once again, though you might not be able to guess the exact year, you will likely correctly hypothesize that the catalogue dates to the late 1960s and early 1970s. Love, peace, and music. It's all about paying attention to the changing of styles and familiarity with the time frame when those styles changed (Figure 6.10).

Just as you recognize and can accurately, if not absolutely precisely, identify the period an object dates to because of your familiarity with the recent history of your own culture, an archaeologist can do the same with ancient cultures he or she is familiar with. When someone hands an archaeologist in the New World a relatively long, finely made, stone spear point bearing a concave channel or "flute" (as in a fluted column in building) that begins as the base and reaches to about half-way up the weapon's length, he or she will instantly suggest that the spear point dates to sometime between twelve thousand and eleven thousand years ago. There's no magic, psychic power, or intuition here, only a familiarity with that style of artifact. Fluted points have been found throughout North America. Wherever they have been found in archaeological context, the dates derived on associated organic remains through radiocarbon dating indicate something in the neighborhood of about 11,800 and 11,200 years ago. When someone hands me a fluted point, devoid of site context and lacking any association with directly datable material, I nevertheless am pretty confident when I suggest that the weapon likely dates to sometime in the twelfth millennium B.P.

# Study Questions

1. What is chronometric or absolute dating? What is relative dating?

2. What are the most common relative dating techniques in archaeology?

3. Discuss the use of degree of artistic sophistication as a dating method in archaeology.

4. Discuss stratigraphy. How does the concept of the law of superposition allow us to relatively date archaeological occupations?

5. Discuss the relative sequence revealed by the test pit excavated in Avon, Connecticut, as detailed in this book.

6. "The deeper something is, the older it is." Can we apply this simple rule in archaeological dating? Why or why not?

7. Can stylistic change through time be used to date archaeological sites?

8. How does seriation work? What is the assumption at the core of seriation?

9. Discuss the application of seriation. Use the example provided for the seriation of beverage can containers in the second half of the twentieth century. Use the example of New England gravestone designs.

10. What are the most common methods of chronometric dating?

11. List the most important radiometric dating techniques used in archaeology.

12. How does radiocarbon dating work? Where does C-14 come from? How does it get into living things? Why does C-14 decay? How does that decay provide a natural clock or calendar that can be used in dating archaeological material?

13. The accuracy of radiocarbon dating relies on what turns out to be a faulty assumption: There has always been a constant ratio of stable C-12 to unstable C-14 in the Earth's atmosphere. How do tree rings provide a workaround, at least for the last 11,000 years or so?

14. What is the calibration curve? How is it applied to radiocarbon dating?

15. What are varves? How has the analysis of varves contributed to improving the accuracy of carbon dating?

16. How does potassium-argon dating work? What can actually be dated using this technique?

17. List some of the radiation damage dating techniques. How do those apply to archaeological specimens?

18. Tree rings are easy enough to understand when we're dealing with a living tree; count the rings to see how old the tree is. But how does this help us date ancient archaeological sites?

19. What is the process behind establishing a master sequence of tree rings for a given region? How does a master sequence enable the dating of an old, now long-dead tree found incorporated into an ancient structure?

20. I have dated charcoal found in a fireplace at the Wood Lily site through radiocarbon dating to about 3,000 years ago. I have concluded from this that the site itself was occupied about 3,000 years ago. What was my reasoning?

21. How do you know the approximate age (perhaps to the correct decade) of an older automobile that had just driven by? How does your reasoning apply in archaeology?

# UNIT 7

By the time we were done with our survey of Peoples State Forest in 1986, we had excavated more than a thousand test pits. The three-thousand-year-old site we called Wood Lily (for the beautiful flowers that marked the point on Center Road where we started the test pit transect that ended up in the middle of the ancient settlement) was only the first of more than twenty prehistoric archaeological sites we discovered that summer in Peoples through the process of subsurface testing (Figure 7.1).

In a few more instances that summer, site locations were predicted with a reasonable degree of accuracy. In all of the other cases, in hindsight anyway, discovering buried sites where we did was not terribly surprising and could have been predicted. These sites were found in places in the forest where it would have made perfect sense for small groups of **foragers** to have settled for short periods of time while hunting animals, fishing, collecting seeds or nuts, or just overnighting while passing through.

In addition to locations used by ancient Native Americans, six sites were identified in our pedestrian survey of the forest associated with people of European descent who had begun moving into the area in the late eighteenth century. These sites included the remains of two separate mill buildings, with associated dams impounding flowing stream water and their "raceways" directing water to the mill wheels, as well as a couple of house foundations (Figure 7.2).

During our walkover in one section of the forest, we encountered a series of very small, irregular, and rather crudely made stone-lined foundations and cellar holes. We were disabused in a hurry of our initial reaction that we had made a spectacular discovery here when we exited the forest onto the nearby road and noticed a brass plaque memorializing the site we had just

**Peoples State Forest**

PREHISTORIC SITE LOCATIONS

**FIGURE 7.1** Outline of Peoples State Forest with sites we located in our 1986 survey. (*Kenneth L. Feder*)

**FIGURE 7.2** This late eighteenth-century foundation is one of several historical sites located in Peoples State Forest and identified in our pedestrian survey. (*Kenneth L. Feder*)

"discovered." Even if our discovery was not extraordinary—everybody in town already knew about the village remains—the story behind the place was spectacular. The foundations were the remains of houses from the Lighthouse, an eighteenth- and nineteenth-century village of people at the social and economic margins, a mixed group of people of Native, European, and African descent. We were to spend several years investigating the site (Figure 7.3; Feder 1994).

But the detailed investigation of our sites was to take place in the future. Our job in the summer of 1986 was to conduct an archaeological survey and produce a map identifying for the Connecticut Historical Commission the location of archaeological remains within the borders of Peoples State Forest. The thirty-three sites we identified fulfilled the goal of this element of the project. Our secondary mandate was to determine the approximate size of the sites and to provide a preliminary description, including how long ago the sites had been occupied and the activities carried out by their inhabitants. Our strategy to accomplish these tasks involved excavating additional test pits in the vicinity of the original units in which archaeological material had been recovered to get a broader perspective of the remains at

**FIGURE 7.3** One of the simple stone foundations located in the late eighteenth-century, early nineteenth-century village called the Lighthouse, in Peoples State Forest. (*Kenneth L. Feder*)

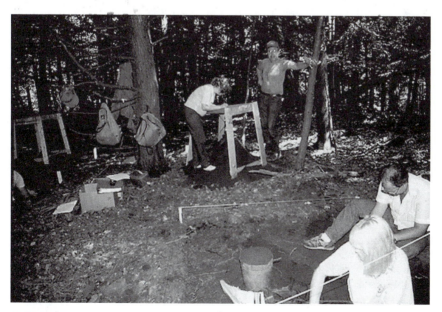

**FIGURE 7.4** Students excavating at the Wood Lily archaeological site in Peoples State Forest. (*Kenneth L. Feder*)

each site. We did precisely this at the aforementioned three-thousand-year-old occupation we called the Wood Lily site.

This preliminary work convinced us that the Wood Lily site possessed great potential to help illuminate the lives of the ancient people of north-central Connecticut. We returned to the site in the summers of 1987 and 1989 to conduct a more detailed investigation through **archaeological excavation.** During both summers my crew consisted of students who were pursuing training in archaeology, students who were not interested in pursuing archaeology as a career but who wanted to work on an excavation, and a number of nonstudent volunteers who simply were interested in archaeology (Figure 7.4).

 ## How Can the Location of Archaeological Sites Be Accurately Predicted?

There are a series of commonsense techniques that archaeologists employ in **site survey,** the process of searching for the locations where archaeological material can be found (Feder 1997b). In a fundamental way, to find sites the archaeologist needs to understand the ways in which a past people utilized territory by identifying features of the landscape that were deciding factors in developing a land-use pattern. Based on the understanding of how a group of people used their landscape, archaeologists then investigate places that would have been attractive to past people for settlements or other kinds of use.

Remember that human beings decide, on the basis of a constellation of characteristics, where to establish villages, situate burial grounds, locate hunting camps, place manufacturing activities, fish, gather firewood, plant gardens, and construct mills for grinding grain or milling lumber. Humans have even decided which places to avoid (for example, no-man's land between hostile groups or locations believed to be inhabited by evil spirits). Obviously, many land-use decisions were based on practical concerns. A hidden overlook near an animal trail is an obvious place for a hunting camp. A fall-line where rapids create a situation conducive to fishing during the seasonal upstream migration of anadromous fish like salmon provides an opportunity for the exploitation of a rich source of food. The area along a narrow section of a stream that can be easily impounded and controlled so that the water can be used to turn a water-wheel, whose energy can in turn be used to power a grist-, saw-, or carding mill, will be appealing to people who use the energy of flowing water to power their industry. A topographically flat area with organically rich soil is attractive to agricultural people. A spot near an ancient volcano with an abundant deposit of obsidian easily flaked into sharp-edged tools will draw people who rely on stone for their tools and weapons. A place with gentle topography, a reliable source of good drinking water (a spring or a permanent watercourse), an abundant source of wood for construction and fuel, with natural protection (a surrounding

**FIGURE 7.5** Called Montezuma's Well, even though the Aztec ruler Montezuma (or Moctezuma) had nothing to do with it, this body of fresh water in Arizona was such an attractive resource that ancient people even built homes in the cliffs overlooking the water. The arrow indicates some of the walls of their ruins. (*Kenneth L. Feder*)

wetland or adjacent mountain) is a sensible spot for a permanent village (Figure 7.5). Locales that afford useful natural characteristics—remembering that "useful," in our application of the term, is culturally defined and will differ among different groups of people—are logical places for people to have utilized and are logical places to examine in the search for the material evidence of past people.

By examining detailed maps, archaeologists can identify particular places where the confluence of a number of important features of the landscape makes it likely that sites will be found. Each human group develops its own practice of land use—a **settlement pattern**—that depends on a complex interplay of their subsistence focus (whether they are foragers or farmers, hunters or fisherfolk, generalists relying on a broad array of food sources, or specialists focusing on a small number of highly productive foods), mode of technology (whether stone or metal is the predominant raw material for their tools; if they make ceramics; if they rely on wood for construction or on stone, clay, earth, or bone; if they power their industry with flowing water), as well as their yearly pattern of land use and seasonality (whether they are **sedentary,** living in one place all year relying on the resources offered there; **nomadic,** moving from place to place on a regular schedule following the availability of resources; or whether their settlement pattern falls somewhere between sedentary and nomadic). If a people's settlement pattern reflects their use of the landscape, then what is left behind as the archaeological manifestation of that pattern has been called the **landscape signature** (Marquardt and Crumley 1987).

In accurately predicting the location of sites, which are then found through the processes of a surface inspection of locations or through digging test excavations, archaeologists are, in essence, deducing the general settlement pattern of a group of people. Archaeologists make such determinations based on commonsense interpretation of the natural environment as well as the locations of known sites and then apply that knowledge to predict the location of undiscovered sites.

Based on what we already know about their subsistence, technology, and level of sedentism, we make location predictions where it would have made good practical sense for the people to have settled or exploited resources and where they likely left evidence of their presence on the landscape. There certainly is no guarantee that every place that *we* think would have made sense to settle or utilize will actually have been used or contain archaeological evidence, but it is a sensible way to structure our search for remains.

## Read More

To find out more about the process of successfully predicting locations of archaeological sites, any of the following resources are helpful:

Dincauze, D. F. 1978. Surveying for cultural resources: Don't rush out with a shovel. In *Conservation Archaeology in the Northeast: Toward a Research Orientation*, edited by A. Speiss, vol. 3, 51–59. Peabody Museum of Archaeology and Ethnology, Cambridge, Massachusetts.

Feder, K. L. 1997b. Site survey. In *Field Methods in Archaeology*, edited by T. R. Hester, H. J. Shafer, and K. L. Feder, 41–68. Mayfield Publishing, Mountain View, California.

Marquardt, W. H., and C. Crumley. 1987. Theoretical issues in the analysis of spatial patterning. In *Regional Dynamics: Burgundian Landscapes in Historical Perspective*, edited by C. L. Crumley and W. H. Marquardt, 1–18. Academic Press, San Diego.

Schiffer, M. B., A. P. Sullivan, and T. C. Klinger. 1978. The design of archaeological surveys. *World Archaeology* 10:1–28.

## How Can Landscape Characteristics Be Examined to Help Identify Places Where Sites Are Likely to Be Found?

Once we locate an archaeological site, our next step is to determine why an ancient people positioned themselves there. Why did they select this particular place to settle in a village, build a mill complex, quarry metal ore, or establish a hunting camp?

Our interest in accurately locating a site on a map can be traced, in part, to the applicability in archaeology of an old real estate cliché: "There are three important factors to consider when determining the value of a piece of real estate: location, location, location." Recognizing the factors that influenced a group's decision to use a specific location on their landscape allows us to explain their pattern of land use. Understanding that pattern allows us successfully to predict the location of other sites in places we have not yet looked. A given place provides people, both modern and ancient, a particular set of benefits. Human beings have always based their decisions to settle or exploit a particular place on their own set of complex calculations concerning the benefits of the location (Feder 1997b; Marquardt and Crumley 1987).

Our task, then, becomes one of assessing as many variables as possible in our attempt to reveal that set of calculations. Our ability to do this is greatly enhanced by an approach called **Geographic Information Systems (GIS).** GIS refers to a form of analysis of spatially distributed information and the production of maps that convey the nature of the relationships among sets of spatially distributed data (McPherron and Dibble 2002; Wheatley and Gillings 2002).

Imagine a grid superimposed over an entire region with a series of measurements (of **continuous variables**) or expressions (of **discontinuous** or **nominal variables**) recorded at each point on the grid: for example, elevation, slope, soil pH (measurable, continuous variables), soil type, and presence or absence of flowing water (discontinuous variables where the value at any given point is not a measurement but a name). Those measurements or records represent a database and may be stored in a spreadsheet where each column represents a spatially distributed variable and each row represents a location on the grid where each variable's expression at that spot is recorded. In other words, each cell in the spreadsheet has a value or name that represents the expression of a given variable (for example, elevation or soil type) at a given place (for example, the X,Y coordinate) on the gridded region being mapped.

In GIS, each variable in the spreadsheet can be isolated and its values at each location where it was measured on the grid can be mapped as a map layer. Additional map layers using other spatially distributed variables can be selectively superimposed on top of other layers. Finally, additional layers indicating the locations of archaeological sites of different ages can be produced and superimposed onto other layers. Along with providing a visual depiction that might allow us to infer the ways in which variables are related, distributional patterns and correlations among variables can be determined using various statistical software packages. A multilayered map, including the locations of archaeological sites, can be statistically analyzed and complex patterns can be exposed indicating the key factors that likely affected the calculations of people who lived in the region during different time periods. Detailed mapping of variables and site locations for a given region with a comprehensive archaeological database can enable the prediction of site locations in a region where little archaeological research has been conducted (Figure 7.6).

GIS doesn't necessarily produce new data, but it allows us to examine data in new ways. Our imperfect and limited minds have a difficult time decrypting vast arrays of data stored in spreadsheets with tens of columns and hundreds of rows. The visual patterning that becomes apparent in the mapping of these data is far easier for our minds to absorb and is a valuable tool in providing insights into how these spatially distributed data might be patterned or correlated.

**FIGURE 7.6** GIS map showing Peoples State Forest with the boundaries of the forest, roads, drainage streams, and archaeological site locations, each making up a layer of the map. (*Keegan Associates*)

## Read More

To find out more about the role of landscape in archaeological analysis see the following resources; in particular, take a look at the book by Wheatley and Gillings on the use of GIS in archaeology:

Feder, K. L. 1997b. Site survey. In *Field Methods in Archaeology*, edited by T. R. Hester, H. J. Shafer, and K. L. Feder, 41–68. Mayfield Publishing, Mountain View, California.

Marquardt, W. H., and C. Crumley. 1987. Theoretical issues in the analysis of spatial patterning. In *Regional Dynamics: Burgundian Landscapes in Historical Perspective*, edited by C. L. Crumley and W. H. Marquardt, 1–18. Academic Press, San Diego.

McPherron, S. P., and H. L. Dibble. 2002. *Using Computers in Archaeology.* McGraw-Hill, New York.
Wheatley, D., and M. Gillings. 2002. *Spatial Technology and Archaeology: The Archaeological Applications of GIS.* Taylor and Francis, London.

# How Are Archaeological Sites Named?

Archaeological sites have long been named in a number of traditional and informal ways. When sites are located on private lands, it is common to name the site after the landowner. For example, the Glazier Blade Cache site mentioned previously was named after Mr. Ron Glazier, on whose property the site was located. Sites are often named after their discoverers or according to a local landmark. One example is the Vail Site in Maine, named after its discoverer, local hunting guide and amateur archaeologist Francis Vail. The Ragged Mountain Rockshelter site is descriptively named; it is located in a rockshelter (a long and narrow overhang of rock) on Ragged Mountain in Barkhamsted, Connecticut. Sites are sometimes given colorful, even whimsical names that reflect their appearance: Cliff Palace in southern Colorado, indeed, looks like a palace secreted in a niche just under a cliff; Mound City in Ohio consists of about two dozen earth mounds, with the entire grouping surrounded by an earth wall, giving the place the appearance of a city of mounds. Site names can get fanciful and even reflect errors in historical attribution, but these names often stick anyway: Montezuma's Castle (see Figure 7.5) in Arizona doesn't look much like a castle and Montezuma (now usually spelled Moctezuma), the Aztec king encountered by the Spanish in 1519, had nothing to do with it; the Toltecs, a group who preceded the historical Aztecs in central Mexico had nothing to do with Toltec Mounds in Arkansas; the Aztec Ruins in New Mexico were built by Pueblo Indians, not the Aztecs.

With no individual landowner and no particular discoverer, we named the Wood Lily site for the flowers that were in bloom near the road where we started the test pit transect, along which we found the site (recall the narrative introduction to Chapter 3). The most important element in site naming is to assign a unique identifier to avoid confusion with any other site.

Although names are easier to remember than numbers, named sites are also given numerical identifiers. The common names we apply to sites are not as important as their official designations assigned variously by a state archaeologist, historic preservation office, or other official government entity or museum. These official designations are not arbitrary: they provide, in a coded format, information about the site and its location. A national system of site designation includes a numerical prefix that locates the site by state, with states assigned numbers alphabetically. Using this system, the national designation for every site in Alabama, for example, begins with the numeral 1 because Alabama is the first state in an alphabetical listing of all the states. All archaeological sites listed in Connecticut begin with the numeral 6 because Connecticut was sixth in an alphabetical listing of the states before Alaska and Hawaii became states.

The next part of the national archaeological site designator is a two-letter abbreviation for the county in which the site is located. The final part of the designator is simply a number that reflects a tally of the archaeological sites in a given county in the order of their discovery or, often, the order in which they have been reported to the person in charge of maintaining the list for a given state. For example, 6LF21 is the twenty-first site listed in the county of Litchfield (LF), Connecticut (6). The site is known among Connecticut archaeologists as Templeton (for the property owner, not the rat in *Charlotte's Web*) and has the oldest radiocarbon date of any site in the state (10,190 B.P.).

Some states, like my own, do not have many counties, and county boundaries may be geographically insignificant, historically unimportant, and politically meaningless. Counties in some states can exhibit a tremendous amount of variation in terms of size, and certainly counties in some states are much larger than typical counties in other states; I imagine that counties in some states are bigger than some states in their entirety. As a result, some states have moved away from a county-based system of site naming. In Connecticut, the state archaeologist provides official town-based designations for sites, in which each site designator begins with a numerical prefix that reflects the alphabetical position of the town where the site is located. For example, all sites found in the town of Barkhamsted, Connecticut, are assigned a designator prefix of 5 because that town is fifth in an alphabetical listing of Connecticut's 169 towns. After the town location prefix, a number appears that reflects, again, the order in which sites located in the town have been discovered and reported to the state archaeologist.

However a site is named, the designator should be unique and provide information to anyone who reads its name, allowing a researcher to easily determine at least the general location of the site.

## Read More

For a brief discussion of the conventions of site naming see the following book:

Stewart, R. M. 2002. *Archaeology: Basic Field Methods.* Kendall/Hunt Publishing, Dubuque, Iowa.

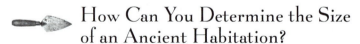 # How Can You Determine the Size of an Ancient Habitation?

Reflecting the spatial nature of the communities, encampments, quarries, industrial zones, and so on that produced them, archaeological sites are spatially bounded. The places that people used had centers and edges, and boundaries that marked the end of these places. In simplest terms, this means that if you were to dig test pits at regular intervals in a series of lines radiating from the geographic midpoint of a site, in some of those test pits you will find an abundance of artifacts and ecofacts, in some test excavations you will find fewer archaeological materials, and at some point along each line you will start digging pits in which no archaeological materials will be found. When you have reached a point where test pits begin producing no artifacts or ecofacts, you have moved past the edge of the place once used by people (at least you have moved beyond the zone where they manufactured, utilized, or deposited elements of their material culture) and passed beyond the margins of the resulting archaeological site.

Think about driving through a large city filled with buildings and people. In the center of the city, the buildings are numerous and close together. As you approach the outskirts of the city, the buildings may be smaller and fewer in number. At the city's margins, there may be less densely occupied suburbs with fewer structures and a less concentrated population. When you reach the edge of the suburbs surrounding the city you may encounter a stretch in which the environs are rural and you do not see any structures or people. Drive far enough and you may encounter the outskirts of the suburbs of yet another city.

Of course, this spatial pattern is not always so neat and simple. Even within the boundaries of a site, you may encounter test pits in which no materials are found. You certainly cannot, on the basis of one or even a few closely spaced pits (perhaps only a few meters apart) in which no archaeological material is found, conclude that you have passed beyond the margins of a site. Consider the analogy we used for determining the edges of a city. In New York City, we certainly could not correctly assume that we had reached the end of the metropolis simply because there were no (or few) buildings when, in our drive we encountered the 843 acres of Central Park. In very short order, as we drive through the park, we would reach the other side and encounter another dense array of enormous buildings, merely having passed from Central Park East to Central Park West.

Inside the boundaries of what any observer would recognize as part of a community, we may come across places where activities were carried out (storytelling or dancing, for example) that resulted in little or no physical evidence of their conduct because the activities themselves did not involve the use of items of material culture. Transform that community into an archaeological site and test pits might provide no evidence for these practices. Remember, archaeologists are dependent to a large extent on people using and losing or discarding stuff. There is no hard and fast rule here—and it would certainly vary depending on the distance between test pits—but, generally, when testing across a site with test pits or borings or cores, when archaeological material runs out along a transect and doesn't pick up again, it is assumed that the line has passed beyond the margins of the site.

Another complication concerns the overlap of different occupations of the same place. We may be able accurately to outline the horizontal extent of a site, but that outline may not necessarily correspond to the spatial extent of an individual occupation of a particular place. The same general spot may have been occupied on more than one and even on numerous occasions; the same appealing features of a spot may have attracted repeated human settlement over a long span of time. Some of those temporally distinct settlements may overlap spatially, but only partially. So we may have a series of sites of varying sizes and spatial patterns superimposed one on top of the other, with part of some of the temporally distinct occupations stratigraphically interdigitated. In such cases, archaeologists must take into careful consideration the stratigraphic level in which artifacts or ecofacts are found. Only in this way can we distinguish the materials found in differing levels and dating to different occupations of the same place, assuring that the materials found in one test pit are from the same stratum and, therefore, belong to the same occupation, as the materials found in another pit.

## Who Gets to Dig at an Archaeological Site?

Many digs in the United States and Canada are conducted by university or college departments of anthropology, archaeology, or history. It is probably fair to say that most of the people who participate in archaeological excavations are undergraduate students at those universities. Many of the students participate as part of their training for a career in archaeology. Students from other academic departments (geology, biology, environmental sciences, or virtually any other area) participate for the unique experience—and credits—they gain. Students can sign up for a **field school** run by the appropriate department at their university or can apply to field programs offered at most other universities and receive academic credit at their home institution. Field schools are treated as academic courses by most universities and may involve classroom work, library research, laboratory, and, especially, field experience. Field schools may run for several weeks or even a few months during which time students receive an intensive introduction—often eight or more hours a day, five days a week—to the methods of archaeological fieldwork.

Beyond learning how to dig, field school participants make a significant contribution to archaeological research. As an undergraduate student majoring in anthropology, I trained at a field school at the University of Cincinnati, where I learned how to excavate a site by participating in the excavation of a thirty-five-hundred-year-old site located in the Ohio River valley. Like my fellow students in that field school, I was doing more than simply training for a career in archaeology. (In fact, the ethical precepts of the archaeological profession preclude the excavation of a site for the sole purpose of training students.) When I learned archaeological field techniques, my work was overseen by experienced graduate students and a professor (Kent Vickery). The grunt work we contributed to the project produced the data that allowed for a detailed study of the nature of an ancient habitation site on the Ohio River (Vickery 1976).

Most of the field research I have conducted over the past twenty-five years would have been impossible if not for the contribution of undergraduate students who, in return for the work they did for me (and their tuition payment) received training in archaeological field research. Every year, the Archaeological Institute of America (AIA) publishes *The Archaeological Fieldwork Opportunities Bulletin,* a comprehensive listing of field schools and projects seeking volunteers (Mozina 2003). If you are interested in participating in a dig, this book is the best place to find opportunities (you can locate information about the fieldwork bulletin by clicking the fieldwork link at that AIA's homepage: http://www.archaeological.org/).

Participation in an archaeological research project is not restricted to university students. Motivated high school students become involved in university sponsored projects and obtain academic credit as well. Many projects also encourage the participation of nonstudent volunteers; I have found that lecturing to historical societies, libraries, and local business or civic groups often generates interest in volunteering from elementary school kids to retired seniors. Depending on volunteers' availability and skills, we encourage their participation. There even are organizations that specialize in providing a formal means by which nonscientists can participate in and contribute to research projects all over the country. The best-known of these is the EarthWatch Institute (http://www.earthwatch.org/). Each year, EarthWatch brings together more than a hundred scientists in seven primary fields of study (endangered ecosystems, oceans, biodiversity, cultural diversity, global change, world health, and archaeology) and thousands of enthusiastic participants. It is the proverbial win/win situation, one in which scientists can accomplish an enormous amount of work (through what amounts to donated labor) and people who always wanted to study the carnivores of South America, help feed children in Estonia, or participate in an archaeological excavation at Pompeii can fulfill their dreams.

In essence, the question posed at the start of this section (Who gets to dig at an archaeological site?) has a simple answer: anyone motivated and willing to devote a substantial chunk of time for the physically challenging but intellectually stimulating, satisfying, and rewarding work of excavation.

## Read More

For a listing of current fieldwork opportunities, investigate the comprehensive annual guide by the Archaeological Institute of America:

Mozina, M. 2003. *Archaeology Fieldwork Bulletin*. Archaeological Institute of America, Boston.

## Study Questions

1. What are the features that make an area attractive to human beings who rely on foraging for their subsistence?
2. What are the features that make an area attractive to those who rely on agriculture?
3. Are sites always located in specific places because those spots provide easy access to subsistence resources?
4. What is the "settlement pattern" of a group of people?
5. Explain the term *landscape signature* as used by archaeologists William Marquardt and Carol Crumley.
6. Describe the landscape signature of Contact period sites of Native Americans in Connecticut (as seen in Figure 4.5).

7. How does GIS work, and how do the features of GIS maps contribute to archaeological analysis?

8. How are archaeological sites named?

9. How is test pitting used in establishing the boundaries of an archaeological site?

10. What might the archaeologist conclude when the number of artifacts found in the test pits located along a transect has declined to zero? What would be the problems with such a conclusion?

11. Suppose, based on the inspiring words of this book, you decided that you wanted to participate in an archaeological dig? Would you be able to do it, even though you have no experience? What are the formats available for participation by nonprofessional archaeologists in archaeological research?

## Excavation and Analysis: Revealing the Past

In the New Testament of the Christian Bible, in the Book of First Corinthians, is a phrase that conveys the difficulty we human beings have in understanding the meaning of our own existence: "For now, we see through a glass, darkly. . . ." In our investigation of the ancient past, archaeologists are usually faced with the same problem. Our goal is to understand ways of life that preceded our own. Often we must attempt to accomplish this goal based on the recovery and examination of a mere handful of objects made and lost long ago. We are, in fact, peering at the past "through a glass, darkly," trying to bring into focus long ago events that have projected often indistinct images into the present.

These indistinct images of past events, activities, patterns, and processes are brought into sharper focus for the archaeologist by recovery and analysis of the physical objects left behind by ancient people. In the process of digging the Wood Lily site, we found the remnants of objects that the people who lived there made, used, used up, broke, lost, discarded, secreted away for safekeeping, forgot about, and so on (Figure 8.1). We found and then carefully recovered those objects through the process of archaeological **excavation.**

At the same time that people were making, using, losing, and

**FIGURE 8.1** A quartz knife photographed in situ, in its exact place of discovery at the Wood Lily site. (*Kenneth L. Feder*)

**FIGURE 8.2** Charred seeds recovered in the Wood Lily excavation. (*Kenneth L. Feder*)

discarding objects that were becoming part of the archaeological record, nature was depositing material at archaeological sites, leaving evidence of the environment of the time period the site was occupied.

Seeds from plants growing in the vicinity, snail shells, insect parts, rodent bones, and **pollen** may become incorporated into the same matrix as archaeological artifacts and ecofacts. The vegetation that produced the seeds, the snails that left behind the shells, the insects and rodents that died, and the plants that rained their pollen down over the site all were part of the environment to which ancient human inhabitants adapted (Figure 8.2). The presence of this natural evidence allows us to reconstruct a past environment.

We worked at Wood Lily, in a sense, in the manner of detectives, collecting the physical evidence left behind by the people who lived at the site. In excavation we take enormous care in removing all of the material that has covered over the site.

Archaeologists excavate slowly and methodically, removing the overburden of soil that has built up over and around the objects that people, mostly unintentionally, left behind. Then, perhaps a bit ironically, we take the site apart, bit by bit (essentially destroying it in order to remove the remains), and take our finds to a laboratory for analysis. Surely you have noticed in television police dramas how, before the dead body is taken to the morgue, before the blood stains are recovered for analysis, and before weapons are dropped into evidence bags, a crime scene photographer takes an abundance of photographs, essentially preserving the crime scene in the form of those two-dimensional images. Archaeologists also take lots of photographs (Figure 8.3) and make lots of spatial measurements and draw lots of maps (Figure 8.4), all in an attempt to preserve the three-dimensional spatial data of an archaeological site that we need to take apart in order to study further. If we are clever enough and—it is not inaccurate to characterize it in this way—obsessive enough in our recording of a site's spatial data, we can put it back together again to examine it more closely.

**FIGURE 8.3** Photo of in situ artifact. (*Kenneth L. Feder*)

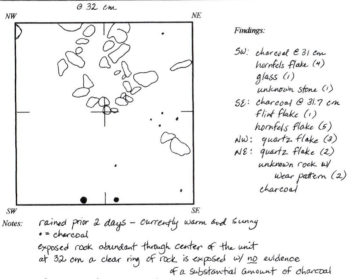

Archaeology Field School - Summer 2003

**Site Location:** Firetown Meadow

**Excavation Unit:** S6 E9

**Level:** 29-32 cm

**Date:** 6/16/03 & 6/17/03

@ 32 cm.

NW          NE

SW          SE

*Findings:*

SW: charcoal @ 31 cm
    hornfels flake (4)
    glass (1)
    unknown stone (1)

SE: charcoal @ 31.7 cm
    flint flake (1)
    hornfels flake (5)

NW: quartz flake (3)

NE: quartz flake (2)
    unknown rock w/
      wear pattern (2)
    charcoal

*Notes:* rained prior 2 days - currently warm and sunny
• = charcoal
exposed rock abundant through center of the unit
at 32 cm a clear ring of rock is exposed w/ <u>no</u> evidence
          of a substantial amount of charcoal
A horizon throughout unit
Diagram shows rock location

**FIGURE 8.4** Map of in situ artifacts.

# Why Do Archaeologists Want to Know about Ancient Environments and How Do They Do It?

Everybody in my family sneezes. Lots. We all are afflicted by respiratory allergies; my wife and both of our children have asthma. I am just allergic. My allergies first emerged when I was a teenager. I was tested and reacted positively to animal dander, dust, grass, and all manner of tree pollen. Essentially, I am allergic to air. My wife began sneezing and wheezing when she was in her twenties and at this point I think she has a closer relationship with her inhaler than she has with most people. Both of our kids are mucous factories and are on medication year-round to prevent the wheezing, sneezing, itchy eyes, and general misery that comes with the territory of respiratory allergies. Though all four of us exhibit allergy symptoms year-round, we suffer the most in the spring. Around our house, there's no need to check the local news for the pollen count; you can come up with a pretty accurate estimate just by looking at our red, sore eyes and by counting the sneezes.

Pollen grains serve a purpose beyond making us miserable; they are the male gametes in plant sexual reproduction. In other words, each pollen grain is the equivalent of a sperm cell, a tiny package with half the genetic instructions necessary to produce the next generation of a species of plant. There are two features of pollen grains that make them especially useful in **paleoenvironmental** reconstruction and, therefore, to archaeologists who hope to understand the environmental context within which a past people developed a way of life. First, under certain depositional conditions, pollen grains can survive for a very long period of time. Pollen grains have been recovered that are hundreds, thousands, and even tens of thousands of years old. Unlike bark, seeds, roots, fruits, wood, and leaves, which decay to dust in a short period of time under most circumstances, pollen is far more likely to survive. In fact, some of the pollen that was produced by trees, bushes, and grasses during the time when an archaeological site was a village of people and that rained down upon middens, trash dumps, and nearby wetlands (where pollen preserves particularly well) can be recovered and analyzed by field scientists long after the trees, bushes, and grasses that produced the pollen have long since decayed away.

The other key feature of pollen is its species-specific appearance. The pollen grains produced by each species are distinguishable in appearance from those produced by every other plant species (Figure 8.5). By studying the morphology of pollen, scientists called **palynologists**—I know, it would be easier to remember if they were called pollenologists, but that's the way it goes—become adept at recognizing the pollen grains of a large array of plant species.

What this all means for site study is that when pollen has preserved and been recovered at or adjacent to an archaeological site from a soil layer that is contemporaneous with the site's occupation, we can begin to put together a list of the plants the site's former inhabitants encountered in their territory and had available for exploitation: to eat, make containers, weave mats, build houses, make rope, burn for fuel, and so on. Beyond simply putting together a list of plant resources in an area during a particular time period, such information may be a preliminary step in reconstructing the overall environment, especially the climate of an area when a site was occupied. Many plant species have a relatively narrow range of acceptable environmental conditions in which they can survive. The presence of a plant species in a place where it cannot now grow—because the current conditions are too hot or too cold, too dry or too wet—is a good indicator that the climate was different when the site was occupied.

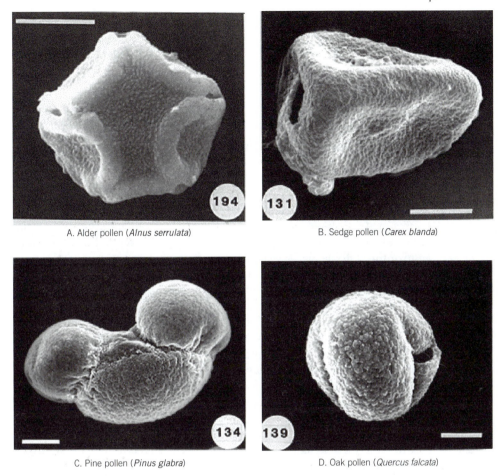

A. Alder pollen (*Alnus serrulata*)

B. Sedge pollen (*Carex blanda*)

C. Pine pollen (*Pinus glabra*)

D. Oak pollen (*Quercus falcata*)

**FIGURE 8.5** Examples of pollen grains: (A) Alder (*Alnus serrulata*), (B) Sedge (*Carex blanda*), (C) Pirie (*Pinus glabra*), and (D) Oak (*Quercus falcata*). (*Courtesy of Gretchen D. Jones, USDA-ARS, APMRU*)

A far more detailed picture of an ancient climate can be constructed, not by simply putting together a species list from pollen grains recovered in a cultural layer in a stratigraphic sequence, but by producing a **pollen profile** in which the actual percentages of recovered pollen grains are calculated for a succession of time periods. Of course, it would be great if these pollen percentages could be neatly and directly translated into species percentages—for example, if 30% of the pollen found falling on a site during a given period was that of pine trees, it would mean that 30% of the vegetation in the vicinity of a site was pine trees—but it doesn't work out that way. Some species produce proportionally larger amounts of pollen than others (pine is one of them) and the pollen of some species is more aerodynamic and flies farther when airborne (pine again). In fact, pine pollen may show up in a given place, even though there are no pine trees in the immediate vicinity, simply because pine trees produce an over-abundance of pollen that can travel great distances on the wind. The percentage of pollen at a given place, therefore, is not simply the result of the abundance of the species, but a complex interplay of factors. Species abundance (what we need to assess to reconstruct a local plant community and an ancient environment) is only one factor in the equation.

Brilliant solutions to scientific quandaries often rely on elegant work-arounds. Palynologists, especially Margaret Davis of Yale, devised a brilliant, simple, and elegant solution to the pollen problem. Instead of attempting to come up with a complex and convoluted way to convert pollen percentages to actual tree or plant percentages directly, Davis (1969a, b) simply took the pollen percentages recovered from ancient strata and compared those figures to the percentages of pollen raining in various locations *today*. Palynologists have calculated modern pollen percentages the same way they figure the pollen count announced on the evening news, using sticky tape to capture modern pollen floating through the air. Where the pollen percentages in the modern and ancient samples were similar, Davis concluded that the ancient and modern plant communities were similar and, therefore, the ancient climate was similar to the modern location with a similar pollen profile.

For example, Davis collected a series of soil cores from the bottom of Roger's Lake in southeastern Connecticut. She recognized a number of natural strata in the cores and determined their ages by radiocarbon dating organic material that had preserved in the respective layers of the soil column. Davis then recovered pollen from each of the column's strata and counted the grains, deriving the percentages of pollen for a bunch of different species in each of the strata in the core, which she then depicted in a graph (Figure 8.6). With these percentages in hand, Davis searched for areas in eastern North America (where Roger's Lake is located) where the modern pollen percentages appeared to be most similar to those she calculated for each of the ancient, dated strata.

The **pollen rain** falling on Roger's Lake around fourteen thousand years ago doesn't match up at all with the modern rain falling at its location today. In fact, today one would have to go far to the north, about as far north as you can go in Arctic Canada, to find a plant community producing a mix of pollen percentages similar to what was falling on Roger's Lake and vicinity fourteen thousand years ago. In the twelve-thousand-year-old stratum from the Roger's Lake core, a mix of pollen percentages was derived that closely matches the profile that today falls in the central region of the east shore of Hudson's Bay. From the ten-thousand-year level in the Roger's Lake core, a mix of pollen was falling that is similar to what today is found around Lake Ontario. It wasn't until the eight-thousand-year-old level that Davis found a mix of pollen similar to what was falling on Roger's Lake in modern times, if we define modern times as about A.D. 1600, before Europeans entered the region, cleared huge swaths of Connecticut's forests, and introduced new plants and crops to the area. Yes, humans too have an impact on the plant communities of a region, and the pollen profile is just one example.

What would it have been like to live in southeastern Connecticut fourteen thousand years ago? What was the weather like? What kinds of plants were

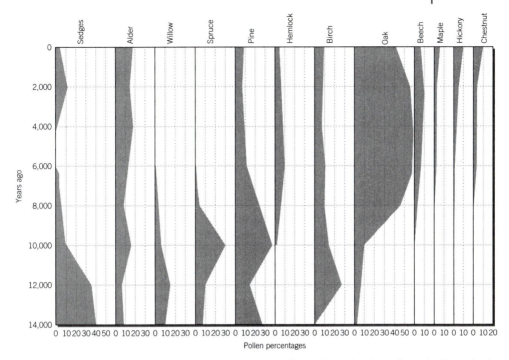

**FIGURE 8.6** The pollen profile at Roger's Lake, southeastern Connecticut, showing a dramatic change in the local plant communities over the last fourteen thousand years. (*Kenneth L. Feder*)

growing? How long were the various seasons? How much did it snow? What animals would have been attracted to the conditions that characterized the area? A visit to the Arctic coast of northeastern Canada would provide the best model for southeast Connecticut fifteen millennia ago. How about twelve thousand years ago? According to pollen analysis, we can begin to answer this question by traveling north to the east shore of Hudson's Bay and examining current conditions there. And ten thousand years ago? The north shore of Lake Ontario provides the best analog to answer our questions.

Remember, the environment, including the climate as well as the plant and animal communities that characterize a location, provides the context for a human adaptation. The environment cannot cause people to behave in a certain way, but it certainly produces limits and possibilities. If we hope to understand the cultural adaptation of a past people, we need to illuminate the setting of that adaptation; we need to understand the conditions to which a past people adapted. So understanding an ancient environment is crucial to our understanding of an ancient culture.

Palynology is an important tool in this effort. Pollen analysis can provide archaeologists with a detailed picture of the plant community with which an ancient human community interacted, along with insights into the nature of the climate that defined the plant community and to which human groups developed cultural adaptations.

## Read More

To find out more about the procedures of pollen recovery and analysis, and for the examples of Margaret Davis's work in Connecticut, see the following sources:

Bryant Jr., V. M., and R. G. Holloway. 1983. The role of palynology in archaeology. In *Advances in Archaeological Method and Theory*, edited by M. B. Schiffer, 191–224. Academic Press, New York.

Davis, M. B. 1969a. Climatic changes in southern Connecticut recorded by pollen deposition at Rogers Lake. *Ecology* 50:409–22.

———. 1969b. Palynology and environmental history during the Quaternary period. *American Scientist* 57:317–32.

Dimbleby, G. W. 1985. *The Palynology of Archaeological Sites*. Academic Press, London.

Holloway, R. G. 1997. Excavation and recovery of botanical materials from archaeological sites. In *Field Methods in Archaeology*, edited by T. R. Hester, H. J. Shafer, and K. L. Feder, 283–97. Mayfield Publishing, Mountain View, California.

Pearsall, D. M. 2000. *Paleoethnobotany: A Handbook of Procedures*. Academic Press, San Diego.

 ## How Is Archaeological Research Like Detective Work?

Archaeological excavation has been likened to the work of a detective. Like all such analogies, it is imperfect, but we can make some useful comparisons between detective work and archaeology. A detective usually arrives at the scene after the crime has been committed. Based on physical evidence that remains at the scene—bullets from a gun, a knife blade, a jimmied lock, a broken window, blood spatters, footprints, fingerprints, even a dead body—a detective attempts to reconstruct the sequence of events that surrounded the commission of the crime. Determining the nature of the crime, when it occured, how it was carried out, "whodunnit," and the motive are all issues a detective attempts to resolve based, at least in part, on the physical evidence left behind and recovered at the scene. If our hypothetical detective were in the board game *Clue*, his or her goal might be to determine that Professor Plum committed the crime in the kitchen with the pipe wrench.

At the Wood Lily site, we conducted our work, not at the scene of a crime but at the scene of a life. Our job was to reconstruct, not necessarily a particular event (though there are many individual events we can reconstruct there), but a series of events that transpired during the time the place was occupied and used by human beings. Like detectives, archaeologists search for physical evidence to reconstruct what transpired at a particular place. In a general sense, we ask and attempt to answer many of the same questions a detective might in solving a crime: What was the nature, not of the crime, but of the lives lived by the people at this place? When was this place occupied? How did the people conduct themselves here? Who were these people? Why did they live here and why did they live as they did? Also like detectives, the raw data archaeologists use in our effort to answer these questions consists of the physical evidence unintentionally left behind by the people whose lives we are hoping to understand.

Continuing the detective analogy: you may be familiar with the French detective Hercule Poirot, the literary invention of the famous mystery novelist Agatha Christie. He's not as famous as Sir Arthur Conan Doyle's Sherlock Holmes or even Christie's other crime solver, Miss Marple, but he's a terrific character nonetheless. Poirot's catchphrase when encountering a crime scene, spoken in his thickly accented English, is "Touch nothing." It is of the utmost importance at a crime scene not to disturb anything, not to contaminate any evidence, not to destroy or lose any of the often subtle clues that might enable the solution of a crime. The importance of "touching nothing" is similar when excavating an archaeological site. Crucial evidence at a site might consist of a barest whisper of pollen, the tiniest flecks of charcoal, the most delicate fragments of bone, or invisible residues of blood on a stone knife. It would be supremely ironic if, in our attempt to find and recover the evidence of past lives at a site, we destroyed that same evidence through lack of care. As detectives of the past, archaeologists make every effort to salvage every scrap of evidence that might inform us of the lives lived at the sites we study.

## How Do Archaeologists Excavate Sites?

You know the old joke that asks the question: "How should you react when encountering an angry grizzly bear?" "Very carefully," is the response spoken only half in jest. The same answer, again only half jokingly, applies to the question posed by the title of this segment: How do archaeologists excavate sites? Indeed, very carefully (Hester 1997a; Stewart 2002).

It is one of the great ironies of archaeological research that we seek out places where the material remains of past human activity have nearly miraculously escaped destruction and dismemberment through natural processes and modern development and, once found, we dig them up and, in so doing, destroy those preserved places.

It is important to understand that sites are not just accumulations of artifacts and ecofacts. Sites are the archaeological manifestations of once-living communities of people. Sites consist of all the artifacts and ecofacts as well as all of the space between them. Remember our discussion of how archaeological sites are formed. Sites come into existence by people losing, discarding, caching, and abandoning material *at particular places* (within their village, hunting camp, farmstead, quarry, mill, cemetery, and so on). The particular places where those deposited objects can be found by the archaeologist often are the places where people carried out tasks: where they made spear points or pottery; where they hunted and butchered animals; where they cooked their food or conducted religious ceremonies; where they spilled their blood in pitched battles fought for reasons we can never know; where they ground grain between massive millwheels, prepared wool for spinning, or milled enormous trees into lumber; where they extracted clay for the manufacture of ceramics; played games; or simply threw stuff away. The fact that a particular object can be found at a particular place, and in spatial association with other objects at an archaeological site, informs us about what transpired at that place within what was a community of people.

Certainly, the last thing we want to do as archaeologists (who hope to figure out what went on in a community by examining the site produced by the

*Firetown*

behavior of the inhabitants) is to destroy this vital spatial component of the evidence. I have already likened archaeology to detective work. Detectives are not merely interested in collecting individual items. A collection of disconnected bits of evidence tells only part of the story of what transpired at a crime scene. Detectives need to know the precise location where each item (bullet casings, glass shards, footprints) was found and their **spatial associations** (which bits of evidence were found together). A bag filled with bullets is only partially informative. A detailed map showing where each bullet was found—specifically in relation to each other bullet, to shattered windows, footprints, and the dead body—along with the bullets themselves (which can be analyzed in a laboratory to determine if they all came from the same gun, if any show traces of blood, and so on) allows for a far more detailed, precise, and accurate reconstruction of the scene than do the bullets alone (Figure 8.7).

Consider an intact, carefully preserved crime scene where everything has been left in place. The mapped locations of the bullets can used to determine the trajectory of the projectiles. Those trajectories can then be traced back to their source and the detective can pinpoint the location from which the shots were fired. That spot, once identified, can be investigated for additional clues that will contribute to the solution of the crime. Compare that intact

**FIGURE 8.7** A detailed analysis of the location of artifacts found in a surface investigation of the place where the Battle of the Little Big Horn was fought has provided researchers with fresh insights into the flow of the battle between Custer and his Seventh Cavalry and the Sioux and associated tribes who defeated him. (*Courtesy Doug Scott*)

and carefully examined crime scene to a bag of bullets collected at the site with no spatial data. If you were a detective, which scenario would you prefer?

Just as a detective must collect all of the individual bits of evidence and return these items to a laboratory for detailed analysis, archaeologists must do the same. And just as detectives must preserve all of the spatial data encoded in those bits of evidence—what material was found where—to thoroughly reconstruct what happened at a crime scene, archaeologists must preserve the spatial data of a site—what artifacts and ecofacts were found where—by careful data recovery and recordkeeping. By accurately and thoroughly mapping the locations of artifacts and ecofacts, we can, in a sense, preserve the three-dimensional (location and depth) data necessary to preserve the spatial organization of a site even as we dismantle it to study its individual components.

## Read More

Archaeologists spend a lot of time agonizing about excavation; how to preserve as much of the information presented at an archaeological site as possible, recognizing that excavation itself can be a destructive process. As a result, an enormous number of publications focus on the problems and challenges of the process of excavation. For three of the best broad and nearly inclusive summaries, see the following resources:

Dancey, W. S. 1981. *Archaeological Field Methods: An Introduction*. Burgess International Group, New York.
Hester, T. R. 1997a. Methods of excavation. In *Field Methods in Archaeology*, edited by T. R. Hester, H. J. Shafer, and K. L. Feder, 69–112. Mayfield Publishing, Mountain View, California.
Stewart, R. M. 2002. *Archaeology: Basic Field Methods*. Kendall/Hunt Publishing, Dubuque, Iowa.

## How Do Archaeologists Keep Track of Where Stuff Is Found at Sites?

We sometimes say in archaeology that through our work we hope to paint a picture of an ancient way of life. It's not a great metaphor, but it does convey a reasonably accurate impression of at least one of the things we hope to accomplish by excavating and analyzing archaeological sites.

Do you remember from art history the pointillism method of producing paintings by placing a series of very short brushstrokes or "points" of paint on a canvas? This interesting method has resulted in some terrific paintings. Georges Seurat is one of the best known pointillists and when you stand back far enough to view his paintings (for example, *Sunday Afternoon on the Island of the Grande Jatte*), the individual points of color seamlessly blend together to convey uniquely beautiful images of Seurat's nineteenth-century France.

Suppose we wanted to study one of Seurat's paintings and further suppose that to do so we simply collected all of the dots of paint from the canvas, removing them from the painting and analyzing them individually. We might learn a lot about the paint Seurat used, but we would never know what the painting looked like, what scene or people the painter depicted. In our desire to study the painting we would have destroyed the story told by the painter.

Suppose now that we still were obliged to remove all of the points of paint from a canvas to study the paint, the canvas, and the technology used to apply the paint to the canvas, but we also hoped to examine and understand the message conveyed by the painter. As we took it apart, piece by piece, paint-point by paint-point, we would need to keep an absolutely accurate and thorough record of where each and every paint-point originated, map them precisely, and then re-create the image in order to study it.

We don't ordinarily need to do this to a painting, but we almost always need to do it for an archaeological site. We usually cannot just leave a site as is. We need to expose it and then remove its individual elements to study and preserve them. In order to preserve the story of a way of life told by the blending of the "brushstrokes" (the artifacts, ecofacts, and features), we must make accurate measurements of their locations. This enables us to put the image back together and tell the story of the life lived by a people at a particular place and time.

The exact location of an artifact, ecofact, or feature is called its **provenience.** When an artifact or ecofact is encountered, it is left in place so that its location can be measured. Large artifacts, ecofacts, and especially features will have a series of locational points measured to provide an outline of their locations that can then be transferred to a map. These locations first may be measured relative to the southwest corner of the excavation unit it which the items were found (used traditionally as the point from which all material found in a unit is measured; see Unit 9). Like all corners of all excavation units at a site, every southwest corner is named and labeled relative to the overall site datum (Figure 8.8).

A measurement relative to the southwest corner provides a measurement for everything found in every excavation unit at a site relative to a single, common fixed point, the **datum** of the site. With all of these locations mapped in, the archaeologist can produce a detailed and accurate map of the locations of artifacts, ecofacts, and features relative to the site datum and, importantly, relative to all other artifacts, ecofacts, and features found at the site.

**FIGURE 8.8** Archaeological excavation unit. (*Kenneth L. Feder*)

Remember that a site is not just a two-dimensional entity. On the one hand, a site occupied for a very short period of time may be represented by a thin layer of material all at the same approximate depth from the modern surface. On the other hand, a site occupied for an extended period—with material slowly accumulated underfoot over years, decades, and even centuries—may be found in a thick band of cultural material of varying depths from the surface. It is not enough, therefore, to take only a two-dimensional reading of the location of an artifact, ecofact, or feature. We also need to measure the depths from which material was recovered in order to place these items in their proper **stratigraphic** context.

One low-tech way of accomplishing this measurement involves the use of a carpenter's bubble level. The level is hung from a string attached to the stake marking the southwest corner of an excavation unit. When pulled taut over the unit and with the bubble centered, that string defines a fixed plane from which we can take depth measurements (Figure 8.9). A tape measure or carpenter's rule held vertically is used to measure the depth of an occupation level or the surface on which an artifact or ecofact rests, relative to the string. The height of all of the strings in each of the excavation units can be determined relative to the elevation of the datum point, enabling the determination of a fixed depth of all archaeological material recovered at the site.

A "medium-tech" way of accomplishing depth measurement involves the use of one of a number of surveying devices, for example, an **alidade**

**FIGURE 8.9** Use of a decidedly low-tech piece of equipment, a carpenter's suspended bubble level, to measure the depth of an excavation unit and to maintain a flat excavation surface. (*Kenneth L. Feder*)

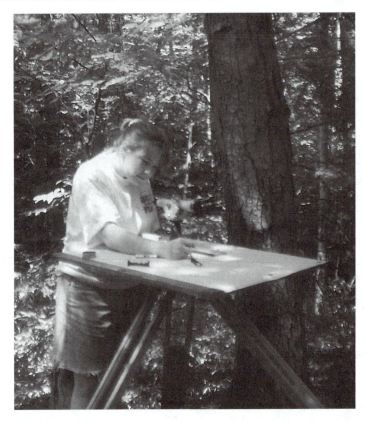

**FIGURE 8.10** The plane table is leveled on top of a tripod and the alidade is placed on the table. The precise height of the crosshairs in the alidade lens is measured and the depth of artifacts can be measured relative to those crosshairs. (*Kenneth L. Feder*)

(Figure 8.10). An alidade is essentially a telescope with crosshairs, mounted on a flat base that can be positioned on a **plane table.**

When the plane table is leveled on a tripod located, for example, directly over datum, the precise height of the crosshairs in the center of the telescope site can be measured (how high the alidade sits over the surface at the site datum). A **stadia rod,** which is essentially a long, rigid ruler, is then placed at the spot where depth or elevation needs measuring. The line of sight of someone looking through the alidade to the gradation on the stadia rod represents a precise measurement of the depth of the surface on which the rod is resting relative to the height of the alidade's crosshairs. Subtracting the measured height of the alidade above the point where it is located from the measurement read on the stadia rod reveals the actual depth of the surface the rod is resting on from the surface under the alidade, which, in this case, is the site datum. The depth of everything so measured at a site can be determined relative to datum. When the site is so large that the alidade must be moved away from datum, as long as the elevation of the point it is being moved to is measured first, all subsequent elevation or depth measurements can be tied back in to the site datum. A higher-tech method involves the use of a more expensive piece of equipment called a **total station,** which includes as its heart a **laser transit,** a device you likely have seen highway engineers use. The laser transit sits on a tripod and looks a bit like those mounted binocular sighting devices you find at scenic overlooks (Figure 8.11).

As in work with the alidade, a fieldworker places a stadia rod on the spot whose depth is being measured. Unlike work with the alidade, instead of actually looking though the transit to obtain a measurement, the device itself sends out a beam of laser light that bounces off the rod and returns to the transit receiver where the precise gradation intersected by the light can be recorded and the exact distance from the transit to the stadia rod can be calculated. These measurements can be automatically adjusted for the height of the transit, stored in the transit's memory, and downloaded to a computer where any one of a number of mapping programs can produce a map showing the natural topography of a site, the positioning of the excavation units, and the locations and depths of every artifact, ecofact, and feature encountered in the excavation. It sounds cool, and it is.

**FIGURE 8.11** A total station is the most accurate of the methods discussed here for mapping the locations and depths of archaeological materials. (*Kenneth L. Feder*)

## Read More

Keeping track of where stuff is found at a site can be time consuming and tedious, but it is extremely important. We can begin the process of recording the location of discovery of archaeological materials by dividing a site into excavation units. For a discussion of mapping the precise location of archaeological material within the established analytical units within the grid, refer to any of the following resources. See especially McPherron and Dibble for the use of laser transits.

Dancey, W. S. 1981. *Archaeological Field Methods: An Introduction.* Burgess International Group, New York.

Feder, K. L. 1997a. Data preservation: Recording and collecting. In *Field Methods in Archaeology,* edited by T. R. Hester, H. J. Shafer, and K. L. Feder. Mayfield Publishing, Mountain View, California.

Knapton, L. K. 1997. Archaeological mapping, site grids, and surveying. In *Field Methods in Archaeology,* edited by T. R. Hester, H. Shafer, and K. L. Feder, 177–234. Mayfield Publishing, Mountain View, California.

McPherron, S. P., and H. L. Dibble. 2002. *Using Computers in Archaeology.* McGraw-Hill, New York.

Stewart, R. M. 2002. *Archaeology: Basic Field Methods.* Kendall/Hunt Publishing, Dubuque, Iowa.

Winans, M. C., and R. C. Winans. 1993. Measuring systems, techniques, and equipment for taphonomic studies. In *Practical Archaeology: Field and Laboratory Techniques and Archaeological Logistics,* edited by B. D. Dillon, 33–38. Institute of Archaeology, Los Angeles.

## Study Questions

1. I use the image of a detective working at the scene of a crime as an analogy for the archaeologist working "at the scene of a life." Explain that metaphor—how is archaeology like detective work?

2. What is the purpose of environmental reconstruction? Remembering that human beings adapt to their environments, why do archaeologists want to know about the environments of the past?

3. What is pollen? How can pollen be used to reconstruct the plant communities that flourished at a particular place in antiquity?

4. What is a pollen profile?

5. Can pollen percentages recovered at or near to an ancient archaeological site be used to directly determine the percentages of various species of plants growing nearby? (I'll give you a hint: No.) Why not?

6. How did Margaret Davis use the pollen percentages she calculated for an ancient time period in the reconstruction of an ancient environment?

7. The pollen rain at Roger's Lake in southeastern Connecticut changed drastically after A.D. 1600, even though there is no evidence of a significant climate change at this time. What else might explain the change in the pollen rain at Roger's Lake at the cusp of the seventeenth century?

8. What does an archaeologist mean by "spatial association"? What might the close spatial associations of objects at an archaeological site tell us about human behavior that produced such a spatial distribution?

9. I hand you a bag of ten stone artifacts. You analyze them. I present you with those same ten artifacts, this time laid out in the exact locations where people left them a thousand years ago. What information is lacking in the first scenario that can be recovered in the second?

10. What is the provenience of an artifact?

11. What are the three dimensions of an in situ artifact?

12. How is the horizontal component of an artifact's provenience measured?

13. How is the vertical component of an artifact's provenience measured? What different tools are commonly used?

### Excavating Wood Lily

Somewhere in the back of your mind, you probably have an image of the vanishing Cheshire Cat from Lewis Carroll's *Alice in Wonderland.* Perhaps you have seen Disney's animated version of the story, where the large, disconcertingly inscrutable striped cat was played with the perfect degree of disinterest by the languid-voiced actor Sterling Holloway. One minute, the cat is lounging on the branch of a tree, chatting with Alice and then, bit by bit, piece by piece, he slowly fades into translucency, and then invisibility, until all that remains is his fading smile. Finally, even the all-knowing grin vanishes without a trace. At first, you can still hear Holloway's hypnotic voice, but that too fades out and finally nothing at all is left of the cat.

Envision that bit of animation, as the Cheshire Cat slowly fades into invisibility. Now reverse that sequence in your mind. Instead of disappearing, the Cheshire Cat bubbles forth into existence, manifesting itself first as just a smile, adding the face, the torso, legs, and finally the tail. At last, as Alice might have put it, we have a complete and "proper cat." With that reverse animation in mind, you have a nice analogy for what it is like to be an archaeologist and slowly uncover a complete artifact in the process of excavation. One of my students, Carolyn White, surely experienced this as she worked in excavation unit N25W4 on a steamy July day in 1989.

We had found lots of small, discarded fragments of chipped stone at Wood Lily. These bits of debris, called **debitage,** are largely produced in **percussion flaking,** where a **hammerstone** or antler hammer is used to detach flakes from a **core** by striking it. Interestingly, although entire, perfect specimens of tools may be more aesthetically pleasing and end up in museum displays, often we can learn more about the process of tool

**FIGURE 9.1** Two pieces of the same, nearly five-thousand-year-old spear point, found at the Alsop Meadow site in Avon, Connecticut. The point had broken, probably while it was being manufactured, and its two halves discarded, only to be recovered within several centimeters of each other in the same stratigraphic layer of the site. (*Kenneth L. Feder*)

making through analysis of discarded material: the rejects and mistakes. Errors may, in a sense, freeze a moment in time and preserve a step in the tool manufacturing process that might otherwise become obscured by subsequent steps in tool making.

During a television interview, a rather bored reporter offhandedly inquired on camera about the scientific validity of conclusions archaeologists might reach concerning people and events of long ago based simply on what amounted to their trash. At that moment, I had excavated two sections of a spear point that pretty obviously had broken during the final stages of its manufacture (Figure 9.1). I suggested to the reporter that, while it might be true that we would never know the name of the artisan who produced the broken weapon I held in my hand, I could fairly accurately guess what the tool maker had said upon accidentally snapping the spear point in two at the end of a long and exacting process of tool making. I'm not sure that's the best example of the kinds of insights we gain from the discovery of broken rather than perfect specimens, but it is, nevertheless, a good story.

Carolyn White was expecting little beyond additional debitage when she began excavating that July morning deep in the woods at the Wood Lily site. Like the reappearing Cheshire Cat who teased Alice by revealing nothing more than a toothy grin or who sometimes fully materialized in all his tubby glory, it is impossible to know, as your trowel first makes contact with an object, if the artifact will turn out to be nothing more than a tiny chip of stone no bigger than what the trowel initially exposes, which is valuable in its own right, or something quite a bit more. Exchanging her hard-edged metal trowel for a piece of soft bamboo carved into a flat blade to avoid damaging the artifact, Carolyn began the process of exposing what she presumed would be a small stone chip.

She recognized almost immediately that the piece of stone was made of flint, a favorite raw material for tool making at the Wood Lily site and virtually anywhere this rock type was available to ancient people. Flint flakes rather easily; more importantly it flakes regularly, consistently, and predictably. Finally, flint can be flaked into relatively durable, extremely thin, almost dangerously sharp edges. Striking a piece of flint with the right kind of **percussor** at the right place and at the appropriate angle produces an edge that is perfect for tools intended for cutting and piercing soft materials like animal hide and flesh.

# What Is an Excavation Unit and How Is It Labeled?

Imagine an enormous piece of graph paper laid out across a landscape and you have a pretty good idea of the way in which excavators divide an archaeological site into spatial entities called **excavation units**—but you needn't call them that in the field, where the term "squares" will suffice (Figure 9.2).

Archaeological sites vary widely in size, from just a few square meters to several square kilometers. Very small sites can be excavated in their entirety, and a human mind—even that of a mosquito-bitten overworked archaeologist—can take them in all at once. Most sites are far too large for that and need to be excavated and analyzed in manageable bites. The excavation unit is the manageable

**FIGURE 9.2** Archaeological site overlain by a site grid defining 2-meter by 2-meter excavation units. Wooden stakes have been placed firmly in ground at the corners of each unit of the grid and the lines have been defined by sturdy string nailed into the tops of the stakes. (*Kenneth L. Feder*)

bite, usually square in shape (that's why we call them "squares"). At one time, the standard size of an excavation unit was the "6-foot square": a square 6 feet long on each of its sides (there even was an instructional film about archaeological excavation called, appropriately enough, *The Six-Foot Square*). Almost all archaeologists have shifted to the metric system, which, once mastered, truly is more sensible than the English system, with much more easily convertible units, and the standard size of an excavation unit has become 2 meters on a side (an area, rather obviously, of 4 square meters). Depending on site size and conditions, a unit may be smaller or larger and may not even be a square at all but a rectangular trench. Some historical archaeologists in the United States have argued for retention of the English system of inches, feet, and yards in excavating historical sites. These researchers have a point: the features they excavate (house foundations, mill races, iron foundries, and so on) were built to specifications of the English system, so it makes sense to excavate these features using the same measurements of the system that was utilized in their construction.

Whatever the shape or precise size of an excavation unit—or the system of measurement employed—the motives for digging in regular, small-scale units are the same: the method divides the physical labor of excavating a site into manageable units and provides a framework by which the locations of all recovered materials, at least at the level of the excavation unit, can be expeditiously recorded. That framework is a site grid, the enormous, imaginary piece of graph paper mentioned at the beginning of this section.

The designator for each unit is its location on an orthogonal grid, a series of equally spaced parallel lines intersected by another set of equally spaced lines parallel to each other and perpendicular to the first set of lines (in other words, a grid with all right angles). The grid is commonly oriented north/south, east/west, although the actual orientation of the site or of the landscape to be excavated may cause this to vary. However the grid is oriented, one point on the grid where two of the perpendicular lines intersect is labeled the **datum;** on a standard graph this is called the origin, and represents the 0,0 location. Ordinarily the datum is placed at a margin of the site, or even offsite. Every location—each grid point as well as the precise positioning of each artifact, ecofact, and feature found within the site—is keyed into the location of the origin of the grid in terms of its distance to the north or south and its distance to the east or west of the datum point.

This method keys everything within the site relative to an arbitrarily designated 0,0 point, and in so doing we can then place all site locations within an absolute spatial frame of reference. The precise geographic location of datum can be calculated to great precision in terms of, for example, longitude and latitude, though more commonly exact location is measured in reference to the **Universal Transverse Mercator (UTM),** a military grid system based on the metric system and used by cartographers. In some cases, the site datum can be readily referenced to a nearby physical benchmark, a permanent marker (often of concrete), whose location has been accurately measured and recorded and that appears on maps of an area. Also, the precise location of datum can often be determined by use of a **Global Positioning System (GPS)** unit—some of which are small enough to hold in your hand—that use satellites orbiting the Earth to calculate a nearly exact location on the planet.

Each excavation unit is designated by its location on the grid relative to the datum or 0,0 point. By tradition, an excavation unit may be labeled by the coordinates of its southwest corner. For example, a 2-meter by 2-meter square unit whose four corners are demarcated by the points on the grid 20 meters north/38 meters east, 22 meters north/38 meters east, 20 meters north/40 meters east, and 22 meters north/40 meters east (all measurements north or east of datum) is most often designated: N20E38, that point being the southwest corner of the unit. When artifacts or ecofacts are found in a unit, they are bagged together when removed from the soil and the bag is clearly marked with the unit designation along with the stratigraphic slice or the depth from which the material in the bag was recovered. In this way, though the archaeologist has removed the specimens from their position in situ, the location and depth of their recovery has been recorded and preserved.

## Read More

The crucial task of recording where objects are found at a site can be time consuming and tedious. We begin the process of recording locations by dividing a site into excavation units. For a discussion of the process of laying out a site grid and labeling individual analytical units, see the following sources:

Dancey, W. S. 1981. *Archaeological Field Methods: An Introduction.* Burgess International Group, New York.

Feder, K. L. 1997a. Data preservation: Recording and collecting. In *Field Methods in Archaeology,* edited by T. R. Hester, H. J. Shafer, and K. L. Feder, 113–42. Mayfield Publishing, Mountain View, California.

Knapton, L. K. 1997. Archaeological mapping, site grids, and surveying. In *Field Methods in Archaeology,* edited by T. R. Hester, H. J. Shafer, and K. L. Feder, 177–234. Mayfield Publishing, Mountain View, California.

Stewart, R. M. 2002. *Archaeology: Basic Field Methods.* Kendall/Hunt Publishing, Dubuque, Iowa.

 # Why Do Archaeologists Save All the Tiny Scraps of Stone, Bone, and Other Stuff?

Archaeologists can fairly be characterized as packrats. As a group, we can be awfully obsessive about recovering, saving, and taking back to the lab every tiny scrap that might conceivably be the result of human activity in the past. I have, on occasion, wondered to myself when taking an inordinate amount of time to recover some tiny bits of animal bone or burned nut fragments or stone flakes, what the ancient people would think if they could see this grown person so zealously, almost fanatically, picking up tiny, seemingly insignificant pieces of what they would perceive as their garbage. It is important to remember that much of what archaeologists so laboriously and compulsively recover is, after all, stuff ancient people thought so little of that they threw it away.

Remember from our earlier discussion that archaeology is not a treasure hunt. Our goal is not to find beautiful objects reflecting a level of artistic skill that we can appreciate today, although it sometimes happens. Our ultimate goal is far broader than the illumination of the aesthetic sensibilities and artistic abilities of ancient human beings: we strive to find out as much as we can about a past way of life and it turns out that the trash people discard provides us with an enormous amount of valuable information that can enable us to reach our goal. Small fragments of bone, little bits of charred seeds, and pieces of shell, corn cobs, squash rind provide significant information about the diet of a group of people.

Even the tiniest flakes of stone removed from a tool to sharpen its edge, shattered bits of a hammerstone, and broken stone preforms resulting from mistakes in the tool making process can illuminate the technology employed by a people to produce the tools necessary for their subsistence. Pieces of pottery smaller than your thumbnail may allow us to reconstruct the type of kiln an ancient people used to fire their ceramics. Even the bodily wastes of people—yes, their feces—in those rare instances when they have preserved, are a treasure trove of information about the diet, disease, and the overall health of the people who deposited these particular ecofacts.

Nearly thirty years after I learned field methods, I now pass along to my own field school students an object lesson I learned. Back in 1972, we students each spent at least one entire day in the lab along with a grad student whose job it was to process the material brought to the facility on each previous day. The grad student first ran us through the procedures employed in the project related to cleaning and inventorying artifacts and ecofacts by laying out some material recovered at the site that had already been processed. When we came to some admittedly small flakes of quartz, one of the other students working in the lab that day—it wasn't me, I swear—said something like: "Oh, are those the things we should be keeping? I found lots but just threw them away. . . ." Ouch. To be sure, there was a large pile of stones discarded behind the lab building, objects that had been brought back from the site and that turned out to be nothing more than rocks, collected a bit overzealously by inexperienced diggers fearful of discarding anything that could be significant. But that's okay. Material collected during excavation that turns out to be noncultural, just rocks or modern seeds or fresh bone, can always be discarded. However, it is far more difficult to re-recover important data from the **backdirt,** the sifted soil piled in mounds adjacent to an excavation unit.

There is a remarkable story encoded into even the humblest of archaeological specimens. The collection of data, not pretty objects, is the goal of archaeological fieldwork and nothing should be overlooked in our desire to illuminate the lives of a past group of people.

# Read More

For a discussion of the reasons for the archaeologist's obsession with recovering all available evidence at a site, see any of the following books or chapters about archaeological methodology:

Baker, B. W., B. S. Shaffer, and D. G. Steele. 1997. Basic approaches in archaeological faunal analysis. In *Field Methods in Archaeology*, edited by T. R. Hester, H. J. Shafer, and K. L. Feder, 298–318. Mayfield Publishing, Mountain View, California.

Dancey, W. S. 1981. *Archaeological Field Methods: An Introduction*. Burgess International Group, New York.

Hester, T. R. 1997b. The handling and conservation of artifacts in the field. In *Field Methods in Archaeology*, edited by T. R. Hester, H. J. Shafer, and K. L. Feder, 143–58. Mayfield Publishing, Mountain View, California.

Holloway, R. G. 1997. Excavation and recovery of botanical materials from archaeological sites. In *Field Methods in Archaeology*, edited by T. R. Hester, H. J. Shafer, and K. L. Feder, 283–97. Mayfield Publishing, Mountain View, California.

Stewart, R. M. 2002. *Archaeology: Basic Field Methods*. Kendall/Hunt Publishing, Dubuque, Iowa.

## How Can You Identify Tree Species from Bits of Burned Wood?

It can be hard enough distinguishing one tree from another when walking around in a living forest. I do okay, at least in the spring and summer, when the trees in the mixed deciduous forest of southern New England where I live and work are decked out in their leafy finery. Maple, oak, birch, and hickory all produce leaves that are distinct and easy to identify after a little practice. Among the conifers, hemlocks are easily differentiated from pine, which is easy to discriminate from spruce, which is nothing like larch.

Come fall, however, things get a lot more challenging for me. The conifers are still pretty easy, but once I get past white birch with its uniquely colored bark, I am pretty much clueless when it comes to separating out the deciduous trees. Without their leaves, I am lost. Now imagine how incredibly more complicated this process of tree identification becomes when we have no leaves or bark, in fact, no living trees at all, but just little fragments of wood and, on top of this, these little pieces of wood have preserved only because they have been burned.

In fact, however, the wood produced by individual genera and sometimes individual species of trees certainly is distinguishable, especially in terms of its microstructure. With the use of reference slides, specimen collections, and photomicrographs, analysts can identify tree species even from small burned fragments (McWeeney 2002).

For example, burned wood samples recovered from the occupation surfaces of two sites we excavated in the past few years were provided to our botanical specialist, Dr. Cindy McWeeney. McWeeny was able to identify the wood of chestnut, oak, and hickory from two sites dating to more than a thousand years ago (Figure 9.3). Because we know that these were not the only three tree species growing in southern New England at the time, we can

**FIGURE 9.3** Cross-section of a sample of oak charcoal exhibiting morphological characteristics diagnostic of wood derived from the genus *Quercus* (oak). (*Courtesy of Cindy McWeeney*)

suggest that the presence of just these three species in the charcoal assemblage resulted from a conscious decision on the part of the ancient inhabitants of the sites. They were selecting, in fact, three tree species that are known to produce a high, even, and steady output of heat. In fact, those of us who use wood to heat our houses know that hardwoods are much better for their steady heat output (and their lower production of creosote to gum up our chimneys).

Identifying the species of trees whose wood was used as fuel in a hearth, fireplace, or kiln provides us with a glimpse into the makeup of a forest in which a past people lived or which they traveled to for its resources. Knowing the tree species selected by a past people also provides insights into their behavior, offering a glimpse into their uses of the resources in their environment.

## Read More

The following guide is a standard for identifying wood remains:

Hoadley, R. B. 1990. *Identifying Wood: Accurate Results with Simple Tools.* The Taunton Press, Newtown, Connecticut.

 ## What Tools Do Archaeologists Use to Expose and Recover Artifacts?

Whenever you see archaeologists on a television drama or in a movie, they're forever using whisk brooms and dustpans to extract the dust of the ages from the precious artifacts that will enable them to solve the vexing mysteries of human antiquity. Something like that. Well, to be honest, I hardly ever use a whisk broom. Here in the forests of southern New England, the soil is mostly moist and rocky and whisk brooms aren't very effective; they just get clogged up and heavily laden with mud. Some of my colleagues, however, swear by whisk brooms, but even they will admit that the most valuable tool in the arsenal of the archaeologist is the venerable mason's trowel: a pointed steel blade, roughly in the shape of a diamond, with a handle welded (never riveted, please) at one end along its long axis (Figure 9.4). Mason's trowels are made by companies like Red Devil and Sears, but the Marshalltown trowel has attained the status of icon in the archaeological community. Marshalltown trowels can last for years, decreasing in size as they are continually resharpened (Flannery 1982). One of the annual awards bestowed by the Society for American Archaeology, in fact, is a plaque adorned with a gold-painted Marshalltown trowel.

**FIGURE 9.4** Though not a Marshalltown, this trowel has lasted a good long time. (*Kenneth L. Feder*)

Whenever I go to the hardware store to pick up some new trowels, I invariably run into a homeowner intent on doing a little masonry work but unfamiliar with the tools needed to build that brick wall around their patio or flowerbed. For some reason, I must appear to know my way around the tool-shed and they will ask me about the best trowel to accomplish the task. I have given up trying to explain the rather idiosyncratic function of the trowels I purchase, so I just go ahead and recommend Marshalltowns. I guess they're as good at laying brick as they are at excavating an archaeological site. At least I've never had any complaints.

In all seriousness, the tools archaeologists use in the field have the primary purpose of removing the soil matrix surrounding archaeological material and then extracting those materials from that matrix. We use whatever works. The trowel, with its blade kept razor-sharp, is an effective tool for scraping soil from the surface of an excavation unit in thin slices and also for smoothing and straightening the vertical walls of the unit. When artifacts or ecofacts are exposed by trowel work, they are left exactly where we found them: we use the Latin phrase **in situ** to characterize an object in its precise place of discovery. Archaeologists everywhere formally apologize to the Latinists among us when we admit that we often refer to objects removed from their place of discovery as being "out of situ," which, I have on good authority, is not proper Latin.

In any event, we leave items in place first just to see if they are in spatial association with other objects yet to be found in the square and second to allow for mapping in the material and then for photography. A unit's vertical walls are scraped with the trowel to provide a smooth, clean profile of the soil at a site, allowing for a detailed examination of its stratigraphy and identifying the precise layer or layers in which archaeological material is found. The trowel is also used in collecting soil samples for analysis in the laboratory. Some archaeologists grind and sharpen a notch in one of the back edges of the trowel for use as a small root cutter and, though I cannot personally recommend it, many of my students extol the virtues of a sharp Marshalltown as a back scratcher for those

**FIGURE 9.5** After the trowel, a typical archaeology tool kit includes these objects: (A) whisk broom, (B) small brush, (C) dental picks, (D) tape measure, (E) tweezers, (F) root cutters, (G) bubble level, (H) 10X loop (magnifier), and (I) compass. (*Kenneth L. Feder*)

hard-to-reach mosquito bites or patches of poison ivy rash.

Plenty of other tools are helpful in carrying out the fundamental task of removing soil from around artifacts and ecofacts and in exposing features (Figure 9.5). Even trowels miniaturized by years of resharpening often are still too large to safely expose very small objects.

Dental picks work well in removing the soil surrounding small bits of charcoal, pottery shards, or tiny stone flakes. Fine tweezers—the kind you can purchase at science supply houses and used in biology labs, not the cheapies you can buy at a drugstore for removing splinters or attending to your cuticles—are useful in picking up very small and delicate remains.

Metal-bladed trowels and dental picks can cause damage to soft material (bone, for instance) and many archaeologists make scraping tools out of bamboo, which generally is hard enough to excavate soil in small bits but soft enough to prevent damage to breakable objects. Toothbrushes, soft paint brushes, and airbrushes (small, soft brushes attached to a rubber or plastic bulb which, when squeezed, sends a puff of air down the bristles of the brush) can be extremely useful in gently prodding soil away from archaeological specimens, both those in situ as well as items newly extracted from the soil. And yes, it is to be admitted that under many conditions, particularly where the soil is dry and easily brushed away, whisk brooms can be extremely useful in removing the matrix above and around archaeological material.

## Read More

For brief discussions of the archaeologist's tool kit (including Kent Flannery's parable about the revered and esteemed Marshalltown trowel), see the following resources:

Flannery, K. V. 1982. The golden Marshalltown: A parable for the archaeology of the 1980s. *American Anthropologist* 84:265–78.

Hester, T. R. 1997a. Methods of excavation. In *Field Methods in Archaeology*, edited by T. R. Hester, H. J. Shafer, and K. L. Feder, 69–112. Mayfield Publishing, Mountain View, California.

Stewart, R. M. 2002. *Archaeology: Basic Field Methods*. Kendall/Hunt Publishing, Dubuque, Iowa.

Winans, M. C., and R. C. Winans. 1993. Measuring systems, techniques, and equipment for taphonomic studies. In *Practical Archaeology: Field and Laboratory Techniques and Archaeological Logistics*, edited by B. D. Dillon, 33–38. Institute of Archaeology, Los Angeles.

# Study Questions

1. How are archaeological sites divided up into manageable bites? Discuss the site grid.

2. How are excavation units at archaeological sites designated and labeled?

3. Where and what is the site datum?

4. Why do archaeologists attempt to recover small, seemingly insignificant pieces of chipped stone, broken ceramics, nutshell, seeds, charcoal, and bone?

5. How can we know what tree species were used for fuel in an ancient fire? (I mean besides sending them to Cindy McWeeney.) Why might we want to know what kinds of wood were being used by ancient people?

6. What are the primary tools that commonly make up the archaeologist's tool kit? What functions do each of these tools serve?

7. What do we mean by the Latin term "in situ"?

8. The standard archaeological tools—trowel, whisk broom, dental picks, toothbrushes, airbrush—serve what fundamental purpose in fieldwork? Why not just dig up a site with a shovel and screen all the dirt?

# UNIT 10

The flint recovered at Wood Lily and throughout our research study area in north-central and northwest Connecticut was nonlocal; we call it an **exotic material.** The geology of our area had not been conducive to the natural production of flint and, therefore, there isn't much of it available in Connecticut. However, about 80 kilometers (50 miles) to the west in the Hudson River valley of New York State, there were (and are) abundant sources of flint. The aboriginal people of Connecticut clearly had access to this flint and obtained it in large quantities.

Flint is a far superior raw material for making sharp-edged tools than any of the locally available rock types (like quartz and quartzite) and assorted volcanics (like basalt) available in Connecticut. When possible, and increasingly after about four thousand years ago, the native inhabitants of Connecticut either traveled to the flint source, or, more likely, had established trading networks in order to obtain this prized **lithic** material. In fact, at some Connecticut sites dating to about one thousand years ago, flint comprises nearly 100% of the lithic assemblage. Flint made up 52.3% of the lithic debitage and about 46.3% of the finished tools found at the three-thousand-year-old Wood Lily site.

When Carolyn White first encountered what she had assumed was a stone flake in the soil, she was fairly certain it was flint because of its color and reflectivity: it was black and shiny, as is the New York State flint, and unlike almost all of the other rock types we might expect to find in southern New England. But remember, at this point in the excavation, all that was exposed to her was a small piece of stone, not unlike the literally thousands of pieces of debitage already encountered and recovered at the site.

As she began to slowly strip the soil from around the artifact, instead of the ends of the flake becoming exposed (as would have happened had the piece been just a small fragment of flint), it became clear that, though extremely narrow, the piece of flint was substantially longer than any of the flakes we had previously found. Also, instead of a randomly shaped piece of stone struck off of a stone **core** while making a tool, it was apparent that this stone had been carefully flaked into a symmetrical form. Excavation slowly revealed a long, narrow shape that must have been painstakingly chipped. It was quickly clear to Carolyn that she had found not simply a piece of debitage, but a precisely shaped, carefully flaked tool, or at least a large part of one.

The excitement of the unknown is a fascinating part of excavation. When you begin exposing an object, you really have no idea how much of it is intact. As you slowly and carefully remove the soil from above and around it, taking great care to leave it in place in order to preserve its **spatial context** and **stratigraphic** positioning, you are aware that at any point in this process the broken edge of a tool may be exposed as you scrape away the soil and there may be nothing more.

The rest of the tool may be somewhere else in the site. If you are lucky, another digger may find it and the two fragments will fit together or **conjoin.** The tool may be somewhere else entirely, never to be found; perhaps the tip broke off when the spear was thrown and only the base, still attached to the retrieved wooden handle, was returned to the village that is now the archaeological site you are excavating.

As Carolyn slowly and carefully followed the path of the stone in the soil, it became apparent that, broken or not, she had found at least a substantial part of the object. After a little more work, it was clear that she had found not just most but an entire, unbroken stone tool.

The tool she had uncovered was a complete drill (Figure 10.1). The tip and edges of the drill bit evidenced the tool's pattern of use, matching the **wear patterns** on other stone drills found by archaeologists and mirroring those seen on replica tools of a similar form used experimentally for drilling.

The bit was long and delicate, exquisite, really. The base of the drill flared out to facilitate its attachment to a handle, likely of wood, that had not preserved in our acidic New England soil. The artisan who had produced this tool had been a master, knowing precisely where to apply pressure—almost certainly with the narrow, durable tip of a deer antler (a tine)—to the edge of the stone blade without snapping the bit in two. The tool maker obviously knew exactly how to apply pressure to remove small flakes from the bit's edge to produce a light yet strong, symmetrical, functional, and, at the same time, quite lovely piece of stonework. It is a tool that I continue to use three thousand years after the lithic artist produced it, not for drilling, of course, but as a model in my **experimental archaeology** course of the craft of stone tool manufacture or **knapping.**

**FIGURE 10.1** The beautifully crafted, complete flint drill found at the Wood Lily site in Peoples State Forest, Barkhamsted, Connecticut. (*Kenneth L. Feder*)

The flint drill may have been the finest example of stone tool making found at the Wood Lily site, but it was far from being the only such example. In fact, in two field seasons of excavation, we recovered fifty-three complete or partial stone tools at the site. Among those were the bits or tips of four more drills (Figure 10.2).

The diversity of functional tool types found at a site is used by archaeologists as an indicator of the range of activities that were carried out there. In the logical process employed by archaeologists, it is the degree of diversity of activities carried out at a site, as exhibited by the diversity of the functions reflected by the tools recovered, that allows us to deduce the kind of community we are exploring: a village site where adult men and women as well as children lived and where a broad range of tasks were carried out with an equally broad array of tools; or perhaps more specialized sites like hunting or gathering camps, military encampments, quarry sites, or sacred places, all where the diversity of functional tool types would have been far more restricted, reflecting a narrower range of activities.

**FIGURE 10.2** The nearly complete Wood Lily flint drill is shown in the center of this photograph. The four additional drill fragments recovered at Wood Lily are also shown. (*Kenneth L. Feder*)

Based on the diversity of material we recovered at Wood Lily, we concluded that it was a small village, a habitation site. Because we found lots of debitage (the debris of the process of stone tool making), as well as the instruments by which these waste flakes were struck from cores, we knew that tool making was a significant part of the repertoire of activities carried out by the site's inhabitants.

We didn't find any artifacts directly related to cooking or eating at the site—no pots or plates—but this doesn't mean that food preparation and eating weren't important activities here as well. The age of Wood Lily (three thousand years old) places the site at the very end of the **pre-ceramic** period in southern New England. The oldest **ceramic** objects recovered by archaeologists in Connecticut are about three thousand years old (Figure 10.3). The oldest dated ceramic objects we have found in the

**FIGURE 10.3** A fragment of pottery (called a sherd) found at an archaeological site in the Farmington Valley in Connecticut, which has been dated to about 2,500 years ago. The rough exterior surface resulted from pressing a cord-wrapped paddle into the pot when the clay was still wet. Cord marking may have served a utilitarian function—strengthening the bonds between the clay coils used in building the pot—as well as an artistic one—creating an interestingly textured surface on the finished vessel. (*Kenneth L. Feder*)

**FIGURE 10.4** A soapstone quarry located in north-central Connecticut. The two vaguely circular pedestals seen here are what was left when hemispheres of soft soapstone were carved out of the bedrock (Swiss Army knife added for scale). Those hemispheres of soft stone would have been hollowed out to produce bowls. (*Kenneth L. Feder*)

Farmington River Valley are about five hundred years more recent than that; we have **thermoluminescence** dates from ceramics found at another site in the valley of about twenty-five-hundred years ago.

In our part of America, ceramic technology was not independently invented, but it moved into our area from the south and west. We found no stone bowls at Wood Lily either. **Steatite,** also called **soapstone,** is a soft rock that the native people of North America used, where it was available, to carve sturdy cooking vessels that, although generally quite bulky, have marvelous heat retention qualities (Figure 10.4).

**FIGURE 10.5** This cluster of stones and burned soil are the remains of a hearth at the Wood Lily site. Careful analysis of the soil matrix in and around the stones provided us with burned wood—used in radiocarbon dating the site—and bits of bone as well as seed and nut fragments used in reconstructing the diet of the site's inhabitants. (*Kenneth L. Feder*)

But we found no soapstone at the site. In all likelihood, the people at Wood Lily used perishable materials like bark, wood, or reeds to make containers for storing and cooking food, and none of them have preserved in the acidic soil of southern New England.

So, while we believe that Wood Lily was a habitation site, it is not surprising that we found no pottery. We did find cooking **features** at the site, however, and some evidence of food remains (Figure 10.5).

Based on our analysis of these remains, it was clear that the people who lived at Wood Lily three millennia ago had eaten deer meat, acorn and hickory nuts, and also had collected and eaten the seeds of a number of different kinds of plants that grew in abundance near the stream that marked the eastern margin of their settlement (Figure 10.6).

**FIGURE 10.6** Charred nutshell fragments like these were found in the hearths excavated at the Wood Lily site. (*Kenneth L. Feder*)

# What Are the Characteristics That Make a Rock Type Attractive to Tool Makers?

No later than about 2.5 million years ago, and likely substantially before this, our most ancient hominid ancestors had recognized that by manipulating objects in their environment they could make tools that were sharper, stronger, harder, and more durable than those that nature had provided them in the form of their teeth, fingernails, and muscles. Stone likely was among the first of the raw materials that these ancient ancestors relied on for the production of sharp and durable edges for cutting, piercing, scraping, sawing, pounding, and grinding.

It is clear from the archaeological record that these pioneers in stone tool technology learned that not all rock types were equal in how easily they could be made into useful tools. These most ancient ancestors became, in a sense, "experimental geologists" who figured out by trial and error, on the one hand, which rocks were too difficult to break or too soft or crumbly to make into useful tools and, on the other hand, which rocks broke in predictable and consistent ways, producing desirably thin, sharp, and durable working edges.

By studying ancient artifacts and identifying the particular rock types used by people in different times and places to make chipped stone tools, and by experimenting with those same rock types in an effort to replicate the stone tool making process, archaeologists have identified the key characteristics that made a lithic raw material attractive to tool makers (Crabtree 1982; Kooyman 2002; Luedtke 1992; Whittaker 1994).

The best rock types for making cutting, piercing, or scraping tools are **vitreous,** or glass-like. At some point during your childhood, you probably dropped a glass or a bottle on a hard surface, it shattered, and your mother or father was panic-stricken, concerned that you might badly cut yourself on the sharp glass shards. Indeed, glass tends to break into very thin, extremely sharp fragments which, though dangerous to a barefoot kid who has just broken a drinking glass, is exactly the attribute someone making a spear point or butchering tool would find advantageous. In fact, making stone tools can be likened to controlled glass breakage.

Along with producing very thin, sharp edges when it breaks, glass also breaks consistently and predictably. It exhibits **conchoidal** fracture in which an applied force literally flows through the homogeneous material like ripples across a pond (Figure 10.7). The stone tool maker takes advantage of the consistent and predictable way that a force passes through materials that exhibit this fracture pattern to control the size and shape of the resulting flake.

If you consistently strike, with a hard object, a piece of glass or a glass-like rock (1) that has a less-than-90-degree angle between the surface you are striking (the **striking platform**) and the surface from which the flake is actually being removed, and (2) with a consistent amount of force, (3) at the same distance away from the intersection of the striking platform and the surface from which the flake is being removed, and (4) if you apply that force by striking or pressing the rock at a consistent angle (the so-called **angle of applied force**) you will produce flakes of a consistent size and shape. After a lot of practice, a **knapper** can predict with a great degree of accuracy the size and shape of a flake before the core is struck and then can control the size and shape of the flake to be removed by altering the angle at which the force is applied and the precise point of impact between the hammer and the core. Bruce Bradley, an archaeologist and a lithic technology expert, has produced a terrific video that takes the viewer through the steps of making stone tools (Bradley, 1989). At one point in the video, Bradley draws an outline on a sheet of paper of the tool he intends to make, a bifacially flaked spear point with side notches to aid in hafting the stone tip onto a wooden shaft. After completing the work, he superimposes the end product on the drawing he made before he began knapping. Like all great knappers, Bradley nitpicks his own work, but, in truth, the tool is a remarkably good, if not perfect, match. One point of this exercise is to show that stone tool manufacturing is not a random or informal process. An experienced stone tool maker doesn't simply smash two rocks together and hope for the best: instead, tool making is a highly controlled and predictable process— well, for people with the skill of Bruce Bradley, anyway.

Nature produces a form of glass in volcanoes. Usually black and translucent along thin edges, **obsidian** is a remarkable and remarkably beautiful natural material (Figure 10.8). Obsidian was an important raw material for making stone tools wherever ancient people could find it, though its sharp edges can be very delicate and will break quite easily. Some other rock types are glass-like but to lesser

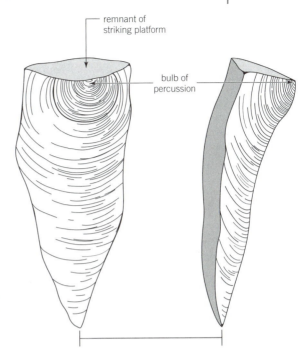

**FIGURE 10.7** Drawing of a long flake of stone removed from a rock that exhibits a pattern of conchoidal fracture. The force of the blow that detached the flake from the rock passed through like ripples on a pond, leaving remnants of those ripples on the surface of the flake. (*Kenneth L. Feder*)

**FIGURE 10.8** Obsidian blades. (*Kenneth L. Feder*)

degrees than obsidian. Flint, chalcedony, jasper, and chert are not natural glass but consist of tiny crystals cemented together. The crystals in these rock types are so small, they are invisible to the naked eye and are described as **cryptocrystalline** (literally, "hidden crystals"). Because the crystals in cryptocrystalline rocks are so small, an applied force is not diverted along the intersections of the crystals as it passes through the stone, as is the case in rock types like quartzite, where the individual crystals making up the rock are much larger (Luedtke 1992). As a result, the knapper—and not the rock—has a great deal of control over how the force he or she applies passes through the stone and, therefore, how the stone breaks. Cryptocrystalline rocks also exhibit conchoidal fracture. An applied force passes through them in a controllable fashion, enabling experienced knappers to peel consistently sized and shaped thin, sharp flakes off a struck core. These rocks also are useful raw materials for stone tool makers.

## Read More

To find out more about the technical qualities that make a rock attractive to the stone tool maker, check out the following resources. Crabtree's venerable *An Introduction to Flint Working* is, essentially, a dictionary of terms and still the best place to start on this subject. Bradley's video will leave you in awe of his skill and you will come away with a visceral appreciation for the intelligence it took for our ancestors to invent stone tool technology.

Bradley, B. 1989. *Flintknapping,* Produced by INTERpark and Primitive Tech. Enterprises. Cortez, Colorado.

Crabtree, D. E. 1982. *An Introduction to Flint Working.* Idaho Museum of Natural History, Pocatello.

Kooyman, B. P. 2002. *Understanding Stone Tools and Archaeological Sites.* University of New Mexico Press, Albuquerque.

Luedtke, B. E. 1992. *An Archaeologist's Guide to Chert and Flint.* Archaeological Research Tools 7. University of California Press, Los Angeles.

Whittaker, J. C. 1994. *Flintknapping: Making and Understanding Stone Tools.* University of Texas Press, Austin.

## How Can You Determine the Source of a Raw Material Used by Ancient People?

There is a movement in law enforcement to include chemical tags in dangerous substances to allow for the precise tracing of those materials to their sources when they are used for nefarious purposes. For example, one strategy is to add a minute amount of a different nonreactive substance to the TNT sold by each of the legal suppliers of the explosive. Then, if a terrorist or more mundane criminal were to use some of that TNT in an illegal act, traces of the tagging substance would be found in the blast residue and the explosives used in the crime could be traced to a particular supplier, who would be legally obliged to keep records of who purchased the material. In theory, this would allow for the identification of whoever purchased the explosives.

In a sense, nature has placed its own version of a unique chemical tag in many of the materials and substances used by ancient people. As in the forensic application, those natural tags are unique to each raw material source and can be used to trace a material from a site where an ancient people used it to make something back to the place where they directly or indirectly obtained it.

Obsidian from two different volcanic regions may look just the same to the naked eye, and even under the microscope, but there very well may be slight differences in their chemical makeup. The same holds true for the beautiful gemstone turquoise, where each source may present a crazy quilt of colors and each, as well, exhibits a unique **chemical signature** distinguishable from every other turquoise source. Stone, clay, and metal sources may have unique profiles of trace contaminants that have little or no affect on the appearance, utility, or other qualities of the material. When those materials are found at archaeological sites, made into spear points, pots, or knives, the trace element profile of the raw materials from which these artifacts were made can be determined and compared to the known profiles of the potential sources of those raw materials (Figure 10.9). When a match is made, an artifact at a site can be associated with the geographic source where the raw material from which it was made most likely originated.

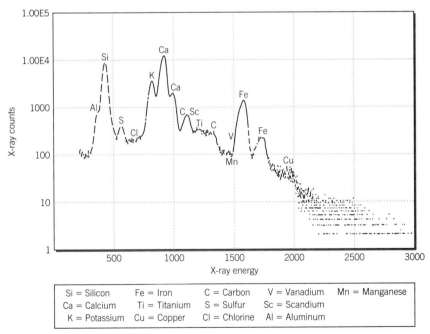

| Si = Silicon | Fe = Iron | C = Carbon | V = Vanadium | Mn = Manganese |
| Ca = Calcium | Ti = Titanium | S = Sulfur | Sc = Scandium | |
| K = Potassium | Cu = Copper | Cl = Chlorine | Al = Aluminum | |

**FIGURE 10.9** A reading of the chemical signature of the clay used to make a prehistoric pot as determined by PIXE (particle induced x-ray emission). Although the raw materials from which an artifact type was made (the stone used to make spear points, the clay used to manufacture pottery, or the gemstone carved into an effigy) may look similar on the outside, their chemical makeup may differ enough to indicate that they originated from different sources. That same trace element analysis may enable the archaeologist to trace the raw material to its geographic source. (*Courtesy of Harold Jull*)

There are several ways in which we can determine the chemical profiles of sources and artifacts and by which we may reveal minute traces of elements that might serve as unique markers. One such procedure is **neutron activation analysis,** which can detect the presence of a wide range of substances (http://www.osp.cornell.edu/vpr/ward/NAA.html) down to extremely small amounts, measured in "parts per million" and even "parts per billion." Neutron activation analysis has been applied in the attempt to trace the sources of artifacts made of obsidian, turquoise, flint, clay, and copper. For example, the seventeen known sources of native copper in the United States and Canada—this is copper found in a naturally pure form, not as an ore—have been studied using the technique, and the chemical signature of each major source has been determined (Rapp et al. 2000). The same procedure can reveal the trace element signature of archaeological specimens, compare the results to the seventeen copper sources, and determine a best match. Using this analysis, we can determine where ancient people in North America obtained their copper and begin to construct trading networks that facilitated the movement of the raw material to various locations where people could make that copper into tools, jewelry, and weapons.

## Read More

The following sources offer interesting examples of the use of trace element chemistry to trace the source of raw materials used by ancient people (clay and copper):

Juli, H., J. Trimble, and M. Monce. 2003. Trade and tribal boundaries in late prehistoric southern New England: A proton induced x-ray emission (PIXE) analysis of Connecticut prehistoric ceramics. *Northeast Anthropology.* In Press.

Rapp, G., J. Allert, V. Vitali, Z. Jing, and E. Henrickson. 2000. *Determining Archaeological Sources of Artifact Copper Source Characterization Using Trace Element Analysis.* University Press of America, Lanham, Maryland.

 ## How Do Archaeologists Figure Out How Ancient People Made Their Tools?

An enormous chasm separates modern people, including people with higher degrees in anthropology, and the ancient folks whose lives we anthropologists hope to illuminate. We are separated, not by intellectual capacity (ancient, anatomically modern human beings were as intelligent as modern people and had our same potential to figure things out), but by vast stretches of time, unimaginably different environments, and at times seemingly irreconcilable cultural differences. Archaeologists attempt to bridge this chasm by recovering elements of the material culture of the ancient people and by developing various strategies to unlock the secrets coded into those objects. We collect lots of direct evidence in the form of end products of the tool making technologies of ancient people (for example, we find their spear points and pots). How though do we figure out the often complex technological processes by studying the end results?

The term "back-engineering" is used to identify the sneaky strategy by which modern industries attempt to discover how their competitors manufacture their products—and then incorporate those methods into their own products. Essentially, back-engineering is figuring out how your competitor made a product by obtaining it and then taking it apart to figure out how your competitor put together the product in the first place.

Archaeologists employ a form of back-engineering to figure out how ancient people made their tools. We examine the end products of ancient technologies along with abandoned steps in the process (half-finished spear points, broken pieces of unfinished pottery, abandoned or incomplete construction projects) and then we try to put the technological process back together. For example, the process of making stone tools, specifically spear points, often proceeds in a series of steps beginning with the removal of a sizeable flake from a core by striking that core with a **hammerstone** in the process called **percussion flaking.** Once removed from the core, the large flake can be thinned by additional percussion, though this may be accomplished with a softer hammer, like the blunt end of a piece of deer or elk antler. The soft hammer may be used for additional shaping as well, making the spear point symmetrical and assuring an aerodynamic quality to the projectile. Finally, the edge may be thinned to razor sharpness and notches may be fashioned on the base to facilitate hafting onto a wooden shaft. The tool maker accomplishes these tasks not by percussion but by direct application of pressure with the pointed tip of a hard antler tine in the process called **pressure flaking.** Though each step in this process may obscure or eliminate many or even most of the scars left by previous steps, a careful examination of the finished spear point (or knife, scraping tool, drill, saw, or engraving tool) often reveals some elements of the flaking patterns of those previous steps.

**Ethnography** and **ethnohistory** may also provide information helpful in the reconstruction of an ancient technology. For example, although the manufacture of stone tools may be an alien technology to most of us, there are people—perhaps not in the present but in the not-so-distant past—for whom making stone tools was a crucial part of life. One of the most famous examples is a man by the name of Ishi. Ishi was a Yahi Indian, living a traditional way of life until he was found near death in northern California in 1911 (Kroeber, Kroeber, and Gannett 2002). Ishi was a highly skilled stone tool maker, one of the few Native Americans in North America in the early twentieth century who still possessed this traditional skill. After being nursed back to health, Ishi spent the rest of his short life (he died in 1916) sharing his skills with interested scientists (Figure 10.10). It would not be an exaggeration to say that we owe to Ishi much of what we know about stone tool making in general among Native Americans (you can find photos of some of the tools Ishi made at http://hearstmuseum.berkeley.edu/exhibitions/ncc/4_2.html).

**FIGURE 10.10** Ishi making stone tools using the pressure technique. Ishi's knowledge continues to contribute to our scientific understanding of stone tool making. (*Phoebe Hearst Museum of Anthropology*)

Finally, archaeologists also employ a hands-on approach to the analysis of tool making technologies in a process called **experimental archaeology.** Combining the information decrypted from ancient tools and provided by ethnography and ethnohistory, some researchers have attempted to recover ancient tool making technologies through trial and error by actually trying to make the tools themselves (Coles 1997). Employing authentic raw materials, archaeologists have experimented with various methods and produced some stunningly accurate replicas of ancient tools. In Europe, François Bordes spent much of his professional life decoding ancient stone tool technologies and then testing his conclusions by actually applying them through replication. In America, Don Crabtree (1982) was responsible for solving many of the mysteries of stone tool making, again through the process of actually applying various methods and deducing which were the most likely to have been used by ancient people. Dozens of Bordes's and Crabtree's students—and dozens upon dozens of subsequent generations of archaeologists—continue to refine the knowledge base developed by these mentors. Today, archaeologist and lithics expert Bruce Bradley, among many others, carries on in the tradition of Bordes and Crabtree, replicating stone tools and passing down this recaptured skill to the next generation of lithic replicators (http://www.primtech.net/; Figure 10.11).

**FIGURE 10.11** Ancient technology expert Bruce Bradley is shown using an antler hammer as a percussor to remove flakes from a nodule of stone in the process of stone tool making. (*Courtesy of Bruce Bradley*)

I teach a course in experimental archaeology, focusing on stone tool replication. Through the course, students engage in an extremely valuable experience. Clearly, those who have actually spent time attempting to make stone tools have an enormous conceptual advantage in archaeological fieldwork. Students who have made stone tools have a much easier time recognizing lithic artifacts, particularly waste flakes, in the field than those who haven't. When you spend an entire semester producing dozens of tools, and thousands of fragments of debitage, you get a very good feel for what such flakes look like as compared to stone broken by natural processes. Students also gain a unique perspective: they recognize the specific features of stone tools and their manufacturing waste products recovered at an ancient site because they have produced nearly identical stuff with their own hands. And, I have to admit, it is a real charge to find instances in which ancient people experienced the same problems with a rock and sometimes made the same mistakes that you make on a regular basis.

Experimental archaeology is not just about stone tools. Experiments have been conducted in ancient pottery making, house construction, musical instruments, cooking, in fact, in every imaginable art, craft, and technology (Coles 1997). A series of large-scale experiments were conducted for public television and were aired in Great Britain and the United States. The videos are great fun and include experiments in which a small replica of an Egyptian pyramid was built (Barnes 1997c), an Egyptian obelisk was erected (Barnes 1997b), Inca stone masonry was replicated (Barnes 1997a), the Roman Colosseum was assessed (Page and Cort 1997a), and one of the Stonehenge trilithons (two large upright slabs, each weighing 100,000 pounds, with a smaller cross piece balanced on top of the two uprights) was replicated (Page and Cort 1997b: Figure 10.12). Ultimately, it must be admitted that, while it is a scientifically valuable approach, experimental archaeology also is great fun, providing both an intellectual and a visceral appreciation for the technological abilities of past people.

# Read More

Experimental archaeology provides insights about ancient technologies in a way that no other analytical process can. To learn more about the ways in which archaeologists—and historians and engineers and musicians and so on—have employed experimental archaeology, read any of the following books and view the videos:

Barnes, M. 1997a. Inca. In *Secrets of Lost Empires*. Nova. WGBH, Boston.
———. 1997b. Obelisk. In *Secrets of Lost Empires*. Nova. WGBH, Boston.
———. 1997c. Pyramid. In *Secrets of Lost Empires*. Nova. WGBH, Boston.
Coles, J. M. 1997. *Experimental Archaeology*. Academic Press, London.
Crabtree, D. E. 1982. *An Introduction to Flint Working*. Idaho Museum of Natural History, Pocatello.
Kroeber, T., K. Kroeber, and L. Gannett. 2002. *Ishi in Two Worlds: A Biography of the Last Wild Indian in North America*. University of California Press, Berkeley.
Page, C., and J. Cort. 1997a. Colosseum. In *Secrets of Lost Empires*. Nova. WGBH, Boston.
———. 1997b. Stonehenge. In *Secrets of Lost Empires*. Nova. WGBH, Boston.

**FIGURE 10.12** Replicating one of the trilithons at Stonehenge involved moving two 50-ton, 24-feet-tall slabs of concrete (top), erecting them (bottom), and then raising a 16-ton lintel to rest on top. All of the twentieth-century workers on the project came away with an enormous amount of respect for the abilities of people who lived nearly five thousand years ago. (*Courtesy, Horizon, BBC Science*)

## How Did Ancient People Make Stone Tools?

As mentioned earlier, researchers approach this question of the manufacture of ancient stone tools in three ways: (1) by examining the tools for traces of their various manufacturing steps (the back-engineering approach), (2) by examining similar technologies practiced by people who lived in the not-too-distant past (ethnographic and ethnohistorical research), and (3) by experimental replication. More than a century of such research, particularly in terms of replication, has resulted in a vast body of knowledge related to the manufacture of stone tools in particular, resulting in a detailed vocabulary (Crabtree 1982) and a tremendous amount of experience in actually making stone tools. In a sense, twentieth- and twenty-first-century scholars have, by the careful examination of archaeological specimens, trial and error, and ethnohistorical research, reinvented and, it is hoped, authentically recaptured ancient stone working technologies.

Stone work begins with a nucleus of stone, a core of good, chippable rock. It helps if the core has facets (distinct sides or faces, like in a cut gemstone) at least a couple of which meet at an angle of less than 90 degrees (a rounded, upside-down cone of rock with a flat top is ideal for many purposes). In the process of **percussion flaking,** the **knapper** applies force with a **percussor,** which can be a **hammerstone,** usually a spherical nodule of rock that comfortably fits in the dominant hand, or a propitiously shaped antler baton or hammer. The percussor does not need to be harder than the core because geometry, not just hardness, controls breakage. A rounded hammerstone, a rock without the facets or angles you look for in a core, can be extremely durable and nearly indestructible. Such a hammerstone can easily break flakes of stone from a harder rock that does have facets or angles.

With the hammerstone held in the dominant hand—right hand for righties, left hand for lefties—and holding the core or **object piece** in the other, the tool maker strikes the core at the margin of one of its flat surfaces, called a **striking platform,** near to where it forms a less-than-90-degree angle with another of its faces (Figure 10.13). The **angle of applied force** (determined as the angle between the striking platform and the trajectory of the hammerstone as it strikes the core) can vary and controls whether the flake is short and thin (an acute angle of applied force) or long and thicker (an angle of applied force closer to, but not exceeding, 90 degrees). When struck correctly, the force of the blow moves down through the interior of the core, close to the face of the rock. If strong enough, the force exceeds the **elastic limit** of the rock and literally peels a thin, sharp flake from the core. This process can be repeated many times and a large number of similar flakes can be removed from the core.

These stone flakes may be extremely sharp and can even be used without further modification as cutting, piercing, or scraping tools. If, however, the desire is to craft a symmetrical, more complex tool (perhaps one that is aerodynamic and intended for use as a projectile tip or point in a spear, dart, or arrow), additional work needs to be accomplished. Some additional thinning and shaping may be necessary and the knapper may shift to a smaller hammerstone or a softer percussor, like the blunt end of an antler. Further edge straightening and thinning may be done by **pressure flaking,** where the pointy end of an antler, called the tine, is aligned against the edge, force is applied simply by pressing against the edge, and small flakes are literally pushed off the faces of the larger "parent" flake (Figure 10.14). The overall shape of the parent flake can be modified in this way, the edges can be straightened and thinned where

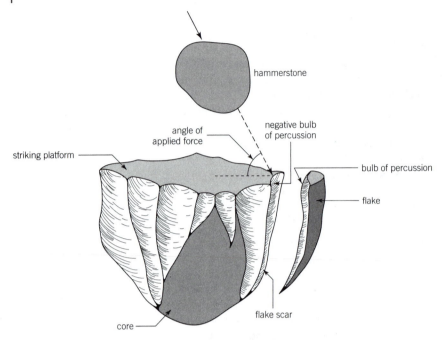

**FIGURE 10.13** Removal of a stone flake from a core. The consistent application of a percussive strike with a hammerstone on the platform of the core can produce a large number of consistently sized and shaped sharp flakes that can be used as is or further worked into specific tools. (*Kenneth L. Feder*)

needed, and a piece of work clearly recognizable as the result of human craft can be produced. Finally, if the toolmaker desires, notches can be carved at the base of the tool in order to facilitate hafting onto a wooden or reed shaft. The notches can be produced by additional pressure flaking.

Stone tool making is anything but easy for a modern person to perfect. After all, unlike our ancient counterparts, we haven't been rehearsing the skill since childhood. In my experimental archaeology course, I first have the students attempt to replicate the oldest tools made by our hominid ancestors: the industry is called **Oldowan** after their place of discovery, Olduvai Gorge in eastern Africa. It takes my students some time to produce respectable, big, crude chopping tools and sharp slicing flakes that would be recognized as fairly legitimate by an actual member of the species *Homo habilis*, the makers of such tools as much as 2.5 million years ago. Students usually get pretty excited by their new skill until I remind them that *Homo habilis* had a brain size less than half that of a modern human being. That pretty much dissuades most of my students from taking their chopping tools home and putting them on their refrigerators. It is fair to say, however, that there are some lithic specialists in archaeology today who are masters of the craft and who can fabricate stone tools that are the technological and artistic equal of any produced in the ancient world. Bruce Bradley is one of those knappers, having attained a remarkable

**FIGURE 10.14** Pressure flaking involves the application of, rather obviously, pressure, along the margins of a flake to thin (and, therefore, sharpen) the flake's edge or to alter the edge to a desired shape. (*Kenneth L. Feder*)

level of mastery of the art of stone tool making. Some of his handiwork is on display at his homepage (http://www.primtech.net/), where visitors also can purchase a videotape demonstrating, as words cannot possibly adequately convey, the fascinating process of making stone tools.

## Read More

Obviously, you cannot become a proficient replicator of stone tools by reading a couple of books or by viewing a videotape. But it's a start, and any of the following resources will provide you with some intellectual insights into the process:

Bradley, B. 1989. *Flintknapping*. Produced by INTERpark and Primitive Tech. Enterprises. Cortex, Colorado.

Crabtree, D. E. 1982. *An Introduction to Flint Working*. Idaho Museum of Natural History, Pocatello.

Kooyman, B. P. 2002. *Understanding Stone Tools and Archaeological Sites*. University of New Mexico Press, Albuquerque.

Whittaker, J. C. 1994. *Flintknapping: Making and Understanding Stone Tools*. University of Texas Press, Austin.

# Why Are Archaeologists So Painstaking and Slow in Excavation?

Most people find it terribly surprising how long the various components of archaeological fieldwork take. Visitors to my excavations often are amazed when they learn from two seemingly intelligent, industrious, and hardworking students, as they are troweling a level at the bottom of a 2-meter by 2-meter excavation unit no more than a couple of feet deep, that they have been working in that one spot for two weeks. I can remember as a field school student our crew being called in to recover some woolly mammoth bones accidentally uncovered by a home builder. The archaeologists arrived with their trowels and dental picks, ready to excavate the often tiny and always delicate fragments of ten-thousand-year-old elephant bones and tusks. The construction people were appalled at the low-tech approach we were employing; a backhoe operator told us he could get the bones out in just a minute or two. He promised he would be "real careful." We turned down his generous offer and continued, using the time-honored tool kit of the archaeology field-worker.

There are a number of commonsense reasons why archaeologists take so much time and are so careful in excavating sites. Like the ten-thousand-year-old woolly mammoth bones, much of the evidence that makes up the archaeological record is delicate and fragile, already largely broken up in the process of being transformed from its behavioral context to its archaeological context and then by natural processes in the soil. A backhoe may be quick, and the operator may be extremely efficient, careful, and perfectly good at removing an archaeologically sterile overburden of soil stratigraphically above a site, but even an expertly employed backhoe is simply incapable of safely recovering archaeological material.

Along with being fragile, a fair proportion of the archaeological record consists of tiny bits of evidence. As indicated a number of times in this book (it is an archaeological mantra of sorts), archaeological research is not a treasure hunt and sometimes even the smallest, most unimpressive fragments of artifacts and ecofacts may be enormously informative and contribute to our understanding of some aspect of an ancient people's way of life. It is time consuming to expose and recover all of these small objects, measure them in their locations, and then bag them to return for further analysis in the lab, but it is more than worthwhile in our effort to understand an ancient way of life, especially one that has left behind little more than the tiny fragments we recover.

Finally, the fundamental irony of archaeological fieldwork has already been discussed: when we excavate a site, we destroy it. Ordinarily, we get only one shot at discovery, recording objects *in situ*, and recovery. It is a professional obligation to accomplish these tasks responsibly and that means carefully, which in turn almost always means slowly. Whatever the time period and whatever the culture, there are a finite number of archaeological sites and each one that is lost through development, erosion, looting, or well-meaning but inadequate archaeological research diminishes the database proportionally. It is our duty, therefore, to excavate archaeological sites as carefully as possible and, furthermore, the reason we try to leave parts of unthreatened sites unexcavated, saving them for future archaeologists with more sophisticated methods for discovering and recovering the precious undisturbed evidence.

## Read More

For more detailed discussions of the importance of careful archaeological excavation, any of the following sources will provide important additional information:

Baker, B. W., B. S. Shaffer, and D. G. Steele. 1997. Basic approaches in archaeological faunal analysis. In *Field Methods in Archaeology*, edited by T. R. Hester, H. J. Shafer, and K. L. Feder, 298–318. Mayfield Publishing, Mountain View, California.

Hester, T. R. 1997a. Methods of excavation. In *Field Methods in Archaeology*, edited by T. R. Hester, H. J. Shafer, and K. L. Feder, 69–112. Mayfield Publishing, Mountain View, California.

———. 1997b. The handling and conservation of artifacts in the field. In *Field Methods in Archaeology*, edited by T. R. Hester, H. J. Shafer, and K. L. Feder, 143–58. Mayfield Publishing, Mountain View, California.

Holloway, R. G. 1997. Excavation and recovery of botanical materials from archaeological sites. In *Field Methods in Archaeology*, edited by T. R. Hester, H. J. Shafer, and K. L. Feder, 283–97. Mayfield Publishing, Mountain View, California.

Stewart, R. M. 2002. *Archaeology: Basic Field Methods*. Kendall/Hunt Publishing, Dubuque, Iowa.

 ## How Do Archaeologists Figure Out the Function of an Ancient Tool?

You might expect, or at least hope, that the function of an ancient tool would be self-evident, that you could determine the use of a tool just by looking at it. Although it is true that form readily identifies function for some tools, this is not universally the case. Most of us would be hard pressed to figure out the use for many of the tools even in a modern toolbox based simply on what they look like. Suppose you had never seen a hammer and were confronted with one for the first time. A quick perusal of its form, feeling its heft and its balance in the hand, probably would give you an accurate estimation of the tool's function. But how about a screwdriver? Suppose you had never seen one before and suppose additionally you had never seen any kind of a screw. How easily could you figure out a screwdriver's use? Would you accurately deduce that it was a tool for installing or removing a particular type of metal fastener (the screw)? Maybe. You might just as likely decide that it was a weapon of some sort, intended for stabbing an enemy and inflicting great harm or even death. Now consider how much more difficult it is to identify the function of a tool when dealing with those made by practitioners of a different, quite alien, and ancient culture.

Identification difficulty often forces archaeologists to rely on direct evidence of tool use rather than simply a tool's appearance. Direct evidence of use takes the form of wear traces that accumulate on tools during use. As you know, metal tools can become dull and scratched and can even sustain damage to

**FIGURE 10.15** Patterns of edge damage resulting from tool use as defined experimentally by archaeologist Lawrence Keeley: (A) deep scalar scars (large, left; small, right), (B) shallow scalar scars (large, left; small, right), (C) step scars (large, left; small, right), and (D) half-moons. (*After Lawrence Keeley, 1980*)

their edges through vigorous use. That brand new Swiss Army Knife that can effortlessly slice through material will quickly dull. The alteration through use to a metal knife's edge can be examined and recognized under magnification, and the same applies to stone tools. When stone tools are used to cut into or through raw materials like wood, animal hide, bone, antler, or even other stone, the surface of the tool sustains varying kinds and degrees of unintentional alteration and damage. That damage may manifest itself as scratches called **striations,** as a smoothing of the surface called **polish,** as microflakes called **scalar scars** because they look like little fish scales peeled off of the surface of a tool, **step scars** because the scars terminate abruptly at 90-degree angle "steps," or as little nibbles taken off an edge called **half-moons** because of their shape (Keeley 1980; Figure 10.15).

So, the edge of a tool, whether it is a finely made utensil or a simple, unintentionally modified flake that exhibits any one of the **wear patterns** mentioned bears evidence of use. The question then becomes: What kind of use? Again we are faced with a challenge. Although the wear on the working edge of a stone tool is visible, at least under magnification, the function of the tool still is not intuitively obvious just by the appearance of the damage rendered by its use. Attempts to overcome this challenge resulted in a brilliantly clever piece of research initially conducted nearly thirty years ago. Archaeologist Lawrence Keeley was able through experiment to provide a series of prototypes of wear patterns for the various uses of stone tools ancient people may have employed (Keeley 1980).

Keeley began by making a large sample of stone tools with various kinds of edges. He then used each of these tools on a series of different raw materials, including wood, animal hide, bone, antler, and stone, performing a wide range of functions, including cutting, scraping, sawing, piercing, engraving, axing, wedging, and adzing (Figure 10.16). Through this work, Keeley produced an extensive sample of models of wear patterns, covering as broad a range as possible of the combination of raw material of the tools, tool morphology, material used on, and mode of use—how the working edge of the tool was applied to the material it was used on.

Keeley found a number of unique results in terms of the appearance of the wear patterns on the used tool edges, depending on how they were used and on what material. For example, an edge used to saw wood tended to exhibit striations running parallel to the edge on both faces, with narrow and shallow scalar scars also on both faces. On the other hand, drilling a hole in a piece of bone (say, to make a flute) resulted in a tool with a very different wear pattern, in this case a brightly polished surface on the high-points of the tool, those edges directly in contact with the bone. Knowing the broad range of possible wear pattern outcomes from the experimental models, it is possible to accurately identify the function and use of an archaeological specimen. In essence, when an ancient tool exhibits wear patterns that look just like those seen on one of Keeley's models, it is reasonable to deduce that the artifact was used to perform a function similar to that of the experimental model.

Keeley went beyond assumption in his research and actually conducted a blind test. He made another set of tools, this time passing them along to a colleague, who used the tools in a variety of ways undisclosed to Keeley and maintained accurate records of how he used the tools. The colleague then returned the tools to Keeley, who compared them to his original tools (the set used in making models of wear patterns). Using those models, Keeley accurately identified the usage patterns for the second set of tools more than 85% of the time. In other words, in more than eight times out of ten, Keeley accurately deduced how a tool was used, and on what raw material, by comparing its wear patterns to those he had produced in his tool use prototypes. Keeley's experiment in wear pattern production and subsequent refinements in the original research have allowed archaeologists to objectively assess the wear patterns on ancient tools and to confidently identify the ways in which they were used by ancient people.

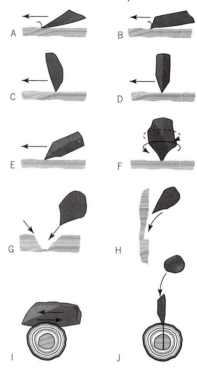

**FIGURE 10.16** Models of stone tool use employed by Lawrence Keeley in his use-wear experiments: (A) whittling, (B) planning, (C) scraping, (D) graving (high angle), (E) graving, low angle, (F) boring, (G) chopping, (H) adzing, (I) sawing or cutting, and (J) wedging. (*After Lawrence Keeley, 1980*)

## Read More

The experimental program of Lawrence Keeley is a model for the interpretation of tool use through the application of replicative experiment. His book is the best place to start to expand your understanding of how archaeologists interpret use-wear patterns on stone tools by actually creating them:

Keeley, L. 1980. *Experimental Determination of Stone Tool Use: A Microwear Analysis.* University of Chicago Press, Chicago.

# How Do Archaeologists Figure Out the Function of a Site?

Ancient people used the landscape in various ways and for various purposes. They settled in villages, established hunting or fishing camps, located quarries, constructed mills, positioned burial grounds, and so on. A people's land use strategy is called a **settlement pattern.** But how are the individual elements of a settlement pattern identified? In essence, once we find a site, how do we determine what the location was used for, what activities were carried out at a given place, and what role a particular site played in an overall settlement pattern?

A site's function is defined by the range of individual activities that can be recognized at the location. A community of people that included men and women, old and young, can be assumed to have conducted a broad range of activities that involved the use of a broad range of material objects. The archaeological site that such a community produces will likely exhibit a broad range of artifact types. It is reasonable to assume the inhabitants made stone tools needed in the daily conduct of life; fired ceramics required for cooking and storage; conducted maintenance activities like tool sharpening, basket-mending, and kiln cleaning; prepared and cooked sustenance in the form of food; disposed of trash; buried the dead; and so on. Concentrations of debitage, broken hammerstones, incomplete tools, cooking hearths, pottery kilns and concentrations of pots broken in the firing process, trash middens or dumps where inedible elements of food resources were deposited, burials of loved ones, and house remains together imply the broad range of activities one would expect to find at a site where an entire community of people lived their lives. Although there is no fixed statistic by which the range of site activity is measured, when a large number of household activities are reflected by a wide range of artifact, ecofact, and feature types, the site's function as a village is recognized. These are the kinds of things a community of people leave behind and that represent the archaeological remains of the community.

Along with a community of households where people carried out their daily activities, human groups also used areas away from their primary habitation for specific purposes. For example, a particular location where a valuable resource could be found and extracted may have attracted human activity that resulted in an archaeological site. A place where obsidian, flint, copper, clay, turquoise, salt, nut foods, or spices could be found might become the focus of human activity as people quarried, extracted, or gathered these materials. Tools lost or broken in resource extraction might be found, defining the activity. Locations where fish might be readily collected may show evidence of this in the form of fish trap remains, weirs, concentrations of fish bones, fish hooks, and fish gutting knives. Cemeteries, quite obviously, will have concentrations of human remains. Hunting camps may show the bones of animals hunted and butchered on site, weapons broken in the hunt, and perhaps some stone waste flakes reflecting tool maintenance. A people reliant on flowing water to power their industry may have constructed mills, the archaeological manifestations of which are represented today by breached mill dams, raceways that channeled the water stored in the millpond, the foundation of the mill building, and perhaps even remnants of the millwheel itself, and elements of the machinery for which the water provided power. Obviously, subgroups of a community may have spent a considerable amount of time away from their home bases at the kinds of locations just described—and many others. The kinds of artifacts found at such locations and, at the same time, the kinds of artifacts *not* found, will help the archaeologist define the nature of the activities performed.

Although a culture might have had, as part of its yearly pattern of settlement, a large village in which multiple families spent a season or more together, at certain times of the year individual family groups may have dispersed across the landscape when that became a better strategy for efficiently finding food. In this case, various sites reflecting the settlement pattern of a group of people at a particular time may exhibit the same or similar degree of artifact diversity and deduced breadth of activity, the only difference in sites being that of overall size. In other words, within a pattern of settlement, the archaeologist may find a pattern of a single large village and several smaller settlements, all with similar clusters of artifacts. Differences in the overall size of sites and, where it can be determined, the number of hut or house remains, may provide key clues concerning the function of each individual site within the context of an overall settlement pattern.

The point is that a site's function is defined on the basis of the activities that were carried out, and that we can recognize on the basis of the artifacts, ecofacts, and features found there.

## Why Is Pottery of Such Great Importance to Archaeologists?

Consider the discussion in the section on gender and archaeology (see pp. 259–261). I point out—and, to be honest, poke fun at—the fact that lithics tend to be studied by male archaeologists and ceramics tend to be studied by female archaeologists. From that discussion, it would be reasonable to conclude that I am self-aware of the stereotyping that goes on in my field. I would never allow that bias to color my thinking or affect how I teach or write. Well, it grieves me to report, in the spirit of full disclosure, that in preparing this book, for a time I was guilty of the same bias in the focus of my discussion on ancient technology. In a previous version of the manuscript, though there was lots of discussion of the importance of stone tools and the archaeological value of their analysis—notice that there's an entire section on how archaeologists figure out how people made stone tools—I had included nothing whatsoever about ceramics. Zilch. Nada. I assure you, that was an oversight. Really. I find pottery every bit as interesting as stone tools. Well, almost. Needless to say, one of the reviewers of the manuscript pointed out that, even though there were no ceramics found at the Wood Lily site, ceramic artifacts are an abundant and important component of the archaeological record at many sites. Reviewers are anonymous, so I can't be sure, but I bet that reviewer was a woman. Just kidding.

In fact, I learned stone tool replication in graduate school where my lithic *sensei* was Terry del Bene. That was more than twenty-five years ago, meaning that I have "knocked rocks" for about half my life. Though I make no claim at being particularly proficient at it, I enjoy it and spend much of the semester in my experimental archaeology course teaching lithic replication. Beyond my dabbling in Play-Doh in kindergarten and an ashtray I made in the third grade, however, until recently my knowledge about ceramics was indirect; I had never actually attempted to make anything out of clay. That changed in early 2002, when I enrolled in an adult beginner ceramics class at the Canton Clayworks, a local ceramics studio in Canton, Connecticut.

For the first month or so of my indoctrination to ceramics, I was convinced that I had reached my peak in ceramic ability back in kindergarten and with the ashtray I had made (and that my mother still has), but slowly my eyes, hands, and brain began to work together and I actually began to produce some bowls, plates, and mugs that, though artistically uninspired, actually looked more or less as I intended. There are a number of teachers at the studio, some of whom teach sculptural ceramics (where forms are built by hand), but most students learn wheel throwing from master potter and owner of the Clayworks, Tim Scull. The funny thing is, when you look around at the student projects at the studio and then you look at Tim's pots, you can tell he is our teacher. Tim likes delicate forms with thin walls. He emphasizes technical skill in his pots and insists that his students do the same. Each of our plates, bowls, and mugs have to be made with at least one "foot" and, in the case of plates, two feet. This means that the bottoms of our pots are never flat, but have raised surfaces that diminish the possibility that the pot will stick to the kiln shelf when it is glaze fired. Tim likes traditional Asian ceramic forms and makes a lot of them; sure enough, many of Tim's students attempt ("attempt" is the operative word here) to emulate their teacher. Because the kilns represent a substantial financial investment, Tim insists on controlling the raw materials that he fires. Clay or glaze purchased elsewhere are unknown quantities, and to protect his investment, Tim is in charge of what gets fired in his kilns; everyone in the studio uses clays and glazes Tim provides.

Consider the variables in ceramic manufacture I just touched upon: the manufacturing technique itself (hand building or wheel throwing); the source of the clay; the styles of the pots, including the forms made and designs applied; the finishing of the base; the firing in a particular kind of kiln; and the glazes used. Together, these variables reflect the conditions in one studio and likely will not match precisely the mix of variables at any other studio. In the modern setting, a ceramics expert examining the output of the studio and comparing it to the ceramics produced at other schools would notice such differences—so would an archaeologist comparing the ceramics produced by ancient people.

In fact, Tim is creating an archaeological site. Canton Clayworks is located in a rural town and is surrounded by trees, with a little brook running down the hill at the back of the property. As I have come to learn through the unhappy lessons of a beginner potter, though they are durable containers, pots can break during or after their initial (bisque) firing, while being handled in the glazing process (I hate tongs), during the glaze firing, and when being handled by careless classmates (no names). Tim takes at least some of the broken fragments and tosses them down the hill. Instant archaeological site.

The same sorts of variables—and many more—for the modern pottery being made at Canton Clayworks can be examined in ancient ceramics, from the oldest pottery made in Japan more than eleven thousand years ago to commercial wares made in the last few hundred years. How pots are made (pinch pots, mold-made, coil-made, wheel thrown); which shapes are acceptable; desired vessel sizes; the clay body available and used; the decision to add **temper** to the clay and the kind of temper selected; base and rim treatment; three-dimensional surface treatment (carving, stamping, or pressing into wet clay and incising dry "leather-hard" pots before bisque firing); adding elements like handles or lugs; staining, slipping, or glazing; method of firing—all of these elements and more affect the final outcome of the ceramic process and affect how the resulting archaeological artifacts will look.

As is always the case in artifact analysis, when examining ceramics (from the tiniest of **potsherds** to complete, intact pots) the archaeologist attempts to decode the complex constellation of choices made by the ancient artisan. Once decoded, the analyst can reveal the existence of pottery traditions. In a sense, the pots produced at Canton Clayworks represent a "tradition," where a group of people—a family, of sorts—have all learned from the same potter and share a suite of pottery making behaviors recognizable in their finished products as well as in the broken pieces of those products. The same is true of a pottery making tradition in which a mother (uh-oh, there I go again), who, along with her sisters learned from their mother, teaches her daughter (just as this mother's sisters teach their daughters), and just as these daughters (all sisters or cousins), will teach their own daughters. The precise look of a pot results from a unique clustering of possibilities and decisions made by this family of women and will be discernibly different from those made by other families of women living upriver, on the other side of the mountain, or in an adjacent valley. Ceramic making is learned and ceramics are made within the contexts of the social, political, and economic systems of the group. Those contexts, as intangible as they might be directly, are made tangible in the materials produced by people—pottery is no exception. Ceramics is important to the archaeologist, therefore, because it was important to the people who made it, traded for it, cooked in it, stored stuff in it, and even buried their dead in it.

# Read More

For basic guidebooks on the analysis and interpretation of ceramics for the archaeologist, four terrific sources follow:

Olin, J. S., and A. D. Franklin, eds. 1982. *Archaeological Ceramics.* Smithsonian Institution Press, Washington, D.C.

Orton, C., P. Tyers, and A. Vince. 1993. *Pottery in Archaeology.* Cambridge University Press, Cambridge, England.

Rye, O. S. 1981. *Pottery Technology: Principles and Reconstruction.* Taraxacum, Washington, D.C.

Shepard, A. 1982. *Ceramics for the Archaeologist.* Carnegie Institute of Washington, Washington, D.C.

How Do Archaeologists Investigate
the Spread of Ideas or Inventions?

A culture is an ever-evolving, ever-changing thing, a grand work in progress intended to provide a technological, economic, social, political, and ideological context for a people's lives. Every generation maintains traditions at the same time that its members develop refinements and elaborations of traditional ways of accomplishing tasks or behaving. At the same time, every generation may invent entirely new ways of accomplishing the same tasks. Of course, as conditions change and as new discoveries are made or inventions developed, novel strategies to accomplish new tasks may arise as needed or even before the need is recognized in the first place, with the "need" defined by the invention rather than the other way around.

It is also certainly the case that human groups do not develop in a vacuum. People practicing a particular way of life are not isolated and regularly come into contact with folks practicing similar, somewhat different, or even entirely alien ways of life. The possible results of contact between two different groups of people are many and diverse. One group may wipe out the members of another group, or merely come to dominate them. The two groups may maintain a degree of separation, or one group may become incorporated into the other as peasants or slaves. Two groups may proceed as equals, trading with each other, forming alliances, or even ignoring each other altogether. However each group in this equation outwardly reacts to the other, ideas can transcend virtually any geographical or cultural barriers. Ordinarily, ideas are more mobile than people, and sometimes can move easily between and among different groups—even enemies, even people who don't speak the same language—and elements of the technology of one group of people are commonly adopted by other groups.

Archaeologists are specialists in the examination of culture change over long periods of time. We often can construct chronological sequences for cultures that span decades, centuries, and even millennia. Using absolute dating or determining the stratigraphic arrangement of components of the same culture, we can assess the nature of change in a people's behavior as these changes are reflected in the material record. Refinements or elaborations in the end products of lithic, ceramic, or metallurgical technologies often are apparent in the archaeological record. Ways of crafting tools or ways of adding design elements to pottery—or even ways of building pyramids or temples—may change over time. By comparing artifacts found in different stratigraphic levels of the same site, or artifacts found at different sites produced by the same cultures but with different chronometric dates, archaeologists can illuminate and evaluate changes in technology through time.

The pattern exhibited by sequences of technological change in the archaeological record in a region may be useful in determining whether this change was internally driven or resulted from the movement or **diffusion** of ideas across cultural boundaries. The pattern of technological, artistic, or behavioral change assumed in seriation reflects internal change and the general pattern in a seriation analysis applies in this case. In other words, when the archaeological record shows the first appearance of a technology as relatively rudimentary, evidencing lots of mistakes, changing as the product of trial and error as a group gropes its way toward perfecting a new process, we conclude that the adoption and evolution of the new behavior is the result of internal patterns of cultural evolution. If, on the other hand, a new technology seems to have arrived full-blown and complete, with little evidence of the first halting steps in the development of a new way of doing things (to the people of the archaeological culture being examined), it may be hypothesized that the behavior was invented, developed, and perfected someplace else. In this case, rather than interpreting the culture in question as having developed the new technology independently, we conclude that they adopted it from a source outside of their own culture (Clarke 1978).

Take, for example, a practice as complex as pyramid building in ancient Egypt and Mesoamerica (Adams 1991; Lehner 1997). Archaeological evidence clearly shows that people on both sides of the Atlantic built monumental pyramidal structures. It certainly is valid to question whether these were independent developments or whether the art of pyramid building developed first in only Egypt or Mesoamerica and the appearance of pyramids in the other location is the result of diffusion or borrowing.

In truth, Egyptian and Mesoamerican pyramids are quite different in appearance, in how they were constructed, and how they were used (Arnold 1991; Sabloff 1989). Add to these differences the fact that the Egyptian pyramids are far older: the last of the Egyptian pyramids was built long before even the earliest of the Mesoamerican monuments, so it does not seem likely that one inspired the other. All of this argues for a separate and independent development of the pyramid in Egypt and Mesoamerica. But also consider the archaeological evidence for the development of the pyramid in both places. In both Egypt and Mesoamerica, the archaeological record shows a long developmental sequence of pyramid building lasting centuries and even millennia. For example, Egyptians didn't simply start the process by building enormous, perfectly constructed pyramids. They started small, with square-block structures called *mastabas* over the tombs of their rulers. In fact, the first large-scale burial monument for a pharaoh wasn't a pyramid at all, but consisted of a series of mastabas of decreasing size placed one on top of the other (Figure 10.17).

After this "stepped pyramid" of the pharaoh Djoser, a subsequent ruler, Sneferu, began the construction of a larger but similar structure that he decided to finish as a true pyramid, filling in the steps. This first attempt at a true pyramidal form failed and the project was abandoned (Figure 10.18). All that remains today is the central core of the structure and the heaped-up remains of its surface; it is, in fact, usually called the "Collapsed Pyramid," though there likely was no catastrophic collapse, merely an abandonment and deterioration over an extended period of time.

Sneferu tried again, but ran into similar problems about halfway through construction. When it became apparent that the surfaces of the second pyramid were too steep to sustain their own weight (cracks had formed toward the bottom, endangering the project), Sneferu's engineers changed the slope of the pyramid toward the top, actually decreasing the angle of the pyramid faces (Figure 10.19). This strategy saved the project but resulted in an oddly shaped

**FIGURE 10.17** The pharaoh Djoser's stepped pyramid represented an obvious next step in ancient Egypt in the evolution from older single-level mastabas. (*M. H. Feder*)

**FIGURE 10.18** The "Collapsed Pyramid," a construction project abandoned when cracks appeared at its base, likely the result of a too-steep angle of the pyramid's facing. (*M. H. Feder*)

pyramid, bend inward at the top—not surprisingly, today the structure is called the "Bent Pyramid."

Sneferu's third attempt at pyramid building succeeded (Figure 10.20), employing from the beginning the less severe angle used at the top of the "Bent Pyramid." This sequential pattern of improving technology—in this case over

**FIGURE 10.19** Called the "Bent Pyramid" for obvious reasons, the angle of the slope of this pyramid was altered midproject, probably as the result of problems with steep-angled pyramids attempted previously. (*M. H. Feder*)

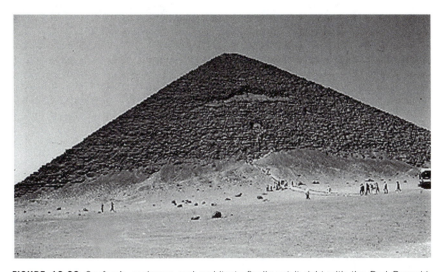

**FIGURE 10.20** Sneferu's engineers and architects finally got it right with the Red Pyramid. The angle of the slope of this pyramid is found in all subsequent pyramids built by the ancient Egyptians, the clear result of trial and error. (*M. H. Feder*)

the course of the life of a single pharaoh—better conforms to a process of internal and independent development rather than to borrowing from elsewhere (Clayton 1994).

Mesoamerican pyramids show much the same process, beginning with small, pyramidal platforms topped with temples, like the Temple of the

*Egypt*

*Maya*

Magician at the site of Dzibichaltun, located in the north of the Yucatan Peninsula (Figure 10.21), and culminating with the enormous, awesome pyramids of Tikal, Palenque, and Chichen Itza (Figure 10.22). Relying on the same basic model, a similar analysis can be performed for everything from the development of agriculture to ceramic and lithic technology.

**FIGURE 10.21** The small stepped platforms built at the Maya site of Dzbichaltun in the northern Yucatan Peninsula, Mexico, were pale harbingers of the magnificent pyramids that were built later in Maya history. (*Kenneth L. Feder*)

**FIGURE 10.22** The Pyramid of the Feathered Serpent is one of the most beautiful of those constructed by the Maya, the culmination of a long history of monumental construction projects. (*Kenneth L. Feder*)

The archaeological record shows quite clearly that ancient human beings were intelligent and capable. Certainly they were able to develop new technologies and at the same time recognized the potential of technologies developed by their neighbors and even by their enemies. The archaeologist's challenge rests in trying to figure out which process—independent invention or diffusion, or some combination of the two—was at work in individual cases.

## Read More

For far more detailed discussions of the ancient civilizations of Egypt and Mexico, as well as discussions of the evidence for diffusion between them and of how archaeologists assess the possibility of ancient contacts between civilizations, take a look at these references:

Adams, R. E. W. 1991. *Prehistoric Mesoamerica*. University of Oklahoma Press, Norman.

Arnold, D. 1991. *Building in Egypt: Pharaonic Stone Masonry*. Oxford University Press, Oxford.

Clarke, D. L. 1978. *Analytical Archaeology*. Columbia University Press, New York.

Clayton, P. A. 1994. *Chronicle of the Pharaohs: The Reign-by-Reign Record of the Rulers and Dynasties of Ancient Egypt*. Thames and Hudson, London.

Feder, K. L. 2002. *Frauds, Myths, and Mysteries: Science and Pseudoscience in Archaeology*. McGraw-Hill/Mayfield Publishing, Mountain View, California.

Lehner, M. 1997. *The Complete Pyramids*. Thames and Hudson, New York.

Sabloff, J. A. 1989. *The Cities of Ancient Mexico: Reconstructing a Lost World*. Thames and Hudson, New York.

## Study Questions

1. What does an archaeologist mean by the term *exotic material?*

2. What are the characteristics that make a lithic raw material desirable to a knapper?

3. What is "conchoidal fracture"?

4. Describe the "geography" and geometry of a stone core from which a knapper can produce stone flakes.

5. Describe the "geography" and geometry of a stone flake just removed from a core from which a knapper can produce a tool.

6. How can the analysis of trace element chemistry aid in attempting to track a raw material used by a past people to its geographic source?

7. Walk through the steps to remove a flake from a core by direct percussion.

8. Walk through the steps to thin a flake by pressure applied bifacially.

9. Describe the role played by Ishi in the ability of modern archaeologists to understand the manufacture of stone tools.

10. How does experimental reconstruction aid in our understanding of ancient stone tool technologies?

11. How does experimental archaeology aid in our understanding of how ancient tools were used?

12. Name and describe the kinds of wear or damage that occur on the edges of stone tools.

13. Describe how archaeologist Lawrence Keeley's experiment showed that wear patterns on stone tools were specific to particular kinds of tool use on specific raw materials.

14. How did archaeologist Lawrence Keeley determine how experimental replica tools he had made were used by a colleague? How did the results of his experiment apply to the analysis of archaeological artifacts?

15. Within the context of an overall settlement pattern, a past people may have used different areas of their territory differently. How might an archaeologist figure out and explain these different uses?

16. How does an archaeologist distinguish the differing purposes of different sites within an overall landscape signature? How might an archaeologist distinguish a village, a hunting camp, a seed-gathering station, and sacred place?

17. How do craft objects (e.g., pottery) inform us about a past people's technology?

18. How do craft objects (e.g., pottery) inform us about aspects about a past people's culture, beyond just technology?

19. What is diffusion?

20. How can an archaeologist distinguish between the diffusion of an idea from one source to other groups and the independent invention of a similar idea by different groups?

21. There are pyramids in Egypt and pyramids in Mexico. Did the idea of the pyramid originate in one of those places and diffuse to the other or was the pyramid invented and developed independently in both? How can you tell?

22. Suppose the pyramid in concept and execution was invented only in Egypt and spread to Mexico in ancient times. What would the archaeological investigation of the appearance and development of the pyramid in Mexico show? What does it really show?

Evidence concerning the subsistence base of the former inhabitants at the Wood Lily site was also apparent in the stone tool **assemblage.** Among the whole or partial tools we found at the site, twenty-five were hunting weapons collectively called projectile points (Figure 11.1) and seventeen were half-moon shaped knives that would have served well in butchering the carcasses of hunted animals (Figure 11.2).

The **morphology** of projectile points indicates their function; they are bilaterally symmetrical and aerodynamic. One end—the "business end"—is sharply pointed to pierce an animal's hide and the other often has specific features (notches, tangs, a stem) to enable hafting onto a wooden shaft (a spear, arrow, or dart shaft). The cutting tools at Wood Lily were blunt along their straight, back ends, where they would have been held in the hand or in a handle, and very thin and sharp along their curved working surfaces (Figure 11.3). A careful examination of the edges and tips of projectile points and the cutting edge of knives shows that careful **pressure flaking** was employed in their production (Figure 11.3).

**FIGURE 11.1** Examples of spear points found at the Wood Lily site. (*Kenneth L. Feder*)

Centimeters

**FIGURE 11.2** Examples of sharp-edged stone cutting tools found at the Wood Lily site. (*Kenneth L. Feder*)

Wood Lily was not a permanent village in which people lived year-long or for many years. The subsistence pattern of native New Englanders during the period of occupation at Wood Lily did not allow for such stability. Wood Lily was occupied long before the native people of New England had adopted the historically well-known diet based on maize (corn), beans, and squash. The wild ancestors of these crops were not native to our area—in fact, maize and beans are tropical plants. Native New Englanders did not initially develop these plants, but instead adopted them from cultures to the south and west, and reliance on these domesticated foods developed relatively late in our area. The oldest evidence of maize in New England does not predate A.D. 1000 and it did not achieve preeminence in subsistence here until at least a couple of centuries later.

Some locations provide a rich enough bounty of wild food resources on a year-round basis for a nonagricultural people to settle permanently; unfortunately, southern New England is not one of those places. The inhabitants of Wood Lily, like their neighbors throughout New England in the period

**FIGURE 11.3** Closeup (ten power) of the utilized edge of one of the stone cutting tools found at the Wood Lily site. The irregular nature of the edge is the result, at least in part, of damage produced simply by using the tool in the manner in which it was intended. (*Kenneth L. Feder*)

before a thousand years ago, were **foragers** or **hunter-gatherers.** Most foragers needed to be **nomadic** rather than **sedentary.** They needed to move in relation to the seasonal availability of resources necessary for their subsistence. They needed to adjust their group size as the local natural productivity of specific places changed during the year. During some seasons, populations might have aggregated at particularly rich spots. At other times, smaller groups, perhaps individual families, needed to disperse across the landscape, spreading out when resources available during those seasons were themselves more dispersed.

 ## How Do Archaeologists Know What Foods Ancient People Ate?

As you have read here previously—and incessantly—archaeology is based in large part on scrutiny of the material remains of human behavior. Analysis of a past people's diet is no different. The subsistence pattern of a group of people can be revealed through examination of the physical remains of the foods they ate and that have fortuitously preserved, along with an analysis of the tools they used in the collection, storage, and preparation of those foods.

Many foods eaten by people are processed in such a way as to extract the edible parts from the inedible, which are then disposed of or used for nondietary purposes. For instance, meat may be removed from bone, which is then discarded. The meat may be gone, invisible to the archaeologist, but the discarded bones, with their evidence of cut and slice marks from butchering with stone or metal tools, become part of the archaeological record. Nutmeats are removed from their shells and the shells may be discarded. The shells, and even some of the nutmeat itself, may rest preserved in trash pits and hearths. Kernels of corn are extracted from their cobs, cereal grains (like wheat, barley, rye, and oats) are removed from their stalks, shellfish are scooped from their shells, squash is scraped from its rind. The cobs, stalks, shells, and rinds—along with kernels and grains that were left behind on their stalks—may be discarded in a pile called a **kitchen midden,** relegated to a trash pit, heaped in a dump, broadcast on the surface of a field, or simply left where they fell during processing, cooking, or eating. Archaeologists can find these middens, pits, piles, and scatters; excavate these features; and then identify the foods that made up the diet of the people who produced the archaeological site being investigated.

In a process called **flotation,** archaeologists use the fact that these pieces of bone, seeds, nutshells, rinds, and all have a different specific gravity than water (a fixed volume of the archaeological material weighs either more or less than, but not the same as, the same fixed volume of water). This enables the separation of the archaeological material from its surrounding soil matrix. Archaeologists commonly will collect a 100% sample of a feature's soil. Either in the field or back in the lab, the soil is poured into a container filled with water. The water may be frothed with air from a pump passed through a bubbler—the kind used to oxygenate the water in a fish tank—to aid in the separation process. Material that is lighter and has a lower specific gravity than water (for example, seeds and charcoal) will float to the surface, where it can be skimmed and then dried for identification. Next, the muddy slurry left behind can be poured through fine screening, where materials that are heavier than water and have a higher specific gravity than water (for example, bone) are trapped, can be recovered, dried, and then identified. The water and fine soil particles pass through the screen (Figure 11.4).

In a recent application of this procedure, we recovered organic material from two sites in the McLean Game Refuge in Granby, Connecticut. We then supplied the recovered material to Dr. Cindy McWeeney, an expert in botanical identification and analysis. Cindy was able to identify pieces of charred hickory nutshell, indicating the use of hickory in the diet at a site occupied about a thousand years ago. She was also able to identify the tree species whose wood fueled the fire in which the hickory nuts were roasted: oak, maple, chestnut, and pine.

Many archaeology labs house **comparative collections** of the bones of animals and fish that live in an area, the shells of shellfish that might have been exploited in a region, as well as examples of edible seeds, nuts, and nutshells. Books provide encyclopedic coverage of animal bones, seeds, and nuts, and many contain photographs and drawings that can be used to identify archaeological specimens (for example, *Mammalian Osteo-Archaeology: North*

**FIGURE 11.4** On-site flotation in the Ohio River. The bottom of the galvanized bucket has been removed and a heavy hardware cloth mesh and fine screening have been fastened to the base. The bucket is partially submerged in the river water, then soil is poured in: organic remains float to the top and inorganic material is caught by the wire mesh. (*Kenneth L. Feder*)

*America* by B. Miles Gilbert, 1973). Recovered archaeological specimens, often broken into small fragments, may be extremely difficult to identify, and a good comparative collection can be a very useful tool in recognizing and identifying the sources for the ecofacts found at an archaeological site.

The faunal comparative collection in my lab was produced by a student as part of a year-long independent study course. The student (David Palmer, who is now a dentist; I have no idea if there is any connection between his putting together an osteological comparative collection and his chosen line of work) drove all over the state obtaining the carcasses of illegally hunted animals (out of season, lack of a hunting license, trespassing on private property, taking more than the legally allowed limit) that had been seized by the state Department of Environmental Protection (DEP). He also looked for and collected fresh roadkills. The collection was so inclusive, that I accused Palmer of driving around looking for live animals to run over himself, but he denied it.

Palmer boiled the flesh off the animals and produced a rather thorough "bone library," storing each animal skeleton in its own container. Many students are startled when they open the box labeled "Hockey Uniform" to find, the entire disarticulated (the bones are all separated) skeleton of an adult male deer instead of clothing. At least I tell them it's a deer and not a hockey player. Clearly the project deserved an A, but just to give the student a hard time (that's part of the job description for university professors), I told Palmer that I would only give him an A if, by using his comparative collection, he could identify a small, intact, triangular bone that we had recovered from a two-thousand-year-old hearth at the Loomis II village site in Windsor, Connecticut (which we had excavated the previous summer). I was only kidding, of course, but Palmer immediately rose to the occasion, stating that he knew exactly which bone it was. He reached into the hockey uniform box containing the adult male deer skeleton, rummaged around for a bit, and then pulled out the precise, if a bit larger, match for the archaeological specimen: a phalange, or toe bone, of a white-tailed deer (*Odocoileus virginianus*; Figure 11.5). Certainly I gave Palmer an A for his efforts and we have employed the osteological comparative collection ever since to identify the animal species exploited by people in our archaeological research.

Food remains are, by their very nature, organic—therein lies a problem. Artifacts made of durable, inorganic raw materials (like stone or fired clay) preserve well under virtually all soil conditions, but the same cannot be said for organic remains. Acidic soils, for example, dissolve organics. Biologically active soils are populated by creatures, both multi- and unicellular, whose entire

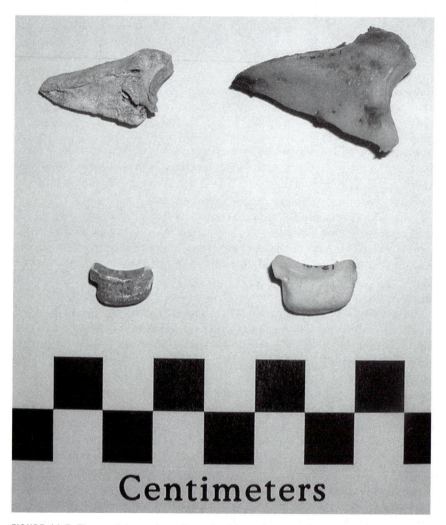

**FIGURE 11.5** The small bone elements on the left are from an archaeological site located in Connecticut that has been radiocarbon dated to nearly two thousand years ago. The two precisely matching bones (except for the fact that they are a little bigger) on the right are from our osteological comparative collection, specifically from a white tailed deer. (*Kenneth L. Feder*)

existence is based on their ingestion and breakdown of organic materials deposited in the soil. These tiny recycling factories care not at all whether some of the materials they are happily munching on are just leaf litter and decomposing old wood or are, instead, valuable archaeological ecofacts. Unfortunately for the archaeologist, these remains all taste equally good to the worms and bacteria that inhabit the soil. So, under conditions of high levels of soil acidity and biological activity, organic remains may not preserve well, if at all.

Fortunately, one form of food processing coincidentally aids in the preservation of food remains: burning. Nutshells or nutmeats deposited in the soil may not preserve well or long under certain conditions, but burning (for example, roasting nuts on an open fire) renders the remains much less susceptible to decay and, apparently, not as tasty to the little critters that would otherwise eat them (Figure 11.6).

Archaeologists may also rely on examination of the tools used by ancient people in the capturing or gathering, processing, and preparation of their foods. Rather obviously, though the scraps of meat and bone may not preserve, the arrow or spear points found by an archaeologist are an indication that hunting played a role in subsistence. Fish hooks, net weights, and the remnants of fish weirs or traps indicate that fishing played a role in the diet. Stone hoes, metal plow blades, or fire-hardened digging sticks indicate that horticulture or agriculture contributed to an ancient people's diet. Apparatus for grinding nuts, seeds, or grain into flour, including manos and metates as well as mortars and pestles, may signify the production of flour as part of the food base of an ancient group. Clearly, the presence of the apparatus used in hunting, fishing, shellfish collecting, plant gathering, or agricultural production indicates that these subsistence modes were employed by a past people, but developing a statistical impression of the importance of each food source is problematic.

When we are lucky and conditions for preservation are just right, we may even be able to detect and recover biological residue, including blood, from the edge of a tool. This residue can sometimes enable a very accurate and specific identification of the animal species the tool was used to kill or butcher.

Lucky for us, ancient people often were not especially fastidious about cleaning the edges of the tools they used in food collection and preparation. As shown, the preservation of organic remains can be problematic in many depositional environments. Luckily, however, plants produce inorganic mineral particles called **phytoliths,** which are highly durable and have a species-specific form. The recovery and identification of phytoliths on tool edges and surfaces provides key clues about the foods collected and prepared by ancient people (Piperno and Pearsall 1998).

If food remains are well preserved, at least a gross measure of the proportional role of each food source in an ancient diet may be suggested. A **faunal analysis** may determine the minimum number of animals present in an archaeological deposit, providing a relative measure of the significance of the animal species used by a people.

Some tools might not obviously imply a particular subsistence component, but reference to ethnographic models and analysis of their wear patterns can help us suggest probable uses and the foods they most likely were used on. For example, so-called **semi-lunar knives** are found at archaeological sites

**FIGURE 11.6** Charred nutshells (acorn and hickory) from a cooking feature excavated at a two-thousand-year-old site located in Windsor, Connecticut. (*Kenneth L. Feder*)

in a wide swath across northeastern North America. These knives, usually made of a thin sheet of slate cut into a half-moon shape, are well known among some native groups in the recent history of the Arctic and sub-Arctic for gutting fish. The tool was held along its straight segment, sometimes in a handle; the curved portion was the cutting edge. Sure enough, when archaeological specimens are examined under magnification, tiny striations are seen parallel to the curved edge, which also exhibits a tremendous amount of polish as a result of use (Figure 11.7). The same kinds of striations are found on replicas used experimentally to cut open fish, supporting the hypothesis that the archaeological semi-lunar knives were used in ways similar to their historical counterparts.

**FIGURE 11.7** Magnification (10X) of the edge of an ulu, a semi-lunar knife. The cutting edge seen at the bottom of the photograph has been dulled, smoothed, nicked, and polished simply by use. (*Courtesy Marc Banks*)

Though it certainly is not the most romantic weapon in the archaeologist's analytical arsenal, food remains that have actually been ingested by, passed through the digestive systems of, and then been excreted by ancient people provide direct if unpleasant evidence of diet. The remains of prehistoric feces, called **paleofeces** or **coprolites,** are preserved, though this is quite rare. Because our human digestive tract is not entirely efficient, some of the material we ingest fails to be entirely digested and is excreted, sometimes with very little alteration and often recognizable. Our bodies are not very good, for instance, at breaking down some forms of cellulose in plant foods and this material passes through our systems, sometimes more or less intact. When human feces have been deposited in a stable, dry environment (where the deposit is not rained on, temperature does not vary widely, and where there are no animals who might like to recyle some of the undigested food), they may preserve for long periods of time. Bones, whole and fragmentary, seeds and seed casings, shells, and even meat cells can be extracted from coprolites. These data are about as direct as we can get in the analysis of an ancient diet. In fact, much of our understanding of the earliest agriculture in the New World is based on undigested food remains found in coprolites excavated in caves in highland Mexico (MacNeish 1967).

And what about the food that actually does become incorporated into your body? I know a lot of people who swear that you can actually see every candy bar they have ever eaten right there on their hips, but that has yet to be tested archaeologically. In fact, however, the chemistry of certain foods does have a measurable affect on the human skeleton. A careful chemical analysis of human bones can reveal at least some general information about a person's diet. We can't count candy bars, but we can reveal some details about the significance of meat in a diet and even the kinds of grains that contributed to subsistence.

## Read More

Here are the references for the specific citations in this section. More citations will be found in the linked segments.

Gilbert, B. M. 1973. *Mammalian Osteo-Archaeology: North America.* Missouri Archaeological Society, Columbia.

MacNeish, R. S. 1967. An interdisciplinary approach to an archaeological problem. In *Prehistory of the Tehuacan Valley: Volume One—Environment and Subsistence,* edited by D. Beyers, 14–23. University of Texas Press, Austin.

Pearsall, D. M. 2000. *Paleoethnobotany: A Handbook of Procedures.* Academic Press, San Diego.

Piperno, D. R., and D. M. Pearsall. 1998. *The Origins of Agriculture in the Lowland Neotropics.* Academic Press, Orlando, Florida.

## Why Do Archaeologists Want to Know the Animal Species Exploited by Ancient People?

Identifying the bones found at an archaeological site certainly allows us to develop a listing of the animal foods eaten by the people who lived there, and that is important in and of itself in attempting to paint a complete picture of the lives of a past people (Baker, Shaffer, and Steele 1997; Chaplin 1971; Gilbert 1973; Hesse and Wapnish 1985; Klein and Cruz-Uribe 1984). But, knowing which animal species were used by an ancient group provides greater insights into the nature of their societies than just what they ate. Importantly, the behavior of different animal species used as food played a role in shaping the behavior of the human groups that exploited them (Binford 1987).

In northeast North America, for example, white-tailed deer played an important role in the subsistence quest. Whitetail are, essentially, solitary animals. The males live by themselves, seeking out the company of females only during the breeding season in November. Sometimes in winter you will see a handful of females browsing together—we once counted nineteen whitetails walking along a trail back behind our house—for the most part, however, the largest social groupings consist of a female and one or two of her offspring; there are no vast herds of white-tailed deer communally traversing the eastern woodlands in a migratory cycle.

The generally solitary nature of whitetails had an obvious impact on the behavior of those human groups that depended on them for their meat and hides. Solitary animals are taken by hunters, rather obviously, one at a time, and it makes sense for hunters to go out singly or in small groups to stalk them. A small social group of hunter-gatherers made up of just a few families with a small handful of hunters can do quite nicely with whitetails. An older buck may provide close to two hundred pounds of meat that, when preserved by drying and combined with other foods (in stews, for example), is sufficient to feed a small group of people for quite some time. The point is, because groups in the northeast were heavily dependent on white-tailed deer for their subsistence, the nature of whitetail behavior molded their hunting behavior and the requirements of these hunting strategies had a significant impact on the size and makeup of their social grouping.

Compare this to another North American species hunted for food, the American bison (*Bison bison*). Bison are gregarious and individual bison herds number in the hundreds and even the thousands. A hunter will almost inevitably run into not a single animal, but many tens of animals. Although a hunter might be able to isolate an individual animal for capture, because bison tend to act in unison to a threat, this might be difficult—and why would a hunter feel constrained to kill only one animal when many can be killed simultaneously, providing a substantial amount of meat and a large number of hides?

A hunting strategy appropriate for the capture of a single deer might not be appropriate for a species that travels in large numbers like bison. And, in fact, unlike deer hunting, cooperative hunts (involving many hunters in an organized effort to kill not just a single animal but tens of creatures and even hundreds in a single hunt) were common among Plains Indians (Wheat 1972). Archaeological evidence shows that such large-scale, cooperative hunts were conducted more than ten thousand years ago. The skeletons of as many as two hundred bison have been found in these mass killings. In some of these hunts, segments of herds were isolated and then herded into quagmires of sand, where they became trapped and easy pickings for hunters with spears (Frison 1974). In other instances, the bison were stampeded over cliffs where the fall would kill most of the animals, who then could be butchered in place. To accomplish this complex, organized, cooperative hunt, a large social group might be called on to participate. Some participants might have the job of isolating a segment of the bison population from the larger group. Some might start fires and make noise in an effort to panic the isolated animals. Others might be charged with the task of directing the panicked animals toward a cliff, while others still might position themselves at the base of the cliff to kill any animals that survived the fall and to begin the task of butchering the animals and drying the huge amounts of meat collected from a kill of that size.

Surely then, the nature of the animals being hunted renders differing hunting strategies appropriate, and human groups will react accordingly. Knowing which animals were exploited by a past people goes far beyond just clarifying their food preferences: it provides an important perspective on how the subsistence base may have contributed to the contours of the rest of their way of life.

Of course, not all animals exploited by people were wild. In some parts of the world, beginning about eleven thousand years ago, human beings began the process of animal domestication. It likely began by a slow process of capture, corralling, and taming wild animals and actually changing them through selective breeding—killing off aggressive, nasty beasts and allowing only those with attractive characteristics to breed (thus passing down those traits to subsequent generations).

In selective breeding, people have usually (but not always) chosen for smaller size and a less aggressive disposition (for safety), a woollier coat (for fiber production), higher milk production (for food), as well as for amount of meat produced. Smaller overall size and smaller teeth and jaws than wild versions of an animal species are physical characteristics that are seen in the archaeological record and interpreted as evidence of selective breeding and domestication. In fact, it is a decrease in jaw size in particular that provides the basis for our recognition of the earliest separation of the domestic dog from the wild wolf (Olson 1985; Pennisi 2002).

Other evidence of domestication is a bit more subtle. For example, the population statistics of wild animals are distinguishable from domesticated stock. Among domestic herd animals, males are nearly always killed off when they are young: very few bulls or rams are needed for breeding and, because they tend be larger and more aggressive, it may make sense to eliminate most of them from a captive population. Females, on the other hand, are kept around for a while: they can produce milk as well as multiple offspring over a long period of time. When Chinese scientists found a population profile in the assemblage of pig bones at Zengpiyan Cave in Guilan Province, it showed that 85% of the animals were males less than two years old, and they concluded that the population represented an early attempt at selective breeding (Chang 1986). Similarly, though they are not morphologically different from the bones of wild members of their species, the bones of goats found at the archaeological site Ganj Dareh in Iran show that the site's inhabitants habitually killed off males when they were still quite young. This elimination indicates a level of control over the breeding process, which implies the existence of a captive population of the animals (Zeder and Hesse 2000).

# Read More

Zooarchaeology, the study of animals whose remains have been found at archaeological sites, has produced a vast literature. The following works serve as guides to identifying animals from their bones and then interpreting the human behaviors that resulted in the deposition of those bones at sites:

Baker, B. W., B. S. Shaffer, and D. G. Steele. 1997. Basic approaches in archaeological faunal analysis. In *Field Methods in Archaeology*, edited by T. R. Hester, H. J. Shafer, and K. L. Feder, 298–318. Mayfield Publishing, Mountain View, California.

Binford, L. 1987. *Bones: Ancient Men and Modern Myths*. Academic Press, New York.

Chang, K.-c. 1986. *The Archaeology of Ancient China*. 4th ed. Yale University Press, New Haven, Connecticut.

Chaplin, R. E. 1971. *The Study of Animal Bones from Archaeological Sites.* Seminar Press, London.

Frison, G., ed. 1974. *The Casper Site: A Hell Gap Bison Kill on the High Plains.* Academic Press, New York.

Gilbert, B. M. 1973. *Mammalian Osteo-Archaeology: North America.* Missouri Archaeological Society, Columbia.

Hesse, B., and P. Wapnish. 1985. *Animal Bone Archaeology.* Manuals on Archaeology 5. Taraxacum, Washington, D.C.

Klein, R. G., and K. Cruz-Uribe. 1984. *The Analysis of Animal Bones from Archaeological Sites.* University of Chicago Press, Chicago.

O'Connor, T. 2000. *The Archaeology of Animal Bones.* Texas A&M Press, College Station.

Olson, S. J. 1985. *Origins of the Domestic Dog: The Fossil Record.* University of Arizona Press, Tucson.

Reitz, E. J. 1999. *Zooarchaeology.* Cambridge University Press, Cambridge, England.

Wheat, J. B. 1972. *The Olsen-Chubbuck Site: A Paleo Indian Bison Kill.* Memoir of the Society for American Archaeology 26, Salt Lake City.

Zeder, M. A., and B. Hesse. 2000. The initial domestication of goats (*Capra hircus*) in the Zagros Mountains 10,000 years ago. *Science* 287:2254–57.

## How Can You Tell What Kind of Animal Was Killed or Butchered with an Ancient Stone Tool?

Regardless of how you might feel about the death penalty (personally, I support capital punishment for telemarketers, but that's just me), one can't help but be given pause by the all-too-frequently aired stories on the evening news of some unfortunate—yet, ultimately, incredibly lucky—man or woman walking out of prison after languishing on death row for ten, fifteen, or twenty years. These innocent people often share in common the fact that after years of professing their innocence, they were finally freed, just before their scheduled execution after being proven innocent through the application of residue analysis. Forensic investigators now recognize that, even years after a crime was committed, a tiny splash of blood may remain concealed on the curve of a serrated blade, a minute clump of the murderer's skin cells may yet reside under the fingernails of the victim, and semen can still be recovered from the clothing of a rape victim. These residues can be recovered and analyzed for blood type and even DNA, enabling investigators to positively rule out innocent individuals—leading to dramatic releases from prison and, in some cases, enabling positive identification of the actual perpetrator of the crime.

The same capillary action by which a tiny droplet of blood may be pulled up along the mechanical polish striations of a stainless steel knife blade acts on tiny droplets of blood to pull them along the interstices of tiny crystals of stone in a cryptocrystalline material, up and away from the cutting edges of a knife blade made of stone. Dried and hidden in tiny cavities and striations on the stone blade, the blood may remain hidden for thousands of years. In certain cases, the blood can be recovered, and the animal species that produced the blood can be identified.

One of the most widely applied techniques for blood residue analysis used in modern law enforcement is **cross-over immunoelectrophoresis (CIEP)**. Precisely the same procedure is used to determine the presence of blood on an ancient weapon and to identify the species that was the source of the blood. The process is based on immunological testing of any residue on a stone tool. The antisera of a number of potential animal sources (including human) are applied to the residue recovered from a tool. Each antiserum consists of antibodies that are species-specific and will, therefore, biologically react to antigens in the blood only of the same species. In other words, when blood residue is recovered from an ancient stone blade, that residue is divided into a number of samples, each of which is then exposed to the antiserum from a different animal species. If the ancient blood is not from the same species as the antiserum, there is no immunological reaction. If, however, the blood residue and the added antiserum come from the same species, the antiserum "recognizes" the antigens in the blood sample and reacts to them.

For example, Loy and Dixon (1998) examined a number of ancient stone tools in Alaska dating to as much as ten thousand years ago. They were able to recover blood residue from the tools, which they then identified as having come from woolly mammoth, bison, bear, sheep, caribou, and musk ox. At the other end of the continent, in eastern Quebec, a series of tools from sites dating to about the same age in the La Martre River valley were examined for blood residue (Chalifoux 1999). The researchers obtained positive reactions for rabbit, deer, bear, sea lion, trout, and rat from the blood residue recovered from a sample of ancient tools from the La Martre sites. At another series of nine-thousand-year-old sites excavated in what is today Yellowstone National Park, traces of blood of deer, elk, rabbit, dog, and bear were identified on stone spear points, scrapers, and scraping tools (Cannon 1995).

Ancient preserved food residues are not restricted to the edges of stone tools. Researchers have also looked for food remains on the interior surfaces of the ceramic vessels in which various foods were cooked, served, or stored. It's a lucky thing, for example, that the people of the ancient Maya civilization of Central America weren't too fastidious about washing out their spouted "teapot" vessels. Researchers have applied a procedure called **high-performance liquid chromatography (HPLC)** to the dry residues recovered from the insides of fourteen of these pouring vessels manufactured by the Maya as long ago as 600 B.C. at the site of Colha, Belize (Hurst et al. 2002). Residues bearing the chemical signature of chocolate were recovered from the insides of three of these vessels. The cacao plant was domesticated by people in the New World and the residues on the Colha vessels predate the previous oldest evidence of the brewing of a chocolate beverage by the Maya by a thousand years. Chocolate-based beverages were a favorite of the Maya and, as the residue analysis shows, they have a long history in Central America. Some argue that maize represents the most significant domesticated crop contributed by the native people of America to the rest of the world: I think that many of us—certainly, any of us who have tasted chocolate—would beg to differ.

When I participated as a student in my first archaeology field school, we made certain to clean every stone tool to make it easier to analyze the edges for use wear. Thirty years later, archaeologists are rethinking the desirability of cleaning those edges before investigating the possibility that biological residues remain that can directly inform us about the animals killed, and as well as the plant foods processed and eaten by the tool users.

## Read More

Any of the examples cited here provide brief, fascinating discussions of the potential of residue analysis in archaeology:

Cannon, K. P. 1995. Blood residue analyses of ancient stone tools reveal clues to prehistoric subsistence patterns in Yellowstone. *CRM* 18(2):14–16.
Chalifoux, É. 1999. Paleoindian occupations on the Gaspé Peninsula. *Northeast Anthropology* 57:69–79.
Loy, T. H., and E. J. Dixon. 1998. Blood residues on fluted points from Eastern Beringia indicate mammoth predation as part of a big-game hunting tradition. *American Antiquity* 63:21–46.

## How Can You Tell What Kinds of Plants Were Collected or Processed with an Ancient Stone Tool?

Much in the way that the residues of animals killed and butchered by ancient people may linger in the nicked edges of the weapons used to kill them and the tools used to prepare them for dinner, plant remains also can adhere to the working edges of utensils for decades, centuries, and even millennia. Recovery and analysis of those remains provide the archaeologist with a database that can allow for the detailed reconstruction of an ancient people's diet.

As mentioned previously, organic residues left by plants often are not particularly durable and bits of wood, fiber, or starch left on an axe blade, mano, or knife likely will disappear as a result of biological activity in the soil in which these artifacts are deposited. However, plants also produce **phytoliths,** a nonorganic residue made up of microscopic mineral particles, more precisely defined as opal silica bodies. Because they are not organic, phytoliths are not eaten or recycled by bacteria or other small organisms, and because they are minerals, phytoliths can be extremely durable, persisting in the soil or adhering to tools for a very long time. Beyond their durability is the fact that different plant genera and species produce a suite of morphologically distinct phytoliths (Figure 11.8). When a researcher trained and experienced in phytolith identification is presented with a sample recovered from the soils at an archaeological site or extracted from the cracks and crevices of ancient tools, he or she can diagnose the species of the plants that grew in the vicinity of the settlement, that were brought back to the community from elsewhere, or that were processed with the tools found at the site.

**FIGURE 11.8** Phytoliths, like pollen, exhibit two characteristics that make them useful to the archaeologist: they are durable and each species produces distinct forms. When phytoliths are recovered from the surfaces of tools, the species of the plants on which the tools were used can be identified. Phytoliths produced by maize are shown here. (Pearsall, Deborah M., *Phytoliths in the Flora of Ecuador: The University of Missouri Online Phytolith Database* http://www.missouri.edu/~phyto/)

Dolores Piperno, Anthony Ranere, Irene Holst, and Patricia Hansell (2000) were able to recover phytoliths adhering to a variety of milling stones excavated at the Aguadulce Shelter site in Panama that dated from between seven thousand and five thousand years ago. Archaeological tools do not come with little tags clearing up questions we have concerning their use, but the shape and heft of the "milling stones" suggested both their name and the fact that they might have been used to grind seeds or roots. In this case, the phytoliths secreted in cracks on the tool surfaces not only showed that the tools had been used to grind plant material, the phytoliths also showed which plants had been processed with the tools. The researchers found phytoliths diagnostic of a number of starchy tropical plants, especially manioc, arrowroot, and yams. Along with milling roots and yams, the people of the Aguadulce Shelter were also processing maize with their grinding stones.

In this specific case, by recovering the microscopic remnants of plants processed by ancient tools, analysis of plant residues is allowing archaeologists to directly address questions related to the origins of agriculture in the New World. More generally, phytolith research is providing a unique avenue of inquiry into the use of plants by past people, often by producing the raw data being used to illuminate the story of the origins of agriculture (Piperno and Flannery 2001 for maize; Piperno and Pearsall 1998 for root crops of South America; Piperno and Stothert 2003 for squash).

# Read More

In each of the following publications, you can read informative accounts of the successful recovery of plant remnants from the surfaces of archaeological artifacts that were used to prepare foods like squash, chocolate, and maize:

Hurst W. J., S. M. Tarka Jr., T. G. Powis, F. Valdez Jr., and T. R. Hester. 2002. Cacao usage by the earliest Maya civilization. *Nature* 418:289–90.

Piperno, D., and K. Flannery. 2001. The earliest archaeological maize (*Zea mays* L.). *Proceedings of the National Academy of Sciences* 98:2101–3.

Piperno, D., and K. A. Stothert. 2003. Phytolith evidence for early Holocene *Cucurbita* domestication in southwest Ecuador. *Science* 299:1054–57.

Piperno, D. R., and D. M. Pearsall. 1998. *The Origins of Agriculture in the Lowland Neotropics.* Academic Press, Orlando, Florida.

Piperno, D. R., A. J. Ranere, I. Holst, and P. Hansell. 2000. Starch grains reveal early root crop horticulture in the Panamanian tropical forest. *Nature* 407:894–97.

## How Can You Determine the Importance of an Animal Species in a People's Diet?

Suppose I dropped you off in the middle of a junkyard and gave you the task of estimating the number of automobiles that had been disposed of there. The problem is, there are no complete cars in the junkyard, only some of their constituent parts. How would you go about the task?

You might begin by looking for major, important components of cars, pieces that are found one per car. The engine block would be one such component. Every car has an engine—and no car has more than one—so you might count the number of engine blocks and suggest that number as a guess for the number of autos abandoned at the junkyard.

Now, suppose I tell you that you can't just rely on engines because some of them had been removed from the junkyard entirely. Luckily, however, other parts of those cars (for example, gas tanks) had been left behind. Every car has a gas tank and you might count those. You couldn't assume that the gas tanks you have counted belonged to different cars from those already counted based on their engine blocks. You almost certainly would be counting some cars twice, once for their engine blocks and once for their gas tanks. Being conservative, and not wanting to overestimate the number of cars, you might assume that, because each car must have had both an engine block and a gas tank, that an engine and tank together still represent only one car. That assumption might underestimate the number of cars—a gas tank and engine block might not belong to the same car, even though you are counting them together as belonging to the same auto—but that's okay; it is more comfortable to come up with a baseline reflecting the minimum possible number rather than a maximum.

If you counted twenty engine blocks and thirty gas tanks in the junkyard, there still must have been a minimum of thirty cars in the junkyard; you would assume that the first twenty gas tanks came from the same cars as represented by the twenty engine blocks (that's twenty cars) but the next ten gas tanks must reflect the presence of ten additional cars whose engine blocks are missing. If you continued this counting of major car components, always assuming that if parts could have belonged to the same automobile, they did, you would come up with a minimum number of cars; there could be more, though you couldn't prove it, but there could be no fewer.

Archaeologists use the same reasoning to come up with a statistic called the **MNI** or **Minimum Number of Individuals** in a faunal assemblage. Although a cooking or trash feature may present the archaeologist with a jumble of bone fragments, a conservative, minimum estimate of the number of animals killed, butchered, and cooked can be determined in much the same way as shown in the junkyard car example. We assume that skeletal elements that are "redundant" (meaning that they could have come from the same animal) did come from the same creature. You may, for example, find the fragmentary, butchered crania of ten white-tailed deer at a site. From this you can conclude with certainty that there must have been at least ten deer killed by the ancient inhabitants. Now suppose that we also recovered thirty right shoulder blades of the same species of deer. Though we couldn't prove it, we assume that ten of those belonged to the deer already represented by the ten crania. The twenty right shoulder blades with no corresponding crania would have to belong to twenty additional deer (we'll assume there were no mutant deer with supernumerary right shoulder blades). So the MNI for deer at the site would be thirty (Figure 11.9 shows a similar analysis for sheep).

We are aided in our MNI calculations by the ability to distinguish the bones of males from females as well as animals who died at different stages of their lives. A right and left lower leg might come from the same deer, but not if one came from a male and the other a female, or if one came from an animal that died young and the other from a much older one.

It is important to understand that through the application of the MNI procedure, we are not hoping to come up with an accurate census of an animal

|  | DEPOSIT | | | |
|---|---|---|---|---|
|  | A | B | C | TOTAL |
| BONE ELEMENT |  |  |  |  |
| Cranium | 3 | 3 | 1 | 7 |
| Mandible | 9 | 24 | 4 | 37 |
| Scapula | 5 | 19 | 2 | 26 |
| Humerus | 4 | 15 | 6 | 25 |
| Radius | 9 | 21 | 8 | 38 |
| Ulna | 3 | 6 | 2 | 11 |
| Metacarpal | 5 | 26 | 6 | 37 |
| Pelvis | 10 | 0 | 0 | 10 |
| Femur | 2 | 4 | 1 | 7 |
| Tibia | 7 | 17 | 8 | 32 |
| Calcaneum | 0 | 0 | 2 | 2 |
| Astragalus | 0 | 0 | 0 | 0 |
| Metatarsal | 10 | 20 | 9 | 39 |

Calculation of the minimum number of sheep recovered from three deposits (A, B, and C) excavated at the Treasury Site, a Saxon farm excavated in London (data from Chaplin 1971). There are 271 individual bones listed here, and each one could have come from a different animal. There could have been, therefore, as many as 271 animals whose remains were represented at the site. But there could have been far fewer; in calculating the number of animals represented at an archaeological deposit, the Minimum Number approach is conservative, assuming that if multiple bone elements could have come from the same individual animal, they did. For example, the 39 metatarsals (foot bones) could have come from fewer than 39 individual animals since each sheep has more than one metatarsal. The 7 crania could have come from no fewer than 7 individuals and the 10 pelvises could have come from no fewer than 10 animals, but some of the crania and some of the pelvises may have come from the same individual animals; in calculating the MNI, it is assumed that the 7 crania and 7 of the 10 pelvises all did come from the same 7 individuals. By the same reasoning, the 37 mandibles could have come from no fewer than 37 animals (some or all of which could have also been represented by the crania and pelvises just enumerated). Based on the above chart, there are the remains of a minimum of 37 animals at the old farm site, though there could have been many more.

**FIGURE 11.9** To determine the minimum number of individuals of an animal species represented at an archaeological site, you need to count all of the different skeletal elements recovered. (*Based on data from Chaplin, 1971*)

population. The MNI statistic merely gives us a valuable impression of the relative importance of each species in the subsistence quest of a past people—it does that rather well.

## Read More

Any of the zooarchaeology guides cited in the section "Why Do Archaeologists Want to Know the Animal Species Exploited by Ancient People?" will walk you through the process of determining the minimum numbers of a particular species represented by the bones recovered at an archaeological site:

Chaplin, R. E. 1971. *The Study of Animal Bones from Archaeological Sites.* Seminar Press, London.
Klein, R. G., and K. Cruz-Uribe. 1984. *The Analysis of Animal Bones from Archaeological Sites.* University of Chicago Press, Chicago.
O'Connor, T. 2000. *The Archaeology of Animal Bones.* Texas A&M Press, College Station.
Reitz, E. J. 1999. *Zooarchaeology.* Cambridge University Press, Cambridge, England.

## How Does Skeletal Chemistry Help Us Reconstruct an Ancient Diet?

I am sure you are familiar with the old expression, "You are what you eat." It turns out that there is more than just a "grain" of truth in that statement. (And it should become clear soon that, I just committed a terrible pun in my use of the word "grain." Sorry. I couldn't help it.) For example, the ratio of stable **isotopes** of carbon and nitrogen have been determined for herbivores and carnivores. It turns out that animals that eat a vegetarian diet have a preponderance of carbon over nitrogen and carnivores have the reverse. Researchers calculated the carbon to nitrogen ratio in bones of an extinct hominid, an individual member of the well-known Neandertals, found in a cave in Croatia. The result resembled the ratio measured for a control group consisting of the bones of an animal whose dietary preference was well known, specifically, a carnivore (and more specifically, the saber-toothed cat). The cats and the Neandertals both had a higher proportion of nitrogen than seen among known herbivores (Richards et al. 2000). This has been interpreted as meaning that the Neandertals relied heavily on meat in their diet.

Even diets that differ only in the kinds of plants eaten may result in human bones that appear identical, but possess a slightly different chemistry. For example, there are at least three somewhat differing photosynthesis processes by which plants use solar energy to produce food, labeled C3, C4, and CAM pathways. Most grasses utilize the C4 pathway that more readily uses carbon dioxide containing an unstable isotope of carbon (C-13) than do those plants (mostly trees) that utilize the C3 pathway. What this means is that C4 pathway plants have a higher concentration of C-13 than do C4 plants. When animals ingest plant food, they incorporate carbon into their bodies, including their skeletons. A preference for or limited availability of plants following one of these pathways will result in a C-13 proportion in the animal's bones that matches the proportion seen in the plants they eat, which can be used to deduce at least a general element of the animal's diet (C3 or C4 pathway plants).

As it turns out, most of the indigenous wild plant foods eaten by ancient Native Americans north of Mexico were C3 plants, with their lower concentration of C-13 (Smith 1995). And, in fact, the bones of Native Americans dating to before about A.D. 1000 (when indigenous plant foods formed the core of subsistence in the Midwest) show a proportionally low concentration of C-13 as well, reflecting the nature of their diet.

The stereotypical American Indian crop is maize, but maize (or corn) is not native to North America. It is a tropical plant native to Mesoamerica, was domesticated there more than 7,000 years ago, and shows up in small amounts at archaeological sites in North America about three thousand years later as a result of **diffusion.** Maize does not follow the photosynthetic pathway of most of the wild plants eaten by the native people of North America. Maize is a C4 plant with a proportionally higher concentration of C-13. In a remarkable turn, after about A.D. 1000, the skeletons of Native Americans found in the Midwest show a marked jump in C-13 proportion when compared to their ancestors. This seems like strong evidence that, although maize had already been introduced into North America no later than 2800 years earlier, it wasn't until after A.D. 1000 that it became a significant and perhaps dominant part of the aboriginal diet whose impact shows up in the chemistry of the bones of native people.

Indeed, you *are* what you eat and the chemistry of human bone is beginning to reveal dietary preferences in remarkable ways.

## Read More

To get more details about reconstructing the diets of ancient people through the chemical analysis of their bones, have a look at the references that follow:

Price, T. D., ed. 1989. *The Chemistry of Prehistoric Bone.* Cambridge University Press, Cambridge, England.

Price, T. D., M. J. Schoeninger, and G. J. Armelagos. 1985. Bone chemistry and past behavior: An overview. *Journal of Human Evolution* 14:419–47.

Richards, M. P., P. P. Pettitt, E. Trinkaus, F. H. Smith, M. Paunovi, and I. Karavani. 2000. Neanderthal diet at Vindija and Neanderthal predation: The evidence from stable isotopes. *Proceedings of the National Academy of Sciences* 97:7663–66.

Sandford, M. K. 1992. A reconsideration of trace element analysis. In *Skeletal Biology of Past Peoples: Research Methods,* edited by S. R. Saunders and A. M. Katzenberg, 153–74. Wiley-Liss, New York.

Smith, B. D. 1995. *The Emergence of Agriculture.* Scientific American Library, New York.

## How Can the Season of a Village's Occupation Be Determined?

As you will remember, in instances where archaeologists rely on chronometric dating methods other than dendrochronology for determining the age of a site, the error factor is usually in the tens and even the hundreds of years. It may seem paradoxical then for me to say that, even though most chronometric dating methods are not precise and the plus-or-minus error factor in years can be substantial, I still might be able to tell you the month or at least the season a site was occupied. But there is no contradiction because assigning a month or season of occupation relies on a different set of data than chronometric dating techniques.

Essentially, human beings depend to one degree or another on resources, especially food resources, that are available on a sometimes fairly restricted seasonal basis. Knowing the season or even the month of availability of resources whose remains are found at an archaeological site provides a way to determine the season or month of site occupation. Because some foods can be stored for an extended period of time, seasonal availability does not necessarily restrict the time of occupation to the season or month when the resource was collected. So, this form of analysis indicates the month or season when a group must have been present, but it cannot be used to prove when it was not present.

For example, during fall in the eastern woodlands of North America, oaks produce acorns, and chestnut, walnut, and hickory trees produce their respective nuts (Bernstein 1999). Finding the remains of the shells and nutmeats of acorns, chestnuts, walnuts, and hickory at an archaeological site is a good indicator that the site was occupied in the fall of the year, but not necessarily only in the fall. People can only collect nuts when they are available, which is soon after they ripen and before animals collect them all or they get covered up by leaves and needles. Certainly, nuts left in their shells can be stored for a substantial length of time, so the recovery of nutshells or charred nutmeats is strong evidence that a site was occupied in the fall, but not necessarily exclusively: the site's inhabitants may have harvested large quantities of nuts in the fall, stored a portion of them, and continued to subsist on nuts well into the winter or beyond.

As a result of migratory patterns, some fish species are available in significant numbers over a relatively narrow window of time during the year. Every fall, for example, Pacific salmon make an epic migration, traveling sometimes hundreds of miles from the ocean back upriver and ultimately (and remarkably) home to the streams in which they hatched. Swimming in great numbers, and fighting the river's flow, these fish were easily caught in enormous quantities by people who organized their seasonal schedules around the upstream journey of the salmon each fall. Sites showing evidence of salmon capture were most likely occupied in the fall during the spawning run (Dincauze 1976). Here too, preservation and storage are a possibility—dried salmon can remain edible for a long time. So, the presence of salmon at a site doesn't mean that the site was inhabited only in the fall, but it must have been inhabited at least in the fall to allow for capture of the fish.

In some cases, the ages of juvenile animals hunted by a people can indicate the season of harvest. Unlike human beings, who are sexually receptive virtually all of the time (well, nearly), most animal species have a relatively brief rutting season when females are sexually receptive and fertile and during which can become pregnant. Also, because the females of most species have a rather regular period of gestation, the births of offspring in a population of animals occur in a rather narrow range of time during the year (again unlike humans, whose births are distributed fairly evenly across the year).

Once born, the young of any animal species go through a series of developmental processes that are obvious on the outside—they get larger, their muscles increase in strength, they may grow horns or antlers—and that are also apparent on the inside, including the animal's bones. Changes to skeletons that reflect growth and increasing maturity usually occur at a regular and consistent rate and at relatively fixed times during development. These changes can be used to gauge the age of a subadult animal—we will see the same analytical process applied to human skeletons as well.

We can figure out the season or even the month that an animal was hunted—and, therefore, the season or month the site was occupied—because we know when animals of the hunted species are born and we can determine the approximate age of death from the morphology of the animal's bones. Let me give you an example: the breeding season of the American bison (commonly called the buffalo and technically *Bison bison*) extends from middle to late summer, July through September. The length of gestation for a bison varies from 270 to 300 days, so most bison are born in the three-month period of March, April, and May. Bison do not achieve sexual maturity until about the age of two, and between birth and that time their bones grow, develop, and achieve adult form, following a rather firmly timed schedule. In other words, as a bison matures, its bones progress through a series of somewhat consistently measured changes in appearance so their appearance, in turn, can be used to accurately estimate a developing bison's age.

Now, suppose we excavate an archaeological site where bison meat was a major component of subsistence. Further suppose that where juvenile bison were hunted, they all can be determined to have been about eighteen months old, based on the morphology of their maturing bones. Count forward eighteen months from their births in March, April, and May and you get to August, September, and October (of the following year). Therefore, those eighteen-month-old bison whose butchered bones were found at this site were most likely hunted sometime during those three months, the late summer and early fall. Using just such an approach, archaeologist R. J. Carter (1997) examined the mandibles of roe deer recovered at the 10,700-year-old

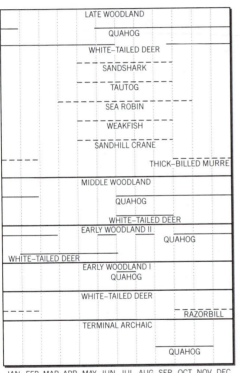

JAN FEB MAR APR MAY JUN JUL AUG SEP OCT NOV DEC

**FIGURE 11.10** Diagram showing food resources recovered by excavators at the Greenwich Cove site located on Narragansett Bay in Rhode Island. The horizontal line associated with each of the species reflects the months during which that species would have been available to the site's residents and, therefore, the months during which the site likely was occupied, broken down by five periods of southern New England prehistory (Terminal Archaic, Early Woodland I and II, Middle Woodland, Late Woodland). (*Courtesy of David Bernstein*)

Star Carr site in England. Carter determined that the ages of the roe deer suggested that they had been killed by the inhabitants sometime during March and April, so the site must have been occupied at least during the early spring.

We don't have any bison in Connecticut, but we do have lots of white-tailed deer. The whitetail rutting season in Connecticut is quite short, beginning in early November. Individual females are sexually receptive for only a few days, but not all at exactly the same time. Overall, the deer population rut lasts usually less than a month. Therefore, most does get pregnant in November. The gestation period for a deer lasts about two hundred days, or a bit less than seven months, so most fawns are born in May or June. The size of the phalange of the white-tailed deer recovered at the two-thousand-year-old Loomis II site in Windsor, Connecticut, indicated an age of about nine months. A nine-month-old deer born in May or June would have been killed in February or March, indicating that, whatever other time of year it may have been inhabited, the Loomis II site almost certainly was occupied in the late winter or very early spring.

Looking at all of the seasonally available foods recovered at a site allows the creation of a seasonality chart (Figure 11.10). The overlapping patterns of seasonal availability allow for a determination of the periods during the year that a site was occupied.

# Read More

Determining the seasons during which a particular archaeological site was occupied relies to a great degree on the analysis of faunal and botanical remains. For detailed discussions of the task of determining seasonality and examples of the process, have a look at any of the following sources:

Baker, B. W., B. S. Shaffer, and D. G. Steele. 1997. Basic approaches in archaeological faunal analysis. In *Field Methods in Archaeology*, edited by T. R. Hester, H. J. Shafer, and K. L. Feder, 298–318. Mayfield Publishing, Mountain View, California.

Bernstein, D. J. 1999. Prehistoric use of plant foods on Long Island and Block Island Sounds. In *Current Northeast Paleoethnobotany*, edited by J. P. Hart, 101–19. New York State Musuem, Albany.

Carter, R. J. 1997. Age estimation of the roe deer (*Capreolus capreolus*) mandibles from the Mesolithic site of Star Carr, Yorkshire, based on radiographs of mandibular tooth development. *Journal of the Zoological Society of London* 241:495–502.

Chaplin, R. E. 1971. *The Study of Animal Bones from Archaeological Sites*. Seminar Press, London.

Davis, S. J. M. 1995. *The Archaeology of Animals*. Yale University Press, New Haven, Connecticut.

Dincauze, D. F. 1976. *The Neville Site: Eight Thousand Years at Amoskeag*. Peabody Museum of Archaeology and Ethnology, Cambridge, Massachusetts.

Klein, R. G., and K. Cruz-Uribe. 1984. *The Analysis of Animal Bones from Archaeological Sites*. University of Chicago Press, Chicago.

Reitz, E. J. 1999. *Zooarchaeology*. Cambridge University Press, Cambridge, England.

Wheat, J. B. 1972. *The Olsen-Chubbuck Site: A Paleo Indian Bison Kill*. Memoir of the Society for American Archaeology 26, Salt Lake City.

# Study Questions

1. What kinds of evidence support the hypothesis that hunting contributed to the subsistence of the inhabitants of the Wood Lily site?

2. What foods do foragers rely on?

3. What is the purpose of "flotation"? Describe the process.

4. What is the purpose of a faunal and floral comparative collection?

5. How might an artifact assemblage suggest, at least qualitatively, the subsistence base of an archaeological group?

6. What are paleofeces or coprolites? How does their analysis assist in reconstructing the diet of a past people?

7. Why is it important to know, not just that an ancient people hunted, but what animals they hunted?

8. How do the strategies for hunting deer differ from those for hunting bison? How might a reliance on deer versus a reliance on bison affect other elements of a culture?

9. How do archaeologists identify the use of domesticated animals by a past people?

10. Why may it not be a good idea to wash archaeological stone tools when they are returned to the lab for analysis?

11. How does blood residue analysis work? Provide a couple of examples where the recovery of blood residues on even very ancient tools has resulted in a precise identification of the animal species being killed and butchered by the ancient people who used the tools.

12. What are phytoliths? How does analysis of phytoliths contribute to our understanding of an ancient diet?

13. Describe the process of determining the minimum number of individuals (MNI) of a particular animal species recovered at an archaeological site. Why do we want to know the MNI?

14. How does an analysis of human skeletal chemistry contribute to our understanding of an ancient diet?

15. How do archaeologists determine the season of a village's occupation?

16. The bones of primarily 18-month-old individuals of an animal species with a rutting season in mid-May and a 2-month gestation period are found at an archaeological site. In which month was the site probably occupied?

Our desire was to reconstruct the **culture** of the people who lived at Wood Lily. Culture is complex, though, made up of all the behaviors and strategies a human group invents and passes down to subsequent generations. Culture, in fact, has been defined as the invented means of adaptation, signifying that culture is an intellectual phenomenon, made up of a web of ideas. The archaeologist's challenge rests in the fact that ideas are nonmaterial and leave no direct impression in the archaeological record, which is material by its very nature as well as by definition. What we have left to examine at Wood Lily, as is the case at all archaeological sites, in essence, are the physical residues of ideas: the objects that were the product of a group's strategies for hunting or storing food or protecting themselves from the elements, and even for organizing their social relationships or worshipping their gods.

Sometimes these physical residues are many and straightforward, like tools used in hunting. Other times these residues are more complex and open to interpretation: a gold ring found on the finger of a skeleton recovered at Pompeii or the crown depicted on the head of an ancient Egyptian pharaoh in ancient carvings can be challenging to translate into their social or political meanings to the ancient people who wore them. And the residues of some elements of human societies simply are not to be found: we did not recover a single object at Wood Lily that we can confidently ascribe to a religious belief system. Yet, because anthropologists have never found a society without a belief system that we can include in the category of religion, we can be pretty confident that the inhabitants of Wood Lily possessed what we would recognize as religion.

Indeed, the archaeological record is limited to material objects and some common human activities—storytelling or dance, for example—may involve no material objects and are, therefore, invisible to the archaeologist looking only at the material record at a site. Like all archaeologists, we are "peering through a glass, darkly" at the three-thousand-year-old Wood Lily village in our direct examination of the archaeological site.

The people who lived at what we call the Wood Lily site reflect in their material culture just what we would expect in southern New England of the Native Americans who lived here three millennia ago. However, although the tools they made, the hearth fires they warmed themselves over, and the trash they discarded are available for us to study, their actual physical remains did not survive the rigors of New England's soil. In our part of the world, high acidity; vigorous biological action on the part of small animals, burrowing worms, and insects; and the voracious appetites of bacteria, along with rough mechanical weathering due at least in part to freezing and thawing, produce a depositional environment not particularly hospitable to organic based material. The act of burning tends to protect bones, seeds, and nuts from various forms of decay, but animal bodies, including those of human beings, tend to last a very short time in our soil; flesh may take only decades to disappear, bones may last only a century or two.

In other regions, human remains fare far better, and skeletons commonly preserve quite well for centuries and even millennia. Under certain circumstances, where the insects and bacteria that recycle our bodies cannot thrive because it is too dry, too cold, or a combination of the two, or where chemicals in the ground serve as a natural preservative, not only will skeletons survive, but so will flesh. In Danish peat bogs, for example, the natural chemical soup in the peat acts as a natural preservative, and nearly intact bodies have been recovered. Complete faces, hands, and fingers with observable fingerprints have preserved for more than four thousand years after burial (or was it disposal?) in the bogs. "Otzi," also called the Ice Man, is a relatively well preserved body that froze nearly 5,300 years ago; tattoos can still be discerned on his body (Figure 12.1; Spindler 1994).

Some cultures did not rely on nature to preserve dead bodies and attempted to preserve the remains of at least some important people. The desiccated, often ghoulish remains of Egyptian mummies testify to the only partial success they achieved in their preservation practices (Figure 12.2).

**FIGURE 12.1** The Ice Man. (© *Reuters NewMedia Inc./CORBIS*)

**FIGURE 12.2** Egyptian mummy. (© *Roger Wood/ CORBIS*)

## Can Archaeologists Figure Out the Social Relationships of Past People?

The Broadway show *Fiddler on the Roof* concerns itself with a community of Jews trying to maintain their unique identity as a small minority in rural, late nineteenth-century Russia. One of the highlights of that show occurs when Tevye, the patriarch of the family that is the focus of the story, sings the song "Tradition" in an attempt to explain how, even under trying circumstances as a beleaguered and oppressed minority, a people can and, in fact, must, remain true to their history, their religion, and their culture. In Tevye's spoken dialogue within the song, he enumerates some of the cultural traditions of his own people and regarding any one of these traditions says: "You may ask; 'How did this tradition get started?' I'll tell you: I don't know. But it's a tradition!" Tevye makes an interesting point here. Traditions are important, not because they necessarily have any particular meaning or rationale today, but because they serve to bind a people together as a community over the long haul.

Human beings carry out their tasks, raise and educate their children, worship their gods, fight their battles, and organize the social fabric of their societies, at least in part, on the basis of tradition, the sources of which most people, like Tevye, have no idea. As children, all human beings become **enculturated** we become practitioners of a particular culture and members of a cultural group. Every day of our lives we are taught how to be a member of our group, both explicitly through training by adults, teachers, and mentors and implicitly by watching those around us and emulating their behavior. We all, to one extent or another, from the most conservative "traditionalists" among us to those who fancy themselves freethinkers and radicals, follow Tevye in embracing many of the traditions and the traditional behaviors of our culture. As an adult and as a parent, I must admit that many of the social rules I balked at as a kid, I now impose on my own children. It's "tradition." Most of us yearn to be accepted as a member of a group, and one way to accomplish this is to behave in a way that tradition demands. Simply by watching our parents go about their daily routines, we are trained in the appropriate behavior of men and women; we acquire food preferences and patterns of food preparation; we worship their gods; we learn how to knit or sew, to take care of an automobile, balance a checkbook, build a house, and so on. Now think about how many of those behaviors coincidentally involve material objects: food itself, utensils, tools, construction materials. We make material things, use them, consume them, and discard them all within the context of our cultural traditions. How these material objects look, how they wear out, and how they end up in the ground as archaeological artifacts and ecofacts all reflect, to one extent or another, our traditional behaviors. Traditions, therefore, are encoded into those objects and in this way are conveyed to archaeologists through the archaeological record.

Take, for example, a simple stone spear point made by a member of a particular ancient society. Certainly, part of the morphology of a utilizable spear point is dictated by functional necessity. A stone intended to tip a hunting spear must have a sharp point to penetrate an animal's skin. Its form should allow it to fly straight and true toward its intended target. Its edges should be thin and sharp enough to cut deep into the prey yet strong enough to sustain the force of impact with the sometimes tough hide of an animal. The butt end of a stone point should be of a shape and form that allow for its hafting onto a wooden shaft so it will not fall off as soon as it strikes its intended victim.

Taken together, however, these functional prerequisites still leave an enormous amount of freedom for the stone tool maker in terms of the shape to make the point and still have it be an effective weapon. Its sharp edges can be straight or serrated, and those edges can be linear or curved. With two straight sides and a base, the point will be triangular, but there is still a choice of equilateral or isosceles. Curved sides work equally well and an effective spear point may look like a willow leaf. The necessity of shaping the base of a point to facilitate hafting still allows for a wide variety of channels or notches: single or multiple; deep or shallow; located along the point's sides, at the corners, or along the base. In many cases, these individual variations do not affect in the least the essential functional characteristics of the weapon. Now imagine all the combinations and permutations of these variables in considering the possibilities of the appearances of perfectly serviceable stone spear points and you see that on the basis of form alone, there is a huge range of acceptable outcomes for a stone spear point maker. It is unlikely in the extreme that there were "laws" concerning what your spear point had to look like. Especially if they came into contact with other groups of people with different traditions of toolmaking, the knappers within a given group certainly realized that there were other shapes that worked just as well as their own, but they tended not to drastically alter their own practice.

When we excavate archaeological sites, it is pretty common to find that during a single period of time, nearly all of the stone spear points look pretty much alike, just variations on a theme. Take, for example, the fluted points of Paleoindians, dating to more than ten thousand years ago. The Clovis variety is found all over the United States and Canada and, wherever they are found, they look much the same: they are more than twice as long as they are wide; their edges begin in parallel at the base and then curve in toward the top; they exhibit channels or "flutes" on both of their faces, which begin at the base and reach up to something less than halfway toward the top. All Clovis points share another common feature; they are concave along their bases. On this characteristic, however, there is some easily recognizable geographic variation. Clovis points in the East tend to have a greatly exaggerated concavity at the base when compared to those found in the West (Figure 12.3). The depth of this concavity reaches its maximum at the Vail site in Maine (Gramly 1982) and Debert in Nova Scotia (MacDonald 1985). We cannot say why this deeply concave base developed, but we certainly can recognize it and wonder about what it signifies.

A particular way of crafting a stone spear point—or ceramic vessel, necklace, house, or burial—is determined by a cultural tradition, passed from the artisan to the apprentice, which may mean, simply, from mother to daughter,

**FIGURE 12.3** Clovis point from the East (left) and West (right) are very similar: they are, in essence, variations on a theme. The most obvious difference in style can be seen at the base of the spear point; both are concave but those from the East tend to be significantly more deeply concave than are those from the West. There may be no functional explanation for this difference; it likely was just a matter of style. (*Casts courtesy of Lithic Casting Lab*)

father to son, or either parent to a daughter or son. In the way things are accomplished in any individual culture (shape of their spear points, shape and designs pressed into their pottery vessels, appearance of items of adornment, configuration of their dwellings, the format of burial chambers) we may ask, like Tevye, "How did this tradition [of stone point making, pot making, jewelry manufacturing, house construction, or burying of the dead] get started?" And, like Tevye, we will be forced to answer, "I don't know." But like Tevye, we understand that these different cultural practices, these ways of doing things within each culture are all part of and the result of "tradition." And therein lies our archaeological application of the concept of tradition. Traditions are passed down within a social system of enculturation. If men make spear points and are taught as boys how to make stone tools by their fathers, then their points will share many of the features of the men from whom they learned the craft. If most of the spear points found at a site share many morphological similarities, it may mean that each generation of stone tool makers learned their trade from their fathers, who learned from their fathers, and so on. All of these men may have shared in a tool making tradition because they were related, descendants of a tool maker who started a particular stone tool making tradition many generations previously.

An archaeologist will recognize the great similarities—or the great differences—in spear points, pots, jewelry, houses, or burials at an archaeological site and may draw conclusions about the nature of the social system of enculturation of the society. For example, if men made the spear points and if all—or nearly all—of the points recovered at a site share the same basic template, it might be the case that all of the men are related to one another, and the tool making tradition reflected in the appearance of their spear points had been passed down in the same family.

In a small social group where the evidence indicates that related men stayed put, they might have had to marry a woman from outside of the group because all of the women born into the group would be related to all of the men. When men stayed in the group upon marriage and their wives left their village of birth to move in with their husband's group, the postmarital residence pattern is called **patrilocality.**

Suppose the spear points found at a site exhibited a great deal of variation and followed no similar template or model. This might signify that the men in the group learned their tool making from different families following different traditions and then brought these differing traditions with them to their new place of residence. In other words, these men came together because of marriage. They left the villages where they were born to live with their wives, who stayed in their own birth-village, a post-marital residence pattern called **matrilocality.** Here, if women made pottery, we might expect them to have followed a common family tradition within which pottery making was taught and passed down.

The remarkable point of all this is simple: even nonmaterial elements of culture like social systems affect and, therefore, become encoded in things as basic as spear points and pottery. Who we are—the families into which we were born and into which we may marry, our position in life, our social standing, economic position, and political power—all may be encoded in the objects we own, the artifacts that are deposited in and around our homes, and even in the graves that ultimately receive us. It is the job of the archaeologists to be clever enough to crack that code.

## Read More

To find out more about the basis for the assertion that social patterns are encoded in the material archaeological record of tools, pots, burial, and so on, and for some examples, see any of the following sources:

Binford, L. 1962. Archaeology as anthropology. *American Antiquity* 28:217–25.
Deetz, J. 1965. *The Dynamics of Stylistic Change in Arikara Ceramics.* University of Illinois Series in Anthropology 4. University of Illinois, Urbana.
Gramly, R. M. 1982. *The Vail Site: A Paleo-Indian Encampment in Maine.* Buffalo Society of Natural Sciences, Buffalo.
MacDonald, G. F. 1985. *Debert: A Paleo-Indian Site in Central Nova Scotia.* Persimmon Press, Buffalo.

### Can Archaeologists Figure Out the Roles of Males and Females in Ancient Societies?

Reading any one of a number of books or articles about human prehistory written fifty years ago might have led one to believe that women evolved rather later than men in the development of our species and then, once they arrived on the scene, did little more than bear and look after children. That might be a bit of an exaggeration, but there's more than just a little truth to it. In the stories archaeologists told of the human past, it would seem that males were responsible for nearly every important development, every great leap forward in technology. Males were responsible for all the important and meaningful tasks needed for the survival of the group: they made stone tools and then wrenched the people's subsistence out of the chaos of nature, hunting ferocious beasts and bringing meat back to camp to supply the group; they traveled on heroic journeys to obtain desperately needed raw materials; they fought pitched battles against their enemies. And, then, when they were done, the men retired to the mysterious depths of spectacular caverns and in their spare time, of course, invented the painterly arts as part of mystical ceremonies of renewal of nature and redemption of themselves.

Though I may have exaggerated these images of what a feminist might call an androcentric view of prehistory, I have not done so to the point of distortion. Especially in popular imaginings of the human past, males are presented as active and females, if they exist at all in these reconstructions, are passive elements, observers of the activities of men, part of the audience, even part of the scenery. In her analysis of more than three hundred artistic recreations depicting scenes of human antiquity, Diane Gifford-Gonzalez (1993) calculated that 100% of the individuals shown hunting, carrying game, or conducting a ritual were males. Nine out of ten of those shown painting an image on a cave wall were males. In the same artwork surveyed, 100% of the adults shown attending to or even just holding or even coming in contact with a child were female. The only activity other than child rearing that women were depicted as engaging in was making hide clothing. Gifford-Gonzalez even jokes about this, calling the typical woman depicted in artistic representations of ancient societies "the drudge on the hide." I had to laugh at that description when, fairly recently, I visited a relatively new series of dioramas devoted to the topic of human evolution at the American Museum of Natural History in New York City. The dioramas are fabulously well made, showing upright loco-motion, hunting, and Paleolithic artistry. And there, in the diorama showing three human ancestors engaged in what the diorama designer surely perceived to be typical tasks, is a male, standing strong and tall, sharpening his wooden spear point, preparing for the fierce, daily battle to provide subsistence for his family. At his feet, is a female sewing—as you may have guessed—an animal hide.

Is this really the way it was or, at least, the only way it was? The truth is that archaeologists focusing on prehistoric societies can determine the sex of a tool maker or of a tool user only in rare circumstances. In a few cases, finger-prints impressed on clay when it was soft (for example, on a piece of ceramic kiln furniture or on the inside of a vessel situated in a position where the sur-face can no longer be reached for smoothing when the top has been constricted) have been preserved when the clay was fired (Figure 12.4). The individual ridges that make up a woman's fingerprint tend to be smaller than those of a male and, therefore, on average, there are more ridges across 1 cm of a female's finger than on a male's. With this in mind, when a fingerprint has preserved, you can determine with a fair degree of accuracy whether the print belonged to a male or female and, by inference, the sex of the person making the ceramic object (Figure 12.5).

**FIGURE 12.4** Fingerprints preserved on ceramic fragment made by African captives in New York City in the eighteenth century. (*Courtesy of Warren Perry*)

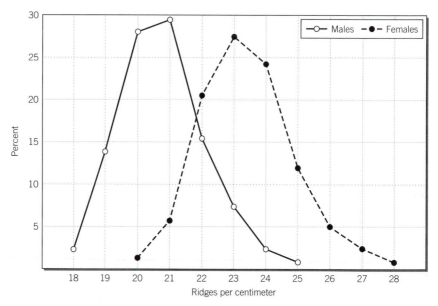

**FIGURE 12.5** Graph showing the bimodal nature of the distribution of the number of individual fingerprint ridges per centimeter. Females, because the individual ridges in their fingerprints tend to be narrower, tend to have a greater number of these ridges than do men. This tendency can be used to identify the sex of an individual who left their fingerprints behind—at a crime scene or on the clay of an ancient pottery vessel. (*From Cummins and Midlo, 1961*)

It must be admitted that at least some of the sex role stereotyping archaeologists are sometimes guilty of results, not from careful consideration of archaeological cultures, but from imposing, likely unconsciously, the biases and assumptions of our own culture. Consider this: my colleague Lucianne Lavin knows more about ancient pottery, especially the kind made by the inhabitants of prehistoric New England, than anybody I know (Lavin 1997, 1998; Lavin and Kra 1994). A few years ago, Luci organized a symposium on ancient ceramics, inviting a number of researchers to present papers specifically on the work they were doing on pottery here in the northeast. Because Luci and I are friends and because she knew that I had recently excavated a site that produced a large number of **potsherds,** she invited me to present a paper on my preliminary analysis of the clay the potters had used to produce their wares. The symposium was an all-day affair, with both a morning and an afternoon session. Although I had received a program several weeks previously and, as a result, knew the identities of all of the participants, I hadn't fully realized one curious fact about the symposium until I carefully scanned the names in the program while waiting for the morning session to start. Of the dozen or so paper presenters, I was, in a fundamental way, unique. All of the other symposium presenters that day were female; I was the only male. A peculiar coincidence, I thought, but one that I have seen repeated since in multiple contexts.

Of course, there is no necessary correspondence between the sex of the archaeologist and his or her research focus, but it does seem, by and large, that the study of stone tools and their manufacture is dominated by males. Read almost any newspaper or magazine account about making and using stone tool replicas and you will commonly see photos of a bunch of hairy guys with bruises and taped-up wounds, having a good old time around a campfire, telling stories about the bison—or deer or antelope or even elephants—they just killed with stone weapons. All the while, they are roasting the meat that they sliced off the bone—with stone tools, of course. Certainly, it is not universal: some of the most important work done in stone tool analysis, especially in the analysis of the marks left on stone tools by use, has been conducted by archaeologist Ruth Tringham (Tringham et al. 1974) and Barbara Luedtke (1992) produced the standard manual on flint and chert, rock types often used to produce stone tools. There are others, of course, but a focus on stone tools, especially their replication, generally has been "a guy thing."

On the other hand, as reflected in the microcosm of the symposium in which I participated, the investigation of ceramics seems (not as strongly, but nonetheless) to be the domain of female archaeologists and archaeology students. For example, all students in my experimental archaeology course conduct a nearly semester-long replicative experiment of their own choosing. I don't push the students in any particular direction, and they more or less have free reign to conduct nearly any replicative experiment whose scope is reasonable in a fifteen-week semester. In the more than twenty years I have taught the course, I would estimate that ten students have designed various experiments in ceramics manufacture, use, and analysis. Every one of those students has been a female. On the other side, it has become something of a running joke in the course that if the experiment involves ancient weaponry of any kind, the experimenter will be a male. Over the same twenty years in my experimental course, there have been about ten students who undertook projects that involved making and using spears, bows and arrows, and spear throwers. Only one of those students was a female.

So what's the deal? Is biology destiny, after all, at least when it comes to the investigation of ancient technology and material culture? Does the apparent correlation, imperfect as it is, between sex and research focus among modern archaeologists essentially repeat the cultural patterns of ancient societies? In other words, are male archaeologists today, through some deep, genetic bond, reflecting a subconscious "brotherhood" with the ancient stone tool makers they study? Are female archaeologists drawn to the investigation of ceramic artifacts because their "sisters" of long ago manufactured these things, and can it all be traced to the fact that both groups—ancient and modern women—have two X chromosomes? Or, is it simply the fact that sex role stereotyping (not in ancient "primitive" societies, but in our modern society of archaeologists) is at the root of this pattern? Are male archaeologists attracted to the study of ancient stone tools because, as males, they are more interested in the things they believe males made? Are female archaeologists attracted to the study of ceramics because, as females, they are interested in the things they believe females made? And do we assume males made stone tools (for use in hunting and warfare) and women made pottery (for use in domestic activities like food preparation and storage), not because of any genetic predisposition but because those are the stereotypes that match the expectations of our own society? Is this just another version of the question, do boys play with toy soldiers and girls play with dolls as a result of the different wiring in the male and female brain or as the result of socialization? And, finally, it occurs to me to ask, who should be the subject of our analysis anyway: ancient people or modern archaeologists?

This brings me to the work of archaeologist Joan Gero (1997), who doubly upsets the applecart I have just neatly set up by being a woman interested in stone tools who also maintains that stone tools almost certainly were made by ancient women. In Gero's discourse on what she identifies as "genderlithics," she makes a number of key points. She points out that, with the exception of certain stone procurement activities that require a significant amount of upper body strength, women are physically just as capable of making stone tools as are men. From my experience in my experimental archaeology course, I must concur. By and large, although strength is needed to flake stone, knowing where to hit a stone core is much more important than brute force. Just as important, Gero cites a number of ethnographic cases on record where women were observed making stone tools, including first-hand accounts of Australian Aborigine women manufacturing stone axes and of Native American women making arrowpoints by utilizing pressure flaking.

The fact that women are physically capable of making stone tools, combined with the ethnographic evidence of women making stone tools in some cultures, forces us to reassess assumptions about sex roles that are based on the stereotyping done by our own culture.

In our own society, we are blurring the distinctions between traditional tasks that were perceived as "women's work" and "men's work," but wasn't there a valid reason for the sexual division of labor in the past? Certainly, males tend to be larger and more heavily muscled than females and this often, though not always, translates into greater physical strength, so it might be advantageous to have men do the work that requires this greater strength. Sexual dimorphism need not be destiny, but it likely is the case that in some societies, men and women had vastly different responsibilities based on men tending to be larger and stronger. Nevertheless, we shouldn't presume to apply recent stereotypes about modern males and females to people of the past. The overall strength of an individual is a flexible characteristic and depends on diet and conditioning. Remember, I have never encountered a woman in my experimental archaeology course who could not make stone tools due to a lack of strength. And check out the incredible archery skills of female Olympic athletes if you are skeptical about the ability of women to master the bow and arrow.

I think we make a mistake if, by default, we assume that if a task required skill, training, strength, guile, cunning, and intelligence, it must have been the purview of males. We should admit that we really don't know. In the end, it is most reasonable to suggest that ancient societies required contributions from everyone, whatever their abilities. Sex is only one factor in a host of character-istics that determine what a person is most capable of contributing to the survival of the group. See all of the chapters in the book *Engendering Archaeology: Women and Prehistory* (Gero and Conkey 1997) as well as works by Roberta Gilchrist (1999), Bettina Arnold and Nancy Wicker (2001), and Diana diZerega Wall (1994) for a diversity of approaches to figuring out the roles of women and men in ancient societies.

## Read More

For a detailed discussion of the ways in which archaeologists can assess the roles of men and women in past societies, start with any of the following sources:

Arnold, B. and N. L. Wicker, eds. 2001. *Gender and the Archaeology of Death*. Rowman and Littlefield, Lanham, Maryland.

Gero, J. M. 1997. Genderlithics: Woman's roles in stone tool production. In *Engendering Archaeology: Women and Prehistory*, edited by J. M. Gero and M. W. Conkey, 163–93. Blackwell, Oxford.

Gero, J. M. and M. W. Conkey, eds. 1997. *Engendering Archaeology: Women and Prehistory*. Blackwell, Oxford.

Gifford-Gonzalez, D. 1993. You can hide, but you can't run: Representation of women's work in illustrations of Paleolithic life. *Visual Anthropology Review* 9(1):23–41.

Gilchrist, R. 1999. *Gender and Archaeology: Contesting the Past*. Routledge, London.

Wall, D. diZerega. 1994. *The Archaeology of Gender: Separating the Spheres in Urban America*. Plenum, New York.

## How Does an Archaeologist Approach Issues of Economic, Social, and Political Inequality in an Ancient Society?

The people who lived at the Wood Lily site were mobile hunter-gatherers. Most such groups are essentially **egalitarian.** Though common usage of that word might imply that everyone is equal in an egalitarian society, this is not actually true. Even within such a society, there almost certainly will be inequality among different categories of people defined and recognized by the group. Only within age and sex categories recognized by the egalitarian group is everyone more or less equal. For example, an egalitarian people may distinguish the following categories of individuals as having different statuses, responsibilities, and attendant expectations concerning how others should treat them: young children, older kids, adolescents, adult males, adult females, elderly males, elderly females. The individuals will not necessarily be "equal" across group boundaries, but within each of these hypothetical subdivisions almost everyone has about the same wealth, status, and authority. Nobody accumulates a disproportionate amount of wealth, no one's social standing is any higher than anyone else's, and, with the possible exception of the leader of a community, no one within the recognized age and sex category has any say or authority over anyone else in the same category.

Egalitarian societies are not beset by anarchy. Especially in small social groups, these age and sex categories and, especially, the family, may provide a more than adequate framework on which interpersonal behavior is based. In most such societies, parents command the respect of their children and control their behavior. Adults in their middle age may have more authority and receive more respect than young adults. Elderly adults may be revered and their advice may be heeded more than that of younger adults. In some cases, males may dominate the decision-making process and, in other instances, females may control the important decisions made by the group.

Certainly, not all societies are egalitarian. Family structure may provide a framework sufficient for organizing a hunting party, digging a well, building a house, or moving a settlement. As a society grows in population, however, it may outgrow the ability of family structure to efficiently organize labor and make decisions. The scale of the projects undertaken by large populations may exceed the organizational capacity of a single family with its kin-based level of control. Building an extensive network of canals to irrigate a valley, constructing an impregnable defensive wall around a settlement, or conscripting an army to defend a region against an aggressive enemy may require the cooperation and coordination of many families, and a social and political structure that transcends the individual family may become necessary.

Societies in which the organization of labor and the coordination of activity are controlled by a structure beyond the family are said to be complex. In contrast to egalitarian societies, **complex societies** confer higher levels of status and authority on certain individuals or groups who can now direct and, to some extent, control people's labor on a large scale, ostensibly for the good of the group. It often ends up, as well, that the group's labor is controlled for the good of those individuals with higher status and authority. Increased wealth may flow into their hands because they can command it and, it must be admitted, because the rest of the people not so privileged may view the greater wealth of those higher in the pecking order as deserved, the legitimate result of higher status.

In some complex societies, disproportionate amounts of status, authority, and wealth become concentrated in permanent and fixed classes of people. These societies become socially (and economically and politically) **stratified.** Just as we talked about sequential strata in soil, in the social application of the term, society may be composed of a pyramid of strata or layers. A tiny fraction of the population (for example, families of the king, emperor, or pharaoh) will reside in the top layer. A larger layer beneath the top represents the nobility. A larger still layer sits beneath the noble class and may be composed of craftspeople, merchants, and military officers. Finally, at the bottom rests the largest layer of all, consisting of the farmers, workers, peasants, and even slaves, whose labors allow for the existence of the economic, social, and politically bounded layers above them.

Differential wealth develops to reflect a society's stratification of status. That differential wealth is reflected in material objects: crowns, jewels, finely worked knickknacks made of rare and precious (therefore expensive) raw materials, larger and elaborate residences, and so on. Material objects are the raw material of archaeological analysis, so it should come as no surprise that archaeologists find evidence of economic and attendant social and political inequality manifested in the archaeological record in terms of the material inequality of the objects found in domiciles and, especially, in graves.

We found no burials of the egalitarian residents of the Wood Lily site. In the site as a whole, there was no evidence at all of the concentration of wealth in the hands of any individual. There were no hoards of precious raw materials in certain site locations, no concentrations of valuables being monopolized by any individuals. In fact, the physical distribution of stuff at the site, more or less equally dispersed across the habitation, is probably an accurate reflection of the society of those who lived there: no place or person was more important than any other.

Compare this to what is demonstrated by the burial of Tutankhamen, the ruler of ancient Egypt between 1333 and 1323 B.C. When discovered in 1922, the mortal remains of the "boy-king" were located in the innermost of three nested coffins. Made of solid gold, the innermost sarcophagus actually contained the young pharaoh's body. It rested in another coffin, constructed of wood and covered with a layer of hammered gold. The outermost coffin was fabricated in the same way; a framework of wood covered in gold. Surrounding the remains of the king, in a series of interconnected rooms, was a virtual warehouse of spectacular treasures. The inventory of the grave goods in Tut's tomb includes an overwhelming array of fabulous treasures: sculptures in gold and alabaster, painted wooden carvings of the gods of ancient Egypt, leopard-skin capes, ebony furniture, gilded storage chests, necklaces and bracelets (some inlaid with lapis lazuli and chalcedony), and gold rings. All of the gifts presented to the dead king are remarkably well crafted and are exquisite examples of the stunning abilities and creativity of ancient Egypt's artisans. A king's treasure, literally, had been crammed into Tut's small death chamber in the Valley of the Kings. The death mask itself is stunning, a breathtaking object of gold and lapis, so perfectly executed that to many people it represents the embodiment of the artistic achievement of ancient Egypt (Figure 12.6).

Tut's burial may be an extreme case, but it is an instructive example for us. Economic, social, and political inequality in life are reflected in the

**FIGURE 12.6** The deservedly renowned death mask of the Egyptian pharaoh Tutankhamen is emblematic of the artistic capabilities of ancient Egypt's artisans, and is a clear material manifestation of the extreme level of economic, social, and political inequality that can characterize complex societies. Suffice it to say that, while pharaohs were buried in this sort of splendor, those whose labors provided for the privileged lives—and deaths—of the noble class of ancient complex societies were not afforded the same—in life or in death. (© Roger Wood/CORBIS)

stuff individuals in complex societies have access to and can accumulate. That stuff, whether it ends up in the archaeological record of someone's abandoned house or in their grave provides us with a snapshot of that inequality, a material representation of a society with rich and poor, leaders and followers, a noble class, peasants and slaves. It is a picture that archaeologists are often successful at recognizing and interpreting.

## Can Archaeologists Reconstruct Ancient Religious Practices?

To the best of our knowledge, human beings are the only species with the ability to recognize the uncertainty of our own fates. As sentient creatures, we are intensely aware of the role played by serendipity (luck, both good and bad) in determining the length and the quality of our lives and the lives of those we love. Also, though other animals may react to the remains of their deceased companions in a manner that we recognize as mournful (elephants and chimpanzees, for example, have been observed behaving in ways that are eerily reminiscent of human mourning), humans are the only species who are cognizant of the essential fact that our lives are finite entities, that each of us dies. This is one reason why I sometimes envy my cats, but that's another story.

To one extent or another, humans also know how to behave to increase the likelihood of well-being as well as success in the tasks they undertake. You may have heard the term "survival instinct," a characteristic pretty clearly evident in human beings: for the most part, we tend to act in ways that materially increase the likelihood of our day-to-day survival. We know how to increase the odds in our favor to be successful in the hunt, grow food, raise our children, and stay healthy and safe. But we humans also know a dirty little secret: life isn't fair. We know that no matter how careful we are, no matter how hard we try, no matter how much we study or practice, there is no guarantee of success. Sometimes, through no apparent fault of their own, people who try hard, work hard, and are sensible and careful, fail anyway, live miserable lives, and die far too young. They didn't deserve their fates, they didn't "have it coming," and they are not paying for their mistakes. They simply got the shaft; no reason, just bad luck. And we all know that it can happen to any of us.

Religion, at least in part, results from recognizing the insecure nature of our fates. There always is a gap between what we can do materially to ensure our success and health and that over which we have no material control. Humans often bridge that gap with the belief that there is a force—a god or gods, spirits, or other supernatural entities—that dictates serendipity, that actually controls that which to us is uncontrollable. That force can mitigate our bad breaks, or at least have reasons for visiting tragedy upon us, reasons that we may someday learn.

With that faith, human beings gain at least a measure of control over the uncertainty that rules life. The uncertainty and volatility that characterize our existence and fuel our fears become less uncertain, less volatile, and less frightening when we believe in a force "bigger" than ourselves, a force with intelligence, a force that can be reasoned with, bargained with, and that ultimately acts in our best interests.

Like every other behavior practiced by people, religion does not fossilize *directly*, leaving a physical impression in the ground that archaeologists need only expose to reveal the behavior. Like most other human behaviors, however, the conduct of religion results in the use of material objects and material consequences that preserve and encode elements of the behaviors. For example, some people may avoid certain serviceable rock types for use in stone tool making and using because the rock is considered to be imbued with a malevolent force. The reliance on a more distant and difficult to obtain rock type without demonstrable advantages may suggest the presence of an ideology that affects the selection of lithic raw materials. In another example, the presence of non-naturalistic, perhaps even supernaturalistic, images etched onto the rock surfaces of a cliff wall difficult to access and distant from any ancient habitation may suggest that the artwork was intended to mark a place sacred to a group of people (Figure 12.7).

Although resource avoidance and the marking of a place with non-naturalistic images are difficult to interpret—and our hypotheses regarding a religious connotation are even more challenging to test—there is a category of archaeological features that seems to be a more direct window into the religious practices, thoughts, and beliefs of an ancient people: burials. The treatment of the dead reflects a people's reaction to the fact of mortality and often manifests key aspects of their religious beliefs.

For example, as much as eighty thousand years ago, a variety of archaic or premodern human beings, the Neandertals, placed the remains of deceased comrades into trenches or pits, occasionally including tools and other objects before covering them with soil (Solecki 1971). More than 25,000 years ago, the people of Sungir', located about 150 km (100 miles) northeast of Moscow, Russia, buried five of their compatriots in what must have amounted to Paleolithic splendor (White 1993). An adolescent boy was buried with a cache of nearly 5,000 beads crafted from the ivory tusks of woolly mammoth. On his chest was a pendant carved from the same ivory. Around his waist was a belt from which its maker had suspended 250 polar fox teeth. Nearby the boy, a young girl had been buried. In her grave were ivory disks carved with an intricate latticework, an ivory pin, and more than 5,000 ivory beads. Nearly 3,330 years ago, a young king who died suddenly was interred in a tomb intended for another. The tomb became a virtual storehouse for the splendid objects whose spirits would be needed in the next life. Alabaster chalices, chests made of ebony and cedar, golden shrines, and a spectacular death mask crafted in sold gold and lapis lazuli are only a handful of the jumble of riches found in the tomb of the Egyptian pharaoh Tutankhamen (Buckley 1976).

As broadly as the grave goods range in the burials of this Neandertal, the children of the Paleolithic, and the boy king of Egypt, they share the love, reverence, or perhaps fear with which the living responded to the deaths of a friend, a child, a leader. Items of great value (made of rare and precious materials, works of great artistry that had taken enormous effort and time to craft)

**FIGURE 12.7** Petroglyphs like those at Bellows Falls in Vermont (top) and Newspaper Rock in Utah (bottom) likely are a reflection of the religious practices of ancient people. (*Kenneth L. Feder*)

*Petroglyphs*

and items that perhaps were believed to be imbued with great spiritual power were placed in these graves. The people left behind may have believed that the spirit of the deceased needed the objects placed in the tomb for use in the afterlife. We know that this belief was the case for ancient Egyptians because they left behind a written record describing their belief in the need for the spirit to have the trappings that surrounded it in life. But we cannot know with any certainty that this was the case for Neandertals or the people of Sungir'.

Perhaps their practice of placing cherished items in a grave was more an act of grieving, something intended to comfort the living rather than provide for the dead. Whatever the case, together these artifacts tell a story of the lives of the dead, and of how the people they left behind commemorated their lives and viewed the passage between life and death—probably the most significant and resonant issue upon which religious belief and practice focuses.

## Read More

Have a look at any of the following references for a wide variety of ways in which the analysis of human burials has provided insights into the ceremonies and religious practices of past peoples:

Arnold, B., and N. L. Wicker, eds. 2001. *Gender and the Archaeology of Death.* Rowman and Littlefield, Lantham, Maryland.

Buckley, T. 1976. The discovery of Tutankhamun's tomb. In *The Treasures of Tutankhamun,* edited by K. S. Gilbert, J. K. Holt, and S. Hudson, 9–18. The Metropolitan Museum of Art, New York.

Pearson, M. P. 2001. *The Archaeology of Death and Burial.* Texas A&M University Press, Austin.

Solecki, R. 1971. *Shanidar: The First Flower People.* Knopf, New York.

White, R. 1993. Technological and social dimensions of "Aurignacian-age" body ornaments across Europe. In *Before Lascaux: The Complex Record of the Early Upper Paleolithic,* edited by H. Knecht, A. Pike-Tay, and R. White, 277–99. CRC Press, Boca Raton, Florida.

Williams, H., ed. 2003. *Archaeologies of Remembrance: Death and Memory in Past Societies.* Plenum, New York.

# How Can Archaeologists Reveal Ways of Life of People Whose Reality Was So Different from Our Own?

Even though archaeologists represent a diversity of cultures, backgrounds, and life experiences, we are, in one important sense, a homogeneous group: we are all residents of the current period of time. I know that sounds odd and obvious. We are alive in the here and now. Of course. But it actually is a significant point. We may speak different languages, reside in different kinds of societies, engage in various traditions, and have dissimilar values, but trained archaeologists are all residents of the modern world. Most of us have attended school, read books, and received degrees in anthropology, history, or archaeology. We drive motor vehicles, buy our food at the grocery and our tools at the hardware store, communicate with cell phones, use computers, and so on. In other words, wherever we are from and whatever our backgrounds, the majority of us are wrapped up in the trappings of the modern world. The people we study, the people who left behind the arrowheads and pots, the temples and pyramids, the mundane trash pits, and the amazing monuments—the people whose lives we hope to illuminate and comprehend—lived in times that were far different from ours. How can we denizens of the twenty-first century, even those of us with advanced degrees in anthropology and years of training and experience in archaeology, ever hope to comprehend the lives of people whose time and reality were so different from our own?

One set of strategies long employed by archaeologists in our attempt to bridge the gap between our own reality and that of ancient peoples—to relate to ways of life and periods of time fundamentally alien to our own—is called **ethnographic analogy.** "Ethnographic" refers to the lives and descriptions of living groups of people. "Analogy" is the comparison of two things that are assumed to be similar in fundamental ways such that knowledge and understanding of one allow for a more complete understanding of the other. Essentially, ethnographic analogy uses the detailed descriptions of living groups of people, or people who lived in a historically recent period, as models for illuminating the lives of ancient peoples. Ethnographic analogy relies on the assumption that information that can be gleaned from the extensively documented lives of people living in recent periods, folks whose lifeways were witnessed and recorded (by explorers, colonists, missionaries, soldiers, doctors, adventurers, traders, as well as anthropologists), can be used to help elucidate the lives of people who lived in antiquity. The descriptions of these living or recent people make sense when it can be shown that the cultures of the two groups—one ancient and the other more recent—likely are similar or, more precisely, analogous.

For example, an archaeologist whose life experience is that of a modern, Western, middle-class individual might excavate a site left behind by ancient hunter-gatherers who lived during a period of extreme cold during the last Ice Age. The realities of the archaeologist and the people who produced the site could hardly be more different. The ancient people needed, on a daily basis, to extract from a capricious natural world everything on which they relied for survival. Hunting large game animals played a major role in their subsistence. They needed to make with their own hands every tool, weapon, and piece of equipment necessary for their continued existence. They were nomadic. Their lives were, on average, short; twenty-five was literally "middle-aged" and it was rare to live past fifty. Infant mortality was high; during her lifetime, a woman might give birth four, five, or more times, yet she might see only one or two of those children survive to adulthood. I do not wish to overstate the case here, but hunger, cold, disease, pain, and early death likely were a much larger part of their reality than the same factors are of our own—at least to those of us living the relatively privileged lives of college students and professors.

But there are people living today, or at least living in the last few hundred years, whose cultures and experiences have been recorded and whose reality was or is a reasonably close match to the Ice Age population just described. There are recent people who were hunters of wild animals and gatherers of wild plants. They made their own tools and weapons. They were nomadic. Life expectancy was short, infant mortality was high. We cannot expect a perfect cultural concordance because the ancient people in the earlier example were inhabitants of Ice Age Europe of 125,000 years ago, and the recent group was the native people of Alaska. It seems reasonable, however, to attempt to extract insights into the lives of the ancient people being studied from recent groups when the material conditions of their existence appear to be fundamentally similar.

Ethnographic analogy takes on many guises. In its traditional application, archaeologists may scour ethnographies written about people with economies and technologies generally similar to those of the ancient people whose sites they were excavating and whose lives they were hoping to illuminate. In the **direct historical approach** in ethnographic analogy, a closer connection is sought between the ancient and modern groups being compared. Ethnographic information about the actual biological and cultural descendants of the ancient people being investigated is used to explain what was found at the archaeological site. For example, in northeastern North America, one group of missionaries, the Jesuits, lived among the Iroquois of New York State. At the same time the Jesuits were attempting to convert the Iroquois to Catholicism, they kept a detailed account of Iroquois lifeways. The resulting multivolume publication, called the *Jesuit Relations* (Greer 2000), provides a wealth of information, albeit not entirely objective, about the lifeways of the Iroquois. The Iroquois and their ancestors have lived in New York State for more than a thousand years and the information recorded by the Jesuits in the seventeenth century can be of enormous value to the archaeologist hoping to understand the lives of the ancestors of the people whom the Jesuits so meticulously documented.

Even soldiers and explorers can provide important information in the direct historical approach to analogy. For example, French explorer Samuel de Champlain visited the New World several times and traveled among the native people of Canada and New York State. Champlain was not simply a passive observer of the Native Americans, he traded with them and even fought alongside groups with which he was friendly against their traditional enemies.

Champlain's voyages and explorations are richly documented in his memoirs and scattered throughout is fascinating information about the native people. Such information is of value to archaeologists investigating the archaeological sites of the Iroquois and their ancestors that date to before Champlain's visit and written account (Champlain 1966). Here's a brief example: in a pitched battle in which Champlain and his men were assisting one native group against another, Champlain was struck in the neck by an arrow. You might think this would have slowed down Champlain in his study of native culture, but he was one tough guy. In his memoirs, Champlain recounts pulling the arrow from his neck, whereupon he immediately provided a detailed description of the raw materials from which the arrow was made!

Archaeologists recognize the many drawbacks of ethnographic analogy when the ethnographic information comes from an individual or group with a particular agenda, for example, missionaries or explorers. Even ethnographic information provided by cultural anthropologists may be of limited value to the archaeologist because ethnographers may not focus on that which so interests archaeologists: material culture. These drawbacks to the ethnographic database have inspired some archaeologists to take the situation into their own hands and conduct the ethnography themselves. In **ethnoarchaeology** or **living archaeology,** the archaeologist becomes the ethnographer, with a particular focus on the archaeological implications of his or her observations (David and Kramer 2001; Longacre 1991; Longacre and Skibo 1994).

Archaeologist Lewis Binford did precisely this in his ethnographic study of the Nunamiut people of the North American Arctic (1978). Binford examined Nunamiut methods of hunting, butchering, preparing, and cooking meat, as well as how they discarded carcasses once they were done extracting everything edible. Binford used the behavior of these living people of the Arctic to provide a model that he then used to interpret archaeological remains at the prehistoric cave site of Combe Grenal in France that was occupied as much as 125,000 years ago (Binford 1987).

Binford used the Nunamiut as a model of the culture of the residents of Combe Grenal, even though the cave is located thousands of miles away from the Nunamiut home territory in Alaska, even though the two peoples are separated by 125,000 years, and even though the Nunamiut are biologically modern human beings and the residents of Combe Grenal were an ancient and archaic variety called the Neandertals. Despite their differences, Binford recognized similarities in material parameters of the subsistence behavior of the two peoples. For example, Binford saw stone tool cut marks on the animal bones recovered at Combe Grenal that were similar to those he had seen in the fresh kills of the Nunamiut. Specifically, Binford recognized that butchering cut marks on the lower jaws of wild cattle, reindeer, and horses at Combe Grenal were a close match in terms of location and orientation to those made by the Nunamiut on caribou jaws. The Nunamiut left those cut marks as a result of their effort to extract the caribou tongue, which they considered a delicacy. Binford concluded from this that the 125,000-year-old Neandertal residents of Combe Grenal extracted tongue meat in a manner similar to the modern Nunamiut of Alaska.

It is difficult, indeed, to bridge the temporal and cultural gaps between archaeologists and those people we study. Ethnographic analogy provides us with one way of attempting to do so.

# Read More

To find out more about the archaeologist's use of the ethnohistorical record and the application of ethnoarchaeology, consult any of the following sources:

Binford, L. 1978. *Nunamiut Ethnoarchaeology.* Academic Press, New York.
———. 1987. *Bones: Ancient Men and Modern Myths.* Academic Press, New York.
Champlain, S. D. 1966. *Voyages of Samuel de Champlain.* Burt Franklin, New York.
David, N., and C. Kramer. 2001. *Ethnoarchaeology in Action.* Cambridge University Press, Cambridge, England.
Greer, A., ed. 2000. *The Jesuit Relations: Natives and Missionaries in Seventeenth-Century North America.* Bedford/St. Martin's Press, New York.
Longacre, W. A., ed. 1991. *Ceramic Ethnoarchaeology.* University of Arizona Press, Tucson.
Longacre, W. A., and J. M. Skibo, eds. 1994. *Kalinga Ethnoarchaeology: Expanding Archaeological Method and Theory.* Smithsonian Institution Press, Washington, D.C.

# Study Questions

1. What does it mean to say that a culture is the adaptation of a particular group of people?

2. What was the point of the reference to the song, "Tradition" from the Broadway musical *Fiddler on the Roof* in my discussion of the archaeological reconstruction of an ancient social system?

3. How might the nature of the social system of a past group of people be encoded in the appearance and styles of the objects they manufactured for everyday use?

4. Explain how the appearance of the ceramics made by the women living in the same village might reflect the fact that their people practice a matrilocal postmarital residence pattern.

5. How might an archaeologist determine the nature of the postmarital residence pattern of a people by examining their material culture?

6. How do traditions of making stone tools or pottery, of burial of the dead, or of crafting baskets reflect the social systems within which such traditions develop?

7. In the division of labor in ancient societies, was biology destiny?

8. What does the work of archaeologist Diane Gifford-Gonzalez show about the stereotyping of sex roles by artists who have depicted ancient people and their lifeways? How are ancient men often depicted? How are ancient women often depicted?

9. Can archaeologists distinguish the labors of men from those of women through the analysis of an ancient material culture?

10. How does the work of Joan Gero call into question the sex-role stereotyping often applied to the making of stone tools by ancient people?

11. What is meant by the term "economic inequality"? How about "social inequality" and "political inequality"?

12. What does it mean when we label an ancient society "egalitarian"?

13. What does it mean when we label an ancient society "complex"?

14. How are equality and inequality reflected in the archaeological record of an ancient group of people?

15. Why are burials so important when it comes to issues of the archaeological reconstruction of social, economic, and political systems?

16. Why are burials so important when it comes to the analysis of equality and inequality in an ancient society?

17. How does such an apparently immaterial part of the human condition—religion—end up encoded in the archaeological record?

18. What do Neandertal burials, a tomb like that of Tutankhamen, or the gravesites at Sungir' tell us about the social, political, and economic lives of the people responsible for them?

19. What is "ethnographic analogy"? Why do archaeologists employ this procedure?

20. What is the "direct historical approach" in ethnographic analogy?

21. What is ethnoarchaeology? Why do archaeologists sometimes get involved in ethnographic research?

P reservation as found in the Ice Man is the rare exception to the norm. When human remains preserve at all, it is usually in the form of skeletons. A human skeleton is of great interest to the archaeologist because it provides, essentially, the autobiography of an ancient person with significant events written thereupon.

## Why Are Archaeologists Interested in Human Bones and Why Is This a Contentious Issue?

The skeletal remains of human beings present archaeologists with an enormous reservoir of information about the life histories of past people, both individually and as groups. The human skeleton, essentially, is a slate onto which the person's significant biological and behavioral patterns and events have been recorded. For the archaeologist whose goal is to reconstruct these life histories, to expose these biological and behavioral group patterns, and to illuminate events experienced by people in the past, the bones of human beings—their "mortal remains"—are vital scientific specimens. The problem, of course, is that these "specimens" are also the often treasured and venerated remains of mothers and fathers, sisters and brothers, grandparents, and great-grandparents stretching back across countless generations. This has become a major and contentious issue that plagues the relationship between archaeologists and the descendants of the people whose bones they have excavated and analyze.

Why are archaeologists so intensely interested in human bones in the first place? This interest is not the result of some ghoulish fixation on the remains of the dead. In fact, archaeologists are enamored of humans bones precisely because skeletons can tell us about the living; who an ancient person was in a broad and sometimes remarkably detailed sense when they can no longer tell us in their own words.

Consider the **demographic** background information that census takers or pollsters might collect to categorize you in the most fundamental ways possible. Certainly, they would want to know whether you were male or female.

Obviously, they would want to know your age. Further, they might ask your "race," nationality, and ethnicity. They might even ask about health issues or nutritional patterns. These variables describe an individual; they describe you. Compiled for an entire population, producing frequencies, proportions, or mean values, these would provide **descriptive statistics,** the numbers that describe and summarize the key characteristics of the population in which an individual lives.

With these descriptive statistics in hand, any other questions that might be posed or factors that might be addressed in a detailed numerical compilation of information about a community, state, or nation—how many years of schooling people tend to complete, income levels of citizens, the number of children people have, their religion, political affiliation, the chronic diseases that commonly afflict individuals, problems of malnutrition, and so on—can be examined for patterns of correlation and causality. Is there a relationship between sex and years of education, between race and income level, between age and political beliefs, income level and disease? Through the various procedures of **inductive statistics,** the correlations between and among the variables that characterize a population can be assessed, allowing us to paint a picture of what it was like for an individual to live in a given society.

**Biological archaeologists, forensic anthropologists,** and **biological** or **physical anthropologists** can assemble the descriptive statistics for the demography of a community by determining the sex, age, health, and even the ethnic affiliations of individuals through careful analysis of those individuals' skeletons.

Consider, for example, some demographic questions. What was the mean lifespan of people in ancient Egypt four thousand years ago? Were the lifespans—as represented by mean age at death—of the pharaoh and his noble classes different from those of farmers and workers? What was the actual ethnic background of the more than four hundred people buried in what was labeled the "Negro Burial Ground" (now called the African Burial Ground) in lower Manhattan? What was the **population profile** of these African captives? Is there evidence on their skeletons of repetitive stress injury typical for people who endure lives of hard physical labor? Is there physical evidence on their bones of physical abuse (beatings, overworking, torture) often inflicted upon slaves? What was the proportion of men to women in Mound 72, the mass grave of the great leader of Cahokia, an enormous Native American population center located on the Mississippi River in Illinois (Iseminger 1996)? Are nutritional differences exhibited between individuals (probably noblemen and women) buried in elaborate tombs containing finely made ceramics and jewelry and those people (likely peasants) interred in simple graves with few or no grave offerings at the Maya site of Altar de Sacrificios? These are but a tiny fraction of the interesting questions that can be posed and answered through the analysis of human remains—and, certainly, the answers to these questions allow the archaeologist to develop a more complete understanding of the lives of ancient people.

Nevertheless, skeletal analysis raises a vexing ethical issue that should not be ignored by any archaeologist. In some parts of the world, the descendant communities stand in opposition to the archaeological study of the bones of their ancestors. This issue is no more vigorously debated than in the United States.

The national organization of professional archaeologists, the Society for American Archaeology (http://www.saa.org), hosted a symposium on this issue at its annual meeting in 1996. Archaeologists, including Native American archaeologists, and Native Americans who were not involved in archaeology, participated. That symposium resulted in a book (*Native Americans and Archaeologists: Stepping Stones to Common Ground,* 1997) in which many and varying opinions were expressed about the role and validity of archaeology within the native community. Consider the perspective of Rebecca Tsosie (1997), a professor of law and a member of the Pascua Yaqui Indian tribe. She contends that it is a basic human right for a people, any people, to be able to pursue their own mode of religious and spiritual fulfillment and that such fulfillment necessarily requires control over the disposition of the remains of their deceased ancestors. Tsosie goes on to reject the notion that Native Americans and their culture are the equivalent of "resources" that are the communal property of all of the citizens of the United States in general and of archaeologists in particular. The remains of Native American ancestors, asserts Tsosie, should belong to their descendants who alone should determine how those remains are treated on the basis of their own tribal traditions and customs. More than a few Native Americans, including some at the symposium, view archaeology in general and the excavation, analysis, and "warehousing" of the bones of their ancestors as just one of a variety of types of colonialism, in this case carried out by scientists instead of the army or cattle ranchers (White Deer 1997).

Gary White Deer (1997:38), a world-renowned artist and member of the Choctaw tribe, has extensive experience in historic preservation on his reservation. He may be right when he points out that archaeologists might be a bit resentful, now that they are obliged by federal statute, in particular, the **Native American Graves Protection and Repatriation Act** (http://www.usbr.gov/nagpra/) to negotiate with "potential specimens." But, as the subtitle of the symposium book suggests, archaeologists and Native Americans need to negotiate "stepping stones to common ground," and that is happening, particularly in those instances where Indians themselves are in control of the archaeological work focusing on their ancestors. As previously indicated, the Navajo Nation, the largest tribe in the United States, has its own archaeology program. The Mashantucket Pequot Tribe in southeastern Connecticut has supported a vigorous archaeological program on its reservation, using some of the money generated by a hugely successful gambling and resort operation to build a cultural center where the archaeological material recovered on the reservation is analyzed, curated, and displayed.

A specific example of archaeologists and Indians working together on the thorny issue of human remains was seen in the analysis of the frozen vestiges of a Native American who died in his early twenties about 550 years ago and was found melting out of a glacier in British Columbia in 1999. His coat crafted of squirrel fur, his bone and metal tools, and a meal of dried fish carried in a leather pouch had been encased in ice, along with the young man himself.

Together, the young man and his meager possessions had lain in the ice for more than five centuries.

Canadian law affords control of ancient archaeological remains to the descendants of the people who left those remains behind. In the case of the "Canadian Ice Man," members of the Champagne and Aishihik "First Nations," whose assent was required, strongly supported a scientific analysis of the remains of the person they called *Kwaday Dan Ts'inchi*—(Long Ago Person Found). "We want to know as much about him as we can. That's what science is for, right?" (Krajick 2002): this may sound like the kind of justification for the analysis an archaeologist might offer, but the words were spoken by Diane Strand, Heritage Officer of the Champagne-Aishihik in an interview in the magazine *Science*. Of course, I should also point out that after extracting sufficient samples for DNA tests still being conducted, the remains of Long Ago Person Found were cremated and his ashes returned to the place were he was found. Obviously, no further analysis applying yet-to-be-developed procedures will be possible in this case.

Dorothy Lippert, a Choctaw Indian and a professional anthropologist, has been an eloquent and uniquely qualified commentator on the debate about the treatment of human remains. As indicated, most scientists view human remains as valuable specimens that can tell us about the life histories of ancient people. As a scientist *and* a Native American, Lippert views the skeletal remains of human beings not as specimens but as the vehicles by which the ancestors of Native Americans can communicate with their descendants: "For many of our ancestors, skeletal analysis is the only way they are able to tell us their stories" (Lippert 1997:126). Lippert goes on to explain skeletal analysis as the process by which ancestors in the past can speak to their descendants in the present in their "voice made of bone." I would only add to this stunning phrasing that ancient people all over the world can speak to us in the present, not only in their "voice made of bone," but of stone, wood, clay, and metal as well. The archaeological record, in its totality, allows for all of our silent ancestors to speak to us and tell us of their lives. Finding those "stepping stones to common ground" between descendant communities and archaeologists is vital for those ancestors to be afforded the opportunity to tell all of us their stories.

## How Can You Determine the Sex of a Person from His or Her Skeleton?

Among mammalian species, human beings exhibit a rather modest degree of **sexual dimorphism.** Human males and females certainly look different on the outside. Some of our body parts—those reflecting our primary and secondary sexual characteristics—clearly are not interchangeable and males tend to possess a larger overall body size than females. However, in many features, the sexes are not as distinct among humans as they are, for example, in one of our nearest biological relatives, gorillas, where males commonly are about twice as large as their female counterparts. On the other hand, the human sexes are far more readily distinguishable than those of the hyena, where males and females are so similar in size, body form, and even in terms of the appearance of their external genitalia that, for the most part, only other hyenas can readily tell the difference.

Sexual dimorphism in mammals is exhibited on the inside as well, where, rather obviously, male and female internal sex organs differentiate the sexes absolutely. The size and general appearance of their skeletons and soft organs also differentiate males from females among mammals. Among our closest relatives, the apes, even with just the bones, the degree of dimorphism is sufficient to insure a nearly perfect identification of and distinction between the skeletons of males and females: their skeletons are absolutely different, or nearly so, and with complete specimens they can always be accurately distinguished.

Sexual dimorphism is less obvious, however, in the human skeleton. Unlike many other species, rather inconveniently for those attempting to identify and differentiate the skeletons of male and female human beings, the skeletons of human males do not possess an absolutely distinguishing element called a baculum or "penis bone." The differences between human male and female skeletons instead are reflected in the measured differences of continuously distributed variables.

Human males, for example, tend to be larger than human females. They usually are taller, heavier, and more robustly muscled, and these differences generally are reflected in the bones of their skeletons. So, though there are no bones unique to either sex, the bones of males within a given human population tend to be bigger, heavier, rougher, and denser than those of the females in the same population as a partial result of genetic predisposition. In other words, a zoologist can *always* distinguish the skeleton of a male sea lion from a female because the male has a penis bone and, not surprisingly, the female does not. On the other hand, a forensic anthropologist can *usually* distinguish the skeleton of a human male from a human female because the individual bones of the male tend to fall on one end of a normal distribution while those of a female tend to fall on the other. There is nearly always substantial overlap, however, and, for example, there are individual males whose bones are smaller and less robust than those of individual females in any group and, therefore, cannot be accurately "sexed" by a forensic anthropologist, biological archaeologist, or biological anthropologist on the basis of size or robusticity alone.

Beyond those bones that contribute to stature, for example, the long bones of the leg (**femur, tibia,** and **fibula**), there are a number of measurements that, individually, help to distinguish human males from females in a population. Taken together, these skeletal elements and features help make the identification of the sex of an individual based on the skeleton extremely accurate. For example, most human males have a discernable ridge of bone over each of their eye orbits (or sockets), located near the eyebrows. Not all human males have a substantial **supraorbital torus,** but within any population males tend to have them and females do not. When a **cranium** (technically, the **skull** consists of the cranium and the **mandible** or lower jaw) is found with a substantial torus, the archaeologist or forensic anthropologist will suggest that it most likely belonged to a male, but there is no certainty based on this feature alone. Another cranial element that tends to distinguish males from females in terms of size and shape is the **mastoid process,** a bump of bone you can feel on your own cranium just behind and toward the bottom of each ear. Several muscles attach to the mastoid process that control extension and rotation of the head and, because the human male head tends to be larger and heavier than that of the female these muscles need to be bigger and, in turn, the male mastoid process tends to be larger (and rougher for firmer muscle attachment) than that of females. Also, the female mastoid process tends to be rather pointy while the male version is flatter. Again, it is not a perfectly distinguishing feature, but it points in a particular direction.

It is in the bones of the pelvis that we find the clearest markers distinguishing human males from females. Although the bones of the rest of the body may be larger and more robust in males than in females, essentially they are functionally the same. In the pelvis, however, we encounter skeletal elements that don't perform the same functions in males and females. The bones of the pelvis provide the attachment points for the leg muscles in both males and females and thus determine our unique method of **bipedal locomotion** (walking on two feet), but in females the pelvis also serves the purpose of providing the walls of a birth canal through which babies can be born. Proportional to other mammals, at birth human babies have enormous heads and, rather unfortunately, as a result of the configuration of the human pelvis that enables us to walk on two feet, the human birth canal is proportionally small. This is one of the features of human anatomy that physical anthropologist Wilton Marion Krogman (1951) referred to as one of the "scars of human evolution."

Nature has dealt with this problem in a number of ways. Compared to other mammals, human babies are born at a proportionally early, immature stage of development to enable them to pass through the constricted birth canal yet still be developed enough to still survive outside of the womb. Nature also seems to have tweaked the configuration of the geometry of the human female pelvis by widening an angled notch on the bone, called the **sciatic notch** after the nerve that passes down the pelvis from the back to the leg. A wider notch opens up the birth canal by a bit, ordinarily just enough to allow for safe passage by the baby during the birth process (Figure 13.1). Though there is quite a bit of variation, in a large sample of human beings, the mean sciatic notch angle for women was calculated to be 74.4 degrees; for males in the same sample, the mean angle was only about two-thirds this at 50.4 degrees (Krogman 1973). Even in this seemingly diagnostic anatomical feature, there was a bit of overlap: the smallest sciatic notch angle for a woman in the sample was about 61 degrees and the largest angle for a man was more than this, about 65 degrees. Though an imperfect yardstick, it is one of the best single measurements by which the sex of an individual can be assessed. If you don't like measuring

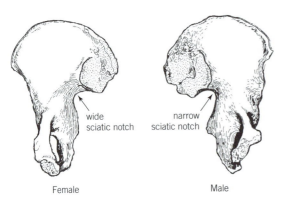

wide sciatic notch

narrow sciatic notch

Female

Male

**FIGURE 13.1** View of the human male and female pelvis showing the sciatic notch, which is diagnostically larger in females than in males.

angles, there even is a literal "rule of thumb": if you can place your thumb straight into the notch and it fits snugly, the pelvis is that of a male; if your thumb can wiggle, it is a female. I suppose, rather ironically, the accuracy of this rule of thumb depends on the size of your thumb which, in turn, depends to an extent on whether you are a male or a female.

In assessing the accuracy of the process of identifying the sex of the individual whose bones we are examining, it is clear that the more skeletal elements of an individual available, the more confident we can be in our conclusion. Having only a long bone to measure or just a cranial fragment inspires less confidence in our identification than if we have long bones and a cranium, and, especially, the pelvis of an individual. Even then, we cannot be 100% accurate, but we do get pretty close to perfection: most forensic anthropologists claim a greater than 95% accuracy rate for the identification of the sex of an individual when the entire skeleton is available for analysis.

## Read More

There are many fine guides to the subjects of forensic anthropology in general, and human osteology in particular, that discuss how an archaeologist can identify the sex of an individual based on his or her bones. The following list includes an old standard (Krogman 1973) and a host of newer, terrific textbooks, manuals, atlases, and guidebooks:

Bass, W. 1987. *Human Osteology: A Laboratory and Field Manual of the Human Skeleton*. Missouri Archaeological Society, Columbia.

Brothwell, D. R. 1972. *Digging Up Bones: The Excavation, Treatment, and Study of Human Skeletal Remains*. British Museum, London.

Burns, K. R. 1999. *The Forensic Anthropology Training Manual*. Prentice Hall, Upper Saddle River, New Jersey.

Byers, S. N. 2001. *Introduction to Forensic Anthropology: A Textbook*. Allyn and Bacon, Boston.

Hillson, S. 1996. *Dental Anthropology*. Cambridge University Press, Cambridge, England.

Krogman, W. M. 1951. The scars of human evolution. *Scientific American* 185:54–57.

———. 1973. *The Human Skeleton in Forensic Medicine*. Charles C. Thomas, Springfield, Illinois.

Rhine, S. 1998. *Bone Voyage*. University of New Mexico Press, Santa Fe.

Scott, G. R., and C. G. Turner II. 2000. *The Anthropology of Modern Human Teeth: Dental Morphology and Its Variation in Recent Human Populations*. Cambridge, University Press, Cambridge, England.

Ubelaker, D. H. 1978. *Human Skeletal Remains: Excavation, Analysis, Interpretation*. Aldine Manuals on Archaeology. Aldine, Chicago.

White, T. D., and P. A. Folkens. 1991. *Human Osteology*. Academic Press, New York.

## How Can You Determine the Age of a Person from His or Her Skeleton?

How old are you? This book is read, primarily, by university students. Although an increasing number of older adults are registering for college courses—in the last few years I have seen a growing number of full-fledged adults in my classes, including parents taking courses at my university alongside their children—by and large, university students are in their late teens and early twenties. That's likely your age range. At that age, in our culture, few of you are all that interested in confronting the certainty of mortality and so it is not surprising, when I assign the "gravestone project" in my introductory archaeology course, that the response is a nearly unanimous, "Yuck!" Except in tragic and mercifully rare circumstances, most college-age people don't spend a lot of time in graveyards, and the prospect of having to collect data from the gravestones in a graveyard, even ones as old as those the project requires (stones erected before 1880) is not often met with a great deal of enthusiasm, at least not initially.

*Gravestones*

I don't send my students to graveyards because of a morbid fascination on my part. Burying grounds actually are fascinating places and, no matter what their age, are archaeological sites. All gravestones, again no matter how long ago they were carved and erected, are artifacts of a particular culture and period of time, reflecting the religious beliefs and attitudes of a past people.

The assignment does not involve any digging but instead requires data collection and analysis. Students collect data from gravestones—the artifacts of the graveyard—including overall size, raw material, shape, and design, as well as the written information on the stones, including name, sex (which often is inferred from name or assigned status like "wife of," or "son of"), year of birth, and date of death. Knowing these two dates allows us to determine the age at death of the person buried beneath the gravestone and then, with a large sample of stones from a graveyard, the mean age at death for the people who lived—and died—in a given town.

Among the various analyses students conduct in the graveyard are a number that can be called **demographic. Demography** is the statistical analysis of a population, including, among a large number of variables, its size, age distribution, longevity, sex ratio, and ethnic makeup. Knowing the demography of a community allows archaeologists to paint a statistical picture of the communities represented in graveyards. The demographic study of a seventeenth-, eighteenth-, or nineteenth-century Connecticut town might not seem all that engaging to you. I know it doesn't, at least not at first, to the students in my class. But something remarkable happens to many young people of college age when they enter an old graveyard and see the overwhelming number of people there who died in their youth, who, in fact, died when they were about the same age as the students collecting the presumed dry demographic data required in the assignment.

Most of us have grown up in a time and in a society in which teenagers and even people well into their twenties are, demographically at least, children. Life expectancy in North America is among the highest in the world. By the reckoning of the U.S. Centers for Disease Control, as of 2001, at birth the life expectancy of a male is 74.4 and of a female is 79.8 (http://www.cdc.gov/nchs/releases/03news/lifeex.htm). You likely haven't thought long and hard about how these numbers, in many ways, have an overwhelming impact on how you live your life. But think about it: male or female, at age eighteen you still have more than 75% of your life to live. You have the luxury of enough time to go to college, make your parents crazy by trying out a wide variety of majors (none of which will get you a well-paying job when you graduate), go to graduate school, "find yourself," experiment with lots of different elements of life, all before you settle down, choose a pathway, and maybe raise a family. Now imagine how entirely different your life, your perspective, your fate would be if you were a member of a society where the mean age at death is half the American average, a reasonable estimate for longevity for many past societies as well as for many modern ones in the undeveloped world. Imagine how different your life experience might be if you grew up in a society where death in childhood was not a thankfully infrequent tragedy, but a common occurrence, a misfortune that touches virtually everyone, at least indirectly. In such a society, at eighteen you would be about half finished with life and suddenly the issue of time would loom large. You would know too many people your age and younger who had died. In such a society, at eighteen there no longer seems to be all the time in the world to grow up, choose a life path, and take on the responsibilities of adulthood. At eighteen, time is already running out in some societies: when you are eighteen years old in a society where the mean age at death is thirty-six, you are already, literally "middle aged."

At some level, many of my students who prowl an old cemetery, at first merely to fulfill a requirement of the project and then, at least for some, out of curiosity about the lives of the people buried there, make that connection and consider how different everything about their lives would be if they had been born three hundred, two hundred, or even one hundred years earlier. Knowing something as simple as the mean age of death in a society (ancient or modern) provides us with a fundamental insight about the nature of the lives of the people who lived in those societies. The analysis of human skeletons allows us to make this determination.

Upon meeting a child for the first time, you probably guess his or her age on the basis of stature. It's obvious enough; kids start off small, get bigger as they get older, and reach maximum height as adults. Until a person reaches his or her full size, stature is a good first indicator of age and the same is true for skeletal remains. The overall height of an individual, based on the length of the bones of his or her skeleton, indicates the approximate age of the person at death, at least in an ordinal sense: infant, toddler, child, teenager, and then adult.

A person's stature in life can be estimated by skeletal measurement, especially of the long bones of the legs. A number of formulas allow for an approximation of an individual's height based on the length of one of those bones, usually the **femur,** the longest of the leg bones. These formulas are different for the two sexes and also vary by ethnicity because bodily proportions may differ among geographic groups of people. The following list shows formulas derived for stature estimation for males and females of European and African descent (Bass 1987):

Female European: Stature ($\pm$3.72 cm) = 2.47 $\times$ femur length in cm + 54.10

Female African: Stature ($\pm$3.41 cm) = 2.28 $\times$ femur length in cm + 59.76

Male European: Stature ($\pm$3.94 cm) = 2.32 $\times$ femur length in cm + 65.53

Male African: Stature ($\pm$3.91 cm) = 2.10 $\times$ femur length in cm + 72.22

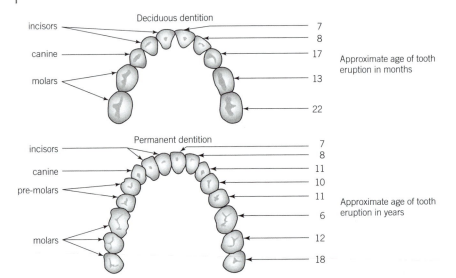

**FIGURE 13.2** Schematic diagram showing the average age at which the deciduous (baby) and permanent (adult) teeth erupt in the human mouth. Reference to this pattern of tooth appearance allows the archaeologist to determine the probable age at death of an individual whose remains have been found at an archaeological site.

Along with a sequence of increasing height, dental development also provides a valuable gauge of level of physical maturity and age. Ordinarily, human children arrive in the world toothless—much to the relief of nursing mothers—and a first set of teeth (the lower central incisors) doesn't begin to emerge until about six-and-a-half months of age. From there, the timing of the appearance of the rest of the baby teeth, called **deciduous teeth,** is fairly consistent across our species until the second upper molars erupt at about two-and-a-half years (when there are twenty teeth in all, Figure 13.2). A child's teeth achieve a certain degree of stasis at two-and-a-half until, at about age six, the first permanent teeth erupt, molars in the lower jaw. Their appearance at about this age is so consistent that they are, in fact, called the six-year-molars. At about the same age, the deciduous teeth (so named because they are shed like the leaves of deciduous, leaf-bearing trees) become fodder for the tooth fairy at a similarly consistent, relatively regular rate and are replaced by the adult or permanent teeth. From age six to about eighteen, the baby teeth all fall out according to a fairly regularly timed schedule, adult teeth replace them, and additional permanent teeth erupt toward the back of an enlarging mouth until there are thirty-two permanent teeth.

The point here is not to prepare you for a career in dental hygiene, but to get across a methodology of age determination. Because of the regularity in timing of the eruption of each of the baby teeth, their shedding and replacement by adult dentition until the thirty-two adult teeth have produced the adult mouth, the mix of deciduous and permanent teeth charts the age of an individual. By reference to a simple table (http://www.tdh.state.tx.us/dental/needknow.htm), the approximate age of a living child or the age at which a deceased child died can be fairly easily and accurately determined based on which teeth are present, the stage of growth of these teeth, and which teeth have yet to erupt into the mouth.

Beyond this, the skeletons of human children are not just smaller versions of those of adults. Their individual bones are readily distinguishable from those of their parents, not just in terms of size, but also in terms of form and configuration. In fact, while the adult human skeleton consists of 206 separate bones, a newborn child's skeleton has well over twice as many, about 450. Children don't have extra bones that are lost in development, but many of the individual bones of an adult begin as separate bone segments and only join fully once maturity and adult size are achieved.

In the **post-cranial skeleton,** the long bones also exhibit a developmental sequence of change that is regular enough to provide a sort of osteological calendar of an individual's lifespan. Just as the cranium of a newborn consists of seven separate bones, each of the bones of their arms, legs, hands, and feet consist of three distinct components at birth and during development. Each of these bones (as well as the clavicle or collarbone) consists of a shaft called a **diaphysis** and two end caps, each called an **epiphysis.** The end caps are flexibly attached to their respective shafts by a strong band of cartilage. Much of the lengthening of these long bones during development occurs at this flexible junction and upon approaching adult size, these cartilage connections ossify, become solid and produce a single, continuous bone where initially there had been three separate boney elements connected by cartilage. Like the development of dentition, this process of ossification during physical development follows a schedule that is pretty consistent among all human children who are not suffering from severe malnutrition (Figure 13.3).

This consistency provides a timetable for estimating the age of a child whose development sadly was halted by death. For example, the **proximal epiphysis** (the upper end) fuses to the diaphysis of the femur at about age seventeen years, while the **distal epiphysis** (lower end) of the same bone fuses to the shaft at about age nineteen. The distal epiphysis of the **humerus** (upper arm bone) fuses at sixteen or seventeen, while the proximal end doesn't fuse until twenty. If you are about that age or younger, x-rays or CT scans of your bones would enable a medical researcher to accurately estimate your age. Therefore, an examination of the progression of the fusion of epiphyses to their respective diaphyses provides an accurate estimate of how old a person was at death.

Changes in the human cranium also reflect a consistent pattern of development. Though we think of the cranium as a hollow, spherical vessel—a single-bone bowl that contains the human brain—in reality we begin life with a cranium of seven separate bones held together by bands of cartilage. Consider the reasons for this. The brain of a newborn human is only about 25% of its ultimate adult size. Compare this to chimpanzees, whose newborn brains are about 40% of their adult size. Even at this very early stage of development, the human baby has a very large head relative to the birth canal it must negotiate and whose size is restricted because of its primary function in the architecture of bipedal locomotion by the mother. To allow for the rather tight fit during birth, the cranium of the fetus is quite flexible. If it were a solid, inflexible sphere of bone, given its size it probably could not pass safely

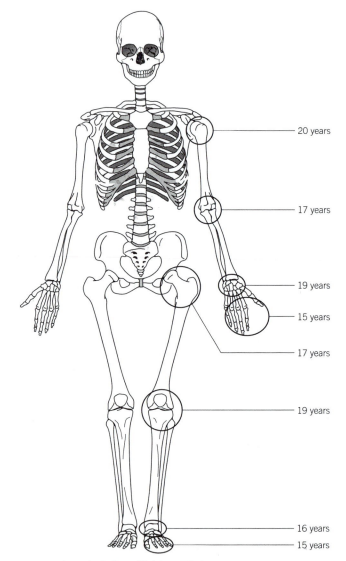

20 years

17 years

19 years

15 years

17 years

19 years

16 years

15 years

Approximate Ages of Epiphyseal Fusion

**FIGURE 13.3** Diagram of the human skeleton showing the average age at which the end caps of the major long bones fuse to their shafts during development.

through the birth canal. Instead, the newborn cranial configuration of seven bone plates connected by flexible cartilage affords the head the malleability needed to safely pass through the birth canal. There are substantial gaps between some of the bone plates, producing two **fontanelles**—the so-called soft spots on a baby's head—that contribute to the ability of the cranium to safely deform during birth. Along with its very small size, therefore, the cranium of a stillborn infant or very young child is quite recognizable because, unlike with the skulls of older children and adults, once the cartilage connecting the cranial plates in newborn or infant remains decays, these plates are no longer connected and often are found as separate pieces.

Unlike all other mammalian species where growth rate slows substantially after birth, brain growth and, therefore, cranial growth in human newborns continues for the first year of life at about the same rate that characterized its pre-birth growth. As a result, the crania of newborn humans continue to exhibit relatively soft connections between the cranial plates, facilitating development as they grow in order to contain rapidly expanding brains during the first year of life. Although the cranial plates don't usually separate in a deceased toddler or older child, the boundaries between the cranial plates are clearly demarcated as rather thick junctions called **cranial sutures.** These sutures continue to fuse slowly during an individual's lifetime and provide a general impression of the age even of an adult based on how thoroughly the sutures have fused (Figure 13.4). As a result, some forensic anthropologists maintain that suture closure provides a viable estimate of age at death to within about a decade. These sutures can become virtually obliterated in the crania of people of advanced age; a cranium with no remaining sign of sutures generally belonged to an individual who died in at least their seventies or eighties.

Physical development, therefore, is marked by fairly consistently timed changes in the human skeleton that can be used to determine age at death for a subadult. Once all of the adult teeth are in and epiphyses fused to their respective shafts, however, accurately aging a skeleton becomes more of a

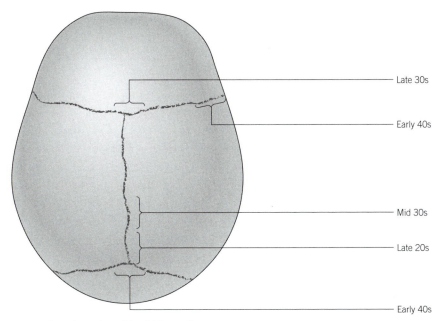

Late 30s

Early 40s

Mid 30s

Late 20s

Early 40s

Approximate Ages of Cranial Suture Closure

**FIGURE 13.4** Schematic diagram of the timing of cranial suture fusion during a human lifespan. Unfortunately, because the rate at which cranial sutures fade varies greatly from person to person, reference to degree of suture fusion is not viewed as a very accurate or precise method of determining an individual's age at death.

challenge and our precision (technically meaning how narrow a range of years we can accurately estimate) declines. As just mentioned, cranial suture closure occurs as we age and, therefore, the degree of fusion or closure marked by the slow disappearance of the suture lines where the cranial plates come together can be used to provide a broad estimate for the age of an individual. Otherwise, with the exception of the clavicle, whose end caps don't fuse until well into the twenties, once an individual passes out of the teens, skeletal changes are not precisely timed steps in physical development but instead reflect the slow, inevitable, and less precisely timed results of bones and joints slowly wearing out during the life of an individual. These degenerative processes do not provide a very accurate skeletal clock because the rate at which they operate varies among individuals, depending on work history, which determines the degree of stress and abuse repetitive use inflicts on various bones and joints. When a sports announcer comments that a physician diagnoses that a thirty-year-old football player has the knees of a sixty-year-old, he or she is expressing this same notion.

Probably the most useful skeletal gauge of adult age occurs at the point in the skeleton where the left and right halves of the pelvis meet in the front. Called the **pubic symphysis,** the two faces of the pelvic bones preserve a record of wear and tear that occurs at a vaguely regular rate during our lives. Through examination of a large sample of human skeletons, some rough models of the appearance of the pubic bones of males and females throughout their lifetimes have been produced. By comparing the pubic symphysis of an archaeological skeleton to the models of known age, a rough estimate, perhaps at a decadal level of precision, can be obtained.

In summary, careful analysis of a complete human skeleton can provide an accurate and rather precise estimate of an individual's age at death, but usually only if the person died in the first twenty or twenty-five years of life. After that, our estimates become less precise, usually allowing for not much better than an estimate of the decade of life in which an individual died. Knowing the mean age of death in a population provides a vital perspective about what it was like to live in a past culture where childhood was short, adulthood came quickly, and death was never a distant tragedy.

## Read More

There are many fine guides to the subjects of forensic anthropology, in general, and human osteology, in particular, that discuss how an archaeologist can identify the age at death of an individual based on his or her bones. The following list includes an old standard (Krogman 1973) and a host of newer, terrific textbooks, manuals, atlases, and guidebooks:

Bass, W. 1987. *Human Osteology: A Laboratory and Field Manual of the Human Skeleton.* Missouri Archaeological Society, Columbia.

Brothwell, D. R. 1972. *Digging Up Bones: The Excavation, Treatment, and Study of Human Skeletal Remains.* British Museum, London.

Burns, K. R. 1999. *The Forensic Anthropology Training Manual.* Prentice Hall, Upper Saddle River, New Jersey.

Byers, S. N. 2001. *Introduction to Forensic Anthropology: A Textbook.* Allyn and Bacon, Boston.

Hillson, S. 1996. *Dental Anthropology.* Cambridge University Press, Cambridge, England.

Krogman, W. M. 1973. *The Human Skeleton in Forensic Medicine.* Charles C. Thomas, Springfield, Illinois.

Rhine, S. 1998. *Bone Voyage.* University of New Mexico Press, Santa Fe.

Scott, G. R., and C. G. Turner II. 2000. *The Anthropology of Modern Human Teeth: Dental Morphology and Its Variation in Recent Human Populations.* Cambridge University Press, Cambridge, England.

Ubelaker, D. H. 1978. *Human Skeletal Remains: Excavation, Analysis, Interpretation.* Aldine Manuals on Archaeology. Aldine, Chicago.

White, T. D., and P. A. Folkens. 1991. *Human Osteology.* Academic Press, New York.

## How Can You Determine the Health of a Person from His or Her Skeleton?

I am quite certain that from anybody's perspective other than my own it must have been quite hilarious: it was the first day of field school and I was leading a team of intrepid neophytes out for their first archaeological experience. My intention that day was to walk them along the river where many of our sites were located, out into a farmer's plowed field where we would walk the furrows scanning for artifacts that had been exposed by the plow blade. It was supposed to be simple and uneventful, and it was, until it came time to instruct the crew on the safest way to cross over a rather innocuous little brook in our hike to the plowed field.

In truth, it would have been perfectly fine to walk through the brook. It was only a few inches deep, a few feet across, and rather still. But an old oak that had once grown on the bank of the brook had long ago fallen over, its curved trunk forming an arched, natural crossing. I had passed over the old trunk on numerous occasions without incident and simply wanted to make certain that everyone on the field crew would be able to make the crossing safely. I went over first, warning them that a bit of sand on the top of the oak arch made the footing a little slippery. As I hit the patch of sand, naturally enough, I slipped and began sliding along the curved trunk, but conveniently enough toward the other side of the brook. "Okay," I thought, "I'll simply surf down the tree trunk. My students will be impressed." The only problem with this plan was the fact that waiting for me at the other side were the spiky remnants of the tree's roots, on which I caught my left foot. This, in turn, tumbled me down like a stone, and I landed hard on the outside of my right foot on a rather sharply pointed rock embedded in the soil near the base of the dead oak. I had the presence of mind to get out one final joke—"Well, that's how *not* to get across the brook"—before the first wave of pain hit. I have sprained an ankle or two, and recognize that it can be uncomfortable, but nothing compared to this. I had no choice but to pretend I was perfectly okay, both for the sake of my dignity—did

I forgot to mention how hilarious my students thought my little performance had been?—and for the fact that we were about a mile-and-a-half from our vehicle and only a couple of hours into our field day.

I'll spare you the details of how I managed to walk over plowed fields, eventually back to the truck, and how I was able to drive it back to campus (using my left foot on the brake and gas; lucky for me it wasn't a standard transmission), and then how I managed to make it home. I'll also forgo any discussion of the expression on the face of the emergency room doctor when I explained to him how I managed to mangle my foot, which the x-ray rather clearly indicated I had broken (fractured the fifth metatarsal, to be precise). For about ten years after I had broken the bone, I could accurately predict rain (my right foot would begin to throb just before a storm) and now, more than twenty years later, the break can still be seen on x-rays of my right foot. My fifth metatarsal, in fact, bears eternal witness to my clumsy inability to cross a stream only about 3 feet across and 3 inches deep. And there's the lesson of my less than excellent adventure: our skeletons bear eternal witness to the physical traumas that have afflicted us. Broken bones, fractures, knife wounds, and bullet holes become permanent records of acts of accident and violence, written on our skeletons.

Consider, for example, the remarkably preserved, 5,300-year-old body found by hikers in the Alps in 1991, just on the Italian side of that nation's border with Austria (Spindler 1994). Though for ten years it was thought that the so-called Ice Man had frozen to death while attempting to cross the mountains in winter, recent CT scans have shown the presence of a stone blade deeply embedded in his shattered shoulder blade. The location of the arrow point indicates that it probably killed the Ice Man within a few hours of penetrating his body.

Although skeletons like the Ice Man's bear witness to a quick, violent end, many human skeletons exhibit the results of a much slower kind of violence that inflicts not obvious trauma, but degeneration over a lengthy period of time. For example, the skeletal remains of thirty-six African slaves examined by Ted Rathburn (1987) bore witness to their lives of toil and exploitation. The degenerative bone disease exhibited in their shoulders, elbows, hips, and lower vertebrae in people far too young to have such a degree of damage through normal use indicates hard lives of stoop-and-bend labor in the field. It is one thing to read of the physical exploitation endured by slaves; it is another to see the agonizing results of that exploitation on their mortal remains.

Along with trauma and wearing out of bones and joints as a result of overuse, the human skeleton also can exhibit evidence of a number of diseases. **Paleopathology,** the study of ancient trauma and illness can in some cases even help solve historical mysteries. For example, Nick Bellantoni, the state archaeologist of Connecticut, was called on to excavate an unmarked, eighteenth-century cemetery in Griswold. It was clear during excavation that one of the crypts had been opened about a decade after burial and that the body within the crypt had been perversely violated (Figure 13.5). The ribs and vertebrae were in disarray, the skull had been moved onto the chest, and the bones of the upper legs had been removed from their correct anatomical position and placed crosswise in front of the skull. Needless to say, this is not the standard form of burial in eighteenth- and nineteenth-century New England and

Bellantoni searched for an answer to this rather disturbing puzzle (1997).

He found that answer, in part, in local nineteenth-century newspaper accounts that recorded, of all things, a vampire frenzy in southern New England during this period. Apparently, a handful of people had been accused of vampirism in southeastern Connecticut and Rhode Island. From a modern, informed perspective, the evidence was flimsy: the accused individuals had suffered long, debilitating illnesses and then, upon their deaths, many of those people close to them slowly deteriorated as well, becoming weak, pale, and listless, as if the life force was being "drained" (get it?) from their bodies, and then they too died. The cause was diagnosed as vampirism and it was believed that those who died initially were rising from their graves and draining the blood of their loved ones, dragging them into the unholy world of the vampires. The only cure, it was thought, was the desecration of the presumed vampire's grave and the removal of his or her heart (removing the need for blood) and the disruption of the bones, especially those of the legs, to prevent rising from the graves and walking the night. The grave Bellantoni excavated fit the pattern, with the disturbed ribs indicating that the chest had been broken into and the leg bones moved from their correct anatomical position.

**FIGURE 13.5** This photo shows a direct view into the grave of one of the individuals interred at the Walton family cemetery in Griswold, Connecticut. The skeleton was found as you see it, with both femurs (the thigh bones) removed from their correct anatomical position, and placed crosswise across the person's chest. (*Courtesy of Nick Bellantoni*)

The symptoms of vampirism described in the news accounts sounded quite a bit like those of tuberculosis, an infectious and deadly, not to mention entirely natural, bacterial disease that still affects millions of people each year by attacking their lungs. The extended period of listlessness, exhaustion, and pallor attributed to vampirism all match the symptoms of tuberculosis. The fact that after a family member died others in the family began exhibiting the same symptoms was not the result of the undead slowly draining the blood of their victims, but likely of the infectious nature of the disease and its lengthy incubation period. The person infected with the tuberculosis bacilli coughs and sneezes, spreading the bacilli through the air, which may then be inhaled by others, especially people living in close quarters with the infected person, in other words, close members of the family.

Tuberculosis is easily diagnosed in a living person by examining the infected lungs, but it is far more difficult among those dead long enough to have their lungs turn to dust. However, there is a diagnostic pathology that appears on the ribs of people suffering from tuberculosis. Sure enough, the whitish-gray, pitted lesions that are skeletal indicators of tuberculosis were found on a number of the ribs of the disturbed grave. It seems certain that Bellantoni solved the mystery of the disturbed grave through analysis of the skeleton of the man buried there.

Nutrition also has an affect on the human skeleton. For example, prolonged bouts of severe malnutrition can have a severe impact on development during childhood. The longitudinal (lengthwise) growth of our long bones can actually be interrupted if the deficiency is severe enough, leaving marks on the bones called **growth arrest lines** or, more commonly, **Harris Lines** (named for the researcher who was among the first to ascribe the lines to malnutrition). The appearance of these defects in the bones of adults indicates that their growth had actually halted temporarily during childhood as a result of malnutrition. Their growth resumed only after the bout of malnutrition ended (Figure 13.6).

Malnutrition during childhood may also manifest itself as a cracking or pitting of tooth enamel called **enamel hypoplasia.** Interestingly, hypoplasia occurs in permanent dentition, even though the malnutrition occurs during childhood. The germs of the adult teeth are already in a child's jaw, under the baby teeth. Just recently, my eight-year-old had an x-ray as part of his regular dental checkup. Sure enough, just below the negative images of the teeth he already has in his mouth there were bright little smudges. These are the buds of his permanent teeth that eventually will erupt and replace his baby teeth. It is the growth of the enamel of these forming adult teeth that is interrupted during childhood bouts of malnutrition and the pathology shows up in the adult mouth.

**FIGURE 13.6** Radiograph of Harris Lines, also called growth arrest lines, which are skeletal evidence of malnutrition during childhood. (*Courtesy of Brian Tidey, www.radiographersreporting.com*)

Consider the cemetery, for example, at the Altar de Sacrificios site of the Maya civilization (Saul 1972; Smith 1972). The Maya represent an extraordinary native New World civilization, replete with great temples, pyramids, a written language, and a sophisticated calendar. The Maya also produced a stratified society with great rulers, a noble class, specialist craftsmen and -women, and a vast peasantry. Researchers excavated 136 burials at the Altar de Sacrificios site. The grave goods interred with the Maya at the site reflect a range of wealth and status, probably representative of the different classes of Maya society. It should come as no surprise to learn that in a stratified society of rulers and peasants wealth differences in life are represented in death as well. The graves at Altar de Sacrificios show this, with a few burials resplendent with finely made necklaces and ceramics while most burials are far plainer, reflecting the lower economic status of the person buried.

It is commonly the case in class societies that the wealthy nobility eats well, even when food is scarce and peasants starve, and this is reflected at Altar de Sacrificios. Frank Saul (1972) identified the presence of enamel hypoplasia in the teeth of most of those buried at the site. He categorized the degree of hypoplasia in each of the skeletons along an ordinal scale (absent, slight, medium, pronounced). Researchers made the same kind of breakdown for the graves based on burial wealth (tombs of the wealthy, tombs of the middle class, and graves of the poor). Finally, a table was produced showing the relationship between the two variables, grave wealth and degree of hypoplasia in the same individuals. The results should shock no one: individuals buried in the more elaborate tombs tended to exhibit either no or low levels of hypoplasia, while those buried with no indication of great wealth or status tended to have higher levels of the condition that is caused by malnutrition in childhood. Childhood malnutrition was uncommon among the Maya nobility at Altar de Sacrificios, but the same cannot be said for Maya peasants, whose teeth betrayed a fundamental element of class society.

Certainly, our skeletons are the product of genetics, but equally certainly their final appearance is a product of our life history: the traumas inflicted, the diseases endured, the toil that accompanied our activities in life, and the foods we were able to obtain. A careful examination of an ancient skeleton illuminates a life history; a careful examination of a community of skeletons illuminates the life of the community.

# Read More

There are many fine guides to the subjects of forensic anthropology, in general, and human osteology, in particular, that discuss how an archaeologist can identify the health and nutritional status of an individual based on his or her bones. The following list includes an old standard (Krogman 1973) and a host of newer, terrific textbooks, manuals, atlases, and guidebooks. Also in this list are the specific sources cited in this segment as examples of the application of human osteology in archaeological analysis:

Bass, W. 1987. *Human Osteology: A Laboratory and Field Manual of the Human Skeleton*. Missouri Archaeological Society, Columbia.

Bellantoni, N. F., P. Sledzik, and D. A. Poirier. 1997. Rescue, research, and reburial: Walton Family Cemetery. In *In Remembrance: Archaeology and Death*, edited by D. Poirier and N. F. Bellantoni, 131–54. Bergin and Garvey, Westport, Connecticut.

Brothwell, D. R. 1972. *Digging Up Bones: The Excavation, Treatment, and Study of Human Skeletal Remains*. British Museum, London.

Burns, K. R. 1999. *The Forensic Anthropology Training Manual*. Prentice Hall, Upper Saddle River, New Jersey.

Byers, S. N. 2001. *Introduction to Forensic Anthropology: A Textbook*. Allyn and Bacon, Boston.

Krogman, W. M. 1973. *The Human Skeleton in Forensic Medicine.* Charles C. Thomas, Springfield, Illinois.

Rathburn, T. 1987. Health and disease at a South Carolina plantation. *American Journal of Physical Anthropology* 74:239–53.

Rhine, S. 1998. *Bone Voyage.* University of New Mexico Press, Santa Fe.

Saul, F. P. 1972. *The Human Skeletal Remains of Altar de Sacrificios.* Papers of the Peabody Museum of Archaeology and Ethnology 63, Cambridge, Massachusetts.

Smith, A. L. 1972. *Excavations at Altar de Sacrificios.* Papers of the Peabody Museum of Archaeology and Ethnology 62, Cambridge, Massachusetts.

Spindler, K. 1994. *The Man in the Ice.* Harmony Books, New York.

Ubelaker, D. H. 1978. *Human Skeletal Remains: Excavation, Analysis, Interpretation.* Aldine Manuals on Archaeology. Aldine, Chicago.

White, T. D., and P. A. Folkens. 1991. *Human Osteology.* Academic Press, New York.

## How Can You Determine the Ethnic Identity of a Person from His or Her Skeleton?

Human beings come in a dizzying variety of different shapes, sizes, colors, and configurations, and these different looks appear to vary geographically. In fact, if you were to ask the average American, I would guess that he or she might enumerate three distinct geographic **races** of humanity, labeling them variously as white, black, and yellow; or Caucasian, Negro, and Mongoloid; or European, African, and Asian; or any one of a number of other designations based on appearance or presumed continent of origin. Examined more closely, however, the usual tripartite division of humanity perceived by many Europeans and Americans masks a far greater degree of diversity within our species and makes separate categories seem more distinct than is really the case. In fact, there is at least as much variation within what are commonly called races as there is between them (Park 2002). There are no significant biological boundaries between people, no real genetic barriers, no distinct walls separating us. Human beings do not come in distinct and separate groupings, but instead appear in a broad continuum reflected by a diversity of traits. Yes, there are very light-skinned folks and very dark-skinned folks, but there also are people with every conceivable skin shade in between. The same broad spectrum of expression applies to other human characteristics, like hair color and texture, bodily sizes and proportions, and facial features. As a result, most biological scientists do not consider the common concept of human races particularly useful in describing human variation.

Of course, it cannot be ignored that people do vary in their outward physical appearance and this variation is, to an extent, geographically linked. There are, indeed, patterns of location related to the particular expression of external human physical characteristics—darker skin tones are concentrated toward the equator, people with squat bodies and relatively short arms and legs are concentrated in cold regions—and some of this may be the result of natural selection, with some physical characteristics conferring an advantage under certain environmental conditions. Beyond this, once we delve beneath the features of skin tone, hair texture and color, nose shape, and lip size there are variations in the human skeleton that also statistically distinguish people from different parts of the world. Accurately determining the ethnic identity of a person from his or her skeleton, however, is a far more difficult task than determining age or sex. Forget what you may have heard about people of African ancestry having extra bones in their feet that provide them with an athletic advantage or other such nonsense. In truth, there are very few clear indicators of ethnicity in the human skeleton, though there are tendencies that may be used at least in attempting to approximate the ethnic/geographic origins of an individual.

For example, viewed from the front, the top of the crania of native people of Africa and Europe tend to be rounded, while those from Asia tend to come to a ridge or keel on top. Viewed in profile, the faces of European and Asian natives are quite flat, while those of Africans tend to be thrust forward (**prognathous**), especially at the jaw. The chin profile of Africans tends to be rounded while that of Europeans is pointy, and Asians are in between. Remember, these all are tendencies and not absolutely distinguishing features and, as a result, their utility and accuracy in identifying the ethnic or geographic origins of an individual are not especially high.

A few skeletal features can be used to distinguish ethnicity a bit more clearly, though still only in a statistical sense. For example, the inside surfaces of the central incisors of Europeans and Africans tend to be shaped like flat blades, while those of Asians tend to be shaped more like shovels, scooped in the middle and with ridges on their lateral margins (Figure 13.7). Understand, not all Asians possess so-called **shovel-shaped incisors** and the proportion of this tooth form varies within Asian populations. Generally, however, more than 50% of Asians within a given region exhibit some degree of shoveling and in some populations it is found in more than 90% of individuals. Shovel-shaped incisors are not entirely absent among Africans or Europeans—in fact, for reasons that are in no way clear, shovel-shaped incisors are not all that rare in Sweden—but shoveling tends to be far less common among them. In fact, the very high level of incisor shoveling among Native Americans is interpreted as strong evidence of their Asian origins because that tooth feature is most common in Asia (Scott and Turner 2000).

Certainly, we should not simply throw up our hands and deny that determining the ethnic/geographic identity of an individual from his or her skeleton can be accomplished. On the other hand,

**FIGURE 13.7** Shovel-shaped incisors, like those in this jaw, are quite common among Native Americans and Asians and are rare in native Europeans, Africans, and Australians. (*Courtesy of John Seidel*)

we need to recognize that the degree of variation seen in human bones can make this a very difficult endeavor.

Scientists now have the ability under certain circumstances to extract DNA from bones, in particular, **mitochondrial DNA** (DNA located outside of the nucleus of cells, in the cellular mitochondria). Modern human groups originating in various parts of the world are characterized by their own unique clusters of particular mitochondrial DNA codes. These clusters are called **haplogroups** or **haplotypes.** In some cases, these same haplogroups have been identified in the mitochondrial DNA recovered from ancient bones found by archaeologists. In these cases, the ethnicity of the ancient person can be determined with a level of accuracy not possible by an analysis of gross morphological characteristics. For example, the five haplogroups designated A, B, C, D, and X are quite rare or entirely absent among Europeans, Africans, and native Australians, but are widely seen among living Native Americans and Asians, lending further support for a genetic connection between the native people of Asia and the New World. These same haplogroups have been identified in the skeletal remains of Native Americans (Derenko et al. 2001), further supporting the idea that living Native Americans are the genetic descendants of Asians who entered the New World in antiquity. Where gross skeletal morphology cannot provide an accurate assessment of the ethnic identity or geographic source of an individual or community, genetic analysis can help answer the question far more precisely.

## Read More

There are many fine guides to the subjects of forensic anthropology, in general, and human osteology, in particular, that discuss how an archaeologist can identify the ethnic or geographic origin of an individual based on his or her bones. The following list includes an old standard (Krogman 1973) and a host of newer, terrific textbooks, manuals, atlases, and guidebooks:

Bass, W. 1987. *Human Osteology: A Laboratory and Field Manual of the Human Skeleton.* Missouri Archaeological Society, Columbia.

Brothwell, D. R. 1972. *Digging Up Bones: The Excavation, Treatment, and Study of Human Skeletal Remains.* British Museum, London.

Burns, K. R. 1999. *The Forensic Anthropology Training Manual.* Prentice Hall, Upper Saddle River, New Jersey.

Byers, S. N. 2001. *Introduction to Forensic Anthropology: A Textbook.* Allyn and Bacon, Boston.

Derenko, M. V., T. Grzybowski, B. A. Malyarchuk, J. Czarny, D. Miscicka-Sliwka, and I. A. Zakharov. 2001. The presence of mitochondiral haplogroup X in Altatians from south Siberia. *American Journal of Human Genetics* 69:237–41.

Hillson, S. 1996. *Dental Anthropology.* Cambridge University Press, Cambridge, England.

Krogman, W. M. 1973. *The Human Skeleton in Forensic Medicine.* Charles C. Thomas, Springfield, Illinois.

Park, M. A. 2002. *Biological Anthropology.* McGraw-Hill, New York.

Rhine, S. 1998. *Bone Voyage.* University of New Mexico Press, Santa Fe.

Scott, G. R. and C. G. Turner II. 2000. *The Anthropology of Modern Human Teeth: Dental Morphology and Its Variation in Recent Human Populations.* Cambridge University Press, Cambridge, England.

Ubelaker, D. H. 1978. *Human Skeletal Remains: Excavation, Analysis, Interpretation.* Aldine Manuals on Archaeology. Aldine, Chicago.

White, T. D., and P. A. Folkens. 1991. *Human Osteology.* Academic Press, New York.

## Study Questions

1. What is archaeological demography?

2. What are the descriptive statistics an archaeological demographer might be able to determine?

3. How does a demographic profile of a past society provide insights about the kinds of lives lived by its people?

4. What primary factors are at the core of the controversy between Native Americans and American archaeologists regarding the excavation, analysis, curation, and display of the skeletal remains of the ancestors of those Native Americans?

5. There's a bit of a false dichotomy presented in number 4; there are some individuals who are both Native Americans and American archaeologists. Summarize the opinions of the Native American archaeologists mentioned in this book about the issue of human remains.

6. What protections do the Native American Graves Protection and Repatriation Act afford to the graves and remains of Native Americans?

7. Can Native Americans and archaeologists reach a common ground on the issue of human remains?

8. Which features or characteristics of the human skeleton allow us to identity, with a fair degree of certainty, the sex of the individual whose bones are being examined?

9. What is sexual dimorphism?

10. Why are the bones of the human pelvis the best to examine when identifying the sex of the person represented by the bones?

11. Which features or characteristics of the human skeleton allow us to identity, with a fair degree of certainty, the age of the individual whose bones are being examined?

12. What features of the human skeleton allow us to approximate the age of individuals through their teens and early twenties?

13. What features of the human skeleton allow us to approximate the age of individuals after they have passed their mid-twenties?

14. Which features or characteristics of the human skeleton allow us to assess the overall health of individuals whose bones are being examined? (Well, of course, they are dead, so their health isn't too good, but I mean the history of their health while they were alive.)

15. How does physical trauma manifest itself on human bones?

16. How do nutritional deficiencies manifest themselves on human bones?

17. How does disease manifest itself on human bones?

18. How did paleopathology contribute to a solution to the mystery of the violated grave found at the Walton family cemetery in Griswold, Connecticut?

19. How did an analysis of the burials at Altar de Sacrificios contribute to our understanding of Maya society?

20. How does ethnicity manifest itself on human bones?

# Wood Lily: Portrait of a Life
## Food for Thought

### The Environment of Wood Lily

The world in which the residents of Wood Lily lived, at least the physical environment in which they found themselves, would be readily recognized by any of us alive today in the eastern woodlands of North America. **Pollen analysis** and identification of wood in the fireplaces built by the inhabitants of the village that became the Wood Lily archaeological site show us that the trees growing there some three thousand years ago reflect generally the same mix of species that currently characterizes the forests of southern New England, including especially oak, maple, hickory, pine, and birch (Figure 14.1). That's a good indication that the overall climate at Wood Lily three thousand years ago—long, cold, snowy winters; rainy springs; long, humid, hot summers; and breathtaking, chilly autumns—was much the same as it is now in southern New England.

Although economically important species like chestnut and elm are largely gone due to relatively recent historical fungal infestations (chestnut blight, which began its devastation in the early 1900s, and Dutch elm disease, first identified in the United States in 1930), many of the other tree species of the modern eastern woodlands are the same as those a resident of Wood Lily would have regularly encountered and have had available for use in building a home, crafting a spear, carving a bowl, making a bark container, producing a canoe, or fueling a fire. Even though wooden tools were not found at Wood Lily and no structural remains endured for our recovery, carbonized fragments of wood, burned in the villagers' fire hearths, were recovered and analyzed. Not surprisingly, we were able to determine that their fuel comprised mainly oak and hickory.

**FIGURE 14.1** Typical eastern woodland landscape. A rich and diverse mixture of trees, plants, and animals made the eastern woodlands an attractive place to settle, for both Native Americans and European colonists. (*Kenneth L. Feder*)

### The Wood Lily Larder: Food for Thought

Fruit- and nut-bearing trees common in our contemporary woodlands, like hickory, chestnut, and oak (acorns), would have provided food for the inhabitants of Wood Lily and, at the same time, would have attracted animals that would have been of great use to the people who lived there. The charred remains of acorn and hickory nutshells recovered in cooking features at the Wood Lily site provide direct evidence for the preparation of nutmeats for use in the diet of the site's inhabitants.

The eastern woodlands of North America were—and, in many cases, continue to be—densely inhabited by a host of economically useful animals. A beautiful representation of this was produced by the artist Alan J. Rummler in the 1930s. His painting entitled *The Mammals of Connecticut* was a product of the Works Project Administration (WPA), a federally sponsored program to help put people, including artists, to work during the Great Depression. The mural, which is more than 10 feet wide and 6 feet tall, presents a pretty and pristine eastern woodland scene—though, in all likelihood you wouldn't get the depicted menagerie together in one place at the same time (Figure 14.2).

**FIGURE 14.2** This placid scene of Connecticut mammals was painted by the artist Alan J. Rummler as part of a WPA project to put people to work during the Great Depression. The mural was originally intended for Norwalk High School and the cutout to the right is not a printing error: the mural was intended to bracket a doorway and the missing part of the mural represents the location of a doorway in the school cafeteria.

Clearly visible in Rummler's conception of an unspoiled Connecticut forest habitat are a family of deer, two raccoons, a couple of skunks, a woodchuck, a red fox, eastern cottontail rabbits, grey squirrels, red squirrels, an opossum, and a mother black bear and her cub. Many of the same species of animals depicted by Rummler in his 1930s forest tableau thrived in the wooded world inhabited by the residents of Wood Lily three thousand years before the artist put brush to canvas. In fact, if you could travel through time and bring the residents of the village that became the Wood Lily archaeological site back to our present, they would instantly recognize all of the animals in the painting except the opossum, a relatively recent migrant into New England from the southern states. Other fur-bearing animals common to the modern eastern woodlands (not depicted by Rummler but historically well known in our region and whose remains have been recovered at other archaeological sites in the east) are the beaver, northern river otter, porcupine, weasel, fisher, bobcat, and coyote. Also likely inhabiting the world of Wood Lily's residents were the eastern timber wolf and cougar, both of which are extinct in southern New England today, but are historically well known in

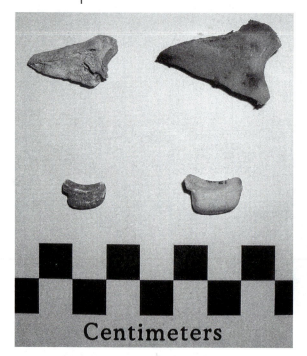

**FIGURE 14.3** Two small bones from the bottom of a deer's leg were recovered at a two-thousand-year-old site. On the right are modern examples of the same bones, taken from the "bone library" in our archaeology lab. (*Kenneth L. Feder*)

the region (before their habitat was dramatically altered and before they were intentionally eliminated because of the danger they presented, primarily to livestock).

Bone fragments recovered at the Wood Lily site show directly that deer contributed significantly to the diet of the site's inhabitants (Figure 14.3). It is likely as well that deer hide, bones, and antler were important raw materials used by the site's residents: the hide for clothing, blankets, and assorted coverings; pieces of the bones might have been shaped into awls, needles, fasteners, and other tools; and the antlers likely were used for **pressure flaking** implements.

There is no direct evidence in the form of faunal remains for the use of small mammals at the Wood Lily site. This likely is due to the high acidity of the soils in New England, a high level of biological activity (lots of bugs, worms, and microbes eating and recycling everything organic they can find), and intensive physical weathering due in part to significant and often rapid temperature changes in the soil and resulting episodes of alternate freezing and thawing. Smaller bones, especially ones not carbonized in a fire during cooking, usually don't stand a chance of preserving in our soils. Nevertheless, it is likely that some of the smaller fur-bearing animals seen in Rummler's painting, along with the other mammals I listed, would have been exploited by the residents of Wood Lily for their meat or for the warmth their fur could provide.

Along with this mammalian bestiary, southern New England is home to more than forty-five reptile and amphibian species, some of which, especially turtles and frogs, are edible and are known to have been used for food by native people in the seventeenth century. Another of Rummler's

**FIGURE 14.4** Artist Alan J. Rummler's companion painting to the *Mammals of Connecticut,* depicting an assortment of the birds of the state and produced for the Norwalk, Connecticut, high school cafeteria during the Great Depression. The blank corner indicates the location of a doorway in the school cafeteria.

paintings, also intended for the Norwalk High School cafeteria, depicts the birds of Connecticut (Figure 14.4). Among the many different species he showed are those whose feathers were used by the native people whose life-ways were described by sixteenth-, seventeenth-, and eighteenth-century European explorers and colonists of Connecticut. Feathers were used to fletch arrow shafts and meat was used as food. Turkeys and ducks especially were used by native people, and may have been on the menu at Wood Lily.

In the background of Rummler's mammal painting lies a body of water, a generic lake representative of those scattered throughout the woodlands of southern New England, specifically, and the eastern woodlands of North America in general. There is no lake in proximity to Wood Lily, but the community was adjacent to a viable, permanent source of flowing, fresh water in the form of a brook, unnamed on modern maps. The brook flows into a larger stream, Beaver Brook, which would likely have provided an abundance of freshwater fish for the site's inhabitants (Whitworth, Berrien, and Keller 1976). **Anadromous** species like the Atlantic salmon, shortnose sturgeon,

**FIGURE 14.5** Historical illustration of native fishing along the coast of Virginia by Theodore de Bry in 1590. Fresh and saltwater fish have made significant contributions to the diets of many past and present peoples.

and American shad live a part of their lives in the salty waters of Long Island Sound and the Atlantic Ocean, but then migrate en masse into freshwater rivers and ultimately into stream nurseries where they produce and deposit eggs before they die. Enormous "fish runs" reported by seventeenth- and eighteenth-century colonists represent eyewitness accounts of these seasonal migrations and would have provided an opportunity for the people living at sites like Wood Lily to collect a tremendous amount of food in the form of fish in a very short period of time, food that they could have preserved by drying (Figure 14.5).

Along with anadromous fish, the brooks, streams, and rivers of the eastern woodlands teem with native fish that spend their entire lives locally in these watercourses. The local fish in Connecticut include a number of varieties of trout, pickerel, shad, perch, sunfish, and a nonanadromous landlocked salmon. Though no fish bones, teeth, or scales were found at Wood Lily, the semi-lunar knives that dominated their stone tool kit would have been efficient implements for slicing open the fish to separate the meat from the bones while preparing the edible part of the fish for drying.

So, Wood Lily was located in an almost stereotypical eastern woodland setting. Imagine a frothy stream skittering among the rocks as it meanders through a dense woodland. A low haze of mosquitoes clouds the air above the wet patches left in the brook's wake. At the bubbling stream edge a lone deer stops for a drink, scattering the brook trout swimming in the water. The doe's eyes and ears are alert to any possible hint of danger, her white flag of a tail twitching at the anticipation of flight. Always busy, hyperkinetic gray squirrels sprint across tree branches overhead. The humid air is pierced by the call of a jay and the honk of geese as they overfly the terrace where the inhabitants of a place live their lives in the pleasant beauty of a woodland summer morning. In all likelihood, these people could never have imagined that three thousand years after their part was played on life's stage, strangers would contemplate their woodland, their stream, and their lives.

## Study Questions

1. What was the environment like when the Wood Lily site was occupied?
2. What plant and animal resources were available for the inhabitants of the Wood Lily site?

# Wood Lily: Portrait of a Life
# Tools of the Trade

### Making Tools at Wood Lily

For a people reliant on stone for a significant part of their tool kit, keeping a ready supply of projectile tips, cutting, sawing, scraping, piercing, and pounding tools on hand—and maintaining the sharpness of their edges—must have been an ongoing process. This explains, in large measure, the nature of much of the archaeological record at Wood Lily and other prehistoric sites in New England before the development of ceramic technology. In a chipped stone tool technology, tools and their edges are not simply ground into shape, they are flaked. This flaking produces a tremendous amount of **debitage,** which can end up discarded on the ground where it fell in a workshop area or anywhere in a site where tools were made or maintained. It is not surprising, therefore, to find waste flakes at any archaeological site where a people who made chipped stone tools lived or carried out a task; in fact, these flakes often are the dominant element in an archaeological assemblage. Wood Lily is a perfect example of this. More than 5,400 waste flakes were recovered in nineteen, 2-meter by 2-meter excavation units at the site. Compare this to the total number of complete or broken chipped stone tools recovered in those same nineteen excavation units: fifty-three, including projectile points, drills, scrapers, knives, and other bifacially flaked tools.

The ratio of waste flakes to tools is often interpreted as an indication of the amount of tool making that was carried out at a site. It should be intuitively obvious that at a site with a small number of waste flakes relative to the number of finished tools not much tool making was done. In the case of Wood Lily, the ratio of waste flakes to tools was substantial at 102.7:1. In other words, statistically, for every finished tool we found at Wood Lily, we recovered a little less than 103 waste flakes. This high ratio of waste flakes to finished tools is a clear indicator that stone tool making was an important activity at the site.

We recovered only a single **hammerstone** at the site, which might seem surprising given the argument just presented that stone tool making was an ongoing process at Wood Lily (Figure 15.1). In fact, I wasn't all that surprised by this, based on my own experience as a knapper. A good hammerstone with just the right heft and shape is not something that tool makers would have

**FIGURE 15.1** One of the few intact hammerstones left behind by the tool makers at Wood Lily. (*Kenneth L. Feder*)

left behind at the site. I maintained the same hammerstone for use in my stone tool replication demonstrations for several years. In truth, I got pretty attached to that rock. An almost perfect sphere of quartzite, I will admit that it got pretty battered after a while, but it worked extremely well in peeling flakes from flint or obsidian cores until its sadly lamented recent demise, when I foolishly attempted to use it to flake a very hard nodule of local basalt, a tough, volcanic rock. Before I killed it, I took that hammerstone with me to all my demonstrations and always brought it back to the lab, so it does not surprise me that the resident knappers at Wood Lily seem to have taken nearly all of their hammerstones with them when they left the site for the last time.

The fifty-three chipped stone tools recovered at Wood Lily were all made on large flakes removed from cores, primarily flint and quartz. Stone tool makers become adept at extracting as many large flakes from a core as they possibly can, but eventually all stone cores get used up and become too small, too battered, or too irregularly shaped to successfully and efficiently remove more flakes. At that point, the core may be discarded. And,

**FIGURE 15.2** After a number of large flakes have been removed to serve as blanks for specific tools, a core like this one from Wood Lily may simply be abandoned. (*Kenneth L. Feder*)

in fact, we found the remnants of seven such **exhausted cores** at Wood Lily (Figure 15.2).

Another category of stone artifacts is called **preform.** Preforms reflect a step in the manufacture of stone tools. A knapper can efficiently remove a large number of flakes from a core as a preliminary step in stone tool making. Next, the knapper may do a preliminary thinning and shaping of the flakes, producing a cache of partially made blanks that can at a moment's notice be retrieved from storage and rather quickly made into whatever tools are needed at that time: a spear point, knife, drill, scraper, and so on. It is a rather more efficient production strategy than one that requires beginning from scratch each time there is a need for a particular kind of tool. We found three preforms at Wood Lily, flakes that had clearly sustained additional work after their removal from cores, chipped on both faces, but only very generally fashioned.

The fifty-three finished tools recovered in our excavation of Wood Lily reflect the diversity of activities conducted at the site. Altogether, we recovered the following finished tools (both intact and fragments): twenty-five projectile points, five drills, seventeen knives, three scrapers, and three piercing tools. With such a tool kit, the residents of the site could have hunted and killed animals, butchered them, removed the hides, prepared the hides for the manufacture of leather cloth, and prepared clothing from those hides.

Along with the chipped stone tools recovered at Wood Lily, we also excavated a single **ground stone** artifact, a tool whose working end was produced not by chipping off flakes, but by grinding the edge down into a useable shape (Figure 15.3). The tool in question has a sharpened, curved edge and appears to be a gouge, a tool likely used to shape wood. I'm calling it a gouge because that's exactly what it looks like and also because

**FIGURE 15.3** A gouge recovered at the Wool Lily site (top). The slightly concave surface on the left is the working edge of the tool. The edge damage that accumulated on the working edge of this tool is visible in the bottom image. (*Kenneth L. Feder*)

of the wear patterns apparent on its working surface. Even with the naked eye, and certainly with a little magnification, a series of scratch marks can be seen on both faces, beginning at the working edge and then running back, perpendicular to that working edge of the tool, just as you might expect in a tool used to gouge into or hollow out a block of wood to make, for example, a bowl or a canoe.

The categories of chipped tools—projectile points, drills, knives, scrapers, and piercing tools—are defined, at least initially, on the basis of morphology (what they look like). Stone spear or arrow points look like their modern, metal counterparts. Stone drill bits also look essentially like

**FIGURE 15.4** Magnified image of the tip of an intact drill recovered at Wood Lily. (*Kenneth L. Feder*)

modern, metal ones. But in each case, and for each specific artifact so categorized, we have also carefully examined its edge with a stereoscopic microscope, using between ten- and eighty-power magnification. Tool use leaves diagnostic damage on the working surfaces of the tools and we looked for these traces on each of our finished tools and fragments. We also looked at a 25% sample of the apparent waste flakes to determine if any of these had been used as ad hoc tools simply because they presented the stone tool worker with fortuitously shaped or sharp edges.

It turned out that many of the flint finished tools (quartz is notoriously difficult for detecting wear pattern) whose function we hypothesized on the basis of form exhibited wear patterns that were in keeping with those functions. What we labeled as drills or drill bits showed the kind of polish we expect in a tool used to bore a hole in a hard material (Figure 15.4).

The tools we labeled as knives exhibited striations on both faces, parallel to the working edge, again conforming to their use as knives (Figure 15.5). Scrapers exhibited striations and other damage evidence on their working edges, but this time perpendicular to those edges, matching our expectations.

**FIGURE 15.5** Magnified image of the edge of a cutting tool. Faint striations can be seen here, parallel to the working edge of the tool, along with evidence of edge damage from rough use. (*Kenneth L. Feder*)

The piercing tools, perhaps used to make holes in leather to allow for a threaded bone or antler needle to pass through in sewing, exhibited a bit of polish exactly as might be expected from constant pressure while twisting through a tough animal hide. Only 5 of the more than 1560 flakes (0.3%) we examined showed evidence of use, a good indicator that the vast majority of artifacts we initially labeled as waste flakes indeed where just that, not tools used by the village residents, but merely the by-products of the tool making process.

The spear points showed little actual wear: the job of these tools tends to be quick and nonrepetitive, so there is little opportunity for damage traces to accumulate on a working edge. Many of these points, however, were found snapped just above the spot where they would have been hafted onto a wooden spear shaft, perhaps indicating that they had broken when thrown at an animal and missed the prey and struck the ground or a tree or when they slammed into the bone inside of the animal.

The overall use of lithic raw materials at Wood Lily showed a nearly equal reliance on stone available locally and stone that needed to be traded or involved travel to obtain. About 52.3% of all of the debitage and tools found at the site was of local quartz and 46.3% was of flint available in the Hudson Valley of New York State. The rest of the lithic assemblage was made up of fractional percentages of local hornfels (0.6%) and basalt (0.4%), as well as a number of not clearly identifiable other materials (0.4%).

## Wood Lily Lives

These statistics and descriptions of what was found at the Wood Lily archaeological site do not represent the destination of the archaeological traveler, but a passport that provides us access to an ancient place and time. A community of people, not spear points, gouges, hammerstones, nut fragments, and deer bones, once lived on the banks of a small brook in a thick woodland in eastern North America. The physical evidence that constitutes the archaeological record at what we have called the Wood Lily site exposes us to shadowy glimpses of a community in which people lived more than three thousand years ago. People lived at this place: they made tools from the raw materials they had at their disposal in order to wrest a living from their environment; they hunted and gathered food for subsistence using those tools; they traded for raw materials or traveled great distances for them; they thrived in a time and a place by developing a way of life, a culture, different from our own but nevertheless familiar and recognizable. The people at Wood Lily represent one small example of the genius of our species at inhabiting an environment, exploiting what that environment has to offer, and developing a way of life in which a people could flourish. Their ancient story is merely a variation of our modern story. It is a story that we can recover by the process described in this book, a story revealed by the science of archaeology.

## Study Questions

1. Describe the stone tool assemblage at Wood Lily.
2. Based on the analysis of its stone tool assemblage, what activities can we conclude were conducted at the Wood Lily village?

# Can We Reconstruct the Past?

Walk through any major natural history or science museum and you are apt to see life-sized dioramas depicting scenes of our contemporary natural world alongside conceptualizations of ordinary moments in human antiquity. I can remember, as a kid, being mesmerized by the animals displayed in these three-dimensional snapshots of nature at the American Museum of Natural History in New York City. The dioramas there were and are amazing, with scores of animals in lifelike poses, brightly illuminated in spectacularly naturalistic settings. Each scene depicted in the dioramas presents animals seemingly playing out a little drama of life and death in nature. These dioramas were to me like magical windows into a host of other worlds and other times. It is truly remarkable still; in the dark, cool, and cavernous great hall of a sprawling building in the heart of a gray, modern metropolis are brightly shimmering portals through which we can see the parched plains of southern Africa, the piercing intersection of snow and sky in the Arctic, and the color-speckled beauty of the autumn woodlands of eastern North America.

Well-done dioramas like the ones at the American Museum of Natural History are splendidly realistic, achingly beautiful, luminous tableaux appearing as actual natural moments frozen in time and space. It would seem that little more was needed than the snap of some omnipotent genie's fingers to instantaneously set in motion the two adult bull moose, forever frozen in their struggle for dominance in a thickly wooded world; for the lion pride to burst from the tall grass and rain death upon the zebras and gazelles nervously browsing alongside the waterhole; for the Gemsbok, locked in their eternal stare, to suddenly come alive and calmly walk out into the grand gallery; or for the two people, looking familiar yet foreign, set against the backdrop of an alien landscape sculpted by a volcano visible in the distance, to resume their arm-in-arm walk, leaving behind two sets of footprints demarcating their immortal stroll (Figure E.1).

Certainly, the animal displays produced today at respected museums are highly accurate, realistic depictions of events, behaviors, and processes that truly occur in the natural world. But what about dioramas that focus on the human past, that depict human ancestors making tools, hunting, burying their dead, creating art, or worshipping their gods? Certainly they are intriguing, dramatic, and even moving, but do these dioramas provide clear glimpses of our

**FIGURE E.1** A volcano erupts in the background of this African landscape as two ancient human ancestors stride over a blanket of ash in this diorama at the American Museum of Natural History in New York City. The artist responsible for this scene has presented a 3.6 million-year-old drama that resulted in the preserved footprints—seen here in the diorama as they were being made—discovered by paleoanthropologists Mary Leakey and Tim White in 1974-1975. (*Photo by D. Finnin/ C. Chesek*)

human world as it once existed, or are they really only clouded and darkened portals into a world that never was? We might ask the same of archaeologists, concerning their ability to accurately craft images of the lives of people in the distant—and not so distant—past.

The dioramas at the American Museum of Natural History that depict our human ancestors present moments from our species' past, both ordinary and extraordinary. In a sense, archaeologists attempt to accomplish something quite similar to the diorama makers, presenting word pictures of all the past places and past times that we study. Like the creators of these dioramas, with their paints, papier-mâché trees, silk leaves, and, of course, stuffed and mounted animals, we hope to be able to produce, in the words we craft, the articles and books we publish, the lectures we present, and the Web sites we design, visions of moments in time. It is our hope, to be sure, that our creations are not just reflections of how we might presume or hope past people lived, not just-so stories that we find comfortable or useful or that affirm our own beliefs or preconceptions, but accurate narratives that expose the lives actually lived by our ancestors, faithful representations of their cultures and their worlds.

Producing dioramas and illuminating the human past alike are difficult and challenging undertakings. The purpose of this book certainly has not been to describe in every detail precisely how archaeologists go about the tasks of discovering places where evidence of the human past exists, recovering that evidence, and then analyzing and interpreting it. Instead, this work has been designed to give you an outline of these processes, a brief taste of how archaeologists attempt to recapture the complexity of human existence, often dating to periods of time that were far different from our own.

As noted earlier in this work, the title of a book by Kathy Schick and Nicholas Toth (1993) about archaeology (*Making Silent Stones Speak*) aptly presents the challenge all archaeologists face in the attempt to describe and learn from the past; the stones (and pots, and bones, and temples, and monuments) we excavate, uncover, and reveal do not speak for themselves. We have to make them speak. This book has been about the techniques archaeologists employ to make the things that have endured in the archaeological record speak to us about the lives of past human beings.

I especially like the phrasing used by well-known paleoanthropologist Pat Shipman in an interview for a documentary about human evolution. In describing some of her highly specialized research looking at the tiny marks left behind on ancient bones by the stone tools wielded by our human ancestors, Shipman talked about having to "coax" information out of the objects in order to reveal the secrets they might possess and share about the ancient people who left those cut marks on the bones. In the end, much of archaeology is focused on doing just that; coaxing from the silent stones and bones, pots, seeds, pits, burials, temples, and monuments the secrets they may reveal about the lives lived by the people who preceded us on life's stage. If we do it well and if we are lucky, the images we resurrect of past people can intrigue, inform, inspire, and even excite us about human antiquity, enabling us, like the diorama makers, to construct, if only in our minds, shimmering windows through which the human past is made visible again.

## Study Questions

1. How is a museum diorama a metaphor for the archaeological reconstruction of an ancient way of life?
2. What is the point, after all, of archaeological research?

# Glossary

**absolute dating:** Dating techniques that provide an actual age in years or a range of years for archaeological artifacts, ecofacts, features, or sites. The precision offered by different absolute dating methods when applied to archaeological sites can range widely. In dendrochronology, for example, the precise year in which a tree was cut down can be determined and, in another example, the maker's mark on a ceramic vessel can be traced to the precise year in which the maker produced a particular style of pottery. At the other extreme, some absolute dating techniques in their archaeological application may provide only a very broad possible range of thousands, tens of thousands, hundreds of thousands, and even millions of years. For example, the potassium/argon dating method may date a volcanic layer overlying archaeological material to 1 million years ago and another layer underlying the site may date to 1.5 million years ago. In this case, we may conclude that the site is between 1 and 1.5 million years old (dating to sometime after the older volcanic flow and before the later deposit. Though the precision is not very high here (the range is a half-million years) this is still an absolute date. Chronometric is another term for absolute dates.

**accession:** A unique designator assigned to each artifact in an archaeological assemblage. An inventory number. With a unique accession number (or some other designator) assigned to each item found at a site, detailed information about each item (its precise location of discovery, depth and date of discovery, and so on) can be recorded on a paper inventory or computer database under its accession designator, allowing the information to be correctly associated with each item.

**activity area:** A general term for a spatially bounded area within a place inhabited or used by people where a particular task or tasks were carried out. Stuff may accumulate where activities were carried out as people lose or simply dispose of material they no longer need or that is of no further use. The discarded objects become artifacts and ecofacts; together they constitute an archaeological feature.

**adaptations:** An adaptation is a "strategy," in the broad sense of that term, for survival. The adaptations of nonhuman animals are primarily biological, the physical characteristics they possess that make survival possible. The primary adaptations of the human animal are literally strategies for survival—behaviors invented and refined by human groups to enable their survival.

**aeolian:** Find particles of clay, silt, and sand deposited by the wind. In some parts of the world, archaeological sites commonly are covered entirely and preserved by aeolian deposits. In some cases, once a community is covered with sand producing a hill, a subsequent group may settle the top of the hill and the remnants of their community may be covered in aeolian deposits as well when is it abandoned. This process can be repeated several times at the same place, producing an enormous hill called a tell, enclosing a sequence of the remains of several communities superimposed one on top of the other.

**alidade:** A surveying instrument that consists of a sighting scope mounted on a flat base. Resting on a leveled plane table, the alidade can be used to sight on a stadia rod to determine the precise depth of the surface on which the rod is resting.

**alluvium:** Material deposited by a flooding river; the soil that blankets the floodplain of a river valley. Technically, alluvium consists of unconsolidated material; sand, gravel, and fine particles of rock. As a result of its fine fabric and rich organic content, alluvium produces soil that is attractive to farmers, both ancient and modern. The regular deposition of alluvium, sometimes in a yearly cycle, can produce a substantial stratigraphic record with deeply buried archaeological material.

**American Antiquities Act of 1906 (http://www.cr.nps.gov/local-law/anti1906.htm):** The law that really set the stage for federal preservation and protection of archaeological sites. This law was short and simple: it explicitly made illegal the destruction or defacement of archaeological sites on federal property and established a fine of up to $500 and a penalty of up to ninety days in jail for its violation. Further, it made digging sites on federal land illegal without a permit; such permits were limited to qualified individuals and issued only when the excavation benefited a recognized university or museum. The law further stipulated that archaeological excavation on public lands was for the public benefit and material excavated needed to be made available to the public in, for example, a public museum.

**anadromous:** Fish, like salmon and shad, that live part of their lives in the sea but return each year to the freshwater stream where they hatched for females to lay their eggs and males to fertilize them and then for them both to die. Their offspring hatch and mature in the freshwater, where they live for between one and three years and then migrate into the ocean. Large spring fish runs mark the point in the fall when the fish swim upstream to reproduce, providing an ample food source for humans poised to exploit it.

**angle of applied force:** In percussion flaking, the angle between the striking platform and the trajectory of the hammerstone as you bring it down on the core or flake. In pressure flaking, the angle between the surface of the flake and the direction of the applied pressure. The angle of applied force should be less than 90 degrees in most circumstances. An angle approaching 90 degrees will tend to produce long flakes, extending down the length of the core; an acute angle of applied force ordinarily will result in shorter, but very thin, sharpedged flakes.

**anthropologist:** Scientists who focus on the broad analysis of human behavior within the discipline of anthropology.

**anthropology:** The holistic study of humanity. Where other social and behaviural sciences tend to specialize and focus on individual elements of human behavior like, for example, economics, political patterns, or social systems, anthropology looks broadly at how human beings behave and how that behavior has evolved. The examination of human physical evolution, cultural evolution, adaptation, and language.

**archaeological context:** Archaeologists can't travel back in time to observe directly the use and meaning of the elements of material culture found through excavation. When these objects are recovered, they are, by definition, in their archaeological contexts: artifacts or ecofacts in the ground, in particular soil levels, in association with other artifacts and ecofacts. Careful analysis of these objects allows for a determination of how these objects were used—their behavioral contexts—by past people.

**archaeological excavation:** The exacting process of revealing the remains left behind by a past people, preserving the physical integrity of the objects revealed, as well as their spatial contexts. By segmenting a site into manageable excavation units; by slowing peeling back the soil in each of those units in small increments by the use of hand tools; by leaving material, at least initially, precisely where found and, by inference, where a past people left the material through processes like discard, loss, and caching; by carefully measuring and mapping in three dimensions, the exact locations where objects were found; and by taking these discovered objects and samples back to the lab for analysis, the information contained within a site is preserved in the process of archaeological excavation.

**archaeological fieldwork:** That portion of archaeological research that is conducted in the field. Examining soil surfaces through walkover or pedestrian survey as well as probing the subsurface through test excavation in the search for sites (survey) and, once found, the intensive investigation of individual sites by excavation.

**Archaeological Resources Protection Act of 1979 (ARPA, http://www2.cr. nps.gov/laws/archprotect.htm):** This federal law expanded and clarified the American Antiquities Act of 1906, protecting archaeological materials located on federal land. Specifically, ARPA prohibits "unauthorized excavation, removal, damage, alteration, or defacement of archaeological resources." ARPA provides stiff penalties for its violation, a fine of up to $10,000 and one year in jail for a first offense and even more severe punishment for subsequent convictions. By passing this law and imposing substantial penalties on those convicted of violating it, the federal government was making an important statement: it takes seriously its responsibility to protect and preserve archaeological resources on federal land; these resources belong to all American citizens as a group, not to any individual, and those who violate the law will be punished.

**archaeological site formation:** Archaeological sites come into existence as the result of human behavior. Sites form by a series of site formation processes that include loss, discard, abandonment, and caching (storing for future use or as a ceremonial deposit).

**archaeology:** The study of the material remains of human behavior. Archaeology is the subdiscipline of anthropology (the study of people) that focuses on the lives of past peoples through the analysis of the things that they made, used, and then lost or discarded and that have fortuitously preserved.

**artifacts:** Any portable object made by a human being. For an archaeological specimen to be an artifact, it must have been intentionally made, not merely the accidental result of human activity. Arrow points, pottery, bone needles, bricks, a mill wheel, and a plow blade are artifacts. Wood found in an ancient fireplace and the unintentionally modified bones of an animal hunted by a human being are not artifacts. Though they bear witness to human activity (burning, butchering marks) the wood and bones in this example were not made into anything. They are, instead, categorized as ecofacts.

**assemblage:** The entirety or individual subsets of the material culture recovered at an archaeological site or sites. All of the artifacts or individual categories of artifacts. One can speak of the artifact assemblage for a particular site and by that mean all of the artifacts. Or, for example, you can refer to the stone tool assemblage or ceramic assemblage, the array of stone tools or ceramic objects found at a site, in a region, or dating to a particular time period.

**backdirt:** The excavated and screened soil that piles up around an excavation unit or test pit. Ostensibly—and hopefully—backdirt is devoid of cultural material, having already been carefully examined by the archaeologist.

**behavioral contexts:** Term given to describe the behavioral meaning of objects in the culture that produced and used them. If an ancient people produced a hunting weapon, for example a spear point, its behavioral context, obviously enough, is that of a tool used in killing an animal in the hunt. Though archaeologists hope to discover the behavioral contexts of the objects found at archaeological sites, it isn't always obvious or immediately evident. Archaeologists first encounter an object's archaeological context.

**Beringia:** The area of northeastern Asia, northwestern North America, together with the Bering Sea that currently separates the two regions, that was a continuous landmass during periods of lowered sea level. The lowered sea level resulted from expanded ice fields in higher elevations and latitudes during the Pleistocene, commonly known as the Ice Age. Beringia was inhabited by cold-adapted plant and animal species and provided a route of migration between the Old and New Worlds. It is thought by most archaeologists that human beings in Asia expanded into Beringia from the west and south, eventually migrating into North America. Native Americans encountered by European explorers in the late tenth century A.D. (the Norse) and late fifteenth century (Columbus and those who followed) were the descendants of these Asian migrants.

**Bering Land Bridge:** The land, currently under the Bering Sea, that was exposed during periods of lowered sea level, and that served as a metaphorical bridge between the Old and New Worlds. At its greatest extent, this "bridge" was, from north to south, likely more than 1500 km (close to 1000 miles) wide, providing a broad and diverse route through its interior and along its southern coast for the movement of people into the New World.

**bifacially:** This refers to how a stone flake has been shaped and sharpened. A stone tool may have two edges or margins and two faces. The distance from margin to margin is the width of a flake and the distance between its faces is its thickness. When a flake is shaped and sharpened by percussion and/or pressure on both faces, it is bifacially flaked. When sharpening or shaping flakes have been struck or pressed from only one of the flake's faces, it is said to be unifacially flaked.

**biological anthropology:** A branch of anthropology, the study of human beings, that focuses on the biological aspects of our species. Among the topics investigated by biological anthropologists are the biological evolution of human beings, the biological variation exhibited by modern human beings, forensic anthropology, primatology (humans are primates and primatologists study the nonhuman primates, including monkeys and apes). Synonymous with physical anthropology.

**biological archaeologists:** Archaeologists who focus on the biological environment in which past people lived and to which they adapted. Biological archaeologists usually focus on the physical remains of animals and plants found at archaeological sites in an attempt to reveal the nature of a past environment and the ways in which the people used that environment.

**bipedal locomotion:** The pattern of walking about on two feet. Among the primates (monkeys, apes, and human beings, along with our evolutionary antecedents), only those in the human line exhibit a pattern of habitual or full-time bipedalism. We know this to be the case both by observing living creatures (of course) and by reconstructing the locomotor habits of deceased or extinct creatures by the examination of their skeletal morphology. The bones reveal how the muscles must have worked which, in turn, reveals how the creature got around.

**C-14 dating:** Carbon-14 dating. Carbon-14 is a radioactive isotope (an unstable variety) of the element carbon. Most carbon is carbon-12. The "12" reflects the atomic weight of the most common configuration of the nucleus of the carbon atom with six positively charged (protons) and six neutral particles (neutrons). Carbon-14 possesses two additional neutrons and is unstable, decaying at a known rate to the element nitrogen. Knowing its rate of decay (its half-life) and by measuring the amount of carbon-14 remaining in a substance, we can determined its age. When found at an archaeological site, the age of the site can be associated with the dated item or items.

**cache:** From the French verb *cacher*, to hide. A cache is, essentially, a stash of stuff placed away for safekeeping—a cluster of spear points, a hoard of coins—that is not retrieved (perhaps intentionally if the items were intended as a ceremonial offering, perhaps unintentionally when the person who deposited the cache died before retrieving the stored material).

**calibration curve:** One of the assumptions underpinning radiocarbon dating is that the ratio of stable carbon-12 to unstable carbon-14 has always been the same. It turns out that this is not the case and that a number of natural processes have served to alter that ratio by increasing or decreasing the rate at which carbon-14 was produced in the atmosphere. Things alive when there was an overproduction (from a contemporary perspective) of c-14 will now appear to be younger and things alive when there was an underproduction of c-14 will now appear to be older than they actually are. This problem has been addressed, at least in part, by determining the radiocarbon dates of individual tree rings. Once a tree ring is added in a living tree, no additional atmospheric carbon is added to it; in other words, if you were to carbon date the first ring in a living, five-hundred-year-old tree, you should get a result in the vicinity of five hundred years old. A comparison of tree-ring dates and radiocarbon dates has been carried out, resulting in a calibration curve, which, in turn, is used to correct carbon dates to tree-ring dates, which are absolutely accurate in terms of calendar dates.

**carbon dating:** Shorthand for radiocarbon dating.

**ceramic:** Objects made of fired clay. Pottery, which usually implies a vessel or plate for cooking, storage, or serving food, is a common end product of ceramic technology.

**chemical signature:** The chemical makeup of a particular raw material (flint, obsidian, copper ore, clay, and so on) at its geographic source (quarry, flow, deposit, mine) as well the chemical constituents of the raw materials of artifacts excavated at archaeological sites. The chemical signature often exhibits a complex array of elements in miniscule or "trace" amounts and may be unique to a particular geographic source. The chemical signatures of artifacts can be revealed and then compared to possible source areas, enabling archaeologists to trace, sometimes quite precisely, the place from which past people obtained the materials, revealing past patterns of resource extraction, movement, and trade.

**chronometric dating:** Dating techniques that provide an actual age in years or a range of years for archaeological artifacts, ecofacts, features, or sites. The precision offered by different chronometric dating methods when applied to archaeological sites can range widely. In dendrochronology, for example, the precise year in which a tree was cut down can be determined and, in another example, the maker's mark on a ceramic vessel can be traced to the precise year in which the maker produced a particular style of pottery. At the other extreme, some chronometric dating techniques in their archaeological application may provide only a broad possible range of thousands, tens of thousands, hundreds of thousands, and even millions of years. For example, the potassium/argon dating method may date a volcanic layer overlying archaeological material to 1 million years ago and another layer underlying the site may date to 1.5 million years ago. In this case, we may conclude that the site is between 1 and 1.5 million years old (dating to sometime after the older volcanic flow and before the later deposit. Though the precision is not very high (the range is a half-million years) this is still a chronometric date. *Absolute dating* is another name for chronometric.

**CIEP:** See crossover-immunoelectrophoresis.

**colluvium:** Imagine a very slow-acting avalanche and you have a picture of colluviation and the production of colluvium. The rock, gravel, sand, silt, and clay that move downhill, along a slope, covering material along the slope and, especially, at the bottom of the hill, is called colluvium.

**comparative collections:** Groupings of samples of animal bones, seeds, nuts, lithic raw materials, and so on that can aid in the identification of materials recovered at archaeological sites. A comparative collection is, essentially, a library of prototypes that serve as the models by which archaeological samples can be judged and identified. Comparative collections are particularly valuable when the archaeological specimens are highly fragmented.

**complex societies:** These are societies in which authority, coordination of activity, and control of behavior are organized at a level beyond that of the family. Complex societies may have ranks or classes, peopled by individuals with greater or lesser wealth, authority, or social standing than those in other ranks or classes.

**compliance archaeology:** Archaeological research conducted to fulfill legal mandates. Federal, state, and local governments in the United States have enacted a wide variety of laws aimed at preserving and protecting archaeological sites. The value of archaeological sites as cultural resources whose study can benefit all citizens has been formally recognized and, especially when these cultural resources are endangered by construction or development, such laws compel developers to have archaeological work conducted to locate endangered cultural resources and, in some cases, to mitigate or diminish the deleterious impacts of development projects on archaeological sites. The archaeological research, in such cases, is conducted to comply with these laws, and thus the term *compliance archaeology*.

**conchoidal:** A variety of fracture exhibited by some rock types. Literally meaning shell-like, with a smooth surface showing concavities and convexities. Rock types like obsidian, flint, jasper, and chalcedony that exhibit conchoidal fracture break predictably and controllably. By a process of trial and error and by a long period of experimentation and repetition, knappers learn how conchoidal fracture is expressed by a rock type and develop an ability to predict and control the fracture to produce stone tools of regular and consistent sizes and shapes.

**conjoin:** To join together. In archaeology, broken fragments of artifacts that can be joined together: the top and bottom halves of a broken spear point, two fragments of a ceramic vessel are examples.

**contexts:** Shorthand for spatial context. The in situ location of an artifact, ecofact, or feature and the materials with which it was found.

**continuous variable:** Any variable in which its expression is a measurement along a continuous scale. The length of projectile points, the cranial capacities of ancient human ancestors, the volume of Egyptian pyramids, and the distance from an archaeological site to the geological source of a raw material used by the inhabitants of the site are all continuous variables because they can be measured.

**coprolites:** Fossilized feces. Because the digestive systems of animals, including human beings, are not 100% efficient, some ingested food is excreted in feces. As a result, the coprolites contain food remains and, therefore, provide data for dietary reconstruction.

**core:** A nodule of stone from which a tool maker detaches flakes by the application of a force, usually percussion, with a hammerstone. In some approaches, the core is essentially sculpted into a tool; in others, the core is merely the source for flakes, the flakes serving as blanks from which tools are then made.

**cranial sutures:** The boundary lines between the cranial plates. When a human is born, his or her cranium consists of seven more or less separate bony plates enclosing the brain. These plates are strongly connected with cartilage and the squiggly lines seen where contiguous plates join are called cranial sutures. The cranial sutures ossify when the skull attains full growth, but the lines do not disappear right away. Bone growth fusing adjoining plates continues during adulthood, eventually obscuring the sutures altogether. The degree of suture closure and disappearance can be used to gauge an individual's age at death, but this is neither terribly accurate nor precise, allowing for an estimation of age sometimes accurate to within about a decade.

**cranium:** The bony enclosure of the brain. Technically, the cranium is that part of the skull that includes the head, face, and upper jaw, but not the mandible (lower jaw).

**crew chief:** The individual archaeological field-worker in charge of a group of diggers. Especially in a large survey project covering a substantial amount of territory, a field crew may have to break up into a number of groups, each of which may cover a separate area. A crew chief will direct the work of a group of test pit diggers or surface investigators, following the directions of the field director.

**crossover immunoelectrophoresis (CIEP):** Forensic analysis in which, in its archaeological application, blood residues are recovered from the edge of a stone or metal tool. These residues are then exposed to a series of different antisera derived from a number of known animal species. The antibodies present in each antiserum will react biologically to the antigen in the blood residue only when the antiserum and the blood come from the same animal species. A positive reaction, therefore, when the antiserum and blood are mixed indicates the presence of blood from the same species as that from which the antiserum was derived, allowing for an identification of the species of animal whose blood is on the tool.

**cryptocrystalline:** Literally meaning "hidden crystals," this refers to the fabric of a rock consisting of individual crystals cemented together where these crystals are too small to be visible, even with a petrological microscope. Where the individual crystals of a rock are relatively large, an applied force (percussion or pressure) tends to shatter the rock along the intersections of the crystals. An applied force to a rock with very small "hidden" crystals moves through the rock in a manner similar to how that force moves through glass— predictably, controllably, producing thin, sharp edges. Cryptocrystalline rock is usually preferred for making stone tools by percussion and/or pressure.

**cultural resources:** A term that reflects the philosophy of the historic preservation movement. Just as we can identify as natural resources elements of our natural environment that make life possible—air, water, plants, and animals—we can also identify elements of the artificial or human-made environment that make life interesting, providing things that we can study, ponder, and from which we can attain knowledge. Ancient archaeological sites, seventeenth-century mill remains, Civil War battlefields, nineteenth-century bridges, and the remnants of early twentieth-century factories are all defined as cultural resources, valuable elements of the human-made environment.

**culture:** The "extra-somatic" means of adaptation. In its broadest sense, culture is a strategy for survival based on ideas, as opposed to physical characteristics of our bodies provided by nature. We can hold a tool in a number of ways because of the inborn, physical characteristics of our hands. We then have the ability to invent a nearly infinite variety of tools that can be used by our hands. Culture is "extra-somatic" or beyond the body; beyond the biological or physical characteristics given us by nature. Culture is still biologically based in that our capacity for culture is based on our enormous intelligence made possible by a large and complex brain. Culture is constituted by all of the behaviors that human beings have invented and passed down to subsequent generations. In a more specific sense, a culture is the particular strategy of survival of an individual group of people.

**culture history:** Essentially, what happened when in a given region. An outline of the major cultural developments—adaptations, subsistence and settlement patterns, technological innovations, culture contacts, and so on—over time. In most world areas, archaeologists have a good handle on the outline of local culture history and simple charts are nearly ubiquitous, showing a column of culture names and developments from bottom (most ancient) to top (most recent).

**datum:** The origin or 0, 0 location of a site grid. A site grid is analogous to a giant piece of graph paper superimposed over a site. Datum is the origin of this imaginary piece of graph paper, and excavation units—and, ultimately, everything recovered at a site—are defined and located in reference to this point.

**debitage:** The wastage produced in stone tool making. Stone tool making is a reductive technology; the maker starts with a piece of stone and sculpts a tool from this core of rock by removing what can be defined as excess. Some of these excess flakes removed in tool making are themselves useful and can be used as tools. But because of size or form, many of the flakes removed in tool making cannot be used and are waste. The waste is called debitage.

**deciduous teeth:** Human baby teeth. These are the teeth that become visible in the mouth during infancy and early childhood and are shed, like the leaves of deciduous trees in the fall, to be replaced by the permanent or adult teeth. The various deciduous teeth—the flat-faced incisors in the front, the pointed canine teeth adjacent to the incisors, and the larger grinding molars to the rear of the child's mouth—erupt through the gum line at a fairly consistent age and are then lost and replaced by the permanent teeth at a similarly fixed point during development. The presence or absence (because they haven't erupted yet or because they have already been shed to make room for the adult teeth) of deciduous teeth is a good gauge of the degree of development of the individual and, therefore, a pretty good indicator of how old the person is—or how old the person was when he or she died, in the case of forensic or archaeological examples.

**demographic:** Anything referring to the "demography" or vital statistics of a population. The basic population data collected and published in the census is demographic: overall population size, longevity, male:female ratio, ethnicity, and so on. Archaeologists approach demography in a number of ways. Those who study cultures with written records may have formal census data available for analysis. When examining the population statistics of prehistoric societies, demographic data is often collected from skeletal remains, whose study may allow for a statistical picture of a group of people if a sufficiently large, representative sample of the ancient population is available.

**demography:** The basic population data collected and published in the census is demographic: overall population size, longevity, male:female ratio, ethnicity, and so on. Archaeologists approach demography in a number of ways. Those who study cultures with written records may have formal census data available for analysis. When examining the population statistics of prehistoric societies, demographic data is often collected from skeletal remains, whose study may allow for a statistical picture of a group of people if a sufficiently large, representative sample of the ancient population is available.

**dendrochronology:** Tree-ring dating. The actual year date a tree was cut down and used, for example, by a past people to build a structure, can be determined by comparing the succession of rings in the ancient tree to those of a broad master sequence whose final ring represents the current year. The master sequence for a given region is constructed by examining a number of trees of overlapping ages. The master sequence consists of a series of rings of various thicknesses stretching back, in some areas, for more than ten thousand years. Tree-ring thickness varies from year to year, consistently across a region as a result of varying temperatures or amounts of rainfall. Ring thicknesses for even a short series of years are not repeated, so any ancient tree found in a region can be placed within the master sequence and the year date of its final ring can be determined, thus dating when the tree died or was cut down.

**descriptive statistics:** The numerical data that summarize the nature of a population. Descriptive statistics can exhibit the central tendency of a data set, for example, the mean, median, or mode of a variable. Your "average" for the semester, more formally, the mean score of all of your individual grades, is a descriptive statistic. The mean length of spear points in a cache, the mean volume of the individual blocks making up the Great Pyramids in Egypt, and the mean cranial capacity (skull volume) of representatives of an ancient hominid species are all descriptive statistics. The standard deviation—a measure of how closely individuals in a sample cluster about the mean—is another descriptive statistic. Where descriptive statistics merely describe a population, inductive statistics provide a way to assess patterns, correlations, and cause-and-effect relationships between and among variables.

**diaphysis:** The shaft of each of the long bones; the individual bones of the legs, arms, hands, and feet. That portion of a long bone between the end caps (epiphyses).

**diffusion:** The movement of ideas across geographic distance and cultural boundaries. When new technologies or styles are reflected in the archaeological record at a particular archaeological site or within a particular region, it may be the result of local and independent invention or development of the new technology or idea, or it may be the result of the borrowing of the new behaviors as a result of diffusion.

**direct historical approach:** An approach in ethnographic analogy in which the culture of a group that represents the descendants of the people whose archaeological remains are being investigated is used as the source for models or analogies used to explain the lifeways lived by the ancient group.

**discontinuous variables:** Variables whose possible expressions are not measurements but names. For example, eye color is a discontinuous variable whose most common possible expressions are brown, blue, and green. Lithic raw material (for example: flint, obsidian, quartzite, quartz, and basalt), temper added to clay (for example: none, quartz grit, sand, shell, ground up pieces of fired clay), and feature type (for example: burial, hearth, lithic cache, foundation, midden) are examples of discontinuous variables. Also called nominal variables.

**distal epiphysis:** Each long bone in your body consists of a shaft—the diaphysis—and two end caps—the epiphyses. In the geography of the body, the distal epiphysis of each of those long bones is the end cap farther away from the trunk (think, "distant" means far from). The end cap closer to or in "proximity to" the trunk is the proximal epiphysis.

**ecofacts:** You won't find this term in the dictionary; it was invented by archaeologists who needed a way to differentiate archaeological specimens that were actually made by people (artifacts) from those that are present at an archaeological site because of human behavior, and that may even show direct evidence of human manipulation, but that were not intentionally made into something by people. Ecofact is what archaeologist Lewis Binford came up with. Ecofacts are elements from the environment (bone, stone, wood, seeds, nuts, shell) that were collected by people for their use (to eat or to warm themselves), but are not themselves tools or manufactured objects.

**egalitarian:** A society in which all of the members within the group's recognized age and sex categories (for example, young children, adolescents, young adult men, young adult women, elderly people) have an equivalent amount of wealth, authority, and social standing. All members of an egalitarian society are not necessarily "equal" and there may be differences in wealth, authority, and social standing among the different groups.

**elastic limit:** Although rock may seem to be hard and brittle, many rock forms actually are flexible, at least at a microscopic level. They are, in fact, "elastic" and deform, if only very slightly, when a force—either percussion or pressure—is applied. Up to a certain level of applied force, the rock will rebound when the force is removed. Once a certain level is reached, a level that will vary within each type of rock and even among different geographic sources of the same rock type, the rock cannot sustain the force and rebound and, instead, breaks. The maximum force a rock can sustain before breaking is its "elastic limit." In stone tool making, the craftsperson exceeds the elastic limit of the rock to remove flakes.

**electrical resistivity survey:** A noninvasive procedure used in archaeological survey where an electrical current is passed through the ground. Variations in soil resistance to the current are used to pinpoint the location of archaeological artifacts or features.

**electron spin resonance (ESR):** Dating method based on the accumulation of energy in the form of electrons in atoms pushed into and then "trapped" at higher energy levels as a result of background radiation. In a given environment and for a given material, the electrons become trapped at a regular rate. The amount so trapped can be measured and the amount of time it would have taken for all that trapping to have occurred once an object was buried can be determined.

**enamel hypoplasia:** Pits and other imperfections in the enamel of the permanent teeth, resulting from bouts of malnutrition during early childhood before those adult teeth appeared in the mouth. The nascent buds of the permanent teeth are present in the upper and lower jaws of newborns, below the buds of the deciduous dentition. Nutritional and other dietary problems (for example, an excess of fluoride) as well as childhood diseases, therefore, can have an impact on the adult teeth long before they erupt. Enamel hypoplasia is one example. Dietary and nutritional deficiencies in individuals, in entire populations, or in only certain segments of a population can be revealed by the discovery of enamel hypoplasia.

**enculturated:** To become a member of a culture, to learn the rules by which a society operates, and to follow them is to become enculturated. Children are born into a culture that is, after all, a set of learned behaviors. As they mature, they grow into their culture—become enculturated—learning every day how to act, how to behave, how to believe, by being surrounded by people who are members of the culture who are acting, behaving, and believing in ways appropriate to the culture.

**Environmental Impact Statement (EIS):** Literally, a formal statement concerning the potential and real affects a given, proposed development or construction project may have on the environment. Mandated by the federal government in the National Environmental Protection Act, an Environmental Impact Statement is often a detailed report prepared by experts in water, air, botanical, zoological, and cultural resources, assessing the possible damage to the environment, in the broadest sense of the word, of a federally funded or mandated project (for example, road construction, pipeline placement, or river dredging). Archaeological sites are defined as cultural resources, of value to all citizens, and worthy of federal concern and protection. Information provided in an EIS may result in an alteration of a proposed project in order to protect archaeological resources, or may lead to the excavation of a site in order to salvage the information it contains before the project proceeds and the site's location is destroyed.

**epiphysis (pl. *epiphyses*):** Each end cap of each long bone in the body. When you are born, each of your long bones consists of three segments: a shaft called the diaphysis and two end caps called epiphyses. The epiphyses are each joined to their diaphysis by a band of cartilage. The proximal epiphysis and distal epiphysis of each long bone permanently fuse to the contiguous diaphysis during a narrowly circumscribed time period of an individual's development. As a result, the age of a subadult individual can be estimated by examining his or her skeleton (by noninvasive imaging of a living person or by directly examining the bones of a deceased individual) and determining which of the epiphyses have already fused to their shafts and which are yet to solidly connect. The long bone epiphyses have all fused by the late teens or very early twenties. Once this has occurred, examining them can tell you only that the individual is at least that old.

**ESR:** See electron spin resonance.

**ethnoarchaeology:** A strategy employed by archaeologists attempting to better understand the ways in which the archaeological record reflects the lives of a group of people. In ethnoarchaeology, the archaeologist lives among a group of people in the manner of an ethnographer, focusing on how the behavior of the living group of people becomes transformed into an archaeological record of that behavior. Investigating how behavior becomes translated into an archaeological entity (a site), provides the archaeologist with insights into the question of how an archaeological entity (a site) reflects the behavior that produced it.

**ethnographic analogy:** Using the description of a living group of people—or a people who lived in the not too distant past and whose lifeways have been documented—as a model for understanding the lifeways of an archaeological group. A recent group whose way of life has been described is considered an appropriate source for comparisons and analogies when the two peoples—those whose archaeological remains we are trying to understand and the more recent groups whose way of life has been described by eyewitnesses—appear to have lived under similar conditions, in generally similar cultural settings.

**ethnographic research:** Ethnography is the observation and analysis of a living group of people. Archaeologists are interested in the study of a living group of people for at least two fundamental reasons: (1) the study of the living descendants of the people who left behind the archaeological materials may provide insights into the meaning and significance of the material and (2) even when no living descendants of the archaeological group can be identified, the analysis of living people, especially those living a way of life similar or analogous to that reflected in the archaeological record, may similarly provide insights into our analysis of the archaeological record.

**ethnography:** The study of a living group of people by living among them, observing their behavior, and participating in their daily activities. The published work describing the research of an ethnographer is also called an ethnography.

**ethnohistory:** Written descriptions of foreign or alien cultures produced, not by trained ethnographers whose purpose was to describe such cultures, but by explorers, adventurers, colonists, traders, missionaries, and others who encountered alien people accidentally while exploring, adventuring, colonizing, trading, or proselytizing. The advantage of ethnohistorical work rests in the fact that they are among the earliest descriptions of many of the world's non-European societies and, therefore, reflect the cultures of non-European people before they were significantly altered by such contact. The disadvantage rests in the fact that those who wrote ethnohistorical descriptions of alien cultures were generally not trained scientists, were not unbiased reporters, and had particular agendas and purposes that often detracted from the objectivity of their observations.

**excavation:** The careful and methodical exposure of subsurface archaeological material. Excavation is usually conducted with hand tools such as trowels, small brushes, and dental picks in an attempt to expose the materials left behind by a past people exactly where these past people left them. See archaeological excavation.

**excavation units:** The individual analytical field unit at an archaeological site. Excavation units are often called "squares" because that is their form; often 2 meters on a side, but they can be 1-meter squares, 6-foot squares, or any other size, and they don't even need to be squares. Excavating in regularly sized and spaced units allows for site excavation in manageable "bites" and makes it easier for the principal investigator—and everyone else—to keep track of where items were found.

**exhausted core:** A stone nucleus that has had a series of flakes removed from it and now is either too small, too battered, or too oddly shaped to allow for the efficient removal of additional flakes.

**exotic material:** Any raw material used by a past people that is not native to their local area. Any raw material that had to be obtained through long-distance trade or by travel to a source outside of the area in which a group commonly moved.

**experimental archaeology:** Answering questions about the cultures of past people by attempting to replicate particular elements of their behavior. Usually applied to material culture, experimental archaeologists attempt to figure out how tools were made and used by actually going through the trial-and-error process of making and using them. Experimental archaeology certainly contributes to our scientific understanding of specific processes of the technologies of past people, but it also does something more: it provides us with a visceral appreciation for past technologies through the humbling experience of actually trying to make and use things similar to objects made by past people.

**faunal analysis:** Examination of the animal bones recovered at an archaeological site. This analysis should provide information about the subsistence base of a group by identifying the animal species being used. Other aspects of a group's subsistence strategy may also be revealed. Did they hunt wild animals or are remains those of domesticated species? Were they capable of capturing only very old and very young animals, or were they successfully hunting animals in their prime? Did they avoid killing females in their prime—females, after all, were important in producing the next generation of animals? Were they thorough or wasteful in their use of an animal's carcass?

**features:** A combination of artifacts and/or ecofacts that together represent a location where an activity took place that resulted in the combined presence of the artifacts and ecofacts. When people carry out tasks in activity areas, they often use material objects and, during the course of the activity, they may intentionally or accidentally leave some of those material objects behind. The remnants of a fireplace characterized by a concentration of charcoal and rocks; an activity area where stone tools were once made and where now battered fragments of hammerstones, waste flakes, and tools broken during the tool making process litter the ground; a human burial with bones and grave goods (the treasured belongings of the deceased provided for use in the afterlife); a platform on which deer meat was once roasted and where now only a bed of burned stones, bits of charred wood, and flecks of bone remain; all of these are archaeological features.

**femur:** The bone of the upper leg; the thigh bone. The femur is the longest of the so-called long bones, which are, exactly as advertised, the long bones of the legs, arms, hands, and feet.

**fibula:** The smaller of the two bones of the lower leg. The larger lower leg bone is the tibia. Feel your shin; that large, flat bone just below the surface of your skin is your tibia. The fibula is behind the tibia, enclosed in muscle.

**field director:** Archaeological field worker in charge of the entire field crew while out in the field. Taking direction from the principal investigator, the field director gives instructions to the crew chiefs concerning the work on any given day.

**field school:** Intensive training, often offered as a course at a university, in archaeological fieldwork and laboratory work. Students may be trained in a diverse array of archaeological methods through a process of learning by doing. In most field schools, students perform much of the grunt labor as they learn common procedures of archaeological survey, gridding, troweling, screening, mapping, recording, photographing, as well as procedures of cleaning, inventorying, and preliminary analysis in the lab. Field schools are conducted all over the world and most offer college credit; many field school opportunities are listed in the Archaeological Fieldwork Opportunities Bulletin published by the Archaeological Institute of America (http://www.archaeological.org/webinfo.php?page=10015).

**floodplain:** A flat expanse of land adjacent to a river or stream. The floodplain is commonly flooded on a yearly basis, particularly in spring as the result of heavy rainfalls and, in the north, meltoff of the winter snowpack. This flooding brings with it a heavy burden of silt—fine-grained material—that is deposited on the floodplain. Called alluvium, this silt consists of fine particles easily moved and deposited by flowing water and very few larger rocks. This can be extremely attractive to farming people, particularly those without machines to help turn over the soil in preparation for planting. This flooding also explains why archaeological material is often found deeply buried, the result of many years of flooding and attendant deposition.

**flotation:** A procedure used in archaeology to separate artifacts and ecofacts from excavated soil—either the soil matrix recovered from a feature or soil samples taken from ancient living surfaces—by the use of water. Flotation is based on the fact that, in the vast majority of instances, the archaeological material that you are trying to isolate and recover from the surrounding soil has a different specific gravity than water (the fixed volume of the archaeological material weighs more or less than but not the same as the same fixed volume of water). This means that when dumped into a pool of standing water (for example, in a basin or bucket) most archaeological remains will separate from the water either by floating to the top or sinking to the bottom. Materials that float (many organics) can be collected by skimming the water's surface. Materials that sink (lithics) can be extracted by draining the water through a fine mesh screen that will allow the water and most of the very fine soil particles, but not the artifacts or ecofacts, to pass through.

**fontanelles:** These are the so-called soft spots on a newborn baby's cranium. There are two fontanelles, one on top toward the front and one farther back where the bony cranial plates do not yet meet in the newborn skull. The presence of these gaps, where the brain is covered not in bone but in a thick layer of cartilage, allows for the flexibility needed in the relatively large newborn human skull in order to pass through the narrow human birth canal. The fontanelles close up during development: the smaller fontanelle at the rear of the skull fuses over at about three months of age and the one toward the front closes at about a year-and-a-half.

**foragers:** Term used to describe a subsistence strategy in which food is provided by any combination of hunting wild animals, fishing, shellfish collecting, and gathering the seeds, roots, nuts, fruits, or leaves of wild plants. All human groups were foragers until the development of food production technologies, where plants and animals were domesticated through a process called artificial selection. The earliest evidence of a shift away from foraging toward food production and, ultimately, full-blown agriculture, occurred in the Middle East sometime soon after twelve thousand years ago and then, independently, in a number of places in the Old and New Worlds sometime later.

**forensic anthropologists:** The word "forensic" refers specifically to the law, and forensic scientists apply scientific procedures to the investigation of a crime. Forensic anthropologists focus on human remains and contribute to our understanding of a past society's demography, including individual longevity, ethnicity, nutrition, disease, and trauma. And, in fact, just like forensic scientists who attempt to solve modern crimes, forensic anthropologists may reveal ancient ones. For example, in the case of the 9,400-year-old Kennewick Man in Oregon as well as the 5,000-year-old Ice Man found in the Italian Alps, forensic specialists found stone spear points embedded in their bodies. In the case of Kennewick, the individual survived to live a long life after impaled; in the case of the Ice Man, the spear wound likely contributed directly to his death.

**four-corners:** The only place in the United States where four separate states meet at right angles. The four states are Arizona, New Mexico, Colorado, and Utah. The region is well known and even world renowned for its extraordinary archaeological heritage exemplified by the Great Houses of Chaco Canyon in New Mexico and the cliff dwellings of Mesa Verde in Colorado.

**Geographic Information Systems (GIS):** Computer mapping programs in which each variable is treated as a map layer. By superimposing layers that might include information about watercourses, topography, soil type, and so on, as well as the locations of archaeological sites, patterns of site location in reference to those environmental variables may become apparent.

**GIS:** See Geographic Information Systems.

**Global Positioning System (GPS):** System of locating precisely any point on Earth, originally developed exclusively for military use, through the use of twenty-four satellites orbiting our planet. Less precise, degraded satellite signals were made available to anyone with a receiver, and as of May 2000, the nondegraded signal became available. With a handheld GPS unit costing just a few hundred dollars, the location of an archaeological site to within just a few meters can be determined, and its location in relation to surrounding resources—resources that may have played a role in a past people's using the location in the first place—can be assessed.

**GPS:** See Global Positioning System.

**ground penetrating radar:** A noninvasive technique used in archaeology where an electromagnetic pulse is passed through the soil. This pulse encounters objects in the soil and is reflected back to a receiver. The radar operator may then be able to interpret the nature of objects that reflected the radar pulse, some of which may represent cultural remains, for example buried walls or foundations.

**ground stone:** Stone tools made, not by striking them with a rock or antler hammer to remove flakes, nor by applying pressure to the edge to push off flakes, but by grinding the stone, often against the surface of another stone, to produce a shape and often a sharp and durable edge.

**growth arrest lines:** Horizontal cracks at the end of the diaphysis of a long bone that persist through adulthood, resulting from a bout of malnutrition during the developing years. Before the fusion of the epiphyses to their diaphysis, the long bone shaft grows out from its ends. If an individual experiences a period of severe malnutrition that growth may stop or at least slow down substantially. If the individual survives and resumes growth when nutrition is restored, a line or lines may appear, sometimes visible on the surface of the bone and sometimes recognizable only in x-ray. The presence of growth arrest lines, therefore, is an indication of nutritional deficiencies in an individual, an entire population, or only in certain segments of the population. Also called Harris Lines, after the researcher who first recognized their cause.

**half-life:** The fixed, regular, and measurable amount of time it takes for one half of the radioactive isotope in a substance to decay into its stable end product or to a step on the path to its stable form. Some radioactive isotopes of elements exhibit half-lives no more than a fraction of a second in length while some half-lives are measured in billions of years. The half-life is, in essence, a natural clock that can be used to date a substance whose age, when found at an archaeological site, can be associated with the site.

**half-moons:** A category of wear traces on stone tools. Unlike scalar scars, which are gouged out on the surface of a tool near the edge, these little crescent-shaped scars along a tool's working edges result when actual bites are taken from those edges during use. A tool that begins with a straight edge may appear serrated after use that produced half-moon scarring. For example, a thin, sharp-edged stone tool used to incise a design on a piece of wood may result in a rapid and significant deterioration of the edge in the form of half-moon scars. The tiny flakes removed in the process may become embedded in the material being worked on and produce striations on the tool as it rubs against them.

**hammerstone:** Tool used in the production of stone tools. The hammerstone is the percussor, the tool used to strike a stone core to remove flakes or to strike a flake in order to thin, sharpen, and shape a tool. The hammerstone needn't be harder than the core; often spherical and, therefore, without facets or angles of less than 90 degrees, a core's geometry provides it with much of its strength and durability.

**haplogroups:** Co-occurring genetic markers that are inherited together, as a unit. The presence of certain recognized mitochondrial haplogroups may distinguish populations of human beings from one another and enable the tracing of historical connections among living peoples.

**haplotypes:** A cluster of co-occurring genetic markers within particular haplogroups that are inherited together, as a unit. The presence of certain recognized mitochondrial haplotypes may distinguish populations of human beings from one another and enable the tracing of historical connections among living peoples. For example, the fact that all five of the mitochondrial haplotypes found among Native Americans are also found in Asia and not in Africa, Europe, or Australia, is interpreted to support the hypothesis of a historical connection between the native people of Asia and the Americas.

**Harris Lines:** Horizontal cracks at the end of the diaphysis of a long bone that persist through adulthood, resulting from a bout of malnutrition during the developing years. Before the fusion of the epiphyses to their diaphysis, the long bone shaft grows out from its ends. If an individual experiences a period of severe malnutrition, that growth may stop or at least slow down substantially. If the individual survives and resumes growth when nutrition is restored, a line or lines may appear, sometimes visible on the surface of the bone and sometimes recognizable only in x-ray. The presence of growth arrest lines, therefore, is an indication of nutritional deficiencies in an individual, an entire population, or only in certain segments of the population. Named for the researcher who first recognized their cause. Also called by the accurately descriptive name growth arrest lines.

**high-performance liquid chromatography (HPLC):** A laboratory procedure for separating molecules in a sample by the application of high pressure. Once separated, the molecules can be identified. HPLC has been used to analyze ancient food residues adhering to interiors of clay vessels.

**hominid:** The taxonomic family that includes human beings and species directly ancestral to humans. The first hominids are characterized by chimp-sized brains and exhibit a skeletal anatomy that enabled upright walking more than four million years ago during the Pliocene epoch. Stone tool making dated to about 2.5 million years ago in the hominids, about the same time the hominid brain exhibited a dramatic increase in size beyond that of any ape species.

**HPLC:** See high-performance liquid chromatography.

**humerus:** The upper arm bone. It is entirely coincidental that at the far end (distal epiphysis) of the humerus is the "funny bone."

**hunter-gatherers:** Human groups that feed themselves by hunting wild animals and collecting wild plants are said to be hunter-gatherers. In most such societies, though hunting provides the bulk of the protein, most of the caloric intake is supplied by plant food and some suggest the term is more appropriately "gatherer-hunters." The term "forager" is preferred by many because it does not implicitly prioritize the importance of any one food source and it is more inclusive, recognizing the possible significance of fishing and shellfish and egg collecting in the subsistence quest.

**igneous:** Volcanic rock formed when enormously hot, molten material in the Earth's interior cooled and solidified; granite, basalt, obsidian, pumices, and so on.

**inductive statistics:** Numerical analysis of patterns, correlations, and cause-and-effect relationships between and among variables. In descriptive statistics researchers can calculate numbers that summarize how a population (of people, spear points, archaeological sites, and so on) scores on a given variable. In inductive statistics, researchers can calculate numbers or formulas that reveal any patterns of how a population scores on a number of variables. For example, inductive statistics may reveal that the measurement for one variable (for example, the thickness of the wall of a ceramic vessel), correlates with another (for example, its age). Knowing, in this example, that older pots have thicker walls may provide insights into the evolution of ceramic technology in a given society.

**in situ:** A Latin phrase meaning "in place." Archaeologists use the term specifically to characterize an exposed artifact that has been left, at least temporarily, in its original location of discovery. In some cases, an in situ specimen is exactly where it was left behind (lost, discarded, cached, abandoned) by a person at some time in the past.

**isotope:** In physics, an isotope is a variety of the atomic structure of an element. All atoms of a given element have the same number of protons in their nuclei but the number of neutrons may vary; different isotopes of an individual element have different numbers of neutrons in their nuclei. Some isotopes of an element are atomically stable, never changing. Others are unstable or radioactive, changing at a regular rate, by a process of decay into a stable end product. The fixed rate of decay of a radioactive isotope forms the basis of radiometric dating.

**K/Ar:** See potassium/argon dating.

**kitchen midden:** An aboveground accumulation or pile of residue from food preparation. Inedible material, spoilage, and excess is thrown on the pile and left to decay. The stuff that does not disappear— depending on the local soil condition this will often be bones, shells, and carbonized remains like seed husks, nutshells, cobs, and rinds—becomes a kitchen midden.

**knapper:** A person who knaps; to strike stone in an effort to shape the stone into a tool or produce flakes that can be used as is or further shaped into tools. A flintknapper refers specifically to a stone tool maker who knaps flint. Knappers are also occasionally referred to as "rock-knockers."

**knapping:** The act of making stone tools.

**lacustrine:** Relating to lakes. Gravel, sand, silt, and clay that accumulate along the shoreline of a lake produce lacustrine deposits that may cover and preserve the archaeological sites resulting from human activity along lake margins.

**landscape signature:** Term suggested by archaeologists William Marquardt and Carole Crumley (1987) for the archaeological manifestation of a settlement pattern. A human group uses its territory and locates its villages, camps, burial grounds, sacred places, and so on in ways that are culturally determined. The spatial distribution of archaeological sites left behind reflecting their pattern of land use is the landscape signature of the group.

**laser transit:** Device used in surveying. Where the old-style transits were visual sighting devices used to measure elevations (depths) and locations, laser transits emit a beam of laser light that bounces off a special stadia rod. The signal is captured by a receiver on the transit where the precise distance and elevation of the point being measured are recorded and stored.

**law of superposition:** The commonsensical rule stating that the relative age of a soil layer (stratum) is determined by its position in an undisturbed vertical sequence of a number of layers (strata). In other words, more recent soil layers are superimposed over older layers. Under most circumstances, this means that deeper layers in a sequence are older than layers higher in the same sequence, but natural and cultural processes can disturb these sequences, so it is best to examine a sequence of layers rather than simply to measure depth to determine the relative age of a stratum. The relative age of archaeological materials can be determined by reference to the soil layers in which they are found.

**literature search:** Primary stage in an archaeological research project in which publications are examined that might discuss previous archaeological research in the proposed project area. In the past, this was fairly straightforward as most regions have a rather limited list of publications in which relevant material might appear. When we started the Farmington River Archaeological Project in which the Wood Lily site was discovered, about the only significant publication in which previous archaeological research in the Farmington River Valley might be discussed was the Bulletin of the Archaeological Society of Connecticut. Today, there is a substantial and growing body of "gray literature," including unpublished reports produced in compliance archaeology projects and nontraditionally published material sometimes available online. In Connecticut, compliance archaeology reports are gathered by the Office of the State Archaeologist and made available to researchers in the Archives and Special Collections of the Thomas J. Dodd Research Center at the University of Connecticut (http://archnet.asu.edu/archives/crm/conn/cttowns/introct.html). Other states and municipalities may handle these materials differently.

**lithic:** Adjective for stone. Any material composed of stone is lithic.

**living archaeology:** A strategy employed by archaeologists attempting to better understand the ways in which the archaeological record reflects the lives of a group of people. In ethnoarchaeology, the archaeologist lives among a group of people in the manner of an ethnographer, focusing on how the behavior of the living group of people becomes transformed into an archaeological record of that behavior. Investigating how behavior becomes translated into an archaeological entity (a site) provides the archaeologist with insights into the question of how an archaeological entity (a site) reflects the behavior that produced it.

**mandible:** The lower jaw. The upper jaw is called the maxilla.

**master sequence:** In dendrochronology, tree-ring sequence, extending in some cases for a period of more than ten thousand years, produced by overlapping the rings of a living tree with a series of successively older trees. Over the course of the time period covered in a regional master sequence, no section of the sequence of ring widths repeats itself. As a result, once a master sequence is established, the ring sequences of newly discovered, long-dead trees, including those cut down and used by ancient people, can be positioned precisely in the master sequence. The exact year of each ring in the master sequence is known because the end of the sequence is rooted in the present, thus the year any tree alive during any time represented in the sequence was cut down can be determined. If people cut it down and used it in a structure, the age of the tree can be applied to the age of the ancient dwelling and archaeological site.

**mastoid process:** In the geography of the skeleton, a process is a bump of bone. Each cranium has two mastoid processes, located at the base on the left and right sides. Feel directly behind your ears, at the level of the earlobes; those are your mastoid processes. The mastoid processes of males and females are a bit different in size and shape (males tend to have larger, rounded processes while those of females are smaller and more pointy). This fact is used to help identify the sex of a deceased individual based on his or her skeleton.

**material culture:** That portion of the human strategy for survival that involves making and using objects: tools, weapons, containers, clothing, houses, items of adornment, art and craftwork, and so on.

**matrilocal:** A postmarital residence pattern in which, upon marriage, a man leaves the community (compound, neighborhood, or village) into which he was born and within which he was raised and moves into the compound, neighborhood, or village in which his wife and her family reside.

**matrilocality:** Refers to a pattern of postmarital residence in which a newly married couple lives in the village, compound, or even the house of the wife's parents. See matrilocal.

**Minimum Number of Individuals (MNI):** This statistic represents a conservative estimate for the number of individual animals represented in the faunal assemblage at an archaeological site. In the MNI calculation, it is assumed that "redundant" skeletal elements, different parts of an animal's body that could have belonged to the same individual—a right front leg and a left rear leg from an animal of the same sex and age, but not two right front legs or two heads—did belong to the same animal. The MNI reflects the minimum number of animals that we can state with certainty are represented in an assemblage.

**mitochondrial DNA:** A type of DNA, separate and distinct from the nuclear DNA, present in the mitochondria of an organism's cells. Unlike nuclear DNA, mitochondrial DNA (mtDNA) of the male and female is not combined in sexual reproduction. The mtDNA of only the female is transmitted to subsequent generations. The simplicity of mtDNA inheritance renders it a valuable tool in examining the relationships between modern populations and, when recovered from ancient bone, the relationships among ancient populations and between modern people and them.

**MNI:** See Minimum Number of Individuals.

**morphology:** We use this term when referring to the form of anything. Biologists use it in reference to the form and structure of organisms and anthropologists use it in the same way, usually applying it to the form of the skeletal remains of human beings and human ancestors. Archaeologists use the term as well, more often referring to the form or shape of tools.

**NAGPRA:** See Native American Graves Protection and Repatriation Act.

**National Environmental Protection Act (NEPA):** Federal law passed in 1969 whose stated purpose was to protect the environment, to minimize negative impacts on the environment by federally funded projects, and to encourage study of the natural world. NEPA is important for archaeologists because the nation's cultural and historical heritage were explicitly included in those elements of the environment that deserved protection and study (http://ceq.eh.doe.gov/nepa/regs/nepa/nepaeqia.htm).

**National Historic Preservation Act of 1966:** This legislation formally established historic preservation as an official policy supported by the federal government of the United States. The spirit of this law is reflected in the wording of its preface, in which the authors expressed the belief that the history of the American people, reflected in part by cultural resources, should be preserved as a reflection of our national heritage. This act also established the National Register of Historic Places.

**National Museum of the American Indian Act of 1989:** Federal law that established a national museum of American Indians to be included as part of the Smithsonian Institution. This museum is currently under construction in Washington, D.C. (http://www.nmnh.si.edu/anthro/repatriation/nmaiact.htm).

**National Register of Historic Places:** Established and authorized in 1966 through the National Historic Preservation Act, the register amounts to an honor role of structures, places (including historic battlefields), and sites that meaningfully reflect significant episodes, events, people, or practices in American history (http://www.cr.nps.gov/nr/about.htm). Sites nominated to and accepted onto the register are deemed worthy of preservation because of their significance in our history.

**Native American Graves Protection and Repatriation Act (NAGPRA) of 1990:** Federal law that confers "ownership" of the biological remains of Native Americans (including Indians and Hawaiians) excavated in federally funded archaeology projects and/or stored in federal or federally funded facilities, to the biological descendents of the people whose remains have been recovered and stored. NAGPRA also requires the return to descendants of those objects that have been kept in federal or federally supported museums, libraries, laboratories, and so on that are deemed sacred by the native people whose ancestors made the objects (http://www.cr.nps.gov/nagpra/).

**NEPA:** See National Environmental Protection Act.

**neutron activation analysis:** Procedure for revealing the chemical signature of a raw material. In neutron activation analysis, samples of a specific raw material (for example, turquoise, obsidian, copper, or iron ore) from a series of geographically distinct sources are irradiated with neutrons. Different elemental constituents in each sample then emit radiation at levels unique to each element. The identity of about sixty different elements can be detected and their concentrations measured (down to trace amounts measured in parts per billion) by the application of this method.

**nomadic:** A way of life in which a group of people regularly move their habitation. A nomadic way of life is not a random existence. Many nomadic groups follow a regular pattern of migration on a yearly basis, consistently moving each season to the same separate location when resources are most abundant there during the course of a year. These nomads essentially follow the geographically shifting abundance of natural resources, moving their residence according to the local availability of wild plant and animal foods.

**nominal variables:** Variables whose possible expressions are not measurements but names. For example, eye color is a discontinuous variable whose most common possible expressions are brown, blue, and green. Lithic raw material (for example: flint, obsidian, quartzite, quartz, and basalt), temper added to clay (for example: none, quartz grit, sand, shell, ground up pieces of fired clay), and feature type (for example: burial, hearth, lithic cache, foundation, midden) are examples of discontinuous variables. Also called discontinuous variables.

**obsidian:** Naturally produced volcanic glass, usually black and translucent at thin edges. Obsidian without impurities breaks very predictably and controllably, producing exceptionally sharp, thin edges. Though these thin edges can be rather delicate and brittle, many ancient people utilized obsidian to make cutting, piercing, slicing, and scraping tools.

**object piece:** In stone tool making, the stone that you are striking with a hammerstone or antler hammer or the stone to which you are applying pressure with a pressure flaking tool. It's simple enough; it's the "piece" of stone (core or flake) that is the "object" of your percussion or pressure.

**obtrusive:** Where past cultures produced large-scale modifications of the landscape and/or constructed buildings of durable material, the archaeological remains of these landscape features and structures are said to be obtrusive: under the right conditions, readily obvious to practically anyone simply walking about these remains. The archaeological visibility of even obtrusive remains, however, may sometimes be obscured by the heavy growth of vegetation. The Maya of Mesoamerica are a good example of this, producing enormous, impressive, durable, and, therefore, highly obtrusive monuments, but in a tropical rainforest environment that has hidden much of their remains in thick vegetation, rendering the archaeological visibility of these features and sites sometimes quite low.

**occupation layer:** The actual layer that was the surface when an archaeological site was occupied. At sites that were not buried, the modern surface also was the occupation layer. At sites covered by alluvium, lake (lacustrine), shoreline (marine), slope (colluvium), or wind-blown (aeolian) deposits the occupation layer is buried and recognizable stratigraphically as the surface upon which the vast majority of artifacts and ecofacts are found and the level where features dug into the soil (trash pits and hearths, for example) begin.

**Oldowan:** The name given the earliest stone tool industry. First found in Olduvai Gorge in eastern Africa, Oldowan tools were manufactured of stone, often quartz or quartzite, pebbles. Using direct percussion, the tool maker struck the stone core, removing a large flake. The flake scar left on the core then became a striking platform for another flake, removed from a facet opposite from the first. The core was then turned around again, using the scar left by the second flake as another striking platform, and another flake was removed. This process was repeated several times, producing a large chopping tool and several sharp, thin cutting flakes. These tools have been dated to as much as 2.5 million years ago and most likely were made by a human ancestor called *Homo habilis.*

**optically stimulated luminescence (OSL):** A variety of luminescence dating; see also thermoluminescence. Buried objects are subject to naturally occurring radiation in the soil. The energy released by radioactive decay may accumulate in rock and clay. If rock or clay is heated to a high temperature by people (rock in a fireplace or clay when fired to make a pot), the energy previously accumulated is released. In other words, the human activity sets the energy accumulation clock to zero. When then buried, energy released by background radiation begins to accumulate again in the rock and fired clay at a regular rate. In optically stimulated luminescence, laser light is used to release the energy so accumulated. The amount of time since the "clock" was set to zero by people can be determined, thus dating the human activity and, therefore, the archaeological site.

**OSL:** See optically stimulated luminescence.

**osteology:** The study of bones. Osteology can focus on the skeletal remains of animals (for example, to determine ancient human use of animals) or of human beings (for example, to analyze the population statistics, dietary features, and disease histories of an ancient people).

**paleoenvironmental:** Relating to the ancient environment of an area. Archaeologists want to understand the nature of the paleoenvironment to which a human group adapted.

**paleofeces:** Ancient, preserved feces. Because the digestive systems of animals, including human beings, are not 100% efficient, some ingested food is excreted in feces. As a result, the paleofeces contain food remains and, therefore, provide data for dietary reconstruction. The term *coprolite* is more commonly used, but technically, coprolites are fossilized and most human deposits are not.

**paleontologist:** Scientist who studies ancient animals, ordinarily through the recovery and analysis of their ancient bones.

**paleopathology:** The study of ancient trauma, infectious disease, and nutritional deficiencies. Such pathologies often leave permanent and recognizable marks on human skeletons. Decades, centuries, and even millennia after death, these pathologies often can be accurately diagnosed, providing insights into the conditions that afflicted individuals as well as entire communities.

**palynologists:** Scientists who study pollen. Palynologists become expert in recovering pollen and identifying the species of plants that produced it. Palynologists can reconstruct ancient plant communities and, by inference, ancient climates, by comparing the pollen profiles derived from ancient pollen assemblages to the pollen rain falling in modern locations with their known climates.

**patrilocal:** A postmarital residence pattern in which, upon marriage, a woman leaves the community (compound, neighborhood, or village into which she was born and within which she was raised) and moves into the compound, neighborhood, or village in which her husband and his family reside.

**patrilocality:** Refers to a pattern of postmarital residence in which a newly married couple lives in the village, compound, or even the house of the groom's parents. See patrilocal.

**pedestrian survey:** The phase of an archaeological survey in which the ground surface is scanned for the presence of archaeological remains. In those parts of the world where soil forms fairly rapidly and covers most small-scale remains, only large-scale, built features—things like stone walls, house foundations, canals, stone-marked graves, monuments—will be visible on the surface and locatable in a pedestrian survey. In those places where soil formation is very slow, artifact clusters, hearth remains, and other small-scale remains may be visible on the surface and can be found in a pedestrian survey. In addition, even in those places where archaeological materials get covered up as a matter of course, other natural processes (for example, erosion along a river or something a bit more catastrophic like an earthquake) may serve to expose buried material that can be found in a pedestrian survey.

**percussion flaking:** A method of stone tool making in which a nucleus of stone is struck with a hammerstone or antler percussor in order to remove stone flakes. Percussion flaking may be used in a primary step in stone tool production in which large flakes that will be worked further into tools are removed from cores and in the intermediate and final stages where a tool is thinned, sharpened, and shaped into its final form.

**percussor:** The tool used in percussion flaking to remove flakes from a core. Ordinarily, the percussor may be of stone (a hammerstone) or of antler. In either case, the percussor does not need to be harder than the rock that makes up the core, it merely must be harder to break. The geometry of the percussor contributes to its durability.

**physical anthropologists:** Practitioners of a branch of anthropology (the study of human beings) that focuses on the biological aspects of our species. Among the topics investigated by physical anthropologists are the biological evolution of human beings, the biological variation exhibited by modern human beings, forensic anthropology, primatology (humans are primates and primatologists study the nonhuman primates, including monkeys and apes). Synonymous with biological anthropology.

**phytolith:** Microscopic, inorganic mineral particles produced by plants. Phytoliths are extremely durable and species-specific. Enormous databases are being compiled that allow the researcher to examine phytoliths recovered in the soils or adhering to artifacts recovered at archaeological sites and to identify the species from which the phytoliths originated (http://www.missouri.edu/~phyto/index.shtml).

**plane table:** A flat table mounted onto a tripod. The plane table can be leveled and serves as the base for an alidade.

**polish:** A category of wear traces on stone tools. Polish appears on the face or faces of a stone tool in applications where the surface(s) continually rubs against the smooth face of the material being worked on. For example, a long, thin stone drill may exhibit smoothing and polishing on high points as a result of rubbing against the material being drilled into. Even without the aid of a microscope, polish can be seen as a smoothed surface on a tool, sometimes dull, sometimes brightly reflecting light.

**pollen:** The male gamete in plant sexual reproduction. The pollen grains produced by different species are morphologically distinct from one another and, under the right conditions, can preserve for millennia. Palynologists can recover pollen grains from the occupation layers at archaeological sites or in areas adjacent to sites where preservation is higher. They can then identify the species that produced the pollen, calculate the percentages of the pollen of the species represented, and then deduce the makeup of the plant communities living in the area of an ancient human habitation.

**pollen analysis:** Figuring out the makeup of a plant community at a particular time and place by the recovery and examination of the pollen deposited there and then. By using modern pollen profiles as models, an ancient pollen profile can be interpreted in reference to modern plant communities. Finally, the climatic conditions that characterize the modern plant community can be suggested as being similar to those that applied when the ancient similar pollen profile was produced.

**pollen profile:** The percentages, usually depicted in a graph, of the pollen of each of the species of plants contributing to the overall pollen assemblage at a given place, at a given time period, compared over time. The increase or decrease in the percentage of individual plant species over time may be a product of a change in climate, either to the benefit or detriment of those species. A change in percentage through time may also result from cultural activity, including forest clearing, the introduction of new species, and farming. Pollen percentages also change through time as the result of the natural process of the evolution of plant communities called succession.

**pollen rain:** The pollen actually falling on a region. Today, the pollen rain may be collected with sticky tape. This sample of the pollen rain is then examined through a microscope in order to determine the percentages of the various plant species contributing to the pollen rain. An ancient pollen rain may be determined by palynologists who recover preserved pollen in soil samples.

**pongid:** The taxonomic family that includes all ape species, both living and extinct. The first pongids date to sometime after fifteen million years ago in the Miocene epoch and they flourished thereafter. Today there are several pongid species including, in Africa, gorillas, chimpanzees, and bonobos (formerly called pygmy chimenzees), and, in Asia, organgutans, gibbons, and siamangs.

**population:** A term used in statistics. The population is the entire group in any data set. The population of sites in a project area means all of the sites, known as well as those not yet (and perhaps never to be) discovered. We rarely have access to an entire population (of sites, particular kinds of artifacts, the skeletons of all of the members of an extinct hominid species). We are able to accurately describe, reveal patterns in, and investigate correlations within a population by analyzing a representative sample of that population.

**population profile:** In demography, a graphic representation of the breakdown of a population of people by sex and age. This graph, also called a population pyramid, depicts the proportion of a population in each decade of life, broken down by sex.

**post-cranial skeleton:** The skeleton below and excluding the cranium.

**potassium/argon (K/Ar):** Dating method based on the decay of an unstable isotope of the element potassium into a stable and inert argon gas. The half-life of radioactive potassium, common in the Earth's crust, is 1.25 billion years, during which time its end product, argon gas, builds up at a regular rate in the rock. By measuring how much argon has accumulated in a lava flow, the amount of time since the lava solidified can be determined.

**potsherds:** Fragments of pottery from a broken pot. Entire, intact pots are rare in archaeology. Most ceramic artifacts recovered are, in fact, potsherds, sometimes simply called sherds.

**pre-ceramic:** Term usually applied regionally to refer to the period of time before the development or adoption of ceramic technology, especially the manufacture and use of pottery. People certainly can store items or cook food without ceramic vessels. In some parts of the world, the presence of soapstone or steatite provided a soft stone that could be carved into fireproof, watertight containers suitable for storing liquids or for use in cooking. Elsewhere, bark and woven containers were made that could hold liquids and that could be heated, not directly over a fire, but by placing heated stones into their contents. Ceramics, however, allowed for the mass production of relatively durable containers and people the world over recognized their utility. The earliest examples of pottery vessels date to a little more than ten thousand years ago in Japan, and between five and six thousand years ago in South America.

**preform:** A product of the process of making a stone tool. A perform represents a flake taken off of a core and then worked in a preliminary, general way into a shape that can be further modified into a number of possible, different, final tool forms, depending on the particular need of the moment. The production of preforms in anticipation of the need to make tools at some point in the future is more efficient and convenient than to have to begin from scratch each time a new stone tool is needed.

**prehistoric:** Adjective modifying any site, culture, artifact, ecofact, feature, and so on that dates to the period before the development of writing. Because writing was not developed or adopted at the same time in all world areas, there can be no universally applied prehistoric time period. Prehistoric refers to a local sequence. In some areas, for example, Southwest Asia, "prehistoric" refers to the time before six thousand years ago when writing was first invented. In other parts of the world, for example, Mesoamerica, "prehistoric" refers to the time before about two thousand years ago when writing was developed there. In yet other parts of the world, for example, America north of Mexico, writing didn't develop independently, but arrived with explorers and colonizers in the fifteenth century A.D. In North America, therefore, "prehistoric" refers to the period before the arrival of the Europeans.

**prehistory:** Literally, the period before the development of true writing or a written system of recordkeeping. The first written language dates to no more than six thousand years ago and the earliest hints at the use of symbols as a form of recordkeeping are about ten thousand years old, so everywhere in the world, archaeological sites that are more than six thousand years old are, by definition, prehistoric. It should be added that not all regions became historic at the same time, so the boundary between prehistory and history is not everywhere the same. The native people of Australia and North America, for example, did not independently develop writing systems, so their story is part of prehistory up until their contact with Europeans just a few hundred years ago. As upright walking, tool making human ancestors date to 2.5 million years ago, human prehistory, therefore constitutes well over 99% of the time human beings and or hominid ancestors have walked the planet.

**pressure flaking:** A method of stone tool making in which relatively small flakes are removed from larger flakes by the application of pressure. Pressure flaking tools are ordinarily made of antler or metal; bone and wood generally are too soft. Because the pressure flaking tool can be positioned precisely at the point where the knapper hopes to remove a flake, pressure flaking is used for the finer work in stone tool making, including precise edge sharpening, flake thinning, final shaping, and notching (to provide a firmer attachment of the stone point to a wooden or reed shaft).

**primary refuse:** Luckily for archaeologists, people tend not to be particularly fastidious about their discard habits. Human beings, including those in the distant past, have always consumed enormous amounts of resources to produce the material objects they needed or wanted and to provide their subsistence. Commonly, a portion of the raw materials from which material objects were made or from which food was extracted were perceived as trash and left just where the objects were made or the food was consumed. At the same time, most tools have a limited useful life and eventually either break or simply wear out and are then discarded. Tools (artifacts) or inedible material produced in food preparation (ecofacts) discarded at their place of manufacture, use, or consumption are called primary refuse.

**principal investigator:** The director of any scientific endeavor, including archaeological research. The researcher who plans the project, obtains funding, directs the conduct of the study, and is responsible for the report or publication describing the results of the research.

**prognathous:** A jaw that protrudes out from the rest of the face. Some human populations are relatively flat faced; viewed in profile their faces are flat from their foreheads down to their chins. Other human groups are relatively prognathous, with their jaws protruding out from the plane of the rest of their faces.

**projectile point:** A sharp piece of stone (usually) that is firmly attached to a wooden or reed shaft that is used as a weapon by throwing or shooting. Projectile is the generic term that includes spear points, darts, and arrowheads. Because the shape and size of a point does not necessarily clarify whether it was used to tip a spear, dart, or arrow shaft, archaeologists generally prefer the term *projectile point* unless they are certain of precisely which kind of projectile was attached to the tip.

**proton magnetometry:** A noninvasive technique used in archaeology in the search for buried remains. The proton magnetometer measures the strength of the Earth's magnetic field at the surface. The magnetometer may detect variations in that field above the locations of buried remains like walls and foundations.

**provenience:** The precisely measured, three-dimensional, in situ location of an artifact, ecofact, or feature at an archaeological site. The provenience may be recorded as a single point for a very small object or as a series of points for larger artifacts and ecofacts and, especially, for the outline of features. Proveniences may be measured initially by reference to the southwest stake of an excavation unit (centimeters north and east of that stake) and depth below a fixed point (the top of the southwest stake or the ground surface at that stake's location). Proveniences are then converted to their location relative to the site datum.

**proximal epiphysis:** Each long bone in your body consists of a shaft (the diaphysis) and two end caps (the epiphyses). In the geography of the body, the proximal epiphysis of each of those long bones is the end cap closer to the trunk (think, "in proximity to" means "near" or "close to"). The end cap farther or more "distant" from the trunk is the distal epiphysis.

**pubic symphysis:** The point of connection or "articulation" between the two halves of the pelvis. Connected by a band of cartilage, the two adjoining faces of the pubic symphysis go through a fairly regular process of change and deterioration during an individual's life. The appearance of the pubic symphysis, therefore, is pretty much time dependent and time consistent, allowing for a fairly accurate estimate of the age at death of an individual.

**races:** A term used to denote different "varieties" of humanity. There is no objective definition for what constitutes a particular race, no set of characteristics that represents precisely one group of people to the exclusion of all other groups. As a result, race is not used as a scientific term and biological anthropologists usually refer to a multiplicity of varieties of human beings, often distributed geographically, but not to a small number (three? four?) of distinct human races.

**radioactive:** A substance that is unstable on the atomic level and that emits energy (radiation) as it decays into a more stable substance. That decay occurs at a fixed, regular, and measurable rate. That rate, once known, provides a natural clock or calendar that can be used to date an object through the measurement of how much of the radioactive substance remains or how much of the stable end product of the decay has accumulated.

**radiocarbon dating:** Radiometric dating procedure that measures the amount of carbon-14 remaining in an item found at an archaeological site to determine its age. Carbon-14 is an unstable isotope of carbon. Its decay rate, expressed as a half-life, is known; therefore, when the amount of carbon-14 remaining in an item is measured, the age of the item can be determined.

**radiometric:** Dating techniques that are based on the regular rate of decay of an unstable (radioactive) variety (isotope) of an element. Because decay rates are known (through measurement), an estimate of how old the object is can be derived from the amount of the radioactive variety of an element remaining, or the amount of the stable end product the radioactive variety decays to. When the life history of the material being dated can be related to past people (for example, when humans cut down a tree containing radioactive carbon and used it in building a structure or when lava containing radioactive argon flowed directly over an ancient village), the date derived from the object being dated is applied to the cultural material.

**random:** Refers to the nature of a sample. A sample is random if there is no bias and every member of a population has the same probability of being selected for inclusion. In the example of a site survey, every location in the project area would have an equal likelihood of being selected for testing.

**relative dating:** Refers to dating methods that place individual artifacts, ecofacts, features, or sites in a chronological sequence, but without a determination of actual age. Applying a relative dating technique allows the researcher to conclude that one site is older than another, or one artifact is younger than another, but does not provide an age in years for sites, artifacts, or any other archaeological materials.

**remote sensing:** Noninvasive process used in probing for archaeological sites without disturbing the soil. Remote sensing includes those procedures that employ instrumentation that is truly remote, like satellite and plane-based cameras. Remote sensing also includes approaches that use devices that can image or probe the characteristics of the subsurface, searching for anomalies that indicate the presence of artifacts or, more usually, patterns of soil disturbance that likely resulted from human activity (for example, burials, trenches, walls).

**representative:** Refers to the nature of a sample. A sample is representative if the various subcategories in the sample are included in the same or very nearly the same as their proportions in the population. A sample of people in an electoral poll is representative if it reflects the same proportion of men and women, rich, middle class, and poor, Democrats and Republicans, and so on as the population from which the sample was drawn. A sample of tested locations in an archaeological survey is representative if the number of pits in each habitat contained in a project area is proportional to the area each of the habitats constitutes of the total project area (if 10% of the project area consists of floodplain, then 10% of the test pits should be located in the floodplain). In a perfect world, an entirely random sample should be also be representative. But the world is rarely perfect and samples may be skewed accidentally. A sample can be made representative by making certain it reflects the characteristics of the population; in the above example, if, by chance only 7% of the test pits ended up in the floodplain, more test pits can be placed there to increase the percentage to the representative 10%.

**representative sample:** Ordinarily, in attempting to understand a given population (the population can be all voters in the state of Nebraska, all redwood trees in California, all archaeological sites in the lower Ohio Valley, and so on) only a fraction of a population—a sample—is examined. In most cases, the entire population of any data set is simply too large and, therefore, too expensive and time consuming to examine so only a part of it, a sample, is actually looked at. To ensure that the conclusions we reach about the subset of the population we can investigate directly also apply to the population as a whole, we make every effort to examine a sample that "looks like" the population. If a sample exhibits the same or very nearly the same characteristics of the population—the same proportions of males and females; Democrats and Republicans; young trees, middle-aged trees, and old trees; village sites, hunting camps, fishing loci, and quarries; and so on—the sample is said to be representative and conclusions reached about the sample likely apply equally well to the larger population as a whole.

**research strategy:** Archaeological research is not random. It is not conducted merely to amuse archaeologists or provide opportunities for students to broaden their experience. At least it shouldn't be. Archaeological research is informed by research goals. Surveys are conducted and sites excavated in an attempt to answer questions about life in the past. The research goal may be designed to answer a very simple, practical question: are there significant archaeological resources that may be destroyed by a planned development project? On the other hand, the research goal may focus on a better understanding of fundamental and very complex issues of human cultural evolution, for example, the nature and causes of the origins of the first complex state societies, commonly called "civilizations." The research strategy of a project consists of the methods by which archaeologists go about the process of reaching these research goals.

**sample:** A term used in statistics to signify that subset or portion of an entire population that the researcher has access to and is analyzing in an attempt to draw accurate and meaningful conclusions about the population as a whole. In most sciences, including archaeology, we cannot recover or it is far too inefficient to study an entire population, but instead we rely on a sample taken from that population. We increase the likelihood that our conclusions about the population based on a sample will be valid by making sure that we have extracted a representative sample of the population.

**sampling strategy:** The approach, in an archaeological survey or excavation, of selecting a fraction of an area or a site to search for the constituents of archaeological sites. The goals of sampling strategies differ on the basis of the research goal of the project as a whole. If an area is to be completely altered in a development project, the strategy may be to intensively sample the entire project area. In other cases, the strategy may be to examine a representative sample, a portion of the project area that closely represents, on a smaller scale, the characteristics of the project area as a whole.

**scalar scars:** A category of wear traces on stone tools. Scalar scars are tiny flake scars, shaped like fish scales, representing the damage caused along a stone tool edge when the pressure applied in use results in the removal of small flakes of stone. Scalar scars usually appear on the face of a tool alongside the edge without deterioration to the edge itself. The same qualities of stone that allow a tool maker intentionally to remove flakes through pressure flaking may result in the accidental removal of flakes through the pressure applied in tool use. For example, the pressure applied when using a steep-edged scraping tool to smooth a wooden shaft in the production of a spear may remove small flakes from the tool's working edge, resulting in scalar scars along that edge.

**sciatic notch:** A deep indentation in the back of each half of the pelvis through which the sciatic nerve travels. The size of the notch affects the overall width of the pelvis. Females tend to have a substantially more widely angled notch, which allows for a wider birth canal. Of all the metrical characteristics of the human skeleton, there probably is the least overlap between the measurements taken for males and females. Because of this, the size of the sciatic notch can be used to accurately (but not perfectly) distinguish the skeleton of a female from that of a male.

**secondary refuse:** People generally are slobs and have a tendency to leave their trash where it first falls to earth (primary refuse). In many instances, however, for reasons of safety (when the discarded material is dangerous: very sharp or even poisonous), or simply for sanitary reasons (the remains are attractive to insects, dangerous animals, a health risk, or they just plain smell bad), people will pick up after themselves and place the trash in a separate trash deposit located a safe and reasonable distance away from where people are actually living or buried in the ground. This trash, removed from its initial place of deposit, is called secondary refuse.

**sedentary:** A way of life in which a human group tends to inhabit a single location during the course of a year. Though active, healthy adults may be quite mobile, leaving home and staying for short periods at locations where resources are collected, they invariably return to their fixed, home base inhabited by less mobile members of society, including the very old, the very young, and pregnant women close to giving birth. A sedentary way of life is made possible by an extremely rich local environment that provides sufficient wild foods for the group year-round and/or by an artificial increase in food resources through food production; in other words, agriculture.

**semi-lunar knives:** Stone or metal knives in the shape of a half moon. The straight part of the half-moon is held or has a handle attached. The curved portion of the tool is the cutting edge. Called an ulu among the Inuit people of the Arctic, the semi-lunar knife was used in butchery, especially fish gutting.

**seriation:** A relative dating technique based on a common pattern of change in material culture. In many cases, when a new way of accomplishing a task is invented or introduced in a society, it is adopted by initially a small fraction of the population and through time slowly increases in popularity until it reaches a peak in its acceptance. At some point, yet another way of accomplishing the same task is invented or introduced and this new way slowly grows in popularity, replacing the previously accepted method, which slowly decreases in use. Individual sites can be dated by measuring the proportions of use of different styles or methods, and from this figuring out where they fit in a general continuum of technological or stylistic change through time.

**seriation graph:** A graphic representation of the level of popularity of a style or method of accomplishing a given task in a society as it changes through time, compared to the level of use of competing styles or methods. A seriation graph is sometimes called a "battleship curve" because of its appearance. Horizontal bars represent the popularity of styles or methods and are stacked in a commonsensical sequence reflecting a pattern of slow acceptance, increasing popularity, maximum use, and subsequent, almost inevitable, decrease as they are replaced by a new approach.

**settlement pattern:** The nature of land use and the resulting distribution across a landscape of habitations, work areas, burial grounds, encampments, sacred places, resource extraction areas, and so on, by a human group. The settlement pattern of a group of people produces a unique archaeological landscape signature reflecting how those people utilized their territory.

**sexual dimorphism:** The nature and degree of difference between the sexes in a species. In some species, there is an extreme level of sexual dimorphism with one sex, usually but not always males, being much larger than females. In other species, there is a very low degree of dimorphism and males and females may be virtually indistinguishable, at least to the naked human eye. Undressed, living human males and females are fairly easy to distinguish and the same can be said for male and female skeletons. Nevertheless, our overall degree of dimorphism falls somewhere between the extremes.

**sherds:** Broken pieces of ceramic objects, usually broken pieces of pottery.

**shovel-shaped incisors:** A form of the incisors, the four flat teeth in the front/center of both the upper and lower jaws. The shovel shape refers to the interior surface of the incisors where there are ridges along the margins giving the teeth the appearance, appropriately enough, of a shovel or spade. Shovel-shaped incisors are very common in Asian populations and in the teeth of Native Americans and are much less common in other populations. The presence of shovel-shaped incisors among human skeletal remains, modern or ancient, is a strong, though imperfect, indicator of an Asian source for the population. It is no coincidence that Native Americans exhibit very high levels of shoveling in their incisors if Asia is the source for their population.

**shovel test pits:** Test pits, sometimes called STPs. Because test pits are usually, but not always, excavated with shovels, archaeologists tend to refer to them as test pits, often preceded by a common expletive.

**silt:** A deposit consisting of very fine mineral particles; technically, between 1/16 and 1/256 mm in size—bigger than sand and smaller than clay particles. Silt is produced by the decomposition of preexisting rock and often makes up a substantial component of alluvium.

**site:** The archaeological term *site* is shorthand for *archaeological site*. An archaeological site is a place that people used in the past—they may have lived there or simply used the place to conduct a specific task or tasks (hunted, buried their dead, engaged in war, conducted a religious ceremony)—and where physical evidence of their use of a place remains in the form of artifacts and/or ecofacts.

**site constituents:** The things that make up the archaeological record and that, therefore, alert the archaeologist conducting a survey that he or she has found a site. Artifacts, ecofacts, and features are among archaeological site constituents.

**site formation processes:** The processes by which the material objects used, manipulated, altered, or manufactured by people become part of the archaeological record. Simply, people lose objects, throw them away, leave them behind, or simply abandon them when they are used up or of no use. These objects become deposited on the ground and in the ground (through intentional burial or placement in pits). By these processes, archaeological sites are formed.

**site survey:** The search for archaeological sites. Site survey often includes historical analysis of a study area, an examination of aerial photographs, a methodical surface inspection, and test excavations, all aimed at discovering the location where people lived in the past and left behind evidence of their presence.

**skull:** The bones of the head, face, and upper and lower jaw. In other words, the skull consists of the cranium and the mandible. The skull exhibits differences between the sexes, it changes in a regular and patterned way from birth through old age, and shows geographic variation in its morphology.

**soapstone:** A metamorphic rock, consisting primarily of the mineral talc, that is highly resistant to and retentive of heat. It is quite soft and can be fairly readily carved with stone or metal tools and, where available, was often used by ancient people to make cooking vessels. In more recent times, soapstone's heat retention capacity rendered it suitable for colonial bed warmers. Called soapstone because of its slippery, soapy feel, its formal name is steatite.

**spatial associations:** The spatial linkages of material at an archaeological site. Items that are found in close proximity to each other and likely were deposited together as a result of their linkage in a behavioral context (as a hammer is linked to a nail) are said to be in spatial association with one another. A key rationale for initially leaving items in place (in situ) upon their discovery during excavation of an archaeological site, as well as providing a reason for the detailed and accurate recording of their exact place of discovery (their provenience), is to insure that spatial associations are preserved, if only on paper, and that the behavioral meaning of those associations can be deduced.

**spatial context:** The location where an archaeological object is found and its spatial associations. Consider three different possible spatial contexts for the same artifact, a chipped stone spearpoint: (1) embedded in the butchered bone of a deer found in a fireplace; (2) one among several spearpoints found together as apparent offerings in a human burial; and (3) in a cluster of stone tools on the floor of the remains of a house. In each case, the spear point's spatial context implies its use and significance in the culture that produced it that cannot be determined simply by its morphology.

**stadia rod:** Essentially a large-format, rigid ruler, usually with metric gradations. The rod is usually collapsible, extending to more than 3 meters in length. The rod is placed on a surface whose precise location and depth are to be measured. The actual measuring may be accomplished with an alidade, old-style transit, or laser transit.

**steatite:** A metamorphic rock, consisting primarily of the mineral talc, that is highly resistant to and retentive of heat. It is quite soft and can be fairly readily carved with stone or metal tools and, where available, was often used by ancient people to make cooking vessels. In more recent times, steatite's heat retention capacity rendered it suitable for colonial bed warmers. Steatite is often known by its common name "soapstone" for its slippery, soapy feel.

**step scars:** A category of wear traces on stone tools. Step scars are tiny flake scars that terminate abruptly, at a right angle, into the face of the rock, giving the appearance of tiny stair steps. Step scars are caused along a stone tool edge when the pressure applied during use results in the removal of small flakes of stone. Step scars usually appear on the face of a tool alongside the edge without deterioration to the edge itself. The same qualities of stone that allow a tool maker intentionally to remove flakes through pressure flaking may result in the accidental removal of flakes through the pressure applied in tool use. For example, the pressure applied to the edge of a stone tool while scraping the meat off of a bone, may remove small flakes from the tool's working edge, resulting in step scars along that edge.

**STPs:** See shovel test pits.

**strata:** Naturally formed and often quite distinct superimposed layers of soil, composed of differing proportions of rock, gravel, sand, silt, clay, and decayed and decaying organic material, as well as cultural material left behind by past people. Different strata may exhibit different colors, textures, and chemical makeup and the boundaries between them may be sharply defined. These differences in strata can be explained by the characteristics of the "parent material" from which the soil layer formed, the agency that laid down the layer (flowing water, wind, vulcanism, slope movement, and so on), the particular environmental conditions present when the layer formed, as well as chemical and physical processes to which the soil has been subjected. The relative position of cultural materials in a sequence of strata is often used to determine the relative ages of those materials.

**stratified (societies):** These are societies characterized by social/economic/political classes or castes into which people are born and, ordinarily, within which they and their descendants remain. These layered societies, with noble classes, merchant classes, workers, and peasants, characterize complex societies.

**stratigraphic:** Refers to the sequence of soil layers superimposed one on top of the other. Stratigraphic levels may result from natural processes of deposition (flooding, blowing wind, soil movement down and across a slope), chemical processes in the soil, and also human activity through movement of soil as well as the accumulation of trash.

**stratigraphy:** Analysis of the sequenced layering of rock and soil. The relative ages of archaeological materials can be determined by the position of the soil levels or strata in which the materials are found by reference to the law of superposition.

**stratum:** The singular of strata; a single or individual soil layer.

**striations:** Scratch marks found on tool surfaces and edges, usually parallel to each other and to the direction of use of a stone tool. Striations are a category of wear traces, a form of damage to or deterioration of a stone tool with use. For example, a durable, sharp-edged stone knife used to cut through bone will usually exhibit striations on both faces, parallel to its working edge.

**striking platform:** The surface of a core or flake—usually flat or platform-like—that the percussor (hammerstone or antler hammer) strikes in an attempt to remove a flake from a contiguous core or flake surface that intersects with the striking platform at an angle of less than 90 degrees.

**supraorbital torus:** A lump or protrusion of bone above the eye orbits, about where your eyebrows are located. Ancient and extinct varieties of hominids had a substantial and, in some cases, continuous ridge of bone over both eyes. In modern humans, the torus is less pronounced and usually not continuous. Within particular groups, human males tend to have larger ridges than females, and this feature is examined when attempting to determine the sex of an individual from his or her cranium.

**survey:** The search for archaeological sites. Site survey often includes historical analysis of a study area, an examination of aerial photographs, a methodical surface inspection, and test excavations, all aimed at discovering the location where people lived in the past and left behind evidence of their presence.

**tells:** Artificial hills that develop, primarily in the Middle East, when sand accumulates around and over abandoned villages. In some instances, subsequent inhabitants of a region elect to construct their villages on the tops of tells. When this happens, the process can repeat itself and the tell grows in size when these subsequent habitations are abandoned and sand accumulates around and over them. In this way, some tells grow to a substantial height, enclosing a succession of villages, one on top of the other, providing a stratigraphic sequence of habitations.

**temper:** Material added to clay to improve its drying characteristics and to improve its strength. Temper commonly consists of sand, ground-up bits of shell, quartz grit, and small pieces of previously fired clay (called grog).

**test pit:** Preliminary excavations carried out in the search for subsurface archaeological evidence. Test pits are excavated in the initial surveying for sites yet to be discovered and also in the preliminary examination of sites in an attempt to ascertain site size and function.

**test pit forms:** Standardized forms for consistently recording information concerning the test pits excavated in an archaeological survey. Test pit forms will include, at least, the name and location of the project, a unique identifier for the pit (a number in a sequence along a transect, for example), a drawing of soil levels encountered with their depths recorded, a listing of any artifacts or ecofacts encountered in the soil levels of the pit and their precise depths recorded, a location of the test unit, the name of the excavator(s), and the date. Using a standardized form insures that every crew member records the same information about each pit and makes life infinitely easier for the person analyzing the results of a survey transect.

**test pitting:** The process of excavating test pits in an attempt to examine a sample of the soil below the ground surface of an area in the search for the archaeological components of sites.

**thermoluminescence (TL):** A variety of luminescence dating; see also optically stimulated luminescence. Buried objects are subject to naturally occurring radiation in the soil. The energy released by radioactive decay may accumulate in rock and clay. If rock or clay is heated to a high temperature by people (rock in a fireplace or clay when fired to make a pot), the energy previously accumulated is released. In other words, the human activity sets the energy accumulation clock to zero. When then buried, energy released by background radiation begins to accumulate again in the rock and fired clay at a regular rate. In thermoluminescence, heat is used to release the energy so accumulated. The amount of time since the "clock" was set to zero by people can be determined, thus dating the human activity and, therefore, the archaeological site.

**tibia:** The larger of the two bones of the lower leg. The smaller lower leg bone is the fibula. Feel your shin; that large, flat bone just below the surface of your skin is your tibia.

**TL:** See thermoluminescence.

**tool kit:** A tool kit is the entire assemblage of tools a past people made and used in an activity or set of activities. Look at the set of tools in your basement used in woodworking—hammers, saws, straightedges and fasteners such as nails and screws—that is a woodworking tool kit. Look at the pots and pans, spatulas, knives, bowls, and even the oven and stove in your kitchen—that is your food preparation tool kit. In the same way, the stone spear points and spear shafts, stone knives, and scraping tools represent the hunting tool kit of a past people.

**topographic maps:** Maps depicting the terrain of an area, including elevations. Archaeologists commonly use topographic maps published by the United States Geological Survey with a scale of 1:24,000. One inch on a map of this scale represents about 2,000 feet. Topographic maps, obviously, are of practical importance in locating archaeological sites. Also, in our attempt to understand how a past people used the landscape, we need to become familiar with that landscape; topographic maps are a useful tool in this effort.

**total station:** Surveying device that uses a laser transit to determine the precise distance and elevation of a point in space. A stadia rod is positioned at a location, the transit emits the beam of light which hits the rod and bounces back to a receiver in the total station. The distance and elevation of the locations being measured are then calculated and stored in the total station where the information can be downloaded to a computer.

**transects:** Lines through a project area along which test pits are excavated or surfaces are examined. Based on the sampling strategy developed for a particular project, transects may be located randomly or situated so as to cut across all of the various habitats found in a research area. The surface is scanned for surface remains and/or test pits are excavated along these transects at regular intervals and the subsurface examined for evidence of archaeological remains.

**unconsolidated material:** Geological deposit in which individual elements are separate and not cemented together. Sand and gravel, for instance, are representative of unconsolidated deposits.

**United States Geological Survey (USGS):** A branch of the United States Department of the Interior. Established in 1879, the USGS has as its job the monitoring of natural resources in the United States. As part of its mandate, the USGS produces topographic maps of the United States of numerous sizes and scales. The USGS maps most commonly used by archaeologists are the topographic quad sheets at 1:24,000 scale. Made from aerial photographs, these maps show major and minor drainages (rivers, streams, brooks), lakes, ponds, wetlands, cultural features (roads, buildings), and provide detailed topographic information. USGS quad sheets serve as good base maps for archaeological survey projects.

**Universal Transverse Mercator (UTM):** A metric mapping and measurement system. The Earth is divided into sixty numbered, north-south zones, each zone representing 6 degrees of the 360-degree, circular Earth when viewed from above the north pole. Measurements of the precise location of any point within a zone are expressed in metric. The boundaries of an archaeological site are often expressed using this system.

**USGS:** See United States Geological Survey.

**UTM:** See Universal Transverse Mercator.

**varve:** Sediments deposited annually in distinct and distinquishable layers along lake and ocean shorelines. Like tree rings in dendrochronology, by counting back varves from the most recently deposited layer (the current year), the precise calendar year date for each varve in a sequence can be determined. A carbon date derived from organic material extracted from a varve can be compared to the year date determined for that varve. When a sequence of such comparisons can be made, any pattern in the possible inaccuracy of the carbon dating technique through time can be assessed; in other words, it can be determined if carbon dates are consistently too old or too young for given stretches of time. Radiocarbon dates can then be calibrated or corrected by reference to the varve chronology.

**visibility:** Archaeological visibility is a relative measure of the ease with which archaeological remains can be spotted in a given area. Areas with high archaeological visibility may be characterized by slow natural processes that tend to cover material left on the surface, so even ancient materials may be exposed on the modern landscape. Vegetation growth also contributes to the degree of archaeological visibility; areas with rapid growth of thick vegetation present low levels of visibility while areas that are sparsely vegetated have higher levels of archaeological visibility.

**vitreous:** Glass-like. Vitreous rock tends to break predictably and controllably, producing sharp edges suitable for making cutting, piercing, and scraping tools. In many world areas, past people made tools from vitreous rock where it was locally available, and traded for it in locations where it was not.

**wear patterns:** The damage that accumulates on the working edge of a stone tool. When a stone edge is used to cut, slice, scrape, or pierce a material (wood, animal flesh, bone, antler, stone, and so on) the edge of the stone tool deteriorates though abrasion and breakage. This deterioration or wear is reflected in striations, polish, and microchippage. Each manner of use, combined with the raw material of the tool and the nature of the material on which the tool is being used, produces a unique pattern of wear on the tool itself. Examining the wear traces on an ancient stone tool, therefore, enables archaeologists to deduce the tool's function; how it was used and on what material.

**Wide Area Augmentation System:** A process added to the standard Global Positioning System that provides for even greater locational accuracy, down to about 2 meters.

# References

Adams, R. E. W. 1991. *Prehistoric Mesoamerica*. University of Oklahoma Press, Norman.

Adams, R. E. W., and F. V., Jr. 1997. Stratigraphy. In *Field Methods in Archaeology*, edited by T. R. Hester, H. J. Shafer, and K. L. Feder, 235–52. Mayfield Publishing, Mountain View, California.

Ames, K. M., and H. D. G. Maschner. 1999. *Peoples of the Northwest Coast*. Thames and Hudson, London.

Arnold, B., and N. L. Wicker, eds. 2001. *Gender and the Archaeology of Death*. Rowman and Littlefield, Lanham, Maryland.

Arnold, D. 1991. *Building in Egypt: Pharaonic Stone Masonry*. Oxford University Press, Oxford.

Ashmore, W., and R. J. Sharer. 1999. *Discovering Our Past: A Brief Introduction to Archaeology*. Mayfield Publishing, Mountain View, California.

Baillie, M. G. L. 1990. *Tree Ring Dating and Archaeology*. University of Chicago Press, Chicago.

Baker, B. W., B. S. Shaffer, and D. G. Steele. 1997.Basic approaches in archaeological faunal analysis. In *Field Methods in Archaeology*, edited by T. R. Hester, H. J. Shafer, and K. L. Feder, 298–318. Mayfield Publishing, Mountain View, California.

Bard, E. 2001. Extending the calibrated radiocarbon record. *Science* 292:2443–44.

Barnes, M. 1997a. Inca. In *Secrets of Lost Empires*. Nova. WGBH, Boston.

———. 1997b. Obelisk. In *Secrets of Lost Empires*. Nova. WGBH, Boston.

———. 1997c. Pyramid. In *Secrets of Lost Empires*. Nova. WGBH, Boston.

Bass, W. 1987. *Human Osteology: A Laboratory and Field Manual of the Human Skeleton*. Missouri Archaeological Society, Columbia.

Beck, J. W., D. A. Richards, R. Lawrence, B. W. Silverman, P. L. Smart, D. J. Donahue, S. Hererra-Osterheld, G. S. Burr, L. Calsoyas, A. J. Timothy, and D. Biddulph. 2001. Extremely large variations of atmospheric 14C concentration during the last glacial period. *Science* 292:2453–58.

Bellantoni, N. F. 2001. Ticked off: Lyme disease and archaeologists. In *Dangerous Places: Health, Safety, and Archaeology*, edited by D. Poirier and K. L. Feder, 3–10. Bergin and Garvey, Westport, Connecticut.

Bellantoni, N. F., P. Sledzik, and D. A. Poirier. 1997. Rescue, research, and reburial: Walton Family Cemetery. In *In Remembrance: Archaeology and Death*, edited by D. Poirier and N. F. Bellantoni, 131–53. Bergin and Garvey, Westport, Connecticut.

Bernstein, D. J. 1999. Prehistoric use of plant foods on Long Island and Block Island Sounds. In *Current Northeast Paleoethnobotany*, edited by J. P. Hart, 101–19. New York State Museum, Albany.

Binford, L. R. 1962. Archaeology as anthropology. *American Antiquity* 28:217–25.

―――. 1968. Archaeological perspectives. In *New Perspectives in Archaeology,* edited by S. R. Binford and L. R. Binford, 5–32. Aldine Publishing, Chicago.

―――. 1978. *Nunamiut Ethnoarchaeology.* Academic Press, New York.

―――. 1987. *Bones: Ancient Men and Modern Myths.* Academic Press, New York.

Biolsi, T., and L. Zimmerman, eds. 1997. *Indians and Anthropologists: Vine Deloria, Jr., and the Critique of Anthropology.* University of Tucson Press, Tucson.

Bowman, S. 1990. *Radiocarbon Dating.* University of California Press, Berkeley.

Bradley, B. 1989. *Flintknapping.* Produced by InterPARK and Primitive Tech. Enterprises. Cortez, Colorado.

Brothwell, D. R. 1972. *Digging Up Bones: The Excavation, Treatment, and Study of Human Skeletal Remains.* British Museum, London.

Bryant, Jr., V. M., and R. G. Holloway. 1983. The role of palynology in archaeology. In *Advances in Archaeological Method and Theory,* edited by M. B. Schiffer, 191–224. Academic Press, New York.

Buckley, T. 1976. The discovery of Tutankhamun's tomb. In *The Treasures of Tutankhamun,* edited by K. S. Gilbert, J. K. Holt, and S. Hudson, 9–18. The Metropolitan Museum of Art, New York.

Burns, K. R. 1999. *The Forensic Anthropology Training Manual.* Prentice Hall, Upper Saddle River, New Jersey.

Butzer, K. W. 1982. *Archaeology as Human Ecology.* Cambridge University Press, Cambridge, England.

Byers, S. N. 2001. *Introduction to Forensic Anthropology: A Textbook.* Allyn and Bacon, Boston.

Cannon, K. P. 1995. Blood residue analyses of ancient stone tools reveal clues to prehistoric subsistence patterns in Yellowstone. *CRM* 18(2):14–16.

Cantwell, A.-M., and D. d. Wall. 2001. *Unearthing Gotham.* Yale University Press, New Haven, Connecticut.

Carter, R. J. 1997. Age estimation of the roe deer (*Capreolus capreolus*) mandibles from the Mesolithic site of Star Carr, Yorkshire, based on radiographs of mandibular tooth development. *Journal of the Zoological Society of London* 241:495–502.

Chalifoux, É. 1999. Paleoindian occupations on the Gaspé Peninsula. *Northeast Anthropology* 57:69–79.

Champlain, S. d. 1966. *Voyages of Samuel de Champlain.* Burt Franklin, New York.

Chang, K.-c. 1986. *The Archaeology of Ancient China.* 4th ed. Yale University Press, New Haven, Connecticut.

Chaplin, R. E. 1971. *The Study of Animal Bones from Archaeological Sites.* Seminar Press, London.

Chartkoff, J. L. 1978. Transect sampling in forests. *American Antiquity* 43:46–52.

Chartkoff, J. L., and K. K. Chartkoff. 1980. *The Discovery of Archaeological Sites: A Review of Methods and Techniques.* U.S. Forest Service.

Chauvet, J.-M., É. Deschamps, and C. Hillaire. 1996. *Dawn of Art: The Chauvet Cave.* Harry N. Abrams, New York.

Childe, V. G. 1942. *What Happened in History.* Pelican Books, Baltimore.

Claasen, C. P., ed. 1994. *Women in Archaeology.* University of Pennsylvania Press, Philadelphia.

Clarke, D., and P. Maguire. 1995. *Skara Brae: Northern Europe's Best Preserved Prehistoric Village.* Historic Edinburgh, Scotland.

Clarke, D. L. 1978. *Analytical Archaeology.* Columbia University Press, New York.

Clayton, P. A. 1994. *Chronicle of the Pharaohs: The Reign-by-Reign Record of the Rulers and Dynasties of Ancient Egypt.* Thames and Hudson, London.

Coe, M. D. 1993. *The Maya.* Thames and Hudson, New York.

Coles, J. M. 1997. *Experimental Archaeology.* Academic Press, London.

Conyers, L. B. 1995. The use of ground penetrating radar to map the buried structures and landscape of the Ceren Site, El Salvador. *Geoarchaeology* 10:275–99.

Conyers, L. B., and D. Goodman. 1997. *Ground-Penetrating Radar: An Introduction for Archaeologists.* Altamira Press, Walnut Creek, California.

Cordell, L. 1994. Ancient Pueblo Peoples. *Exploring the Ancient World.* Smithsonian Books, Washington, D.C.

Crabtree, D. E. 1982. *An Introduction to Flint Working.* Idaho Museum of Natural History, Pocatello.

Cummins, H., and C. Midlo. 1961. *Fingerprints, Palms, and Sols.* Dover, New York.

Dalrymple, G. B., and M. A. Lanphere. 1969. *Potassium-Argon Dating.* W. H. Freeman, San Francisco.

Dancey, W. S. 1981. *Archaeological Field Methods: An Introduction.* Burgess International Group, New York.

David, N., and C. Kramer. 2001. *Ethnoarchaeology in Action.* Cambridge University Press, Cambridge, England.

Davis, M. B. 1969a. Climatic changes in southern Connecticut recorded by pollen deposition at Rogers Lake. *Ecology* 50:409–22.

———. 1969b. Palynology and environmental history during the Quaternary period. *American Scientist* 57:317–32.

Davis, S. J. M. 1995. *The Archaeology of Animals.* Yale University Press, New Haven, Connecticut.

Deetz, J. 1965. *The Dynamics of Stylistic Change in Arikara Ceramics.* University of Illinois Series in Anthropology 4. University of Illinois, Urbana.

Deino, A., P. R. Renne, and C. C. Swisher III. 1998. 40Ar/39Ar dating in paleoanthropology and archaeology. *Evolutionary Anthropology* 6(2):63–75.

Deloria Jr., V. 1995. *Red Earth, White Lies: Native Americans and the Myth of Scientific Fact.* Scribner's, New York.

Derenko, M. V., T. Grzybowski, B. A. Malyarchuk, J. Czarny, D. Miscicka-Sliwka, and I. A. Zakharov. 2001. The presence of mitochondrial haplogroup X in Altaians from South Siberia. *American Journal of Human Genetics* 69:237–41.

Dethlefsen, E., and J. Deetz. 1966. Death's heads, cherubs, and willow trees: Experimental archaeology in colonial cemeteries. *American Antiquity* 31:502–10.

Dillehay, T. D. 2000. *The Settlement of the Americas: A New Prehistory.* Basic Books, New York.

Dillon, B. D. 1993. *Practical Archaeology: Field and Laboratory Techniques and Archaeological Logistics.* Institute of Archaeology, Los Angeles.

Dimbleby, G. W. 1985. *The Palynology of Archaeological Sites.* Academic Press, London.

Dincauze, D. F. 1976. *The Neville Site: Eight Thousand Years at Amoskeag.* Peabody Museum of Archaeology and Ethnology, Cambridge, Massachusetts.

———. 1978. Surveying for cultural resources: Don't rush out with a shovel. In *Conservation Archaeology in the Northeast: Toward a Research Orientation,* edited by A. Speiss, vol. 3, 51–59. Peabody Museum of Archaeology and Ethnology, Cambridge, Massachusetts.

Dixon, E. J. 1999. *Bones, Boats, and Bison: Archaeology and the First Colonization of Western North America.* University of New Mexico Press, Albuquerque.

Dunnell, R. C. 1992. The notion site. In *Space, Time, and Archaeological Landscapes,* edited by J. Rossignol and L. Wandsnider, 21–41. Plenum Publishing, New York.

Ebert, J. I. 1992. *Distributional Archaeology.* University of New Mexico Press, Albuquerque.

Echo-Hawk, R. 1997. Forging a new ancient history for Native America. In *Native Americans and Archaeologists: Stepping Stones to Common Ground*, edited by N. Swindler, K. E. Dongoske, R. Anyon, and A. S. Downer, 88–102. Altamira Press, Walnut Creek, California.

El-Rabbany, A. 2002. *Introduction to GPS: The Global Positioning System*. Artech House, Boston.

Fagan, B. 1994. *Quest for the Past: Great Discoveries in Archaeology*. Waveland Press, Prospect Heights, Illinois.

Fagan, B. M., ed. 1996. *Eyewitness to Discovery: First-Person Accounts of More than Fifty of the World's Greatest Archaeological Discoveries*. Oxford University Press, Oxford.

———. 2000. *In the Beginning: An Introduction to Archaeology*. 7th ed. Prentice Hall, Upper Saddle River, New Jersey.

———. 2002. *Archaeology: A Brief Introduction*. 4th ed. Prentice Hall, Upper Saddle River, New Jersey.

Feder, K. L. 1983. "The avaricious humour of designing Englishmen": The ethnohistory of land transactions in the Farmington Valley. *Bulletin of the Archaeological Society of Connecticut* 45:29–40.

———. 1994. *A Village of Outcasts: Historical Archaeology and Documentary Research at the Lighthouse Site*. Mayfield Publishing, Mountain View, California.

———. 1997a. Data preservation: Recording and collecting. In *Field Methods in Archaeology*, edited by T. R. Hester, H. J. Shafer, and K. L. Feder, 113–42. Mayfield Publishing, Mountain View, California.

———. 1997b. Site survey. In *Field Methods in Archaeology*, edited by T. R. Hester, H. J. Shafer, and K. L. Feder, 41–68. Mayfield Publishing, Mountain View, California.

———. 1999a. Indians and archaeologists: Conflicting views of myth and science. *Skeptic* 5(3):74–80.

———. 1999b. *Lessons from the Past*. Mayfield Publishing, Mountain View, California.

———. 2001. Prehistoric land-use patterns in north-central Connecticut: A matter of scale. In *Archaeology of the Appalachian Highlands*, edited by L. P. Sullivan and S. C. Prezzano, 19–30. University of Tennessee Press, Knoxville.

———. 2002. *Frauds, Myths, and Mysteries: Science and Pseudoscience in Archaeology*. McGraw-Hill/Mayfield Publishing, Mountain View, California.

Feder, K. L., and M. A. Park. 2001. *Human Antiquity: An Introduction to Physical Anthropology and Archaeology*. Mayfield Publishing, Mountain View, California.

Fedje, D. W., and H. Josenhans. 2000. Drowned forests and archaeology on the continental shelf of British Columbia, Canada. *Geology* 28:99–102.

Ferguson, L. 1992. *Uncommon Ground: Archaeology and Early African America, 1650–1800*. Smithsonian Institution Press, Washington, D.C.

Fink, T. M., and K. K. Komatsu. 2001. The fungus among us: *Coccidioidomycosis* ("Valley Fever"). In *Dangerous Places: Health, Safety, and Archaeology*, edited by D. Poirier and K. L. Feder, 21–30. Bergin and Garvey, Westport, Connecticut.

Flannery, K. V. 1982. The golden Marshalltown: A parable for the archaeology of the 1980s. *American Anthropologist* 84:265–78.

Fleming, S. J. 1977. *Dating in Archaeology: A Guide to Scientific Techniques*. Palgrave Macmillan, New York.

Frere, J. 1800. Account of flint weapons discovered in Hoxne in Suffolk. *Archaeologia* 13:204–5.

Frison, G., ed. 1974. *The Casper Site: A Hell Gap Bison Kill on the High Plains*. Academic Press, New York.

Gero, J. M. 1997. Genderlithics: Women's roles in stone tool production. In *Engendering Archaeology: Women and Prehistory*, edited by J. M. Gero and M. W. Conkey, 163–93. Blackwell, Oxford.

Gero, J. M., and M. W. Conkey, eds. 1997. *Engendering Archaeology: Women and Prehistory.* Blackwell, Oxford.

Gifford-Gonzalez, D. 1993. You can hide, but you can't run: Representation of women's work in illustrations of Paleolithic life. *Visual Anthropology Review* 9(1):23–41.

Gilbert, B. M. 1973. *Mammalian Osteo-Archaeology: North America.* Missouri Archaeological Society, Columbia.

Gilchrist, R. 1999. *Gender and Archaeology: Contesting the Past.* Routledge, London.

Gramly, R. M. 1982. *The Vail Site: A Palaeo-Indian Encampment in Maine.* Bulletin of the Buffalo Society of Natural Sciences, Buffalo.

Grayson, D. K. 1983. *The Establishment of Human Antiquity.* Academic Press, New York.

Greer, A., ed. 2000. *The Jesuit Relations: Natives and Missionaries in Seventeenth-Century North America.* Bedford/St. Martin's Press, New York.

Grün, R. 1993. Electron spin resonance dating in paleoanthropology. *Evolutionary Anthropology* 2(5):172–81.

Guzzo, P. G., A. D'Ambrosio, and A. Foglia. 2000. *Pompeii.* Getty Trust Publication, Los Angeles.

Hardesty, D. L. 1997. *The Archaeology of the Donner Party.* University of Nevada Press, Reno.

Harris, E. C. 1979. The laws of archaeological stratigraphy. *World Archaeology* 11:111–17.

———. 1997. *Principles of Archaeological Stratigraphy.* Academic Press, New York.

Harris, E. C., G. J. Brown, and M. R. Brown III, eds. 1993. *Practices of Archaeological Stratigraphy.* Academic Press, New York.

Harrison, G. G., W. L. Rathje, and W. W. Hughes. 1975. Food waste behavior in an urban population. *Journal of Nutrition Education* 7(1):13–16.

Haviland, W. 2001. *Cultural Anthropology.* Wadsworth, Belmont, California.

Hesse, B., and P. Wapnish. 1985. *Animal Bone Archaeology.* Manuals on Archaeology 5. Taraxacum, Washington, D.C.

Hester, T. R. 1997a. Methods of excavation. In *Field Methods in Archaeology*, edited by T. R. Hester, H. J. Shafer, and K. L. Feder, 69–112. Mayfield Publishing, Mountain View, California.

———. 1997b. The handling and conservation of artifacts in the field. In *Field Methods in Archaeology*, edited by T. R. Hester, H. J. Shafer, and K. L. Feder, 143–58. Mayfield Publishing, Mountain View, California.

Higham, C. 2001. *The Civilization of Angkor.* University of California Press, Berkeley.

Hillson, S. 1996. *Dental Anthropology.* Cambridge University Press, Cambridge, England.

Hoadley, R. B. 1990. *Identifying Wood: Accurate Results with Simple Tools.* Taunton Press, Newtown, Connecticut.

Holloway, R. G. 1997. Excavation and recovery of botanical materials from archaeological sites. In *Field Methods in Archaeology*, edited by T. R. Hester, H. J. Shafer, and K. L. Feder, 283–97. Mayfield Publishing, Mountain View, California.

Hotchkiss, N. J. 1999. *A Comprehensive Guide to Land Navigation with GPS.* Alexis Publishing, Leesburg, Virginia.

Hoving, T. 1978. *Tutankhamun, the Untold Story.* Simon and Schuster, New York.

Hurst, W. J., S. M. Tark, Jr. T. G. Powis, F. Valdez, Jr., and T. R. Hester. 2002. Cacao usage by the earliest Maya civilization. *Nature* 418:289–90.

Iseminger, W. R. 1996. Mighty Cahokia. *Archaeology* 49(3):30–37.

Jemison, G. P. 1997. Who owns the past? In *Native Americans and Archaeologists: Stepping Stones to Common Ground,* edited by N. Swindler, K. E. Dongoske, R. Anyon, and A. S. Downer, 57–63. Altamira Press, Walnut Creek, California.

Johnston, R. B. 1964. *Proton Magnetometry and Its Application to Archaeology: An Evaluation at Angel Site.* Research Series. Indiana Historical Society, Indianapolis.

Juli, H., J. Trimble, and M. Monce. 2003. Trade and tribal boundaries in late prehistoric southern New England: A proton induced x-ray emission (PIXE) analysis of Connecticut prehistoric ceramics. *Northeast Anthropology.* In Press.

Keeley, L. 1980. *Experimental Determination of Stone Tool Use: A Microwear Analysis.* University of Chicago Press, Chicago.

King, T. F. 1998. *Cultural Resource Laws and Practice: An Introductory Guide.* Altamira Press, Walnut Creek, California.

King, T. F., P. P. Hickman, and G. Berg. 1977. *Anthropology in Historic Preservation: Caring for Culture's Clutter.* Academic Press, New York.

King, T. F., R. S. Jacobson, K. R. Burns, and K. Spading. 2001. *Amelia Earhart's Shoes: Is the Mystery Solved?* Altamira Press, Walnut Creek, California.

Kintigh, K. W. 1988. The effectiveness of subsurface testing: A simulation approach. *American Antiquity* 53:686–707.

Kitagawa, H., and J. van der Plicht. 1998. Atmospheric radiocarbon calibration to 45,000 BP: Late glacial fluctuations and cosmogenic isotope production. *Science* 279:1187–90.

Klein, R. G., and K. Cruz-Uribe. 1984. *The Analysis of Animal Bones from Archaeological Sites.* University of Chicago Press, Chicago.

Knapton, L. K. 1997. Archaeological mapping, site grids, and surveying. In *Field Methods in Archaeology,* edited by T. R. Hester, H. Shafer, and K. L. Feder, 177–234. Mayfield Publishing, Mountain View, California.

Konefes, J. L., and M. K. McGee. 2001. Old cemeteries, arsenic, and health safety. In *Dangerous Places: Health, Safety, and Archaeology,* edited by D. Poirier and K. L. Feder, 79–106. Bergin and Garvey, Westport, Connecticut.

Kooyman, B. P. 2002. *Understanding Stone Tools and Archaeological Sites.* University of New Mexico Press, Albuquerque.

Kottak, C. 2004. *Anthropology: The Exploration of Human Diversity.* McGraw-Hill, New York.

Krajick, K. 2002. Melting glaciers release ancient relics. *Science* 296:454–56.

Krakker, J. J., M. J. Shott, and P. D. Welch. 1983. Design and evaluation of shovel-test sampling in regional archaeology. *Journal of Field Archaeology* 10:469–80.

Kroeber, T., K. Kroeber, and L. Gannett. 2002. *Ishi in Two Worlds: A Biography of the Last Wild Indian in North America.* University of California Press, Berkeley.

Krogman, W. M. 1951. The scars of human evolution. *Scientific American* 185:54–57.

———. 1973. *The Human Skeleton in Forensic Medicine.* Charles C. Thomas, Springfield, Illinois.

Kromer, B., and M. Spurk. 1998. Revision and tentative extension of the tree-ring based 14C calibration, 9,200–11,855 cal BP. *Radiocarbon* 40(3):1117–26.

Lavin, L. 1997. Diversity in southern New England ceramics: Three case studies. *Bulletin of the Archaeological Society of Connecticut* 60:83–96.

———. 1998. The Windsor tradition: Pottery production and popular identity in southern New England. *Northeast Anthropology* 56:1–17.

Lavin, L., and R. Kra. 1994. Prehistoric pottery assemblages from southern Connecticut: A fresh look at ceramic classification in southern New England. *Bulletin of the Archaeological Society of Connecticut* 57:35–51.

Leakey, M. 1971. *Olduvai Gorge* 3. Cambridge University Press, Cambridge, England.

Leakey, M., and A. Walker. 1997. Early hominid fossils from Africa. *Scientific American* 276(6):74–79.

Leakey, M. D., and R. L. Hay. 1979. Pliocene footprints in the Laetolil Beds at Laetoli, northern Tanzania. *Nature* 278:317–23.

Leakey, R., and R. Lewin. 1992. *Origins Reconsidered: In Search of What Makes Us Human.* Doubleday, New York.

Lehner, M. 1997. *The Complete Pyramids.* Thames and Hudson, New York.

Letham, L. 2001. *GPS Made Easy.* Mountaineers Books, Seattle.

Libby, W. F. 1952. *Radiocarbon Dating.* Chicago University Press, Chicago.

Lightfoot, K. G. 1986. Regional surveys in the Eastern United States: The strengths and weaknesses of implementing subsurface testing programs. *American Antiquity* 51:484–504.

Linck, D., and J. W. Vann III. 2001. Dig fast, die young: Unexploded ordnance and archaeology. In *Dangerous Places: Health, Safety, and Archaeology,* edited by D. Poirier and K. L. Feder, 169–88. Bergin and Garvey, Westport, Connecticut.

Lippert, D. 1997. In front of the mirror: Native Americans and academic archaeology. In *Native Americans and Archaeologists: Stepping Stones to Common Ground,* edited by N. Swindler, K. E. Dongoske, R. Anyon, and A. S. Downer, 120–27. Altamira Press, Walnut Creek, California.

Longacre, W. A., ed. 1991. *Ceramic Ethnoarchaeology.* University of Arizona Press, Tucson.

Longacre, W. A., and J. M. Skibo, eds. 1994. *Kalinga Ethnoarchaeology: Expanding Archaeological Method and Theory.* Smithsonian Institution Press, Washington, D.C.

Lovis, W. A. 1976. Quarter sections and forests: An example of probability sampling in the Northeastern woodlands. *American Antiquity* 41:364–71.

Loy, T. H., and E. J. Dixon. 1998. Blood residues on fluted points from Eastern Beringia indicate mammoth predation as part of a big-game hunting tradition. *American Antiquity* 63:21–46.

Luedtke, B. E. 1992. *An Archaeologist's Guide to Chert and Flint.* Archaeological Research Tools 7. University of California Press, Los Angeles.

MacDonald, G. F. 1985. *Debert: A Paleo-Indian Site in Central Nova Scotia.* Persimmon Press, Buffalo.

MacNeish, R. S. 1967. An interdisciplinary approach to an archaeological problem. In *Prehistory of the Tehuacan Valley: Volume One—Environment and Subsistence,* edited by D. Beyers, 14–23. University of Texas Press, Austin.

Mannikka, E. 1996. *Angkor Wat: Time, Space, and Kingship.* University of Hawaii Press, Honolulu.

Marquardt, W. H., and C. Crumley. 1987. Theoretical issues in the analysis of spatial patterning. In *Regional Dynamics: Burgundian Landscapes in Historical Perspective,* edited by C. L. Crumley and W. H. Marquardt, 1–18. Academic Press, San Diego.

McGimsey III, C. R. 1972. *Public Archaeology.* Seminar Press, New York.

McKee, L. 1995. The earth is their witness. *The Sciences* 35(2):36–41.

McManamon, F. P. 1984. Discovering sites unseen. In *Advances in Archaeological Method and Theory,* edited by M. B. Schiffer, vol. 7, 223–92. Academic Press, New York.

McPherron, S. P., and H. L. Dibble. 2002. *Using Computers in Archaeology.* McGraw-Hill, New York.

McWeeney, L. 2002. *The Charcoal Evidence from the Firetown North and Paine Sites, Granby, Connecticut.* Unpublished ms.

Meltzer, D. J. 1993. Search for the first Americans. In *Smithsonian: Exploring the Ancient World.* Smithsonian Books, Washington, D.C.

———. 1997. Monte Verde and the Pleistocene Peopling of America. *Science* 276: 754–55.

Mercader, J., M. Panger, and C. Boesch. 2002. Excavation of a chimpanzee stone tool site in the African rainforest. *Science* 296:1452–55.

Messenger, P. M., ed. 1993. *The Ethics of Collecting Cultural Property: Whose Culture? Whose Property?* University of New Mexico Press, Albuquerque.

Michels, J. W. 1973. *Dating Methods in Archaeology.* Seminar Press, New York.

Morganti, T., and N. Tartt. 2001. Rabies: A short discourse. In *Dangerous Places: Health, Safety, and Archaeology,* edited by D. Poirier and K. L. Feder, 11–20. Bergin and Garvey, Westport, Connecticut.

Mozina, M. 2003. *Archaeology Fieldwork Bulletin.* Archaeological Institute of America, Boston.

Mueller, J. 1975. *Sampling in Archaeology.* University of Arizona Press, Phoenix.

Nance, J. D., and B. F. Ball. 1986. No surprises? The reliability and validity of test pit sampling. *American Antiquity* 51:457–83.

O'Brien, M. J., and R. L. Lyman. 1999. *Seriation, Stratigraphy, and Index Fossils: The Backbone of Archaeological Dating.* Kluwer Academic Publishers, New York.

O'Connor, T. 2000. *The Archaeology of Animal Bones.* Texas A&M Press, College Station.

Olin, J. S., and A. D. Franklin, eds. 1982. *Archaeological Ceramics.* Smithsonian Institution Press, Washington, D.C.

Olson, S. J. 1985. *Origins of the Domestic Dog: The Fossil Record.* University of Arizona Press, Tucson.

Orton, C. 2000. *Sampling in Archaeology.* Cambridge University Press, Cambridge, England.

Orton, C., P. Tyers, and A. Vince. 1993. *Pottery in Archaeology.* Cambridge University Press, Cambridge, England.

Page, C., and J. Cort. 1997a. Colosseum. In *Secrets of Lost Empires.* Nova. WGBH, Boston.

———. 1997b. Stonehenge. In *Secrets of Lost Empires.* Nova. WGBH, Boston.

Park, M. A. 2002. *Biological Anthropology.* McGraw-Hill, New York.

———. 2003. *Introducing Anthropology: An Integrated Approach.* McGraw-Hill, New York.

Pascua, M. P. 1991. A Makah village in 1491: Ozette. *National Geographic* 180(4):38–53.

Pearsall, D. M. 2000. *Paleoethnobotany: A Handbook of Procedures.* Academic Press, San Diego.

Pearson, M. P. 2001. *The Archaeology of Death and Burial.* Texas A&M University Press, Austin.

Pennisi, E. 2002. A shaggy dog history. *Science* 298:1540–42.

Perry, W., and M. Blakey. 1997. Archaeology as community service: The African Burial Ground Project in New York City. *North American Dialogue* 2(1):1–5.

Piperno, D., and K. Flannery. 2001. The earliest archaeological maize (*Zea mays* L.). *Proceedings of the National Academy of Sciences* 98:2101–3.

Piperno, D., and K. A. Stothert. 2003. Phytolith evidence for early Holocene *Cucurbita* domestication in southwest Ecuador. *Science* 299:1054–57.

Piperno, D. R., and D. M. Pearsall. 1998. *The Origins of Agriculture in the Lowland Neotropics.* Academic Press, Orlando, Florida.

Piperno, D. R., A. J. Ranere, I. Holst, and P. Hansell. 2000. Starch grains reveal early root crop horticulture in the Panamanian tropical forest. *Nature* 407:894–97.

Poirier, D., and K. L. Feder, eds. 2001. *Dangerous Places: Health, Safety, and Archaeology.* Bergin and Garvey, Westport, Connecticut.

Price, T. D., ed. 1989. *The Chemistry of Prehistoric Bone.* Cambridge University Press, Cambridge, England.

Price, T. D., M. J. Schoeninger, and G. J. Armelagos. 1985. Bone chemistry and past behavior: An overview. *Journal of Human Evolution* 14:419–47.

Rapp, G., J. Allert, V. Vitali, Z. Jing, and E. Henrickson. 2000. *Determining Archaeological Sources of Artifact Copper Source Characterization Using Trace Element Analysis.* University Press of America, Lanham, Maryland.

Rathburn, T. 1987. Health and disease at a South Carolina plantation. *American Journal of Physical Anthropology* 74:239–53.

Rathje, W., and C. Murphy. 1992. *Rubbish: The Archaeology of Garbage.* HarperCollins, New York.

Reitz, E. J. 1999. *Zooarchaeology.* Cambridge University Press, Cambridge, England.

———. 2000. *Archaeology: Theories, Method, and Practice.* Thames and Hudson, New York.

Reno, R. L., S. R. Bloyd, and D. L. Hardesty. 2001. Chemical soup: Archaeological hazards at western ore-processing sites. In *Dangerous Places: Health, Safety, and Archaeology,* edited by D. Poirier and K. L. Feder, 205–20. Bergin and Garvey, Westport, Connecticut.

Rhine, S. 1998. *Bone Voyage.* University of New Mexico Press, Santa Fe.

Rice, P. C. 1998. *Doing Archaeology: A Hands-On Laboratory Manual.* Mayfield Publishing, Mountain View, California.

Richards, M. P., P. P. Pettitt, E. Trinkaus, F. H. Smith, M., Paunovi, and I. Karavani. 2000. Neanderthal diet at Vindija and Neanderthal predation: The evidence from stable isotopes. *Proceedings of the National Academy of Sciences* 97:7663–66.

Ritchie, A. 1995. *Prehistoric Orkney.* B.T. Batsford, London.

Roberts, M. 2001. Beneath city streets: Brief observations on the urban landscape. In *Dangerous Places: Health, Safety, and Archaeology,* edited by D. Poirier and K. L. Feder, 157–68. Bergin and Garvey, Westport, Connecticut.

Rye, O. S. 1981. *Pottery Technology: Principles and Reconstruction.* Taraxacum, Washington, D.C.

Sabloff, J. A. 1989. *The Cities of Ancient Mexico: Reconstructing a Lost World.* Thames and Hudson, New York.

Sandford, M. K. 1992. A reconsideration of trace element analysis. In *Skeletal Biology of Past Peoples: Research Methods,* edited by S. R. Saunders and A. M. Katzenberg, 153–74. Wiley-Liss, New York.

Saul, F. P. 1972. *The Human Skeletal Remains of Altar de Sacrificios.* Papers of the Peabody Museum of Archaeology and Ethnology 63, Cambridge, Massachusetts.

Saunders, C., and S. R. Chandler. 2001. Get the lead out. In *Dangerous Places: Health, Safety, and Archaeology,* edited by D. Poirier and K. L. Feder, 189–204. Bergin and Garvey, Westport, Connecticut.

Schele, L., and D. Freidel. 1990. *A Forest of Kings.* Quill William Morrow, New York.

Schele, L., and P. Mathews. 1998. *The Code of Kings: The Language of Seven Sacred Maya Temples and Tombs.* Scribner's, New York.

Schick, K. D., and N. Toth. 1993. *Making Silent Stones Speak: Human Evolution and the Dawn of Technology.* Simon and Schuster, New York.

Schiffer, M. B. 1972. Archaeological context and systemic context. *American Antiquity* 37:156–65.

———. 1975. Archaeology as a behavioral science. *American Anthropologist* 77: 836–48.

———. 1976. *Behavioral Archaeology.* Academic Press, New York.

———. 1983. Toward the identification of site formation processes. *American Antiquity* 48:673–706.

———. 1987. *Formation Processes of the Archaeological Record.* University of New Mexico Press, Albuquerque.

Schiffer, M. B., A. P. Sullivan, and T. C. Klinger. 1978. The design of archaeological surveys. *World Archaeology* 10:1–28.

Schultz, E. A., and R. H. Lavenda. 2000. *Anthropology: A Perspective on the Human Condition.* McGraw-Hill, New York.

Schweingruber, F. H. 1988. *Tree Rings: Basics and Applications of Dendrochronology.* D. Reidel Publishing, Boston.

Scott, D., R. A. Fox, Jr., M. Conner, and J. Harmon. 1989. *Archaeological Perspectives on the Battle of the Little Big Horn.* University of Oklahoma Press, Norman.

Scott, G. R. and C. G. Turner II. 2000. *The Anthropology of Modern Human Teeth: Dental Morphology and Its Variation in Recent Human Populations.* Cambridge University Press, Cambridge, England.

Sebastian, L. 1992. *The Chaco Anasazi: Sociopolitical Evolution in the Prehistoric Southwest.* Cambridge University Press, New York.

Shafer, H. 1997a. Goals of archaeological investigation. In *Field Methods in Archaeology,* edited by T. R. Hester, H. J. Shafer, and K. L. Feder, 5–20. Mayfield Publishing, Mountain View, California.

Shafer, H. J. 1997b. Research design and sampling techniques. In *Field Methods in Archaeology,* edited by T. R. Hester, H. Shafer, and K. L. Feder, 21–40. Mayfield Publishing, Mountain View, California.

Shapiro, G., and J. M. Williams. 1982. *A Search for the Eighteenth Century Village at Michilimackinac: A Soil Resistivity Survey.* Mackinac State Parks, Mackinaw City, Michigan.

Sharer, R. J., and W. Ashmore. 2003. *Archaeology: Discovering Our Past.* 2d ed. McGraw-Hill, New York.

Shepard, A. 1982. *Ceramics for the Archaeologist.* Carnegie Institute of Washington, Washington, D.C.

Shott, M. J. 1989. Shovel test sampling in archaeological survey: Comments on Nance and Ball and Lightfoot. *American Antiquity* 54:396–404.

Smith, A. L. 1972. *Excavations at Altar de Sacrificios.* Papers of the Peabody Museum of Archaeology and Ethnology 62, Cambridge, Massachusetts.

Smith, B. D. 1995. *The Emergence of Agriculture.* Scientific American Library, New York.

Solecki, R. 1971. *Shanidar: The First Flower People.* Knopf, New York.

Spindler, K. 1994. *The Man in the Ice.* Harmony Books, New York.

Staeck, J. 2002. *Back to the Earth: An Introduction to Archaeology.* McGraw-Hill, New York.

Steinitz, M. 2002. Tree-ring dates offer insight on Massachusetts buildings. In *Preservation Advocate,* pp. 1, 6–7, 10.

Stewart, R. M. 2002. *Archaeology: Basic Field Methods.* Kendall/Hunt Publishing, Dubuque, Iowa.

Stiebing Jr., W. H. 1993. *Uncovering the Past: A History of Archaeology.* Oxford University Press, New York.

Stuiver, M., and J. van der Plicht. 1998. Intcal 98: Calibration issue. *Radiocarbon* 40(3).

Sullivan, R. 1998. *The Meadowlands.* Scribner's, New York.

Sutton, M. Q., and B. S. Arkush. 2002. *Archaeological Laboratory Methods: An Introduction.* Kendall/Hunt Publishing, Dubuque, Iowa.

Swindler, N., K. E. Dongoske, R. Anyon, and A. S. Downer, eds. 1997. *Native Americans and Archaeologists: Stepping Stones to Common Ground.* Altamira Press, Walnut Creek, California.

Taylor, R. E. 1987. *Radiocarbon Dating: An Archaeological Perspective.* Academic Press, London.

Taylor, R. E., and M. J. Aitken, eds. 1997. *Chronometric Dating in Archaeology.* Plenum Publishing, New York.

Thomas, D. H. 1998a. *Archaeology.* 3d ed. Wadsworth, Belmont, California.

———. 1998b. *Archaeology: Down to Earth.* Wadsworth, Belmont, California.

———. 2001. *Skull Wars: Kennewick Man, Archaeology, and the Battle for Native American Identity.* Basic Books, New York.

Tringham, R., G. Cooper, G. Odell, B. Voytek, and A. Whitman. 1974. Experimentation in the formation of edge damage: A new approach to lithic analysis. *Journal of Field Archaeology* 1:171–96.

Tsosie, R. 1997. Indigenous rights and archaeology. In *Native Americans and Archaeologists: Stepping Stones to Common Ground,* edited by N. Swindler, K. E. Dongoske, R. Anyon, and A. S. Downer, 64–76. Altamira Press, Walnut Creek, California.

Ubelaker, D. H. 1978. *Human Skeletal Remains: Excavation, Analysis, Interpretation.* Aldine Manuals on Archaeology. Aldine, Chicago.

Van Riper, A. B. 1993. *Men among the Mammoths: Victorian Science and the Discovery of Human Prehistory.* University of Chicago Press, Chicago.

Vickery, K. D. 1976. An Approach to Inferring Archaeological Site Variability. Unpublished Ph.D. dissertation, Department of Anthropology, Indiana University, Bloomington.

Wall, D. d. 1994. *The Archaeology of Gender: Separating the Spheres in Urban America.* Plenum Publishing, New York.

Watkins, J. 2000. *Indigenous Archaeology.* Altamira Press, Walnut Creek, California.

Weymouth, J. W. 1986. Geophysical methods of archaeological site surveying. In *Advances in Archaeological Method and Theory,* edited by M. B. Schiffer, vol. 9, 311–95. Academic Press, Orlando, Florida.

Whalen, M. E. 1990. Sampling versus full-coverage survey: An example from western Texas. In *The Archaeology of Regions: A Case for Full-Coverage Survey,* edited by S. Fish and S. Kowalewski, 219–36. Smithsonian Institution Press, Washington, D.C.

Wheat, J. B. 1972. *The Olsen-Chubbuck Site: A Paleo Indian Bison Kill.* Memoir of the Society for American Archaeology 26, Salt Lake City.

Wheatley, D., and M. Gillings. 2002. *Spatial Technology and Archaeology: The Archaeological Applications of GIS.* Taylor and Francis, London.

White, R. 1993. Technological and social dimensions of "Aurignacian-age" body ornaments across Europe. In *Before Lascaux: The Complex Record of the Early Upper Paleolithic,* edited by H. Knecht, A. Pike-Tay, and R. White, 277–99. CRC Press, Boca Raton, Florida.

White, T. D., and P. A. Folkens. 1991. *Human Osteology.* Academic Press, New York.

White Deer, G. 1997. Return of the sacred: Spirituality and the scientific imperative. In *Native Americans and Archaeologists: Stepping Stones to Common Ground,* edited by N. Swindler, K. E. Dongoske, R. Anyon, and A. S. Downer, 37–43. Altamira Press, Walnut Creek, California.

Whittaker, J. C. 1994. *Flintknapping: Making and Understanding Stone Tools.* University of Texas Press, Austin.

Whitworth, W. R., P. L. Berrien, and W. T. Keller. 1976. *Freshwater Fishes of Connecticut.* Department of Environmental Protection, Bulletin 101. Hartford, Connecticut.

Willey, G. R., and J. A. Sabloff. 1993. *A History of American Archaeology.* W. H. Freeman and Company, New York.

Williams, B., ed. 1981. *Breakthrough: Women in Archaeology.* Walker and Company, New York.

Williams, H., ed. 2003. *Archaeologies of Remembrance: Death and Memory in Past Societies.* Plenum Publishing, New York.

Winans, M. C., and R. C. Winans. 1993. Measuring systems, techniques, and equipment for taphonomic studies. In *Practical Archaeology: Field and Laboratory Techniques and Archaeological Logistics,* edited by B. D. Dillon, 33–38. Institute of Archaeology, Los Angeles.

Zeder, M. A. 1997. *The American Archaeologist: A Profile.* Altamira Press, Walnut Creek, California.

Zeder, M. A., and B. Hesse. 2000. The initial domestication of goats (*Capra hircus*) in the Zagros Mountains 10,000 years ago. *Science* 287:2254–57.

# Index

Note: page numbers in *italics* indicate figures.

## A

Abandonment, 63–64
Absolute dating, 125, 134–135, 314
Accession, 102, *104*, 314
Activity area, 58, 314
Adaptations, 9, 20–21, 314
Aeolian deposits, 75, 314
African Americans, 40
Age, 10–12, 279–286, *284*
Alidades, *177*, 177–178, 315
Alluvial deposits, 77, 315
American Antiquities Act of 1906,
 49, 315
Anadromous species, 301–302, 315
Angkor Wat, 68, *69*
Angle of applied force, 198, 207, *208*, 315
Animals
 artifact relocation, 128–129
 blood residues, 237–238
 comparative collections,
 229–230, *230*
 field danger, *119*, 119–120
 seasonal availability, 245–247
 species importance, 234–236,
 241–243
 at Wood Lily site, 298–301
Anthropologists, 20, 315
Anthropology, 31, 109–110, 315
Archaeological context, 51, 55, 316
Archaeological excavations, 154, 316
Archaeological fieldwork. *See* Field
 training/fieldwork
Archaeological Institute of America, 162
Archaeological Resources Protection
 Act of 1979, 48–49, 316
Archaeological site formation, 59, 316
Archaeologists
 characteristics, 37–40

as detectives, 172–173, 174
popular images of, 36–37
requirements for, 29–31
safety concerns, 117–121
Archaeology. *See also* Experimental
 archaeology; Living archaeology
 accuracy, 311–313
 compliance mandates, 46–47
 described, 8, 17, 316
 first awareness, 24–25
 goals, 186
 irony of, 173
 motivations for, 12, 45–47
 negative findings, 106
 and oral histories, 35–36
 research goals, 108–111,
 115–116
 scope of study, 18–19, 71
Arctic adaptations, 21–24
Argon dating, 140–142
Arnold, Bettina, 32
Artifacts
 age criteria, 72
 care with, 210–211
 in context, 51, 53
 described, 55, 316–317
 versus natural objects, 94
 ownership considerations, 32–33
 preparation for study, 101–102
 preservation imperative, 30
 significance of items, 185–186
 varied nature, 9
 versus written record, 40
Assemblages, 113, 225, 317

## B

Backdirt, 186, 317
Behavioral contexts, 50–51, 55, 317

Bellantoni, Nick, 288–290
Bering Land Bridge/Beringia, 109, 317
Bible, 25–26
Bifacially flaked, 94, 317
Binford, Lewis, 270
Biological anthropology, 274, 317–318
Biological archaeologists, 274, 318
Bipedal locomotion, 278, 318
Bison, 235, 246
Blood, 237–238
Bones, 8–9, 56–57, *57*
Bradley, Bruce, 199, *204*, 208–209
Bristlecone pines, 10–11
Buildings, 145
Bulb of percussion, *208*
Burials, 62–63, 265–267
Burning, 231, *232*

## C

C-14 dating. *See* Radiocarbon dating
Caches, 62–63, 318
Calibration curves, *139*, 139–140, 318
Cans, *130*, 130–131, *132*
Carbon, *136*, 136–137, 243–244
Carbon dating. *See* Radiocarbon dating
Carnivores, 243
Cave paintings, 125–126
Ceramics, 60–61, 195–196, 215–217,
    238, 259, 318
Chaco Canyon, *65*
Chemical signature, 201, *201*, 319
Chemicals, 120
Chimpanzees, 21, *21*
Chocolate, 238
Chronology, 108–109
Chronometric dating, 125, 134–135, 319
Climate, 111, 168–169
Clovis points, 252–253, *254*
Coccidioidosis, 120
Colluvium, 75, 319
Comparative collections, 228–229, 319
Complex societies, 262–264, 319
Compliance archaeology, 46, 114,
    319–320
Conchoidal fractures, 198, *199*, 320
Conjoined fragments, 193, 320
Contexts, 30, 320
Continuous variables, 157, 320
Coprolites, 233, 320
Cores, 57, 181, 193, 203, 207, *208*,
    305–306, *306*, 320

Cranial sutures, 285, *285*, 320
Cranium, 277, 283–285, *285*, 293, 320
Crew chief, 43, 320–321
Croft, Lara, 38
Cross-over immunoelectrophoresis,
    238, 321
Cryptocrystalline rocks, 200, 321
Cultural property, 32
Cultural resources, 30, 321
Culture, 17, 20–21, 31, 249, 321.
    *See also* Material culture
Culture history, 108–109, 321

## D

Dating, 124–125. *See also specific
    methods such as* Absolute dating;
    Radiocarbon dating
Datum, 176, 184, 322
Davis, Margaret, 170
Death, age of, 281
Debitage, 57, 60, 181, 304, 322
Deciduous teeth, 282, 322
Demographic information,
    273–274, 322
Demography, 280, 322
Dendrochronology, 7–8, *8*, 134,
    138–139, *139*, 143, 322–323
Depth determination, 177–179
Descriptive statistics, 274, 323
Detectives, archaeologists as,
    172–173, 174
Diaphysis, 283, 323
Diffusion, 218, 244, 323
Dinosaurs, not archaeological
    territory, 18
Dioramas, 311–313, *312*
Direct historical approach, 269–270, 323
Discard, 60. *See also* Garbage
Discontinuous variables, 157, 323
Distal epiphysis, 283, 323
DNA, 294, 333
Domesticated animals, 236
Drawings, 166, *167*
Drills, *194–195*
Dumps, 61–62
Dylan, Bob, 28–29

## E

Earthwatch Institute, 163
Ecofacts, 51, 55, 56–57, *57*, 323

Egalitarian societies, 261–262, 324
Egypt, 25, *26*, 219–221, *220–221*
Elastic limit, 207, 324
Electrical resistivity survey, 91, 324
Electron spin resonance, 142, 324
Enamel hypoplasia, 290–291, 324
Enculturation, 252, 324
Environmental changes, 170–171
Environmental Impact Statement, 46,
    324–325
Epiphysis, 283, 325
Eskimos. *See* Inuit
Ethnicity, 292–294, *293*
Ethnoarchaeology, 269–270, 325
Ethnographic analogy, 268–269, 325
Ethnographic research, 325
Ethnography, 109–110, 203, 326
Ethnohistory, 203, 326
Excavation, 31, 51, 165, 173–175,
    210, 326
Excavation units, 31, *176*, 183–185, 326
Exhausted cores, 306, *306*, 326
Exotic material, 192, 326
Experimental archaeology, 194, 204, 326

**F**

Fairy stones, 26
Fauna. *See* Animals
Faunal analysis, 231, 326–327
Features, 51, 55, 57–58, *58*, 327
Feces, 233
Federal land, 30, 48–49
Femur, 277, 281, 327
Fibula, 277, 327
Field director, 43, 327
Field school, 162, 327
Field training/fieldwork, 16, 31, 162, 316
Fingerprints, 257, *257–258*
Fish, 245, 301–302, *302*
Flakes, 207–208, *208–209*, 304
Flint, 192
Floodplain, 74, 77, 327
Flotation, 228, *229*, 328
Fontanelles, 284, 328
Food, 227–234, 237–239, 244–247,
    *246*, 298
Foragers, 150, 227, 328
Forensic anthropologists, 274, 328
Four-corners region, 143, 328
Frere, John, 27, *27*
Funding considerations, 112–115

**G**

Garbage, 28–29, 71–72, 228
Garbology, 28–29
Gender roles, 37–38, 256–261
Genderlithics, 260
Geographic Information Systems, 157,
    *158*, 329
Geology, 78–79
Gero, Joan, 260
Glazier Blade Cache, 63, *63*, 94–95, *95*
Global Positioning System (GPS),
    99–101, *100*, 185, 329
Government requirements, 30
Graves. *See* Human remains
Gravestones, 132–133, *133*, 280
Grids, 184
Ground penetrating radar, 91–92,
    *91–92*, 329
Ground stones, 306–307, *307*, 329
Ground truth, 96–97
Growth arrest lines, 290, *290*, 329

**H**

Half-life, 135, 329
Half-moons, 212, *212*, 329–330
Hammerstones, 57, 181, 203, 207, *208*,
    305, *305*, 330
Hantavirus, 119
Haplogroups/haplotypes, 294, 330
Harris Lines, 290, *290*, 330
Hawass, Zahi, 39, *39*
Health, clues to, 287–291, *289–290*
Hearths, *197*
Herbivores, 243
High-performance liquid
    chromatography (HPLC), 238, 330
Histoplasmosis, 120
Historical records, 96, *96*, 269
Hominids, 134, 330
Hoxne, 27, *27*
Human remains, 32, *34*, 47–48, 234,
    250, *251*, 274–275
Humans, 9, 11–12
Humerus, 283, *284*, 330
Hunter-gatherers, 227, 331
Hunting, 234–235

**I**

Ideas, spread of, 218–219
Igneous rock, 140, 331

Impact assessments, 46–47
In situ, 189, 331
Inductive statistics, 274, 331
Injury, 287–288
Insects, 117–119
Interpretation, 35, 38–40
Inuit, *23*, 23–24
Inventions, 218–223, *220–222*
Inventory, 102–103, *104*
Ishi, 203, *203*
Isotopes, 135, *136*, 136–137, 243, 331

**J**

Jade figurines, *56*
Jaw, 293
Journals, 93

**K**

K/Ar. *See* Potassium/argon dating
Keeley, Lawrence, 212, *213*
Khmer, 68, *69*
Kitchen middens, 61–62, 228, 331
Knappers, 198–199, 207, 208, 331
Knapping, 194, 331

**L**

Lacustrine deposits, 74, 331
Lake Suigetsu, 140
Landowners, 95–96
Landscape, 156–157, *158*
Landscape signature, 85–86,
    155, 332
Landslides, 76
Laser transit, 179, 332
Lavin, Lucianne, 258
Law of superposition, 129, 332
Levels, 177, *177*
Life expectancy, 280–281
Lipper, Dorothy, 276
Literature search, 93, 332
Lithic material, 192, 332
Lithic scatter, *61*
Little Big Horn, *174*
Living archaeology, 269–270, 332
Locations, recording of, 175–179
Loss, 59–60
Luck, 264
Luedtke, Barbara, 259
Lyme disease, *118*, 118–119

**M**

Magnetometry, 92
Maize, 226, 244
Malnutrition, 290–291
Mandible, 277, 332
Maps, 157, 158, 173–175, *174. See also*
    Topographic maps
Mastabas, 219, *220*
Master sequence, 143–144, *144*, 333
Mastoid process, 277–278, 333
Material culture, 9–10, 19, 31, 333
Matrilocality, 255, 333
Mayas, *65*, 66–68, *69*, 290–291
McDonald's, *73*
Measurement system, 184
Mesoamerica, 221–222, *222*
Messenger, Phyllis, 32
Minimum Number of Individuals
    (MNI), *242*, 242–243, 333
Mitochondrial DNA, 294, 333
Morphology, 225, 334

**N**

Name assignment, 159–160
National Environmental Protection Act
    (NEPA), 114, 334
National Historic Preservation Act of
    1966, 72, 334
National Museum of the American
    Indian Act of 1989, 33, 334
National Register of Historic Places,
    72, 334
Native American Graves Protection and
    Repatriation Act, 33, 47, 275, 334
Native Americans, 33, *34*, 35, 39, *86*,
    109, 114, 275–276
Neutron activation analysis, 202,
    334–335
New World, 109
Nitrogen, 243
Nomadic people, 155, 227, 335
Nominal variables, 157, 335
Nutrition, 290–291
Nuts, 245

**O**

Object pieces, 207, 335
Obsidian, 199, *199*, 335
Obtrusive features, 64–66, *65*, *69*, 335

Occupation layers, 77, 335
Oceans, 74–75
Oldowan industry, *208*, 335–336
Olduvai Gorge, 66, *67*
Olmecs, *56*
Optically stimulated luminescence
  (OSL), 142, 336
Oral historians, 35–36
Organic materials, 230–231, 250
Orkney Islands, 66–67, *68*
Osteology, 31, 336
Ozette, 76, *76*

P

Painting, 125–126, 175–176, 265, *266*
Paleoenvironmental reconstruction,
  168, 336
Paleofeces, 233, 336
Paleontologists, 18, 336
Paleopathology, 288–289, 336
Palynologists, 168–171, 336
Patrilocality, 255, 336, 337
Pedestrian survey, 53, 68, 337
Pelvis, 278, *278*
Percussion flaking, 57, 181, 203, 207,
  *208*, 337
Percussors, 183, 207, *208*, 337
Perry, Warren, 40
Photography, 166, *167*
Photosynthesis, 243–244
Physical anthropologists, 274, 337
Phytoliths, 102, 231, 239–240,
  *240*, 337
Plane tables, 178, *178*, 337
Plants, 226, 239–240, *241*, 243–244.
  *See also* Pollen
Pointillism, 175–176
Polar bears, 21–23, *22*
Polish, 212, 337
Pollen, 166, 168–171, *169*, 338
Pollen analysis, 297, 338
Pollen profile, 169–170, *171*, 338
Pollen rain, 170, 338
Pompeii, 75, *75*
Pongids, 134, 338
Population, 89, 338
Population profile, 274, 338
Post-cranial skeleton, 283, 338
Potassium/argon (K/Ar) dating,
  140–142, *141*, 338–339

Potsherds, 61, 217, 258, 339
Pottery. *See* Ceramics
Pre-ceramic period, 195, 339
Preforms, 306, 339
Prehistoric, 107, 339
Prehistory, 31, 339
Preservation, 30, 46–47
Pressure flaking, 58, 203, 207–208, *209*,
  225, 300, 340
Primary refuse, 60, 340
Principal investigator, 17, 31, 340
Prognathous jaw, 293, 340
Projectile points, 340
Proton magnetometry, 92, 340
Provenience, 176, 340
Proximal epiphysis, 283, 341
Pubic symphysis, 286, 341
Public land. *See* Federal land
Pyramid of the Magician, *65*
Pyramids, *11*, 219–222, *220–222*

R

Rabies, 119, *119*
Races, 292–294, *293*, 341
Radar, 91–92, *91–92*
Radioactivity, 135, 341
Radiocarbon dating, 135–140,
  318, 341
Radiometric dating, 134–142, 341
Random samples, 89, 341
Rathje, William, 71, *71*
Raw material, 200–202
Refuse. *See* Garbage
Register of Professional Archaeologists
  (RPA), 31
Relative dating, 124, 125–133, 341
Religion, 249, 264–267
Remote sensing, 88, 90–92, 342
Renaissance, 25
Reoccupation, 161–162
Representative samples, 55, 89, 342
Research, 93, 96, 112–116
Research strategies, 53, 85, 342–343
Rituals, 63
Rock, useful characteristics,
  198–200
Romans, 25, *26*
RPA. *See* Register of Professional
  Archaeologists (RPA)
Rummler, Alan J., 298, *299*, *301*

## S

Sacred objects, 33
Sacred sites, 265, *266*
Samples, 343
Sampling strategies, 88–90, 343
Sampling zones, 82, *83*
Saul, Frank, 291
Scalar scars, 212, *212*, 343
Schiffer, Michael, 59
Sciatic notch, 278, *278*, 343
Seasons, 244–247, *246*
Secondary refuse, 61, 343
Sedentary, 155, 227, 343–344
Semi-lunar knives, 231–232, *233*, 344
Seriation, 129–133, 344
Seriation graphs, 132–133, *132–133*, 344
Settlement patterns, 85, 124, 155, 344
Sexual dimorphism, 276–278, 344
Sherds, 61, 344
Shipman, Pat, 313
Shovel-shaped incisors, 293, *293*,
    344–345
Shovel test pits, 88, 97–98, *98*, 345
Silt, 77, 345
Site constituents, 51, 55, 345
Site formation processes, 53, 59–64, 345
Site processes, relative activity, 66
Site survey, 31, 154–156, 345
Sites
    burial processes, 74–76
    cloaking of, 66–68
    in context, 45, 55
    dating overview, 124–125
    depth of burial, 76–79
    described, *50*, 50–51, 345
    digging privileges, 162–163
    excavation care, 173–175
    formation processes, 59–64
    function identification, 214–215
    location identification, 53, *54*, 55,
        64–70, 98–101
    naming conventions, 159–160
    in Peoples State Forest, 151–154,
        *152–153*
    regulation, 47–49
    search techniques, 93–98
    selection, 45–47
    size determination, 160–162
    suspect locations, 85–87
    uncovering, 78

Size determination, 160–162
Skara Brae, 66–67, *68*
Skeletons
    age determination, 246,
        279–286, *284*
    animal counts, 242
    described, 283
    dietary cues, 243–244
    ethnic differences, 292–294, *293*
    health determination, 287–291,
        *289–290*
    sex differences, 276–278
Skull, 277, 345. *See also* Cranium
Slavery, 39–40
Smithsonian Institution, 33
Snakes, 120
Sneferu, 219–222, *220–221*
Soapstone, 196, *196*, 345
Social organization, 234–236
Social structure, 261–264, 267–270
Society for American Archaeology
    (SAA), 37–38
Soil, 77, 91. *See also* Stratigraphy
Spatial associations, 30, 174, 345
Spatial context, 193, 346
Spear points, 147, 252–253, *254*
Squares. *See* Excavation units
Stadia rod, 178, 346
Stalagmites, 140
Steatite, 196, *196*, 346
Step scars, 212, *212*, 346
Stone, sources, 309–310
Stone tools, 25–27, *27*
Strata/stratum, 126, 346
Stratified societies, 262–264, 347
Stratigraphic positioning, 193, 346
Stratigraphy, 126–129, *128*, *141*,
    141–142, 177, 347
Striations, 212, 347
Striking platform, 198, 207, *208*, 347
Style, 129–133, 146–147, *147*
Supraorbital torus, 277, 347
Surveying, 177–179
Surveys, 17, 347

## T

Technology, 129–130, 202–205, *206*,
    218–223, *220–222*
Teeth, 282, *282*, 290–291, 293, *293*
Tells, 77, *78*, 347

Temper, 217, 347
Test pit forms, 53, 347–348
Test pits
    in context, 31, 82
    depth criteria, 78–79
    described, 347
    excavation dangers, 121
    image, 54
    location, 97–98, 98
    sampling strategy, 88
Test pitting, 348
Thermoluminescence (TL), 142, 196, 348
Thunderstones, 26
Tibia, 277, 348
Tool kit, 60, 188–190, 190, 348
Toolmaking
    methods, 206–209, 208–209
    process frozen, 181–182, 182
    processes, 202–205
    refuse, 60
    skills for, 198–199
    at Wood Lily, 304–310
Tools
    chimpanzee use, 21, 21
    differences in form, 252–253, 254
    diversity, 194
    food identification, 231
    gender division, 259
    identification, 211–213
    residues on, 237–240, 240
    shapes, 225
Topographic maps, 44, 45, 99, 348
Total station, 178–179, 179, 348
Trace element chemistry, 200–202
Traditions, 251
Transects, 45, 82, 83, 97, 348–349
Transit, 179, 332
Tree rings. See Dendrochronology

Trees, 134, 187–188
Tringham, Ruth, 259
Trowels, 188–190, 189
Tsosie, Rebecca, 275
Tuberculosis, 289–290
Tutankhamen, 112–113, 263, 263

U

Unconsolidated material, 75, 349
United States Geological Survey,
    107, 349
Universal Transverse Mercator, 184, 349
Universities, 114
Uranium dating method, 140
Use patterns. See Wear patterns
Ussher, James, 26

V

Valley fever, 120
Vampirism, 288–289, 289
Varves, 140, 349
Visibility, 66, 349
Vitreous rock, 198, 349
Volunteers, 163

W

Wealth, 262–263, 290–291
Weapons, 120–121
Wear patterns, 211–213, 212, 227,
    308–309, 308–309, 350
West Nile virus, 117–118
White-tailed deer, 234–235
Wide Area Augmentation System,
    100, 350
Wind, 75
Women, 37–38
Wood, 187